# ON THE TARMAC

## Rules, line-work, shadows and space

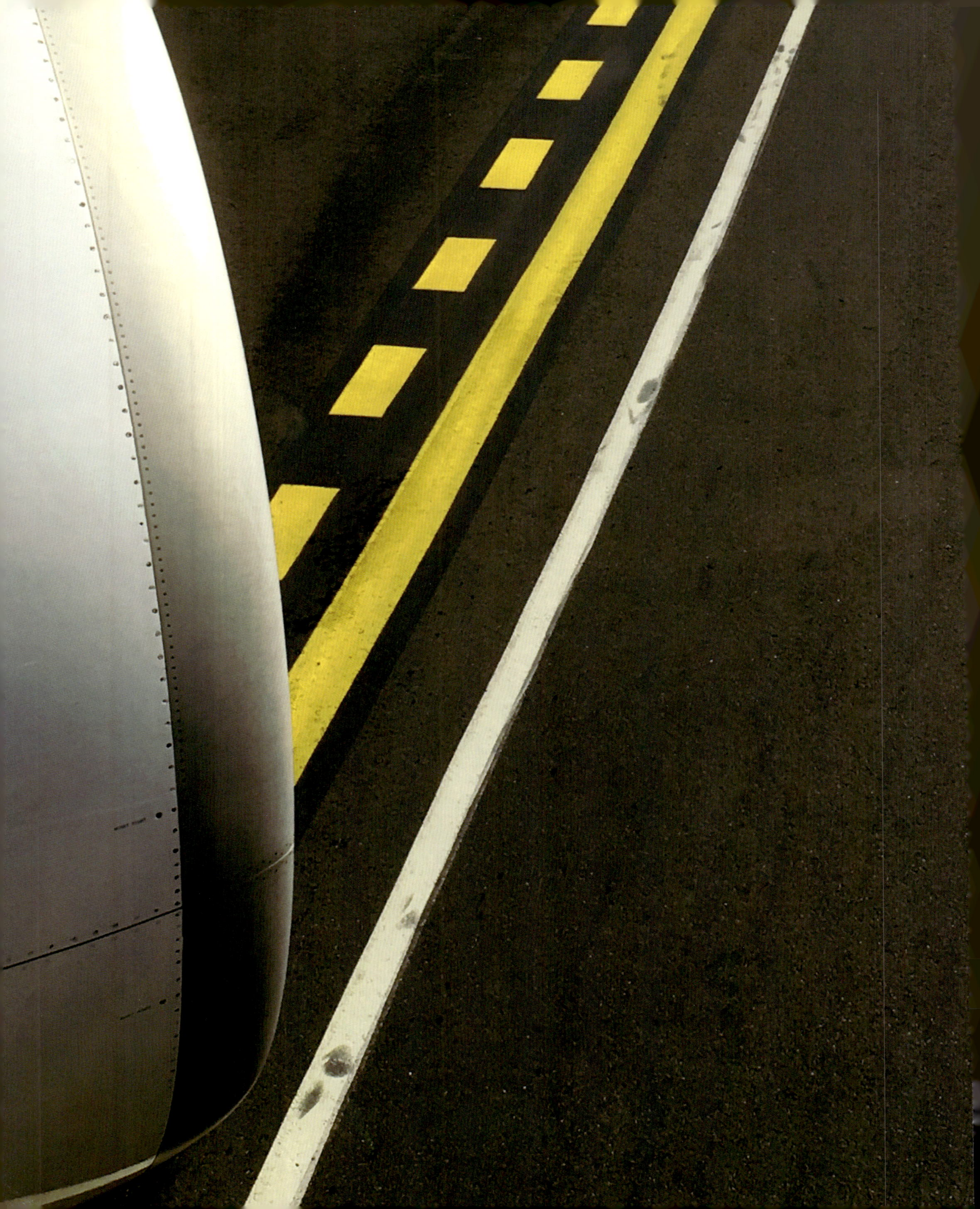

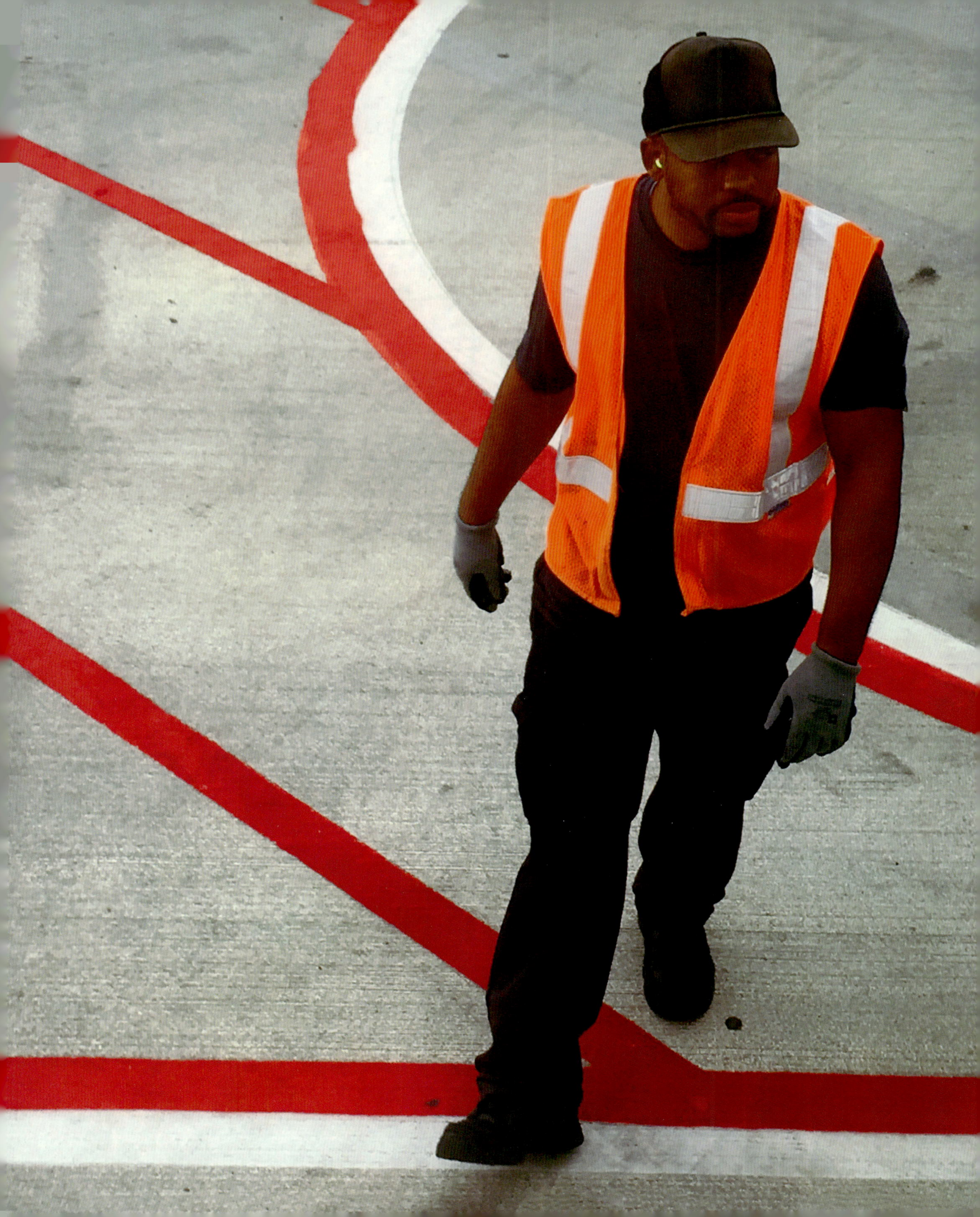

# ON THE TARMAC

## Rules, line-work, shadows and space

**Dennis Pieprz**

Introduction by Philip Barash

**OSCAR RIERA OJEDA**
PUBLISHERS

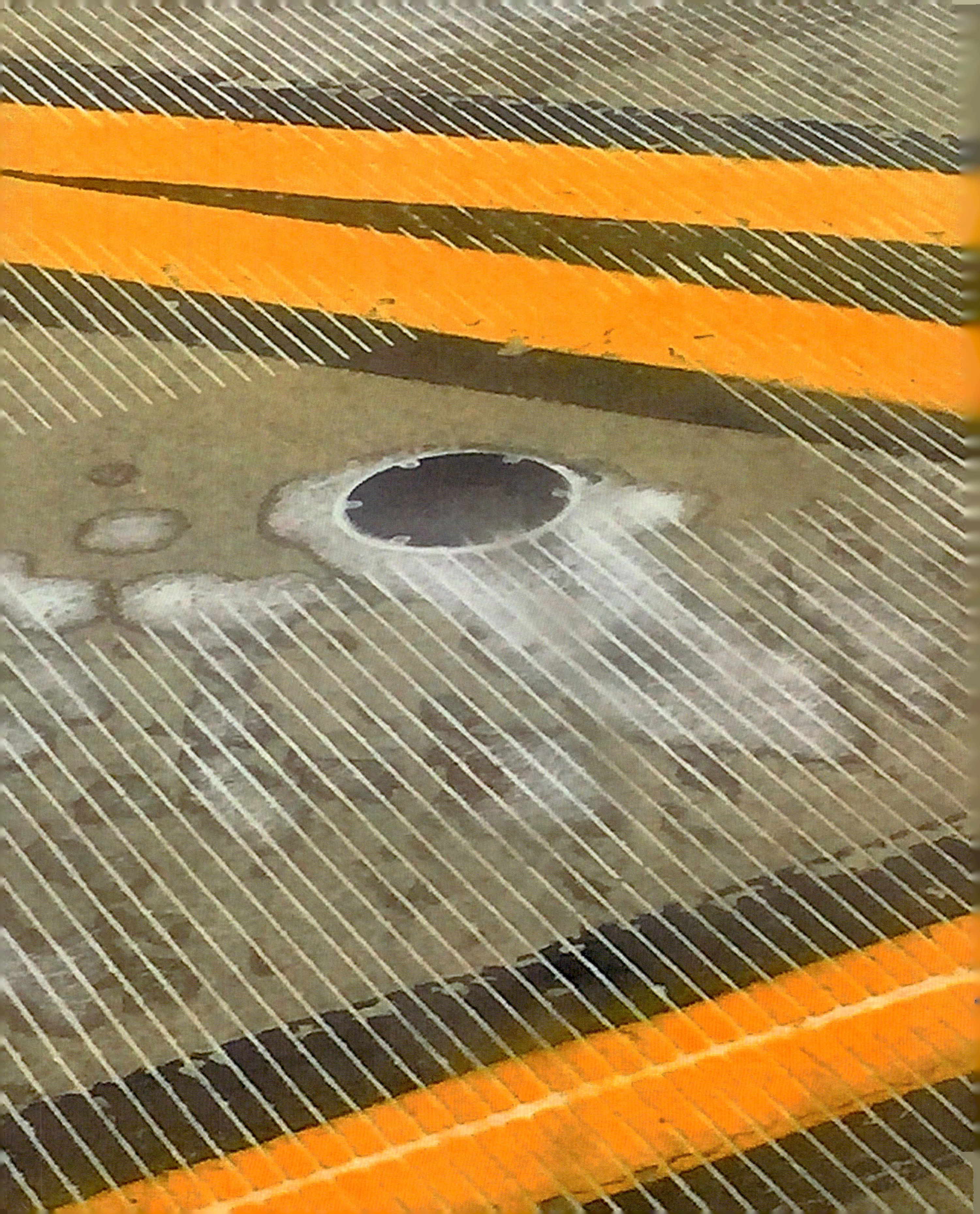

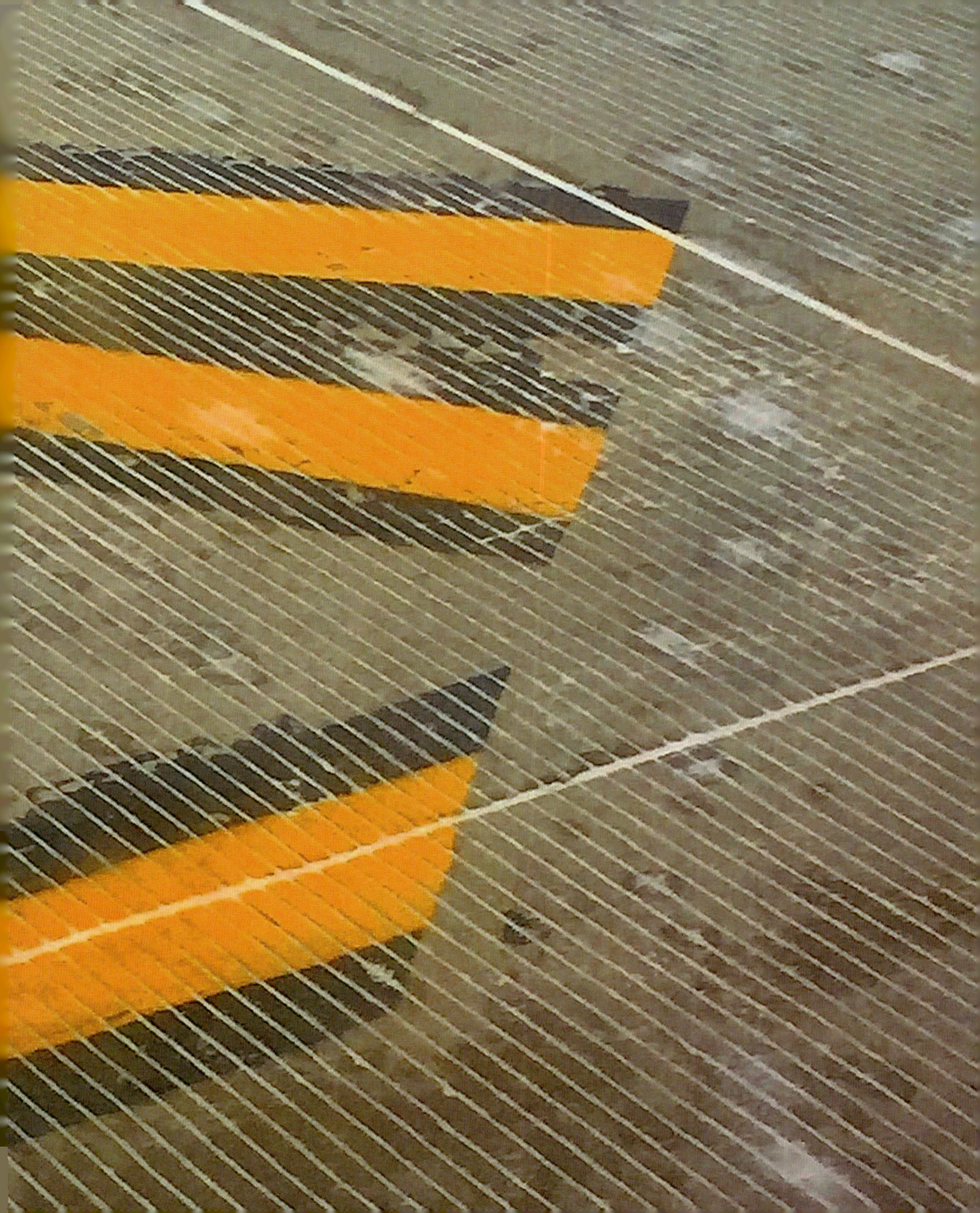

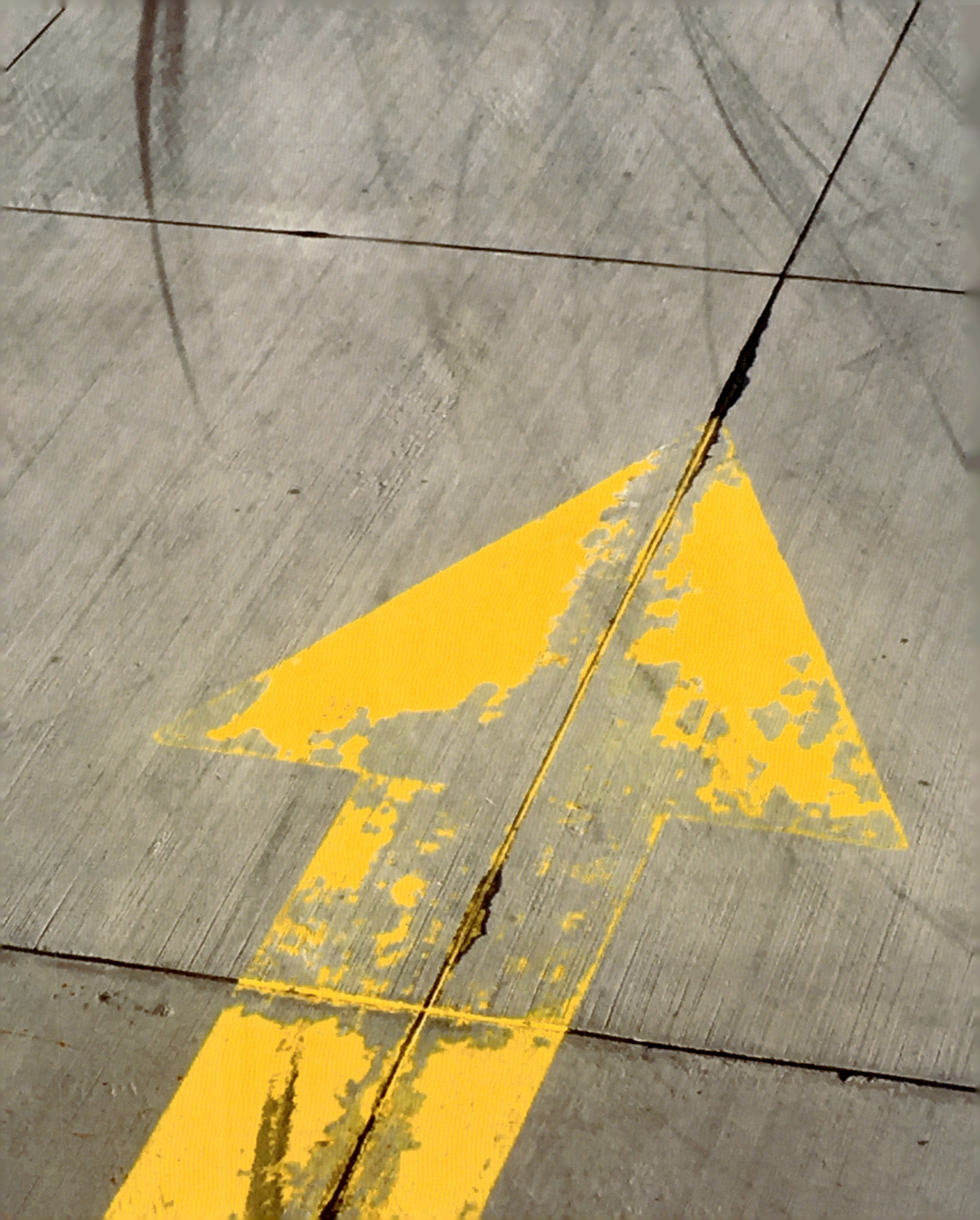

# CONTENTS

# FOREWORD

By Dennis Pieprz

In my travels I noticed an aspect of airports that has become quite an obsession for me. On tarmacs around the globe there seemed to be a "hidden" language of codes and directives, all with a consistency across cultures, locations, and places. With my iPhone, I began to make images of these markings, framing them in ways to create compositions of graphic impact, never quite intended by their makers. In my mind I had the color, from and invention of Malevich, Rodchenko, Scully, Davis and other artist inspirations.

Rules, line-work, shadows and space,
all found on the tarmac...

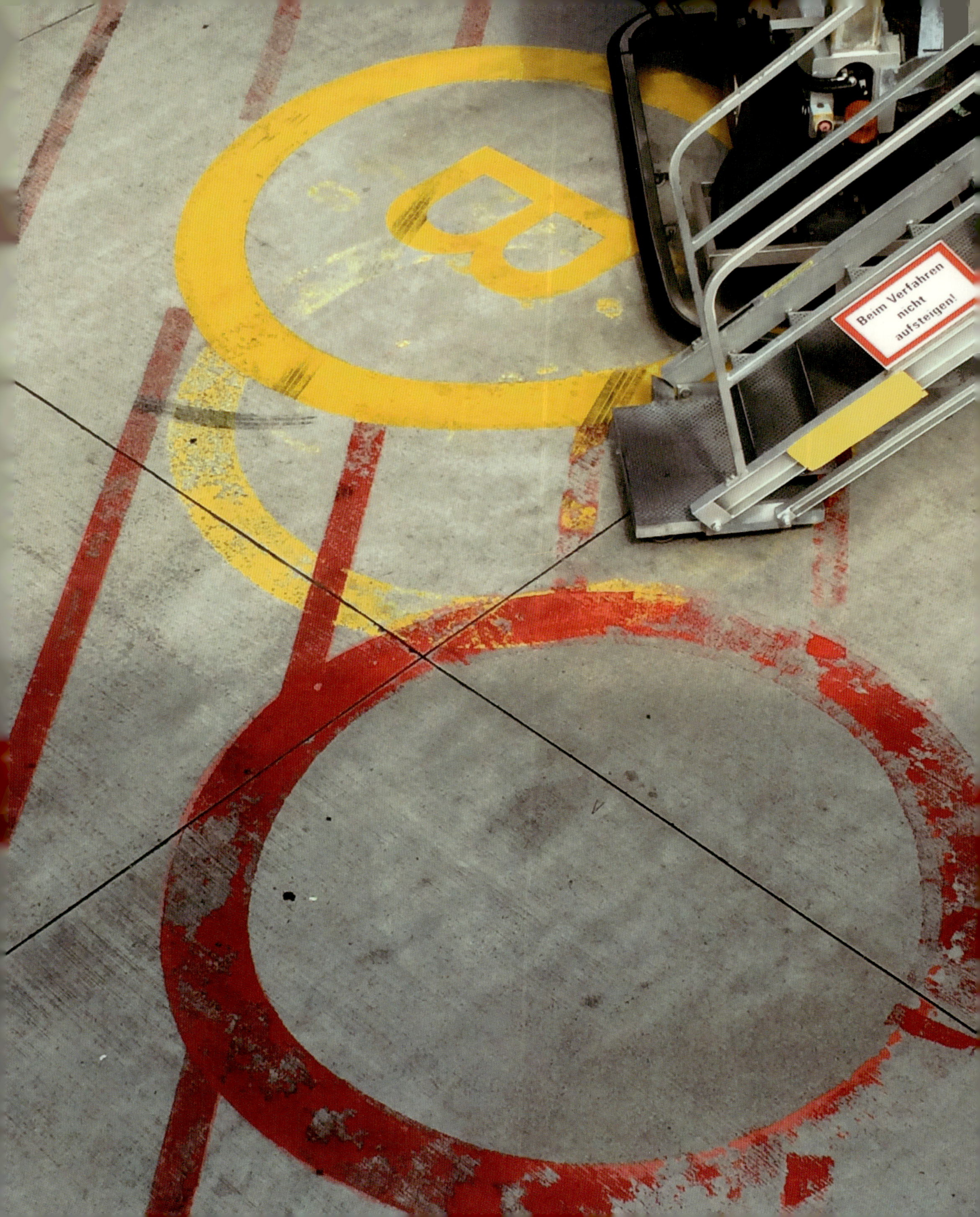
Beim Verfahren nicht aufsteigen!

# INTRODUCTION

By Philip Barash

An entire society has arisen around air travel, with its own hierarchies of elite travelers, its currency of rewards miles, its gilded lounges and its long security lines of bleary-eyed discontents. And it's given us a new language: a visual vocabulary legible only to a priestly few -- pilots and airport operators -- who are entrusted with observing and interpreting this language.

But to those of us who do not belong to this airborne brotherhood, tarmacs are hieroglyphics writ large: an obscure language that greets us as we glide down toward the earth. It is a code both intimately familiar and radically alien.

On the Tarmac is an attempt to break this code: both in the sense of deciphering its meaning and in the sense of causing it to crack apart. Dennis Pieprz's snapshots poke at the tarmac, push it to the limit of legibility, refigure its grammar. The book is full of these kinds of moments, of these "breaks." Intersecting lines morph into abstract patterns. Long arcs bleed off the page, sweeping towards infinity. Industrial equipment gleams in sunshine as if installed in an art gallery. Distorted by raindrops, an airport worker's head appears to double. A propeller stirs the world into a blur. Pieprz captures it all from a window seat with clarity and wit.

In the aggregate, themes begin to unfold, a meta-language of sorts. Themes first suggested themselves in an exhibition hosted by the Boston Society of Architects, where more than 200 images were displayed side by side. (The exhibition prompted the publication of this book; installation photos appear in an appendix in back.) Initially, Pieprz grappled with an organizing schema: should the images be arranged chronologically? Geographically? By some other external logic? But the images contained their own thematic order: affinities of color and shape, for example, dictated sections of the exhibition layout. One row of photos was a gradient of reds, progressing from stripes to firefighting equipment. Another read like a glossary of hand signals. Yet another assembles fragments of yellow lines, which have the urgency of laconic Morse code. These compositions inform a useful commentary: viewed by itself, each image is a snapshot of an esoteric culture. Together, Pieprz's photographs are a mesmerizing portrait of a shared humanity.

Perhaps Pieprz has found a calling as a translator. He's the right man for the job, a native of the skies, accustomed to high altitudes. A renowned urbanist, Pieprz circumnavigates the globe with teams of planners and designers, advancing bold ideas about the future of place. In the course of his work, he spends countless hours taxiing to distant terminals. Armed with boundless curiosity and an iPhone, Pieprz documents his journeys as if collecting postcards. Those long, interstitial minutes after touchdown and before takeoff, for the uninitiated, drag on in social media updates or scrolling through interminable screens of in-flight entertainment options. But to Pieprz, these are times of intense productivity.

For us terrestrials, Pieprz frames images not to convey instructions but to capture vivid patterns and surprising juxtapositions, rigorous geometry and playful shadows. By freeing tarmac markings from their intended meanings, his photos allow other meanings to emerge. They are about catching glimpses of the hyper-local amid globalization. They are about slowing the pace and paying attention. They are about exploring poetry of line work and the ballet of human activity. Most of all, they are about seeking the sublime in the everyday.

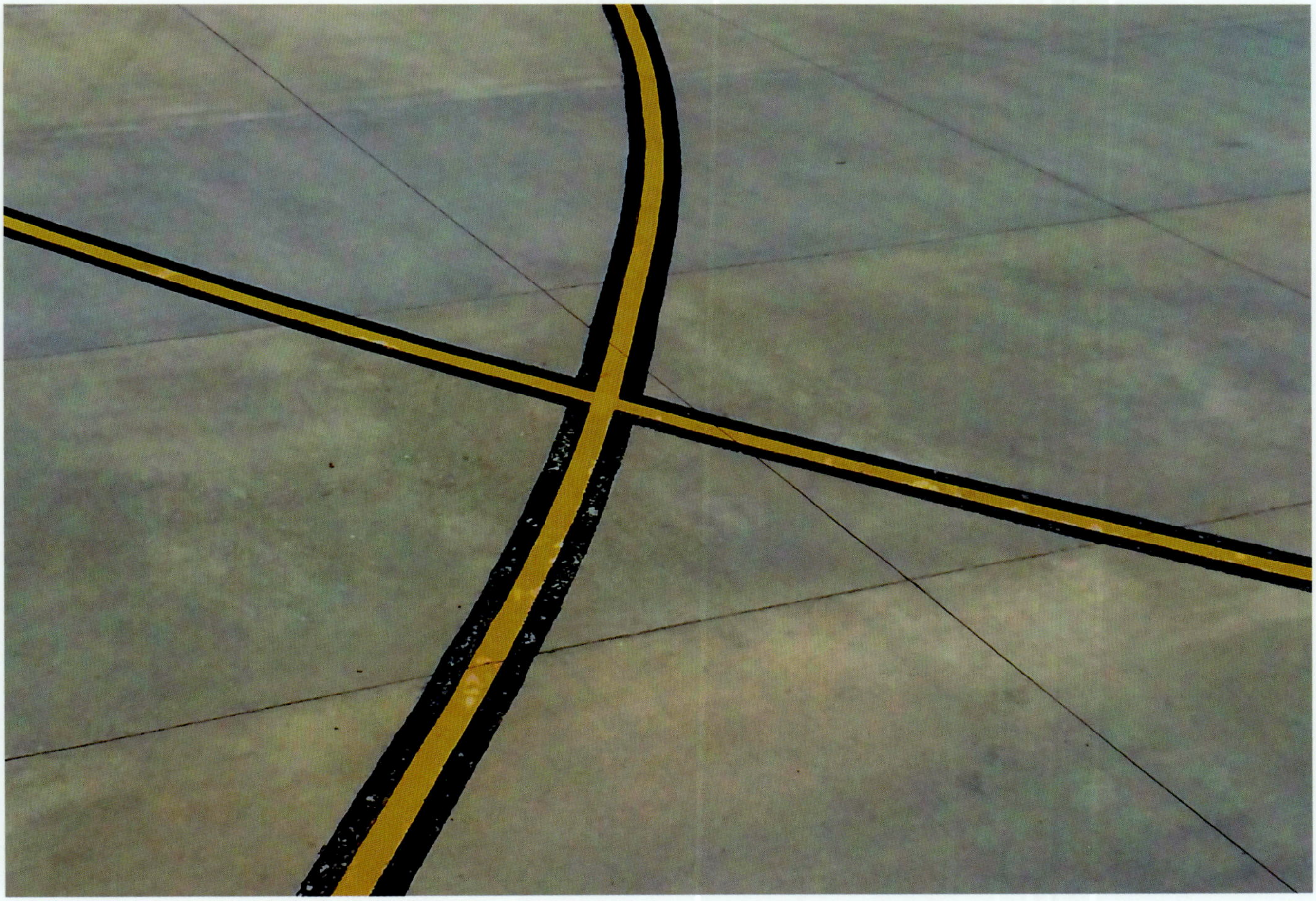

**Philip Barash** is creative director at Sasaki, where he oversees the firm's place branding practice. An accomplished writer, curator, and brand-builder, Barash helps clients define and communicate the vision, strategy and design principles for major real estate developments and public realm projects. • His critical writing about design culture frequently appears in regional and national publications. Recent curatorial projects include the first solo exhibition of iconoclastic designer Jimenez Lai's work and a collection of architectural photography on permanent display at the University of Chicago. Barash explored the intersection of identity and the built environment in the Master of Arts Program in the Humanities at the University of Chicago and studied digital media at the University of Detroit Mercy.

# INTERVIEW

A conversation with Dennis Pieprz

**What was the genesis of your project, On The Tarmac?**

Over the years I've spent a lot of time traveling. I'm interested in culture and what's different about the places I visit. In airports, I've started to notice the language of tarmacs, the instructions that we see for pilots and ground personnel every time we head to and from the runway. There was a fairly consistent language throughout the world; I figured this must be some set of codes and rules, but also noticed that each airport is slightly different. In some countries, the lines are very precise and accurate and in others they're wobbly, and in the heat some of the tarmacs are even melting. With the technology of the iPhone camera, it became very easy [to document], a habit that is part of my travel routine. It's a hobby that turned into a passionate photography game.

**How has your project changed over time?**

This project actually started with my digital camera about five years ago. With the switch to the iPhone, I'd say it's been three years capturing photos in this format. I have 29,000 photos on my iPhone and I picked just 250 of my favorites for the show. Over time, the focus definitely evolved. I used to be completely absorbed by the geometry and lines and lettering and now I've become interested in people and how they interact. The best subjects are the people who guide the planes in. They have these Star Wars-like torches and when you capture them moving around and intersecting with the various geometries it just makes for fascinating imagery. They bring a human touch to the images.

**Where else do you seek inspiration for this work?**

I've always been interested in Russian Constructivist paintings. I was in the Stedelijk Museum in Amsterdam and I saw some of their collection and thought, 'my goodness, this looks like runway markings!' I made the connection and began looking for moments to abstract something ordinary to transform it from mundane to artistic. In this case, I know that the last thing on the minds of the designers and operators of airports is some sort of aesthetic concern when they paint their tarmacs; for them it's all about safety and regulation and control of movement. I wanted to take something like that, something that's super-functional, and look at it in a whole new way. This started as a fascination with tarmac markings and at the time you never thought of it as a photography project to be displayed in a gallery.

**What was it like converting what was meant for digital consumption on Instagram to a tangible artwork that can be displayed?**

Over the holidays last year I decided to do an experiment. I picked some of my favorite images and I used Blurb book-making technology to produce a book, which after many titles, was named On the Tarmac. It was a lot of fun because it revealed the relationship between different photos, geometries, and content. It showed how they might become yet another thing as you look at the pages next to each other, juxtaposing themes and locations. I used the geographical pins on my phone to track every photo by its place. Adding on the layer of place brought a contextual dimension. Suddenly I could compare tarmac language from Boston, Syracuse, Monterrey, and see the collective bring more power to the individual images.

**What are the challenges of your medium?**

Between the iPhone's limitations and the glass barrier of the plane window, you can't get perfect large-scale shots. I've learned to use the dirt or the rain on the windowpane to add a kind of twist to the photos rather than letting the imperfect conditions ruin the images. And while the technology doesn't allow for very large prints, I think that's ok. Each image is no larger than a postcard, which I like. We don't really use postcards anymore but perhaps this is a new kind of postcard.

**How does being an urban designer change the way you view the world and the pictures you capture?**

There are so many big forces going into our work and how we design cities—forces of context, location, culture, program aspirations, systems-thinking. Urbanism also involves geometry of many kinds and there are many ways of being inspired and many ways of working. Sometimes the sweeping geometries and grid-like expressions on the tarmac can be inspiring for my work in cities. It's ultimately one more way of seeing—one more ingredient in the pot.

**Beyond the tarmac, are there other subject areas or fixations that have grabbed you?**

Another area of interest that is somewhat related to flight is the view of cities from above. Obviously, many people are taken by that. I always make sure I get a window seat in front of the wing. I can tell you in America it can be quite horrifying, to see what's out there, because there is so much sprawl and so much waste and lack of adding up to anything. You think of Boston as pretty urban, but when you fly into Boston and you see how spread out it is—or a place like Houston or Dallas or Detroit—it's kind of shocking to see that the sprawl is just everywhere. But flying into places like Manila or Jakarta, or Ho Chi Minh City, you see the informal settlements and the density, and there's a whole other set of problems. It's a related passion to see the macro urban problems from the aerial vantage point but, I think that many people have done that before. I've never seen anyone focus on the Tarmac in the way I have come to do over time. We'll see what's next.

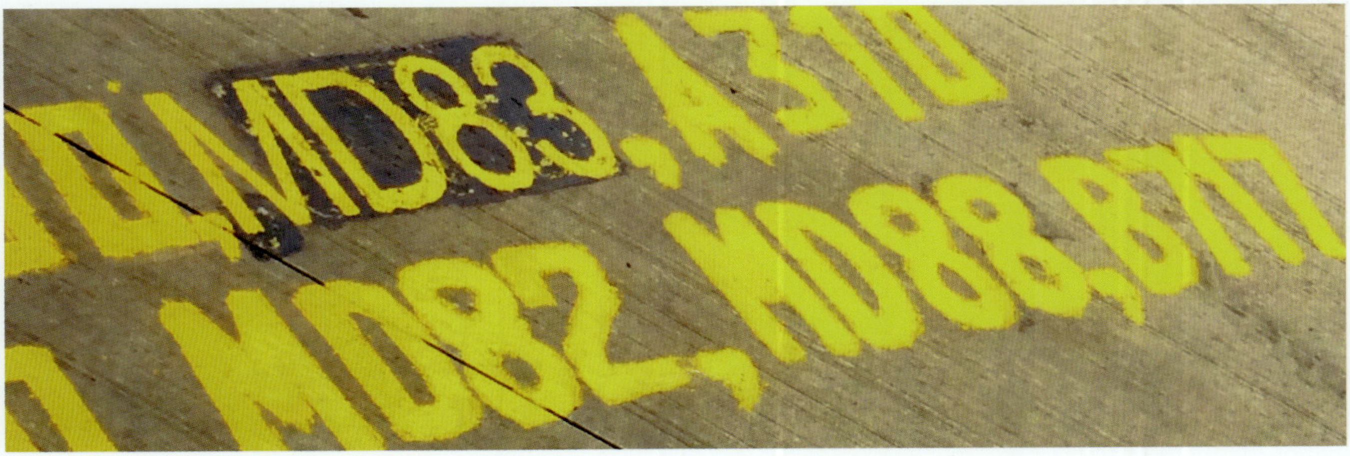

# LOCATIONS

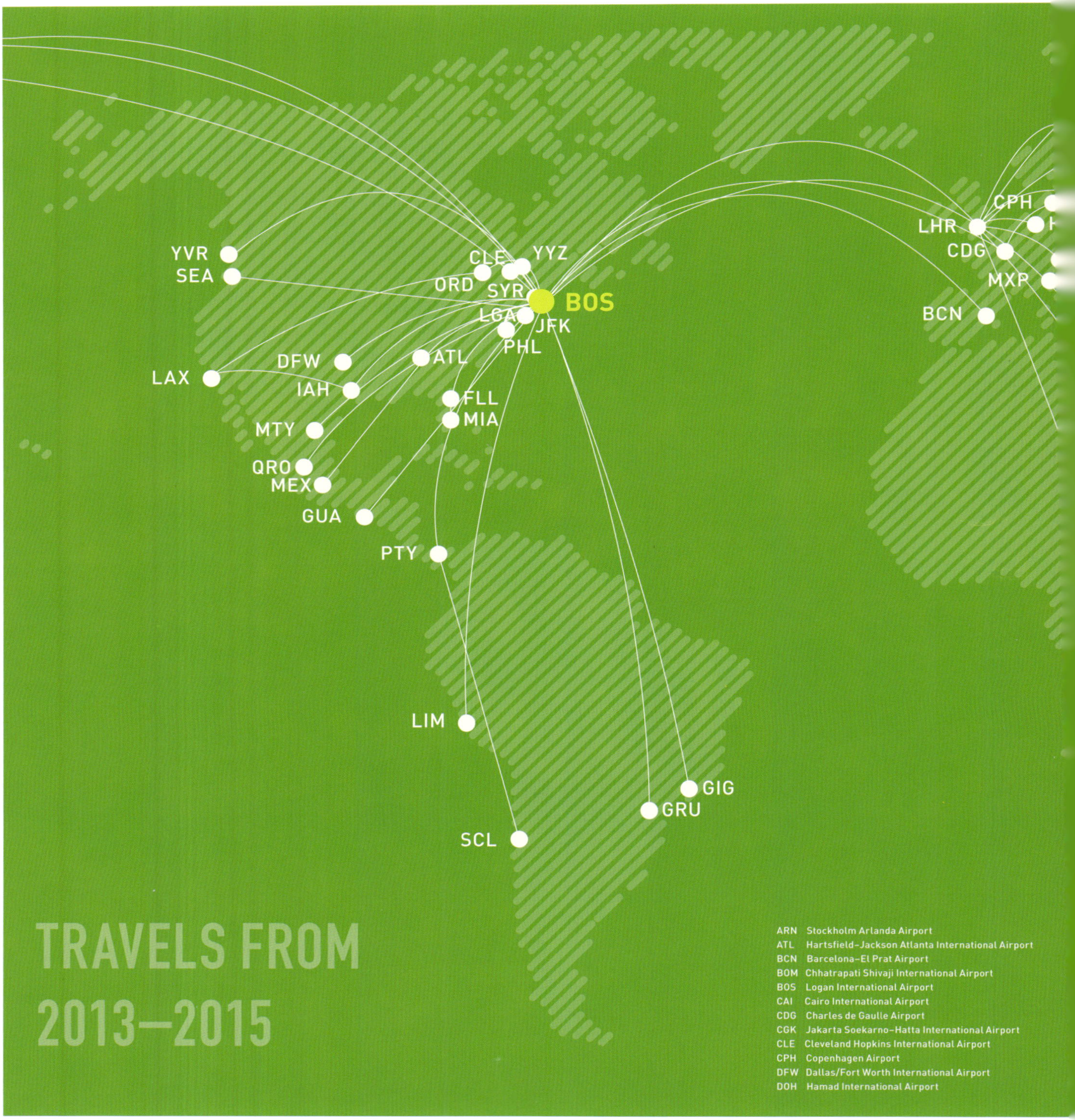


## TRAVELS FROM 2013–2015

| | |
|---|---|
| ARN | Stockholm Arlanda Airport |
| ATL | Hartsfield-Jackson Atlanta International Airport |
| BCN | Barcelona-El Prat Airport |
| BOM | Chhatrapati Shivaji International Airport |
| BOS | Logan International Airport |
| CAI | Cairo International Airport |
| CDG | Charles de Gaulle Airport |
| CGK | Jakarta Soekarno-Hatta International Airport |
| CLE | Cleveland Hopkins International Airport |
| CPH | Copenhagen Airport |
| DFW | Dallas/Fort Worth International Airport |
| DOH | Hamad International Airport |

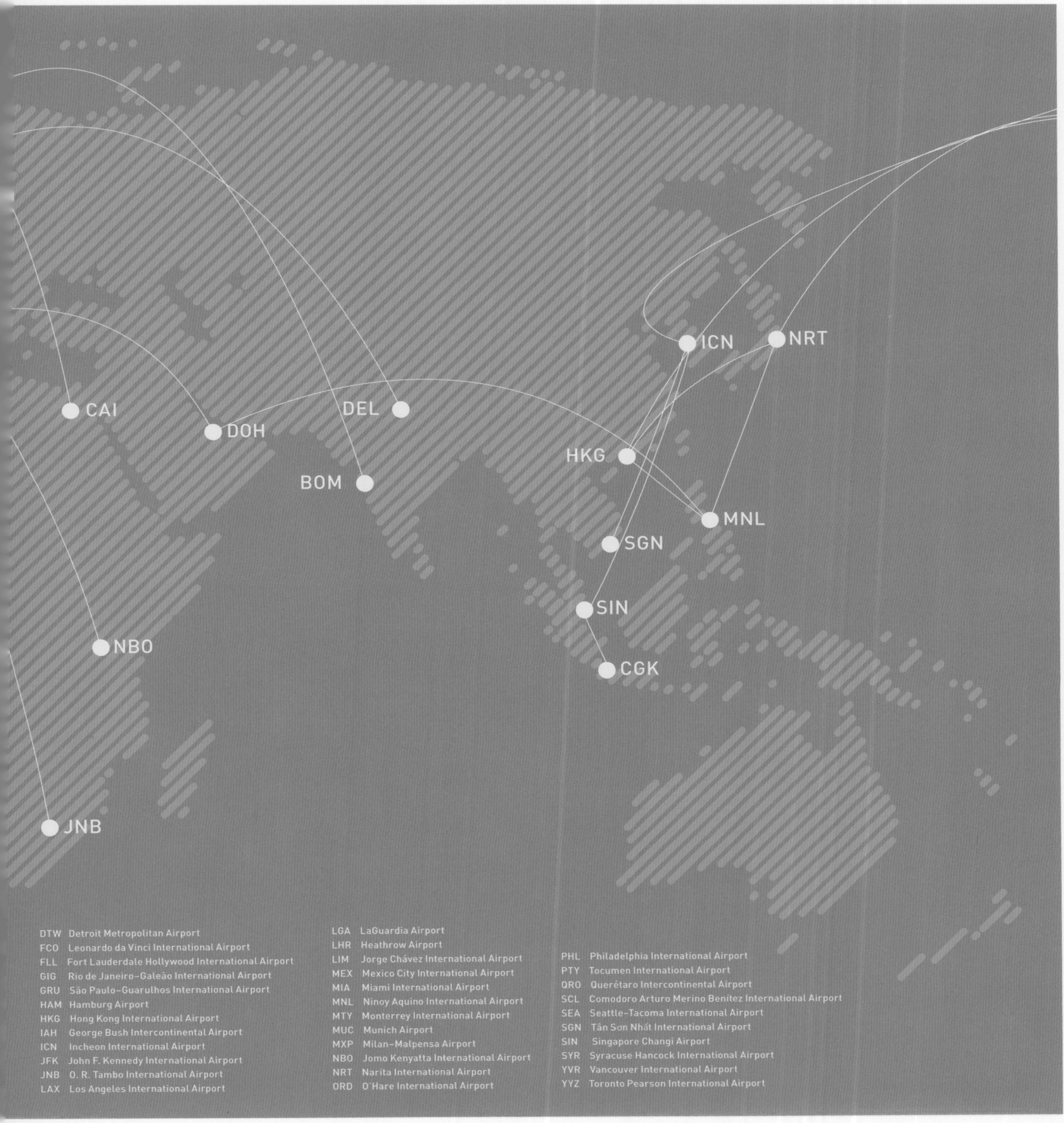


DTW Detroit Metropolitan Airport
FCO Leonardo da Vinci International Airport
FLL Fort Lauderdale Hollywood International Airport
GIG Rio de Janeiro–Galeão International Airport
GRU São Paulo–Guarulhos International Airport
HAM Hamburg Airport
HKG Hong Kong International Airport
IAH George Bush Intercontinental Airport
ICN Incheon International Airport
JFK John F. Kennedy International Airport
JNB O. R. Tambo International Airport
LAX Los Angeles International Airport
LGA LaGuardia Airport
LHR Heathrow Airport
LIM Jorge Chávez International Airport
MEX Mexico City International Airport
MIA Miami International Airport
MNL Ninoy Aquino International Airport
MTY Monterrey International Airport
MUC Munich Airport
MXP Milan–Malpensa Airport
NBO Jomo Kenyatta International Airport
NRT Narita International Airport
ORD O'Hare International Airport
PHL Philadelphia International Airport
PTY Tocumen International Airport
QRO Querétaro Intercontinental Airport
SCL Comodoro Arturo Merino Benítez International Airport
SEA Seattle–Tacoma International Airport
SGN Tân Sơn Nhất International Airport
SIN Singapore Changi Airport
SYR Syracuse Hancock International Airport
YVR Vancouver International Airport
YYZ Toronto Pearson International Airport

# PLATES

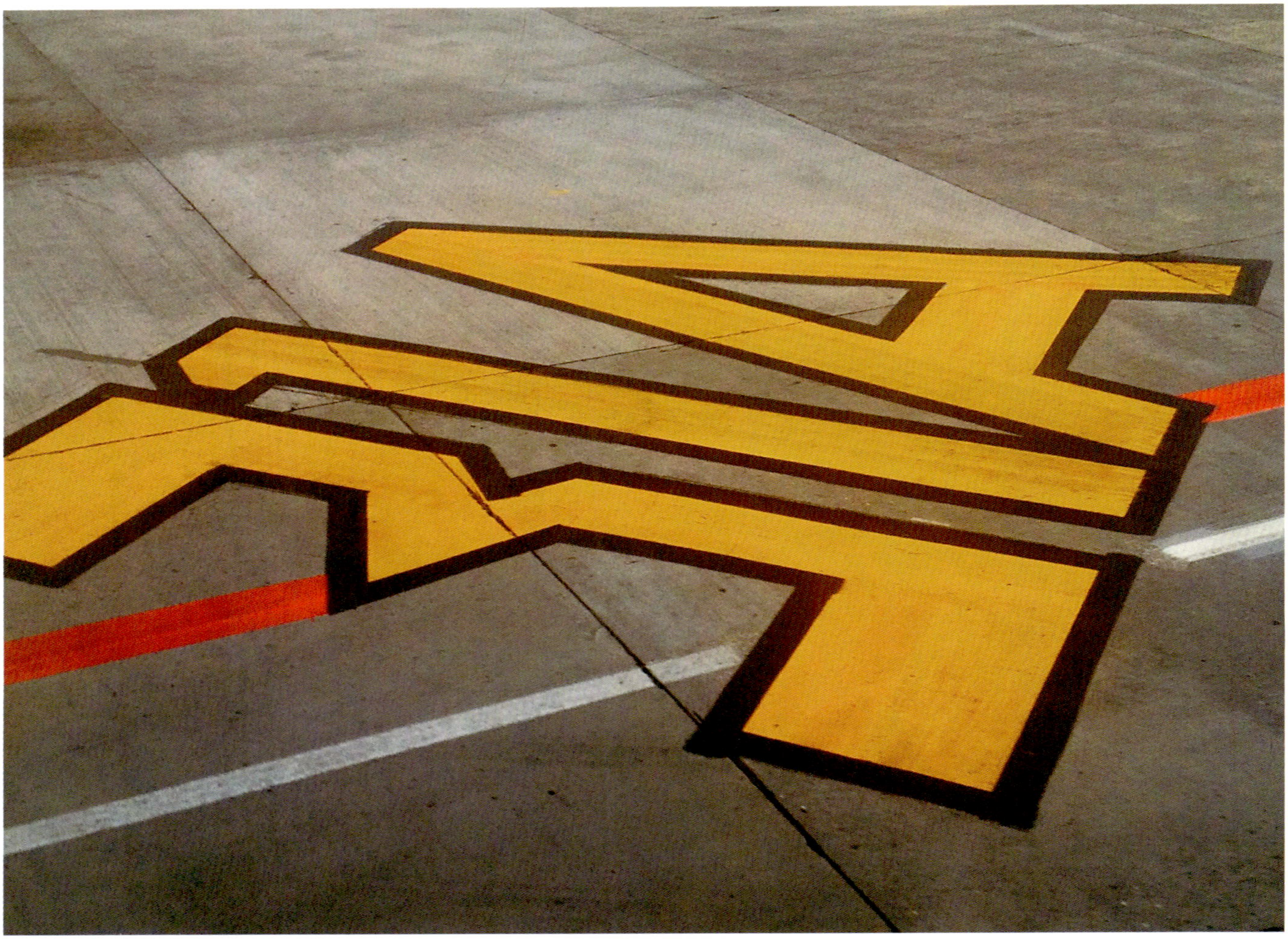

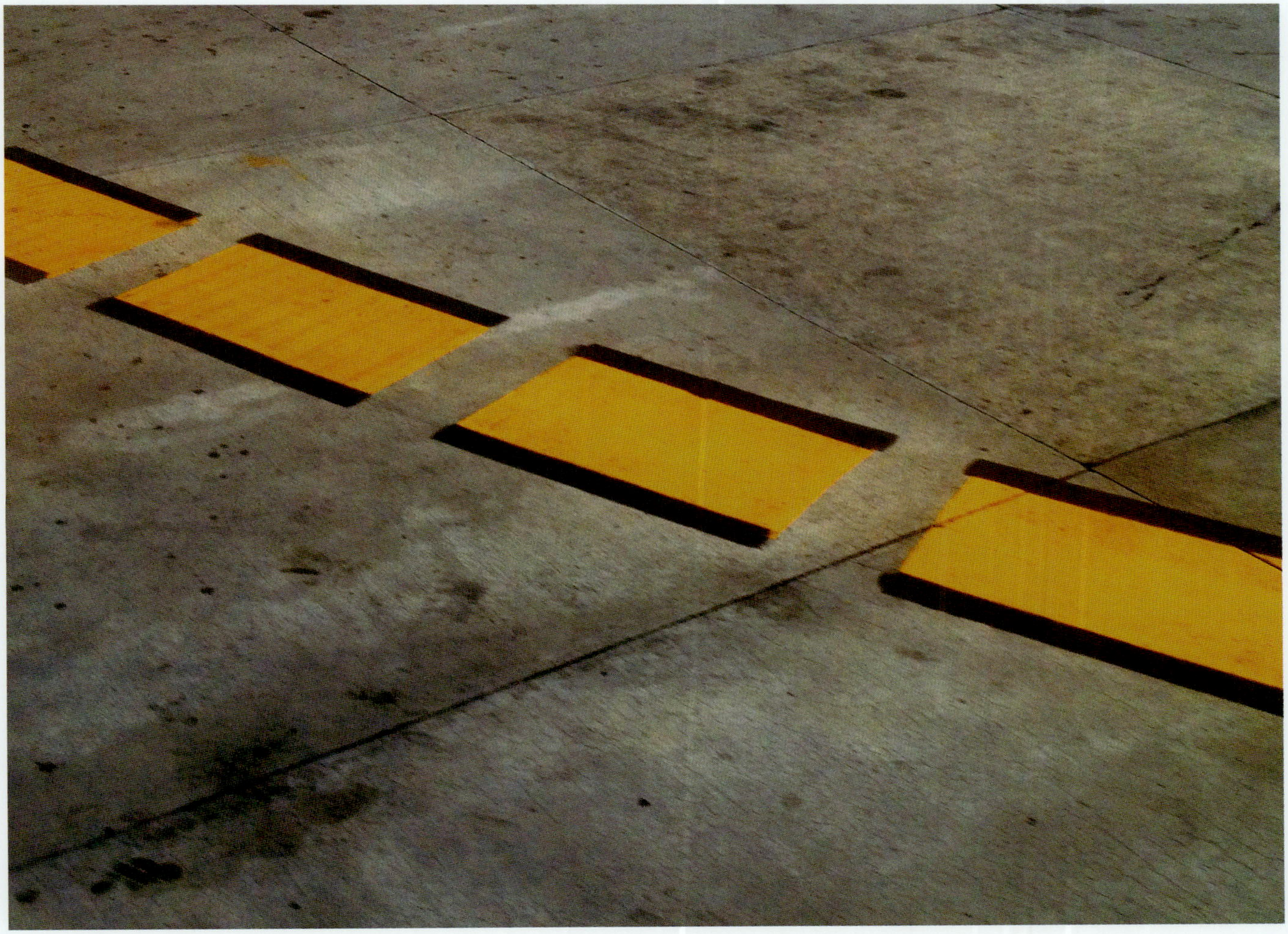

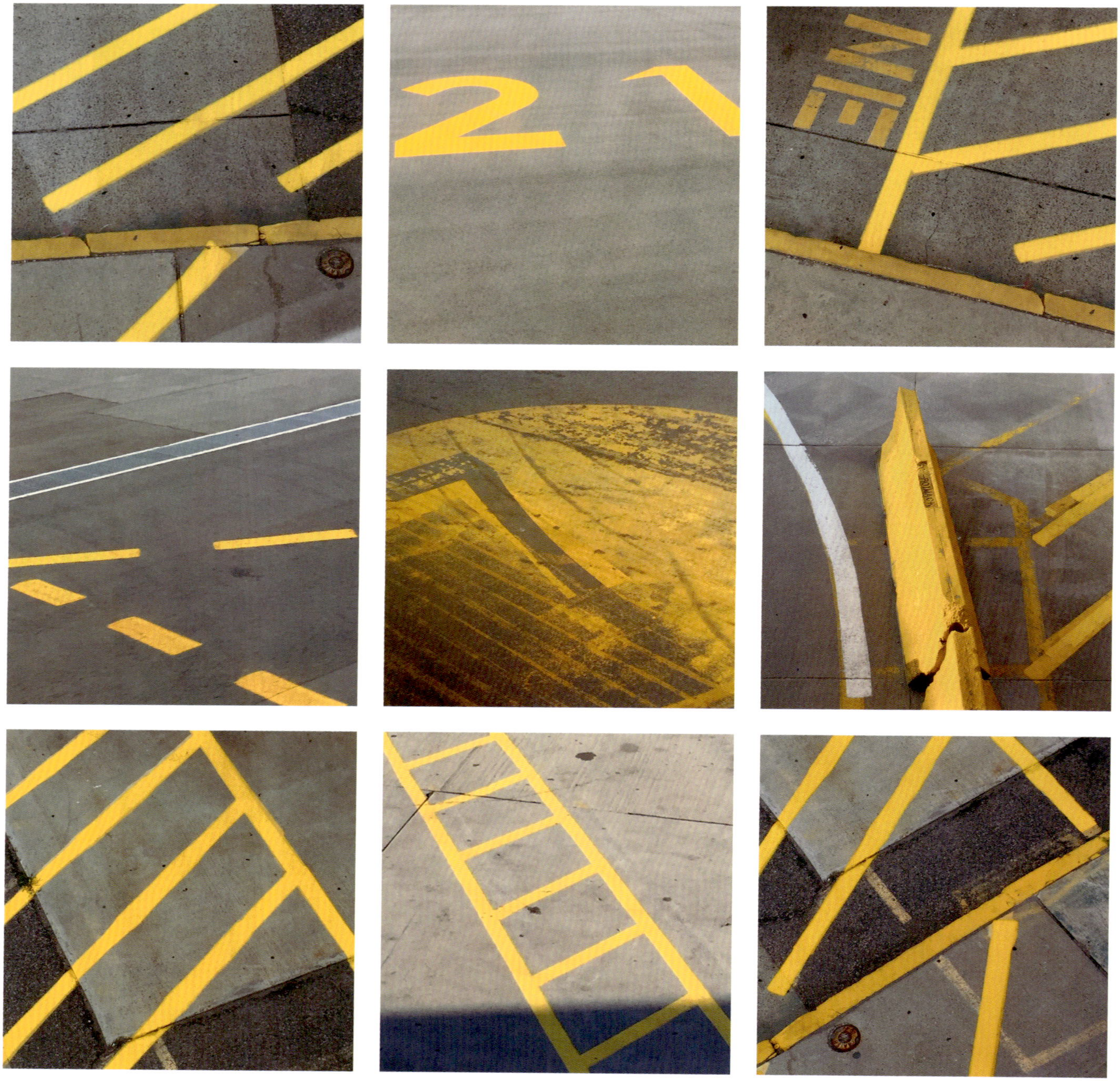

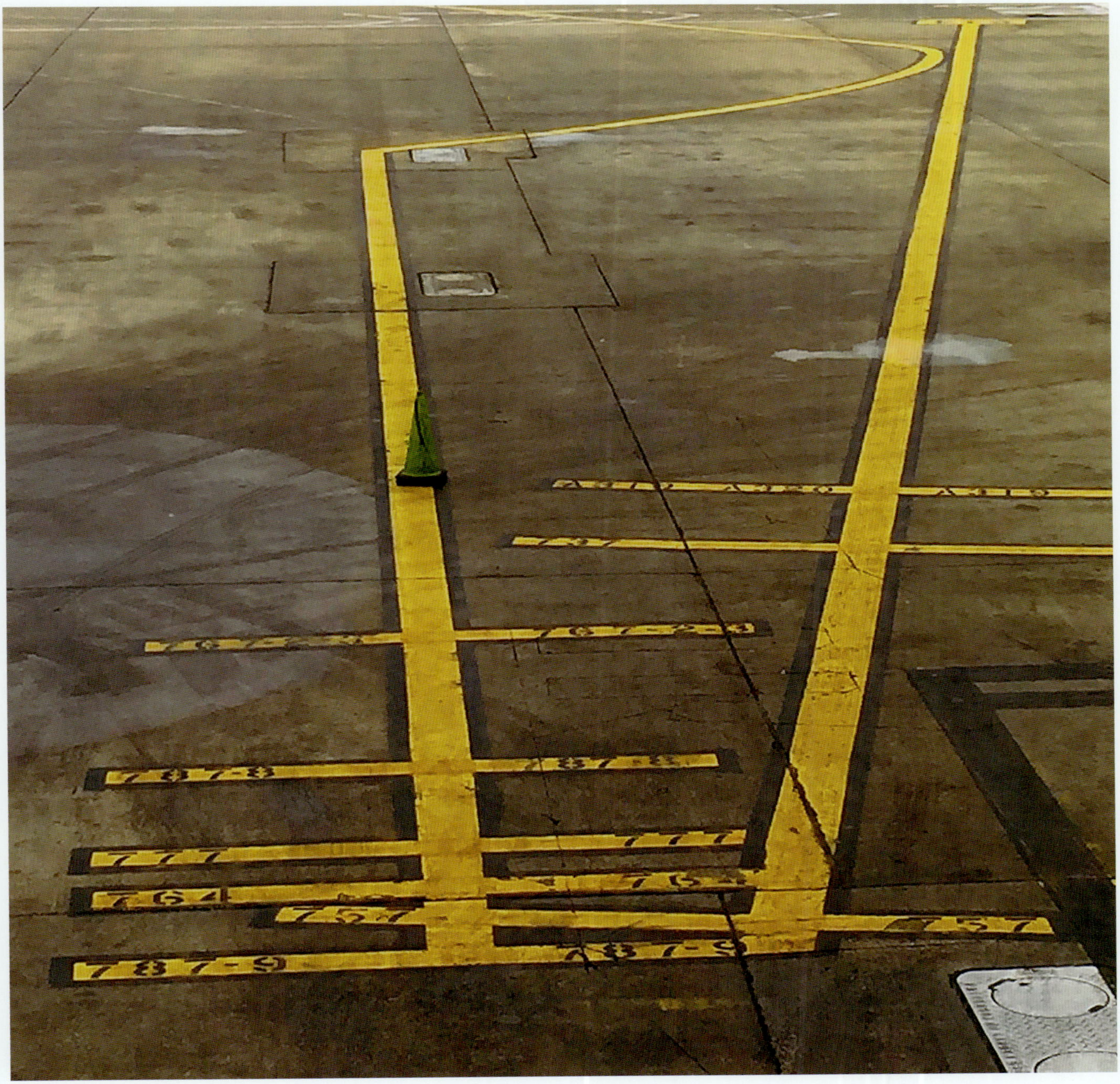
787-8
777
764
757
787-9

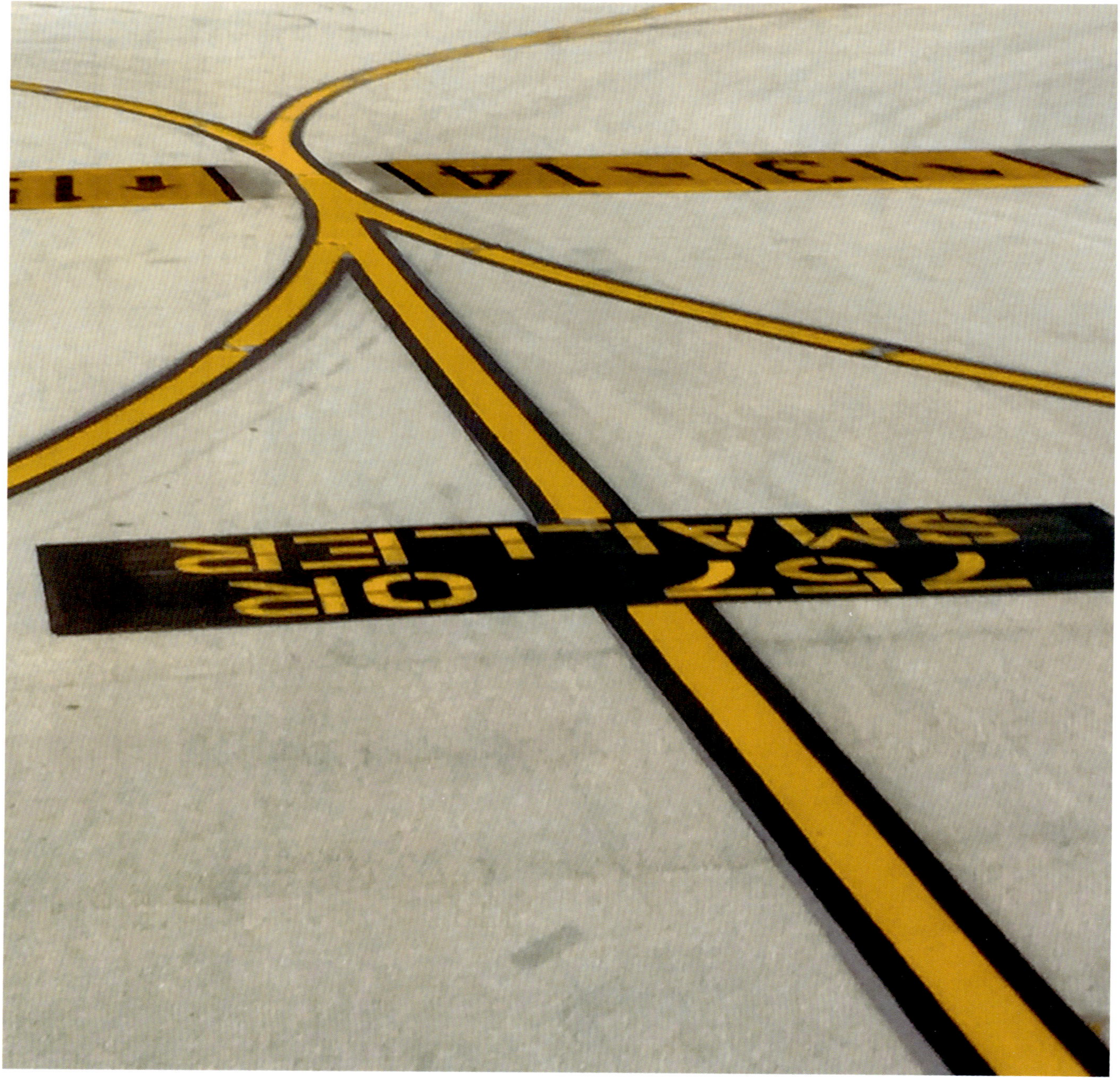
757 OR
SMALLER

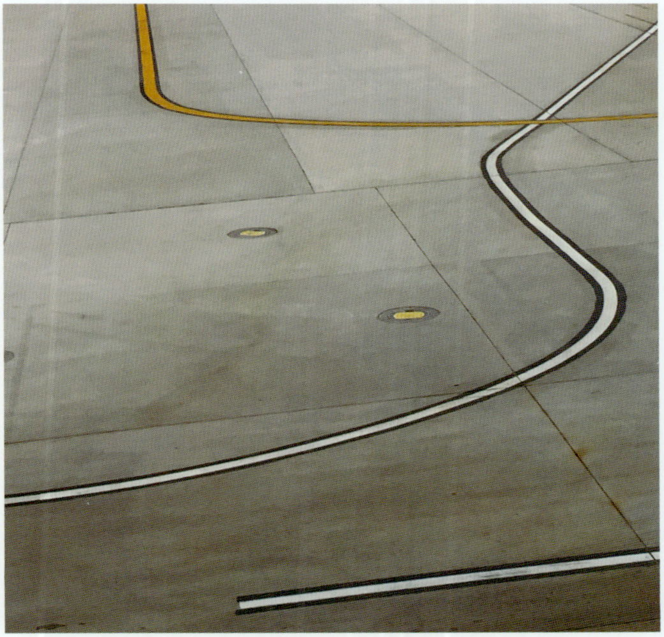

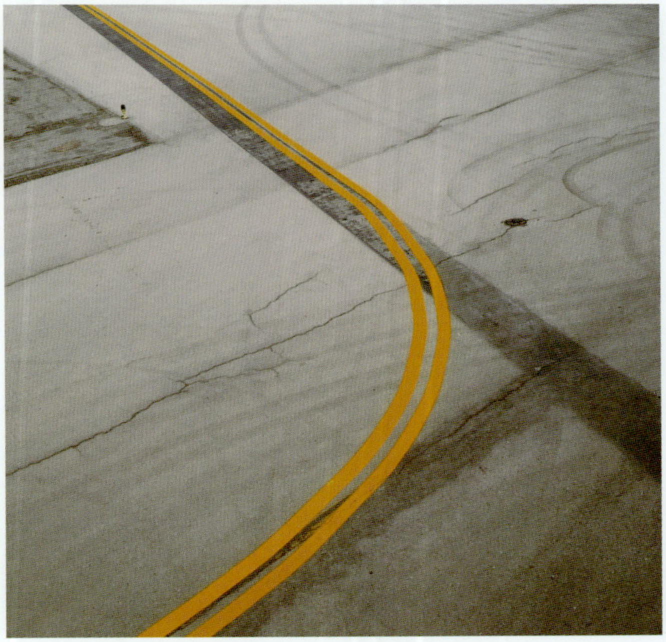

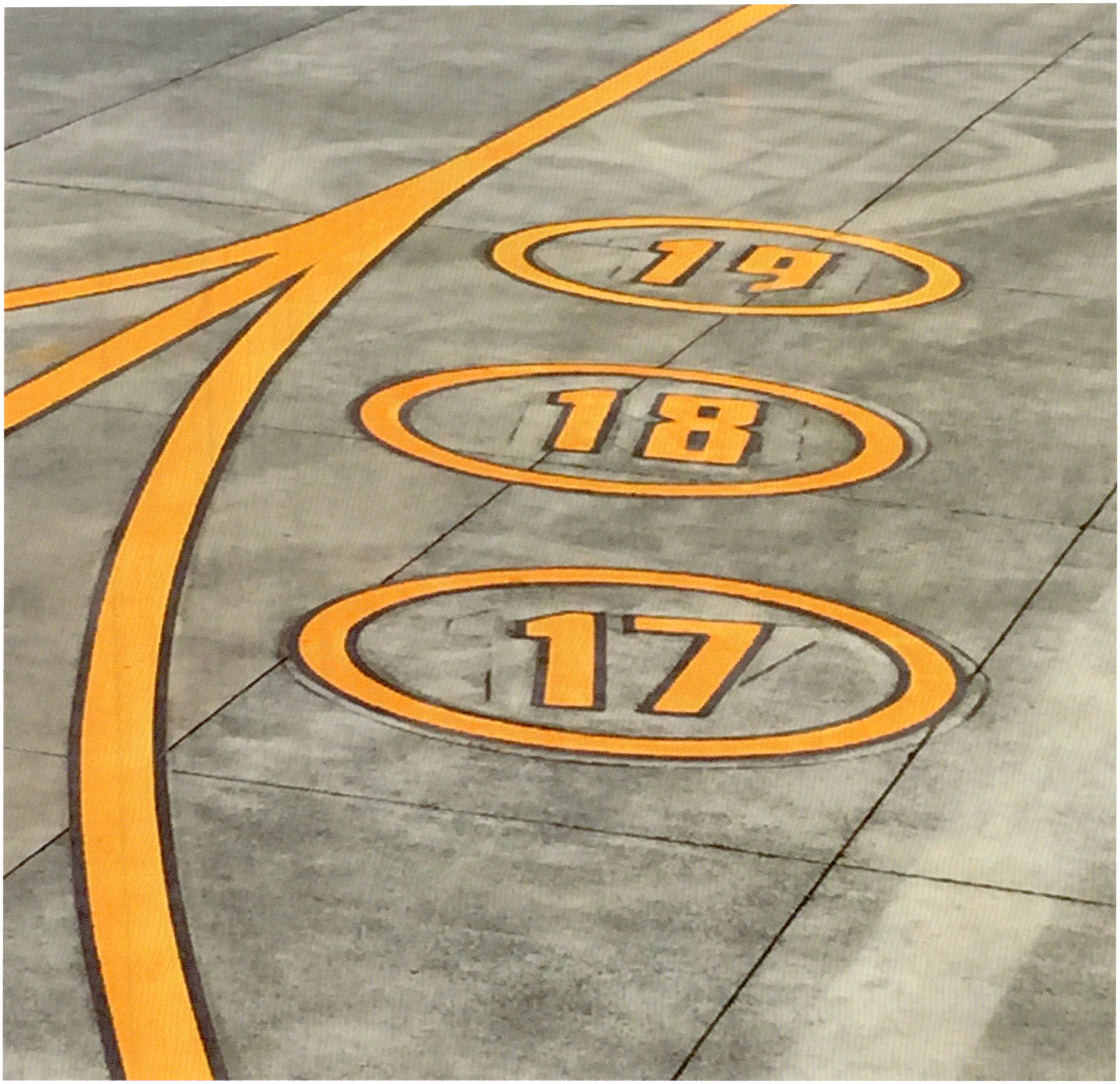
19
18
17

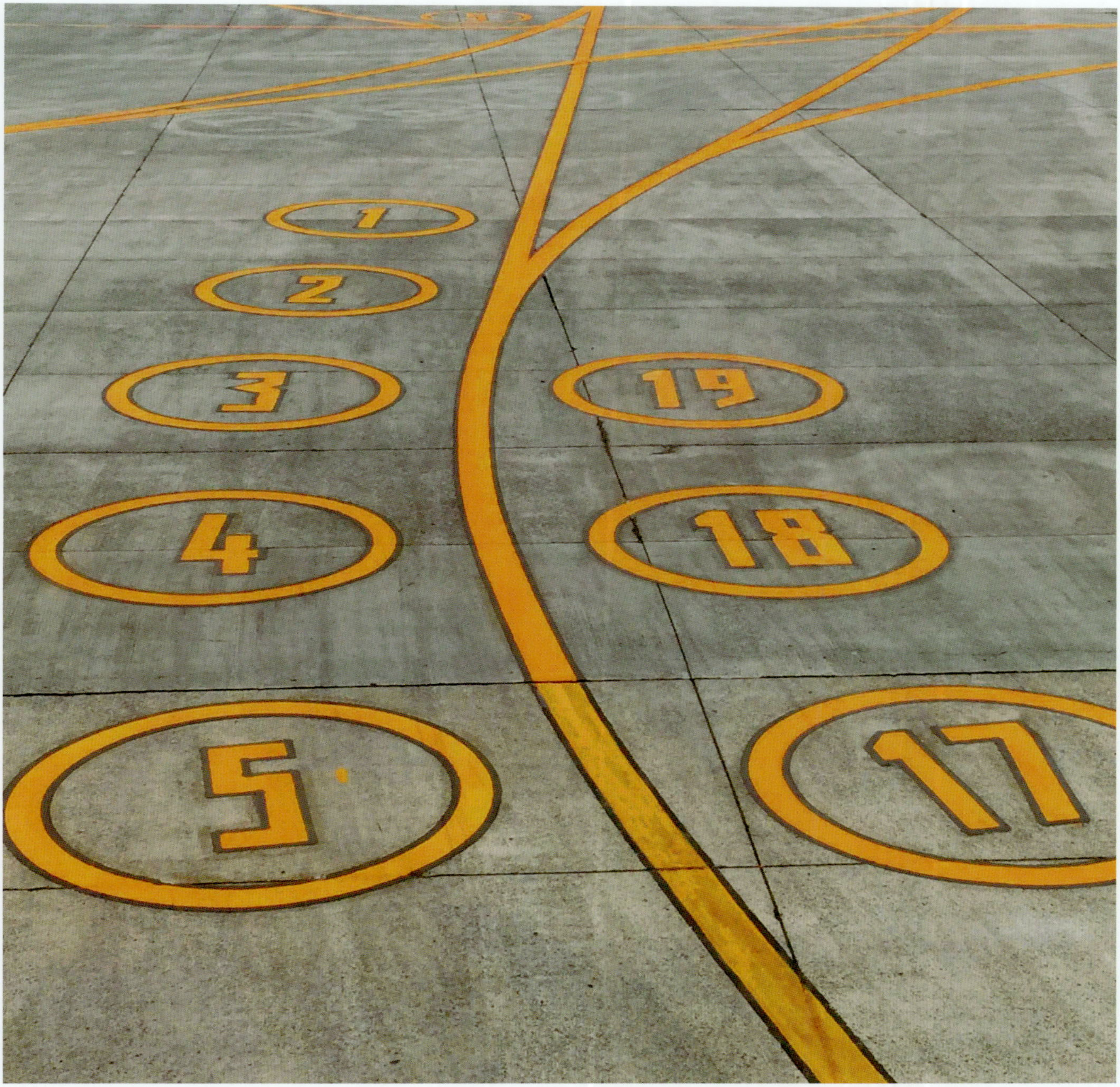
1
2
3
19
4
18
5
17

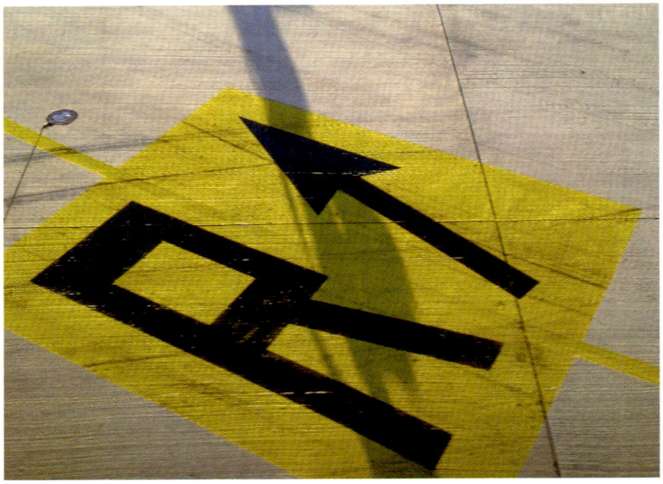

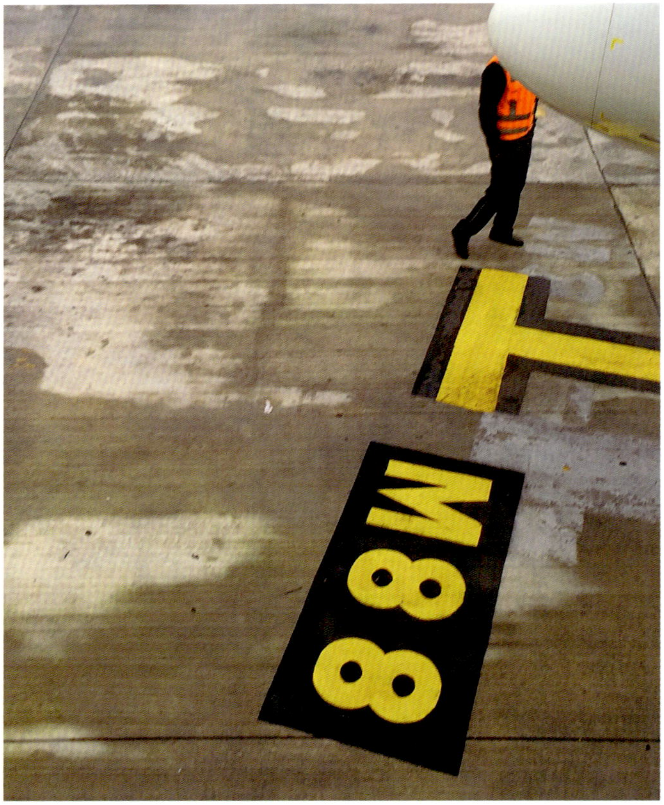

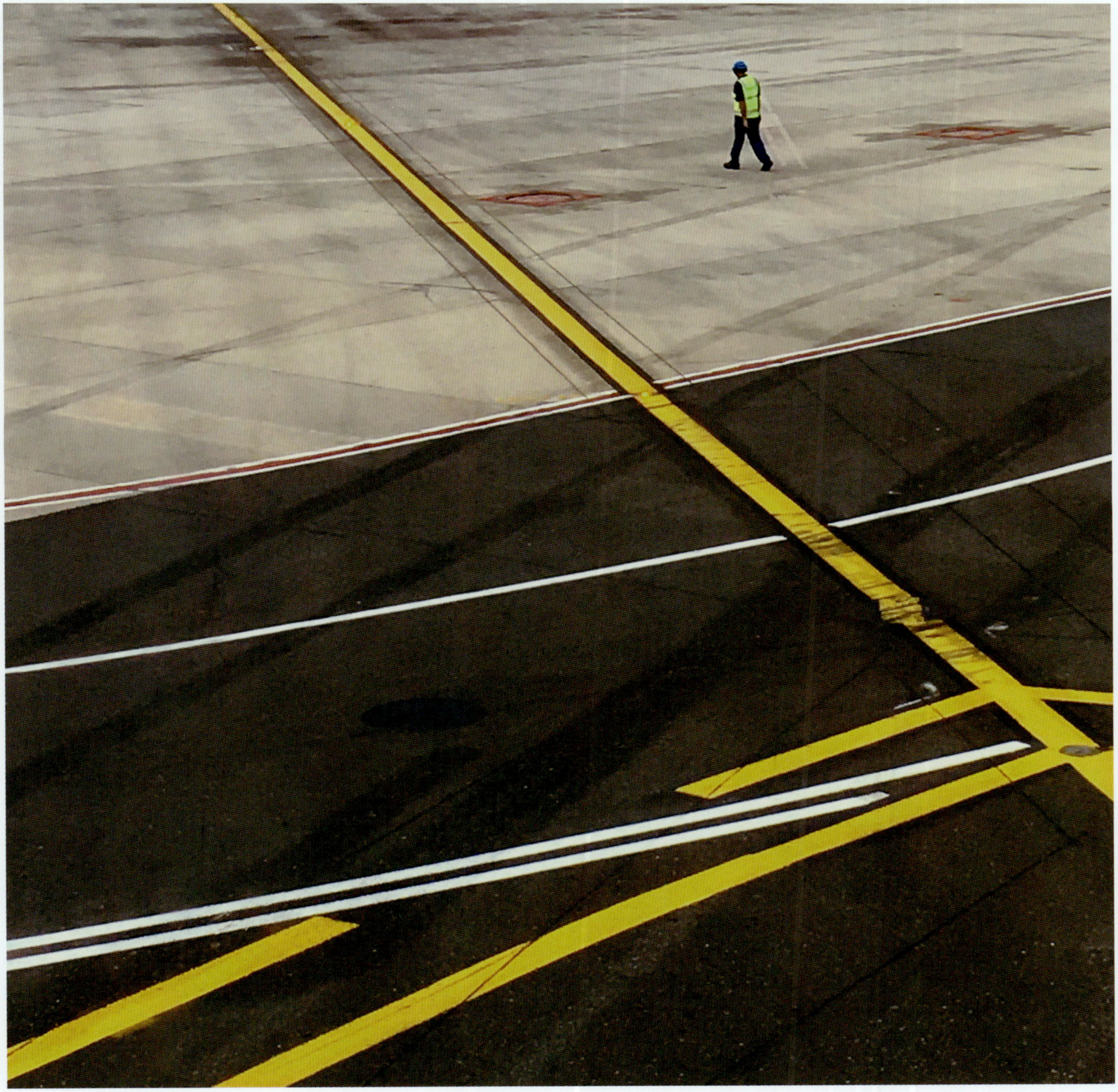

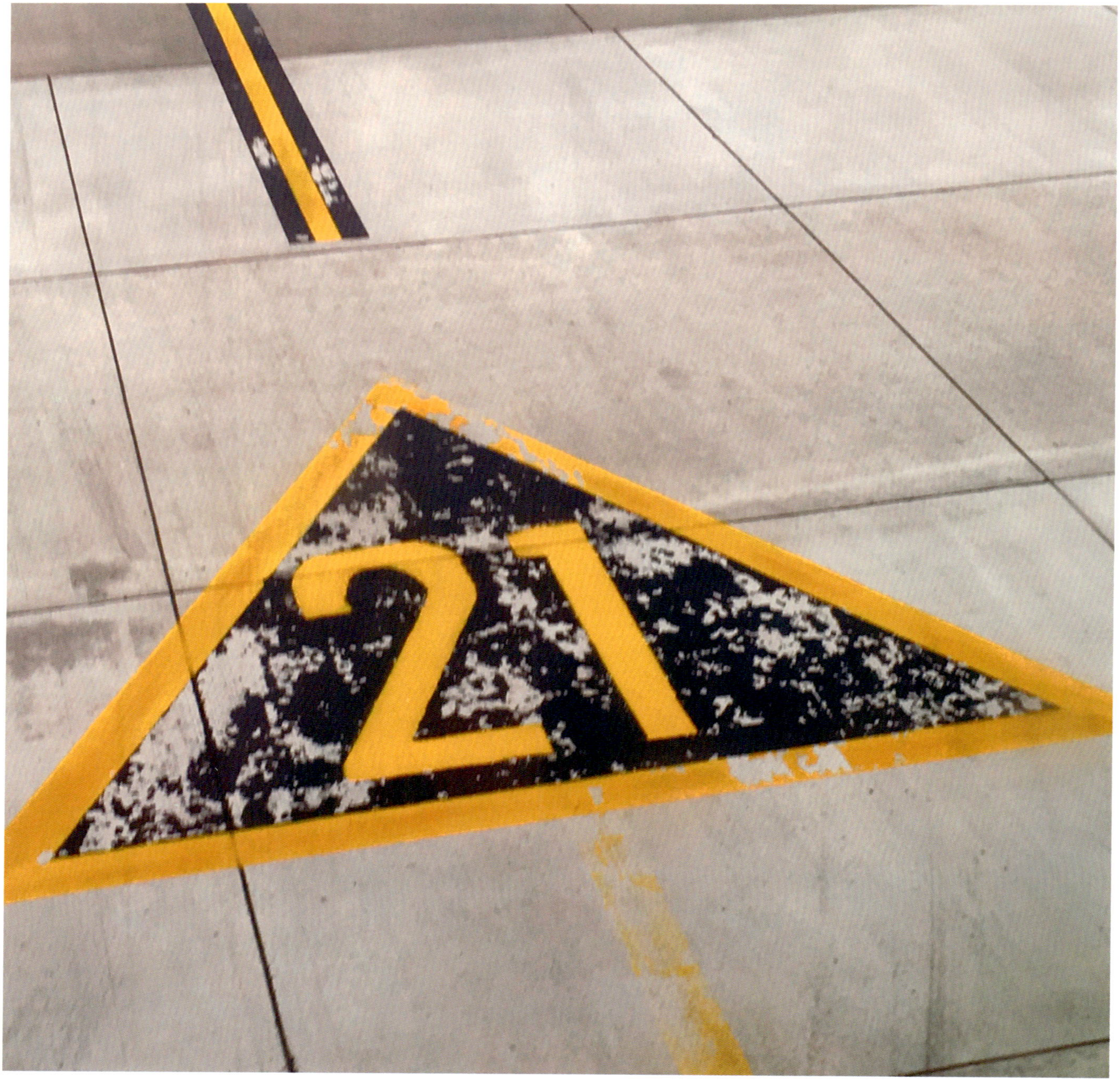
21

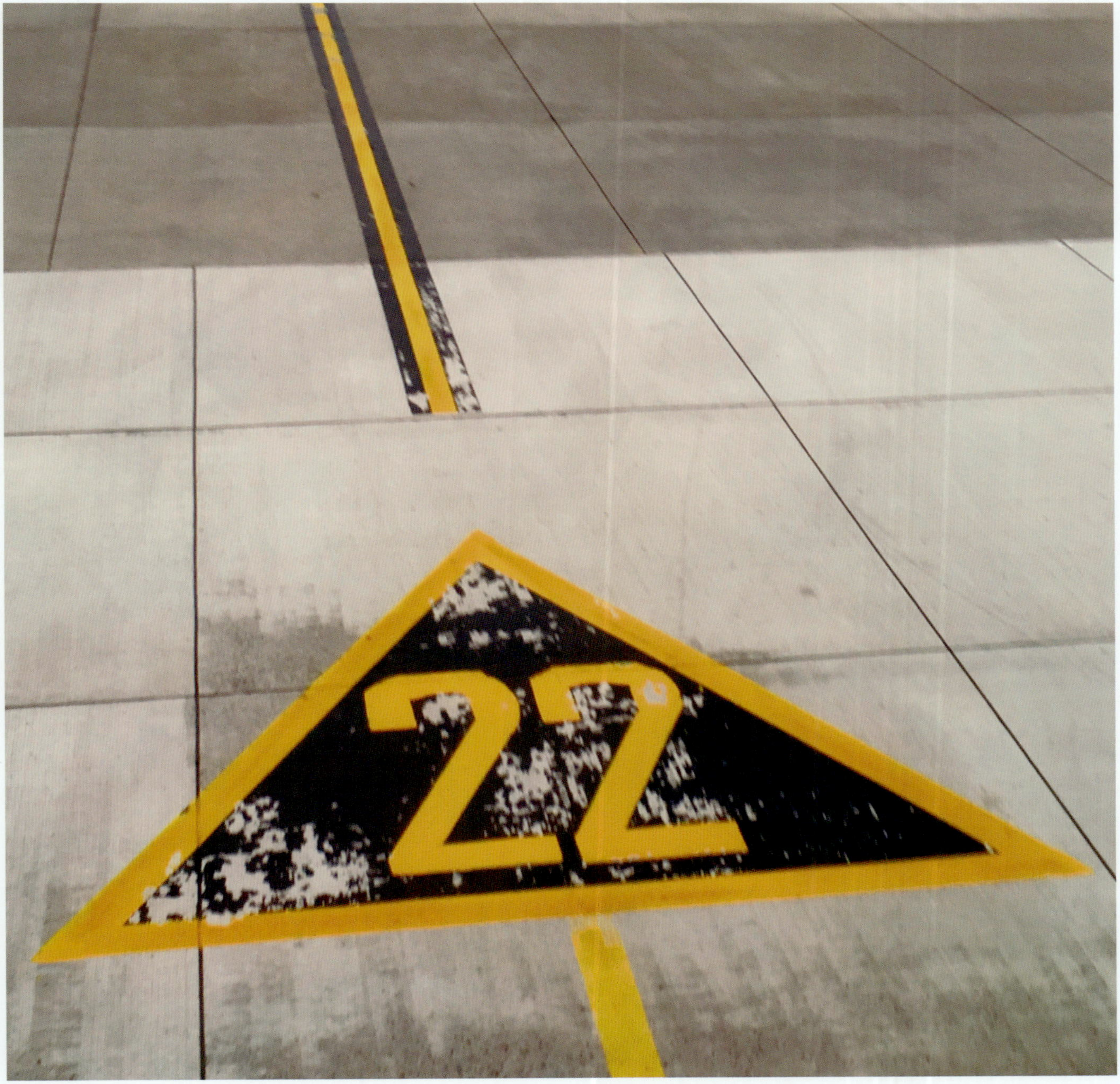
22

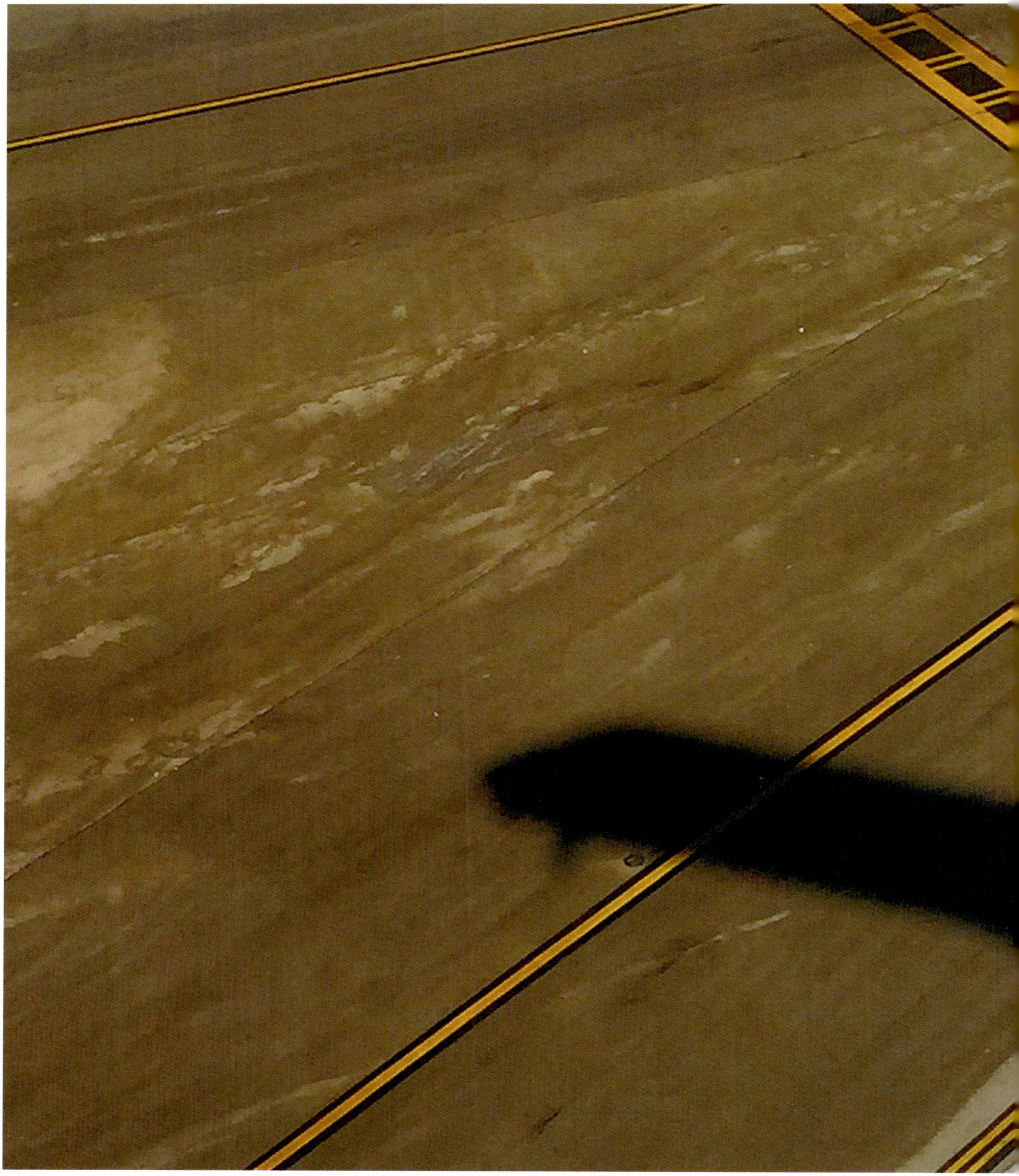

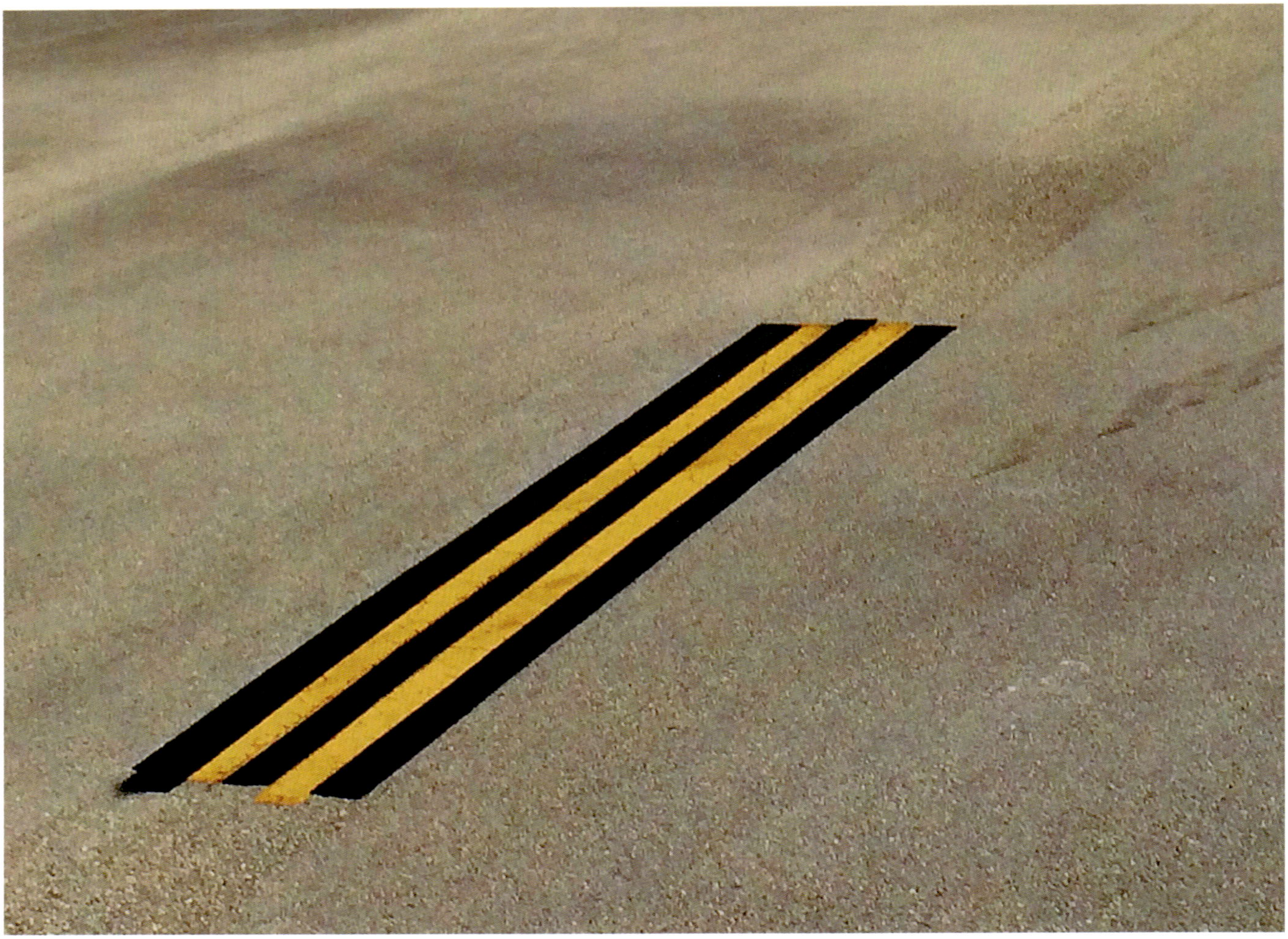

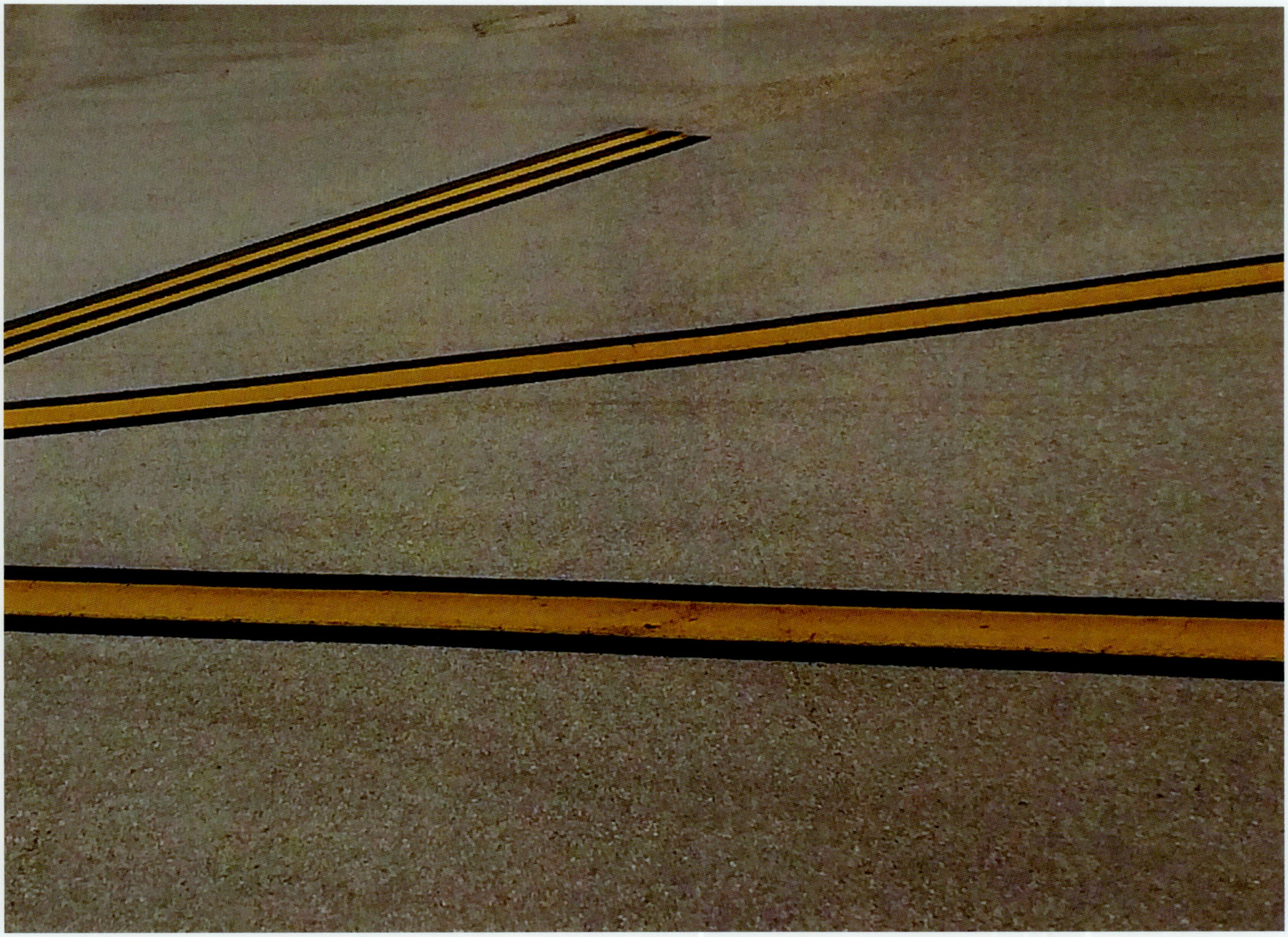

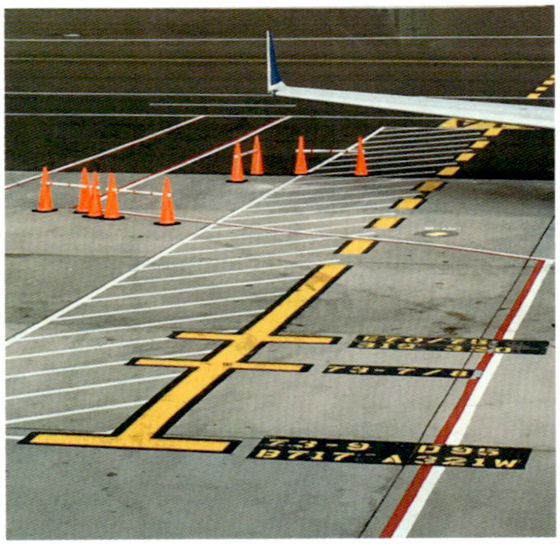
73-9
B717-A321W
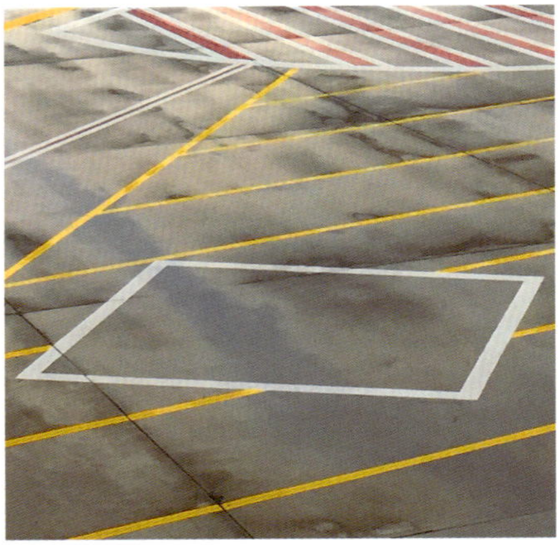
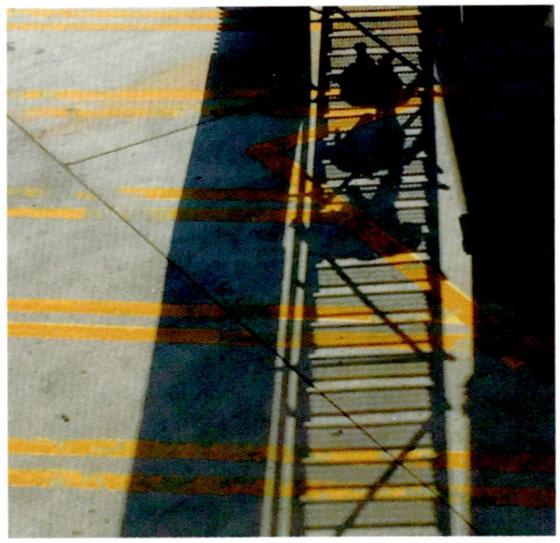
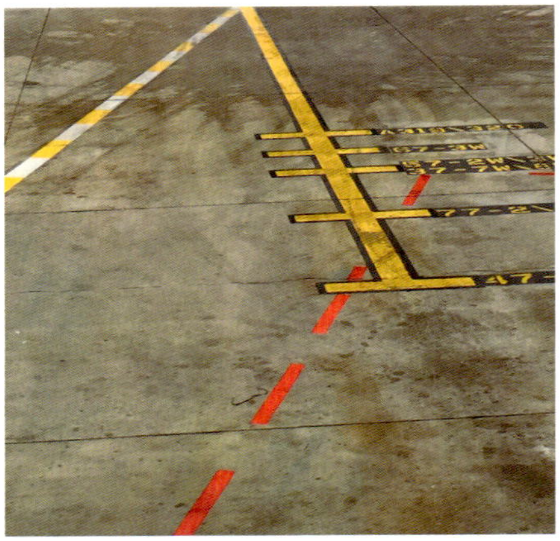
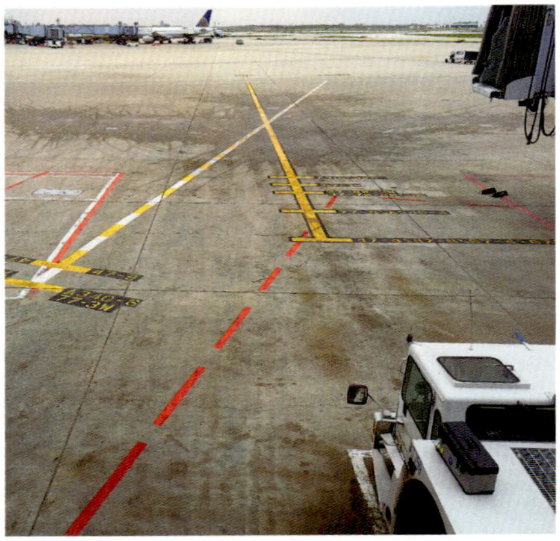
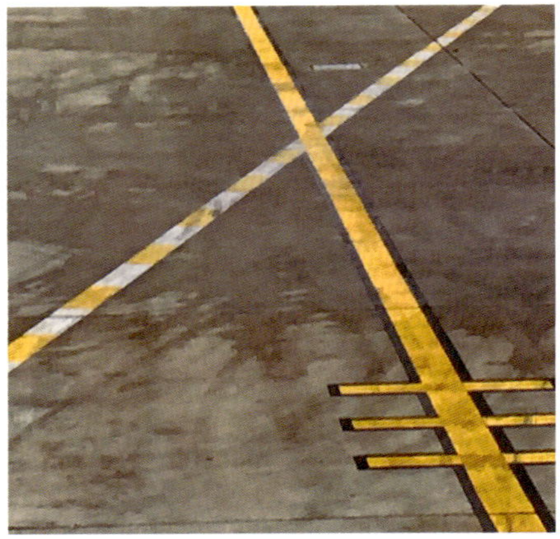
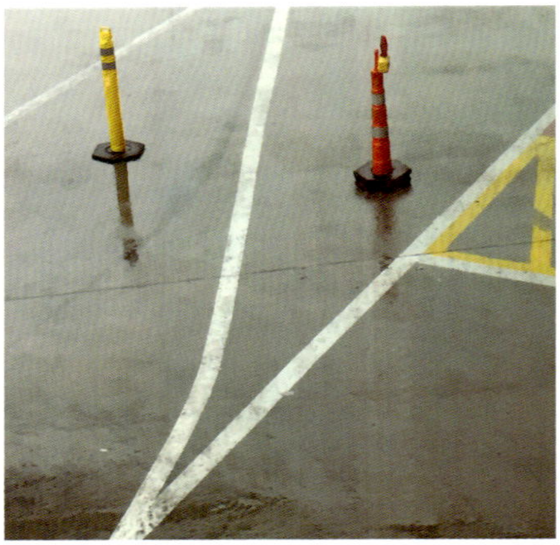
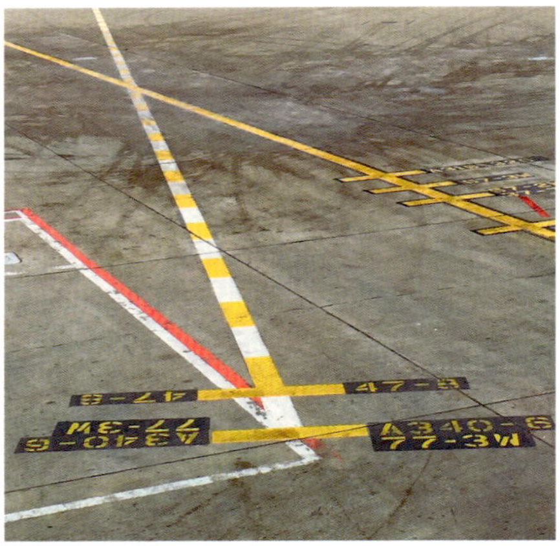
47-8
A340-6
77-3W
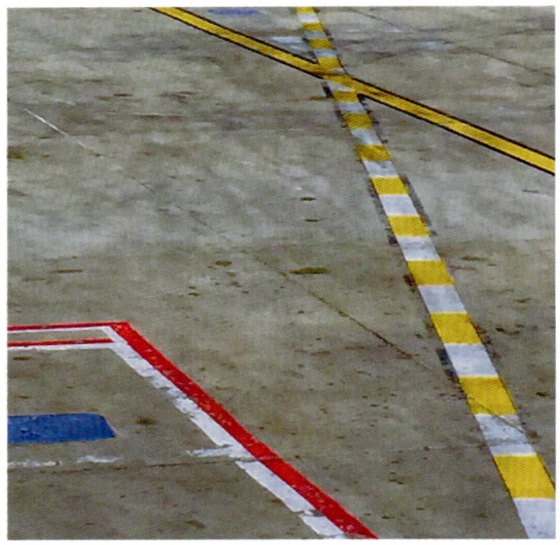

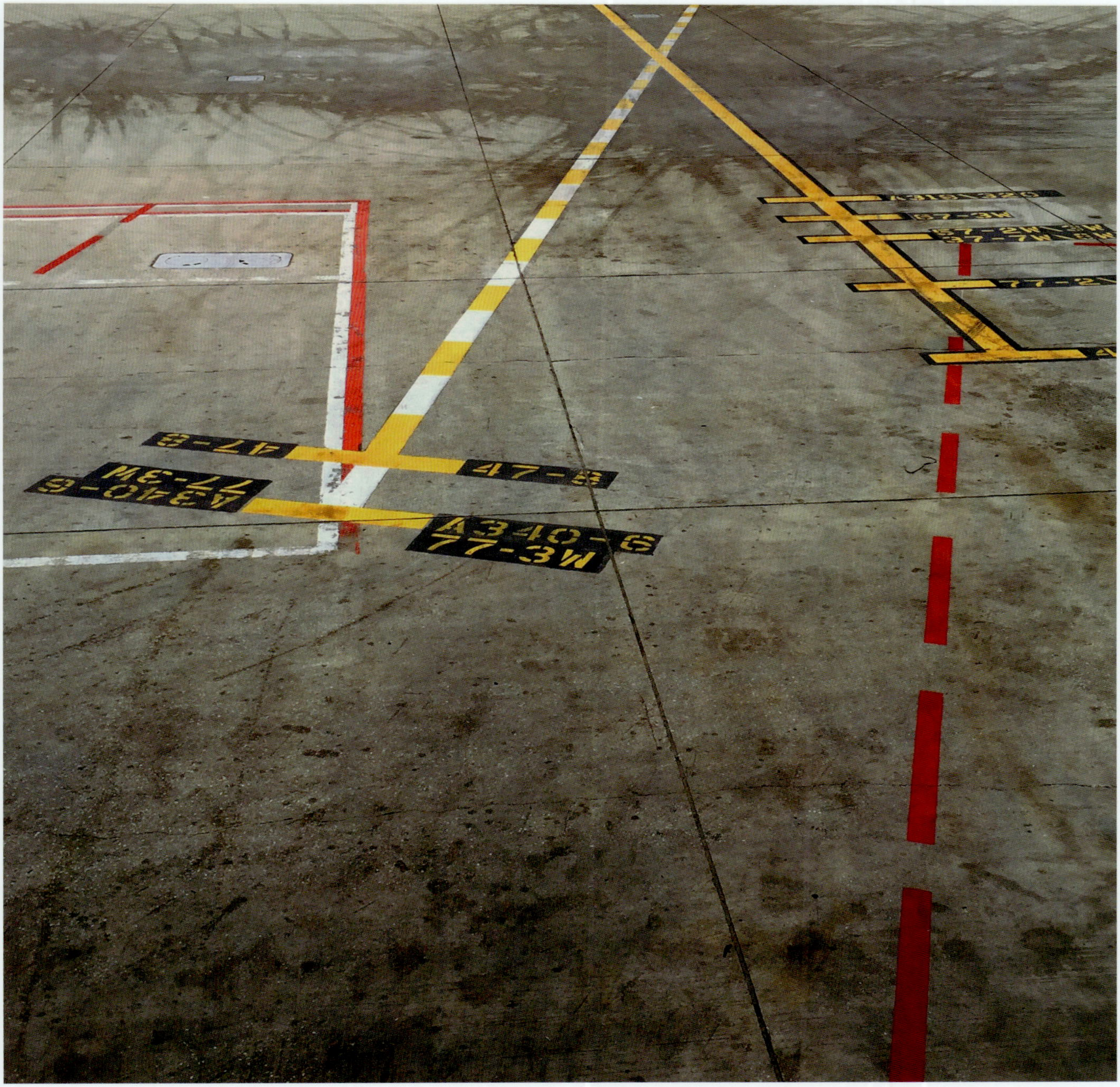
47-8
A340-6
77-3W

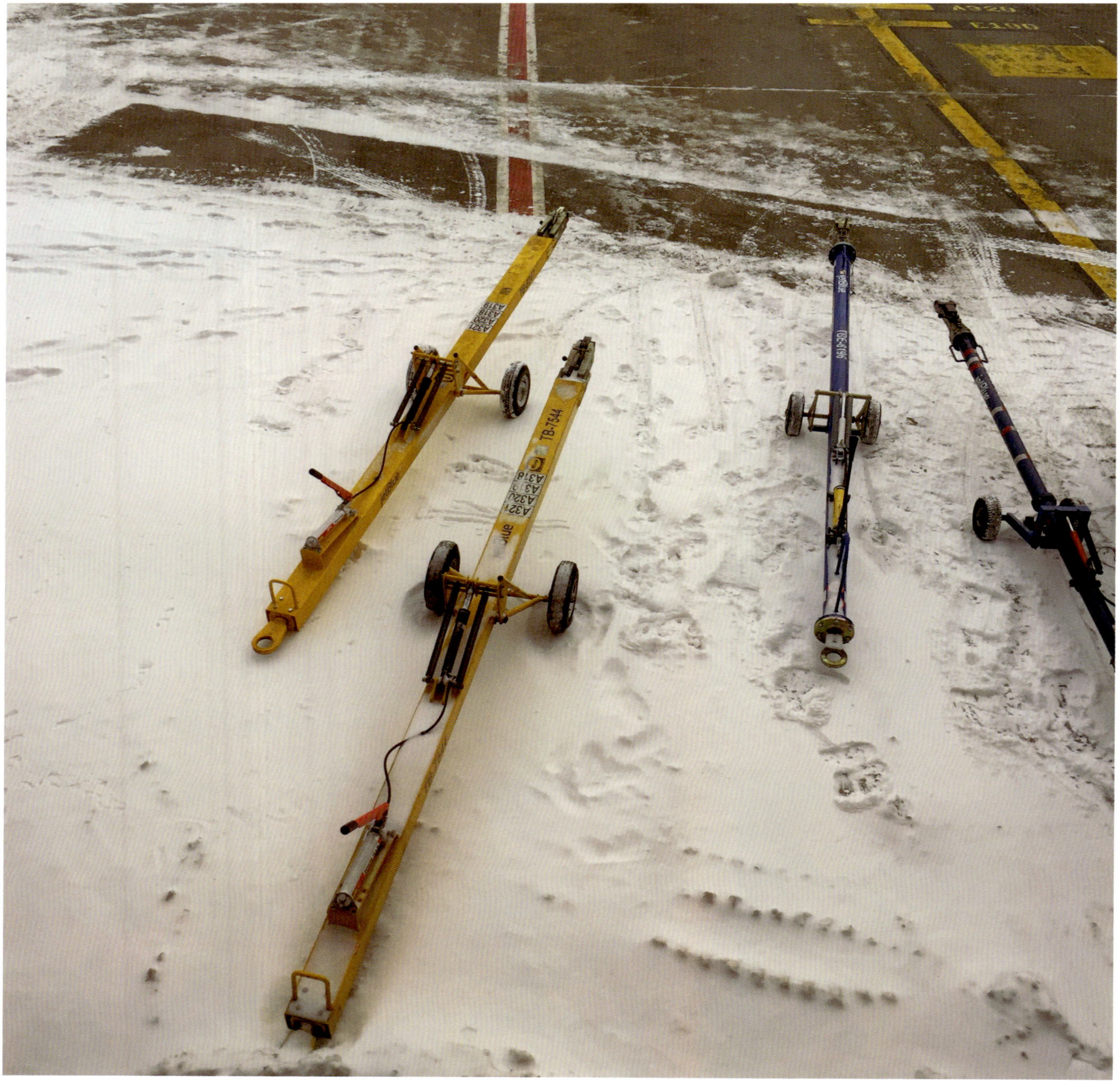

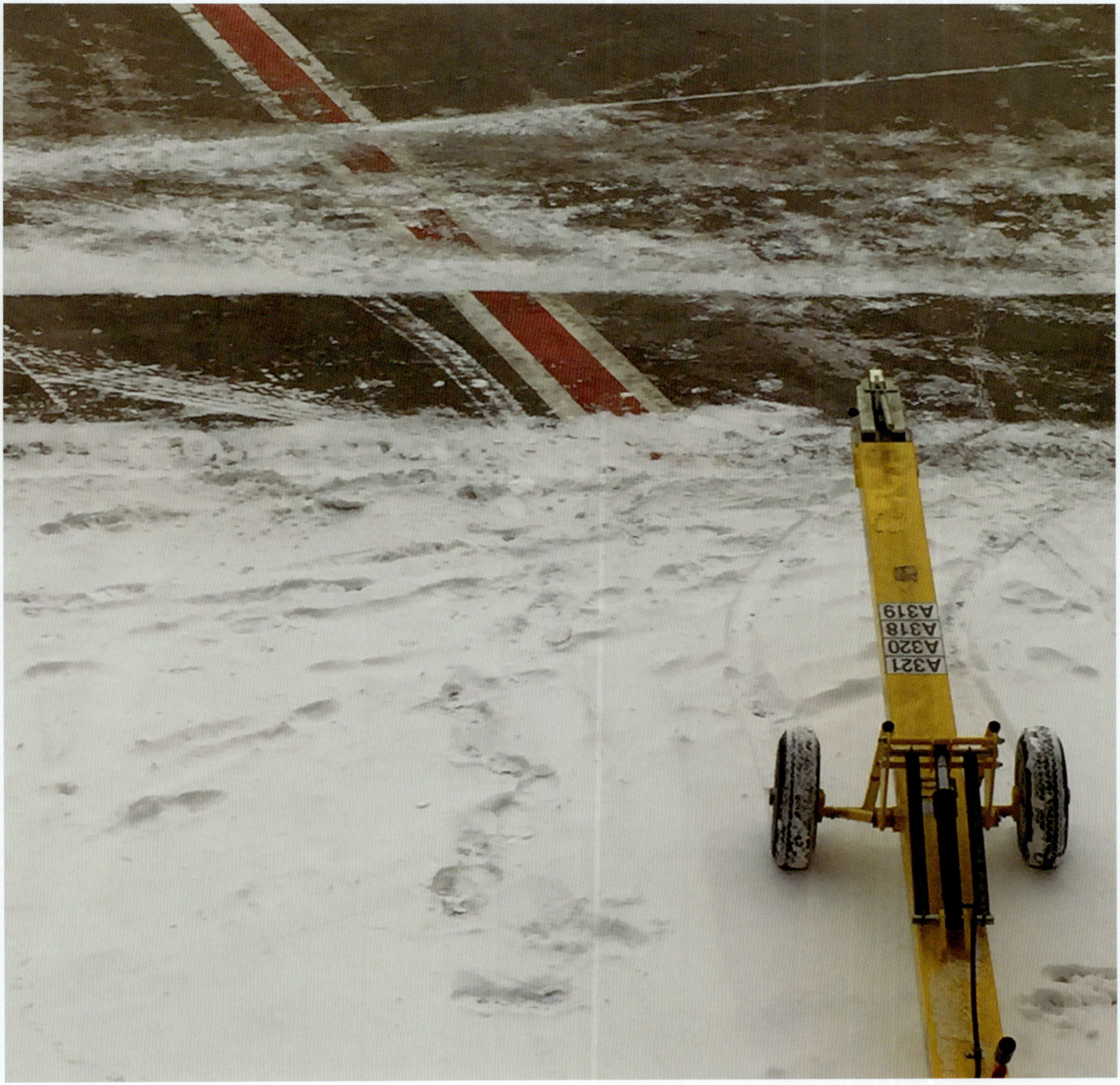
A319
A318
A320
A321

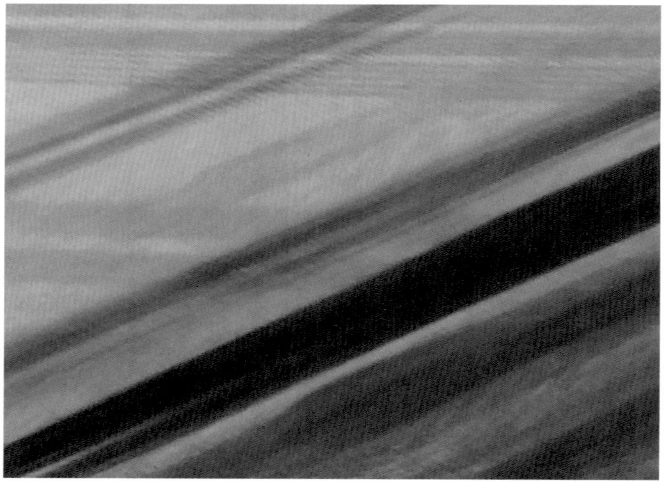

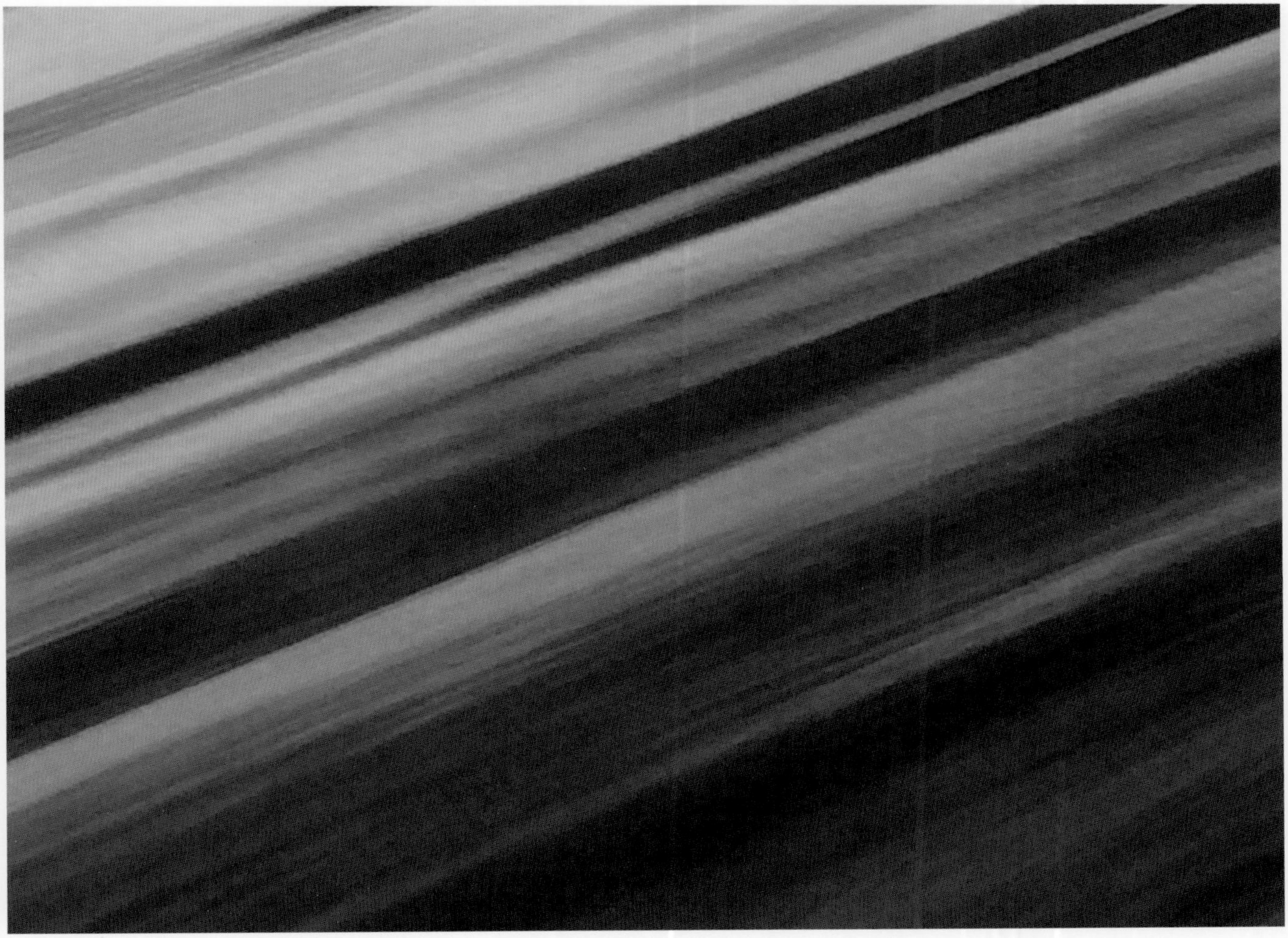

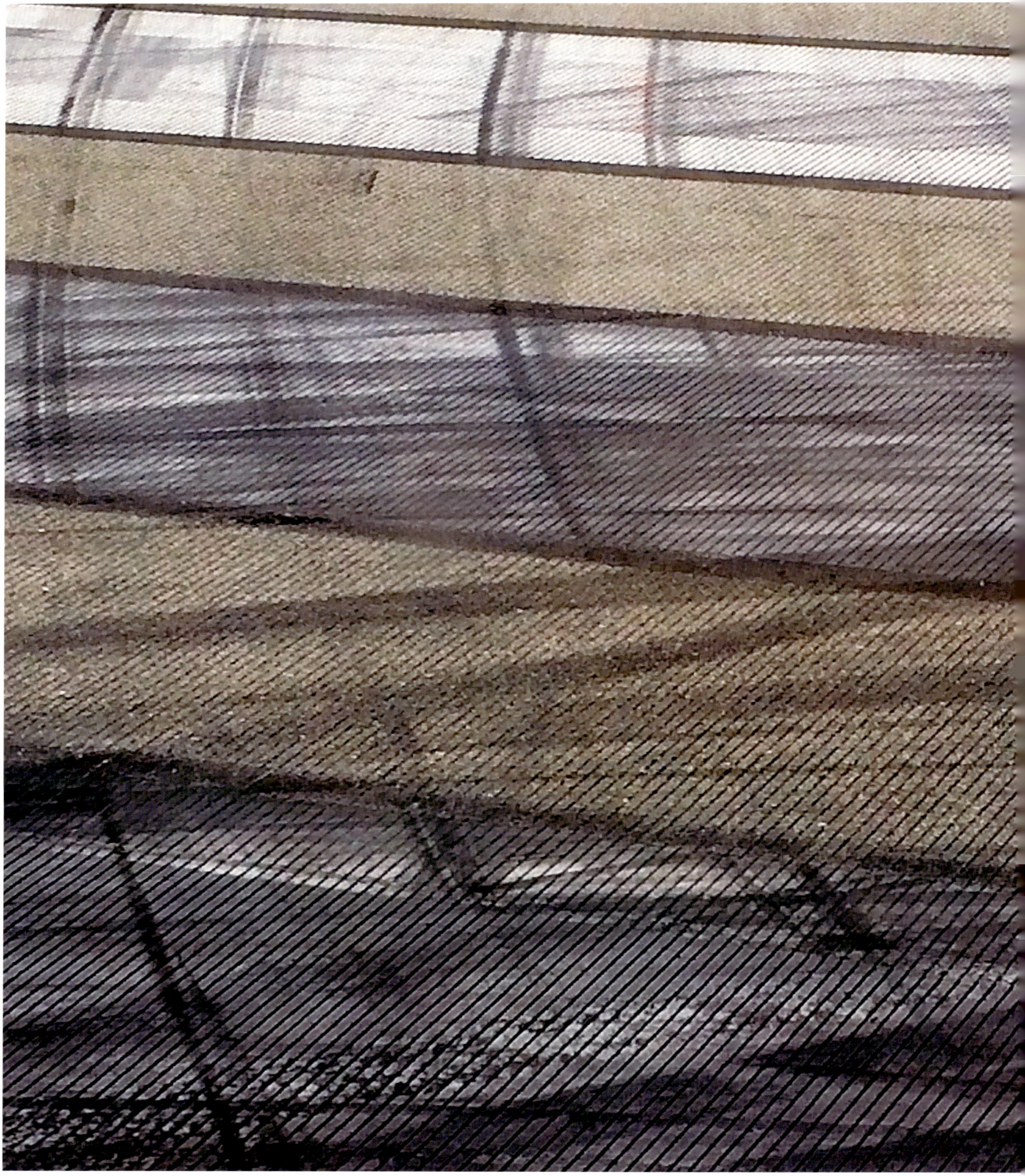

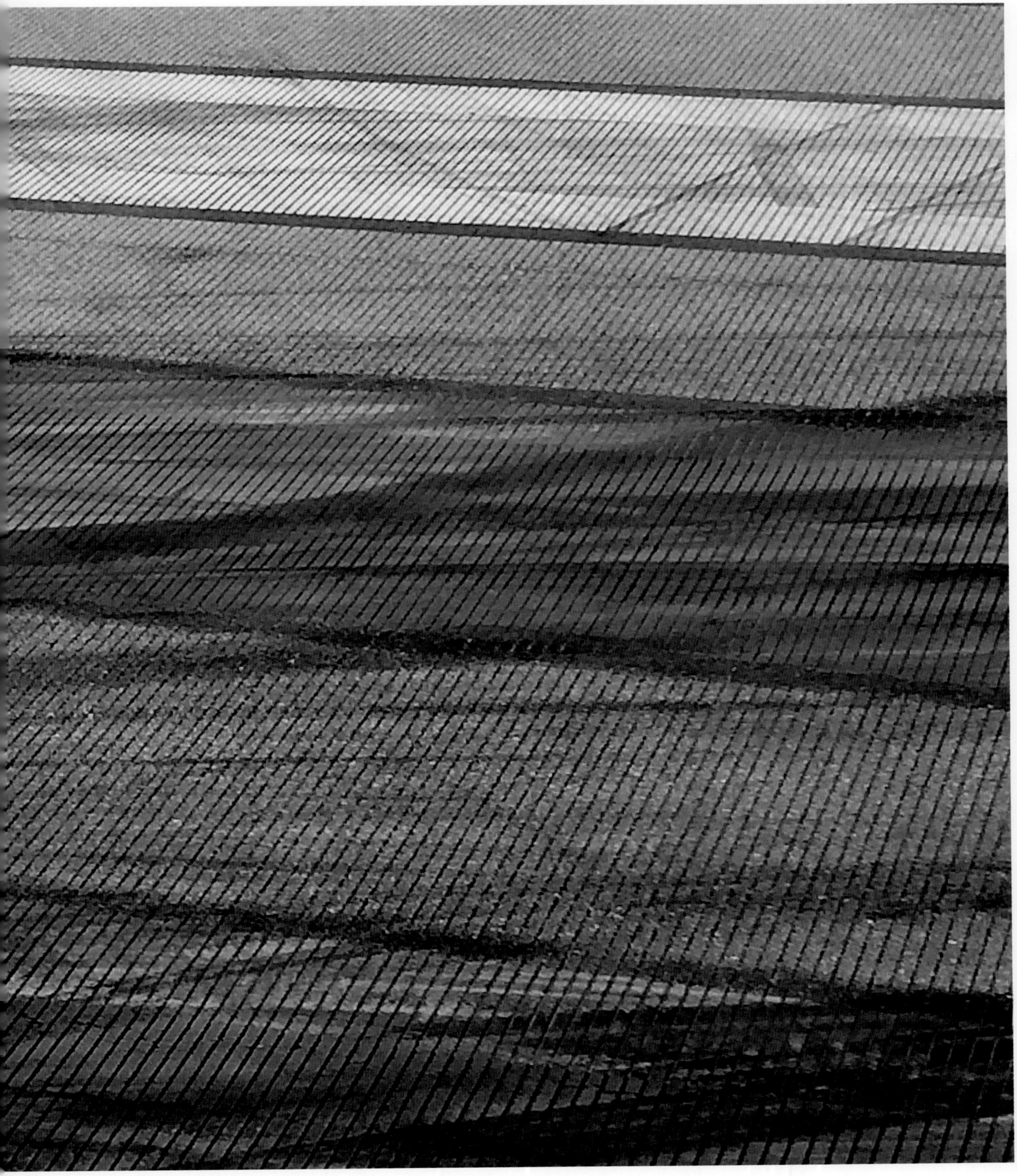

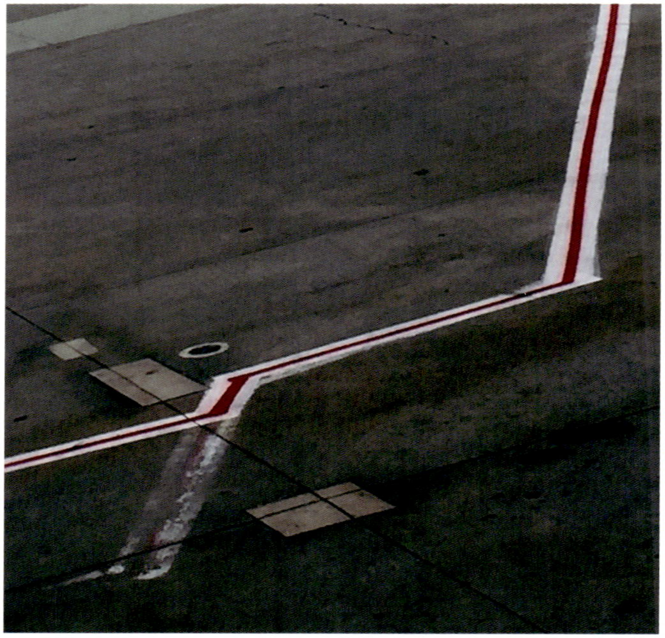

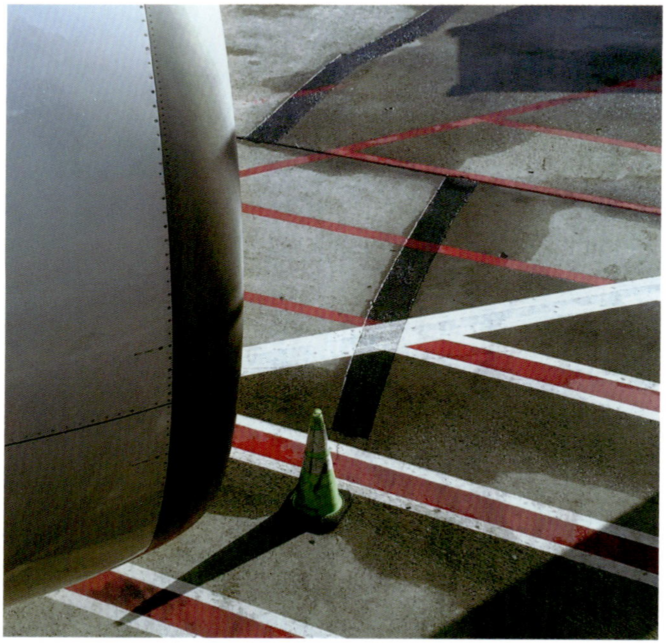

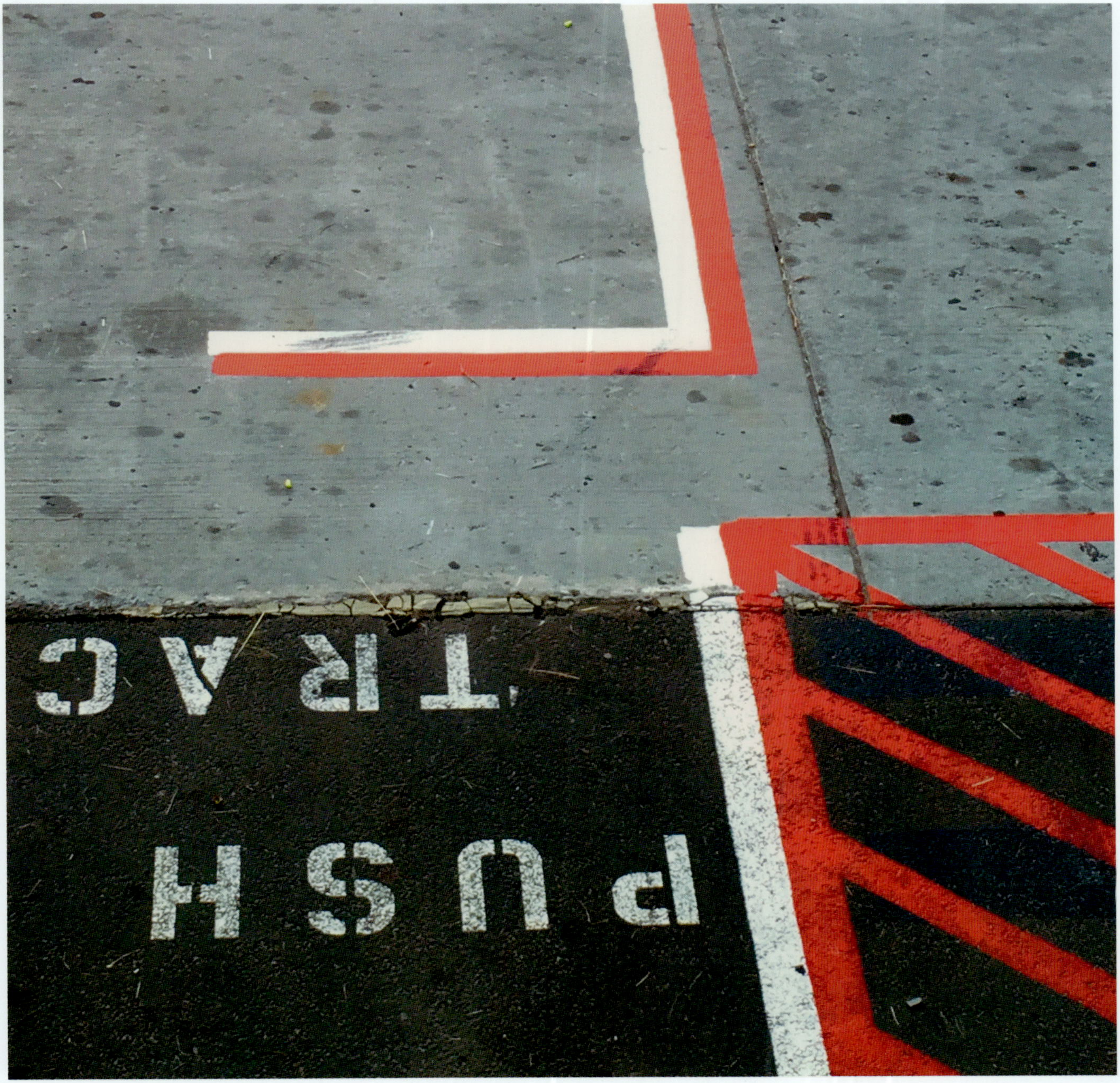
PUSH
CART,

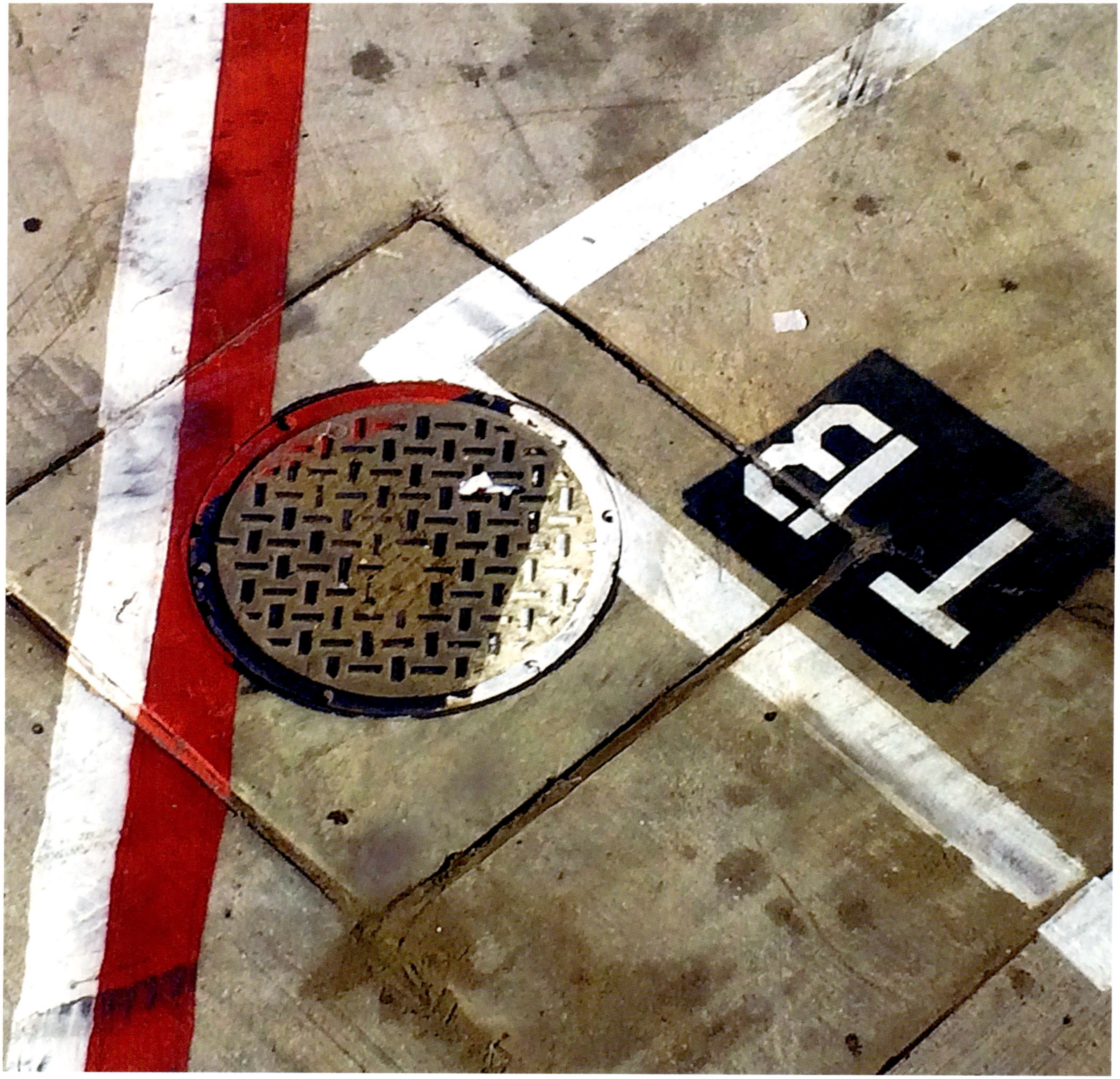

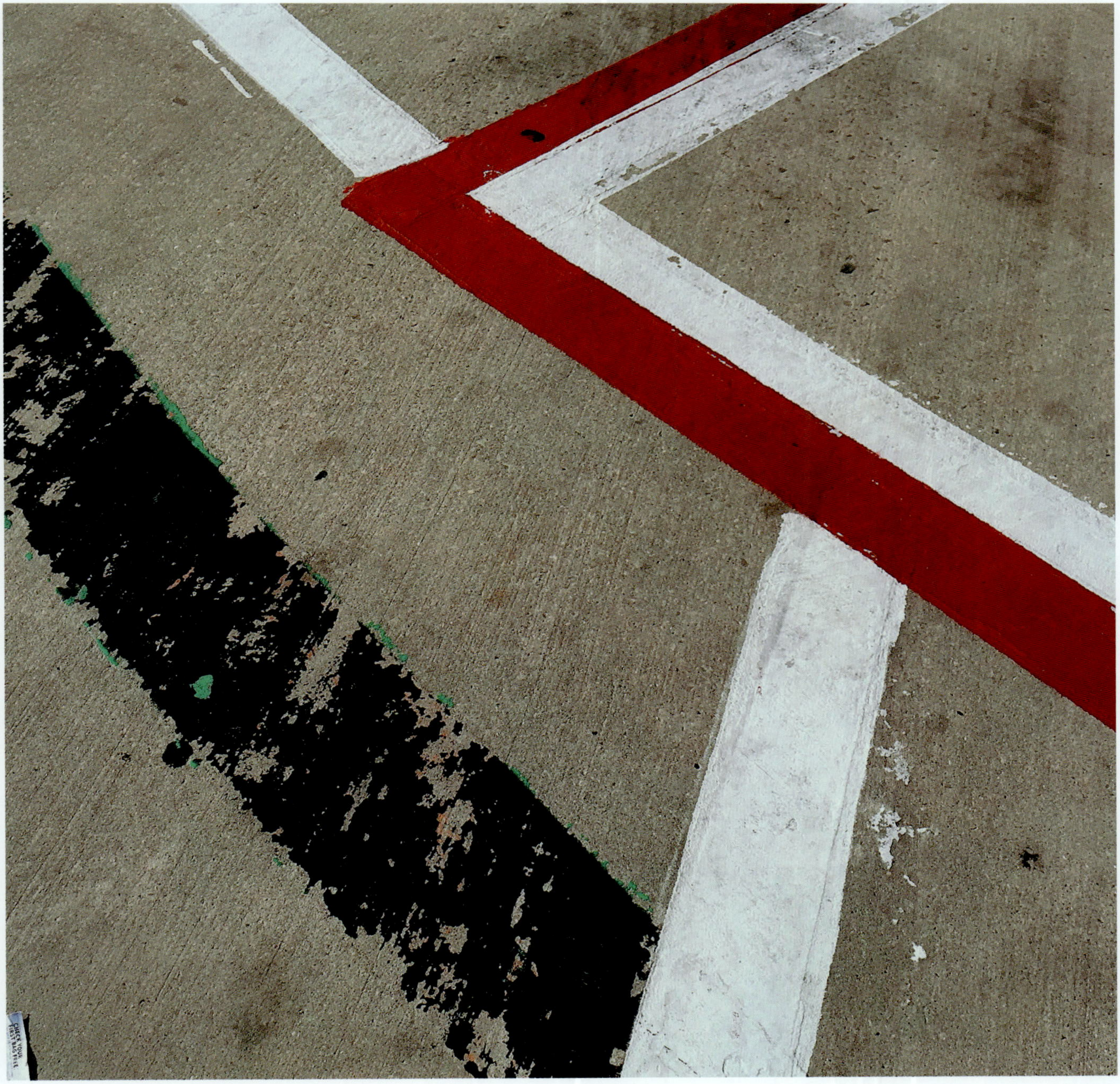

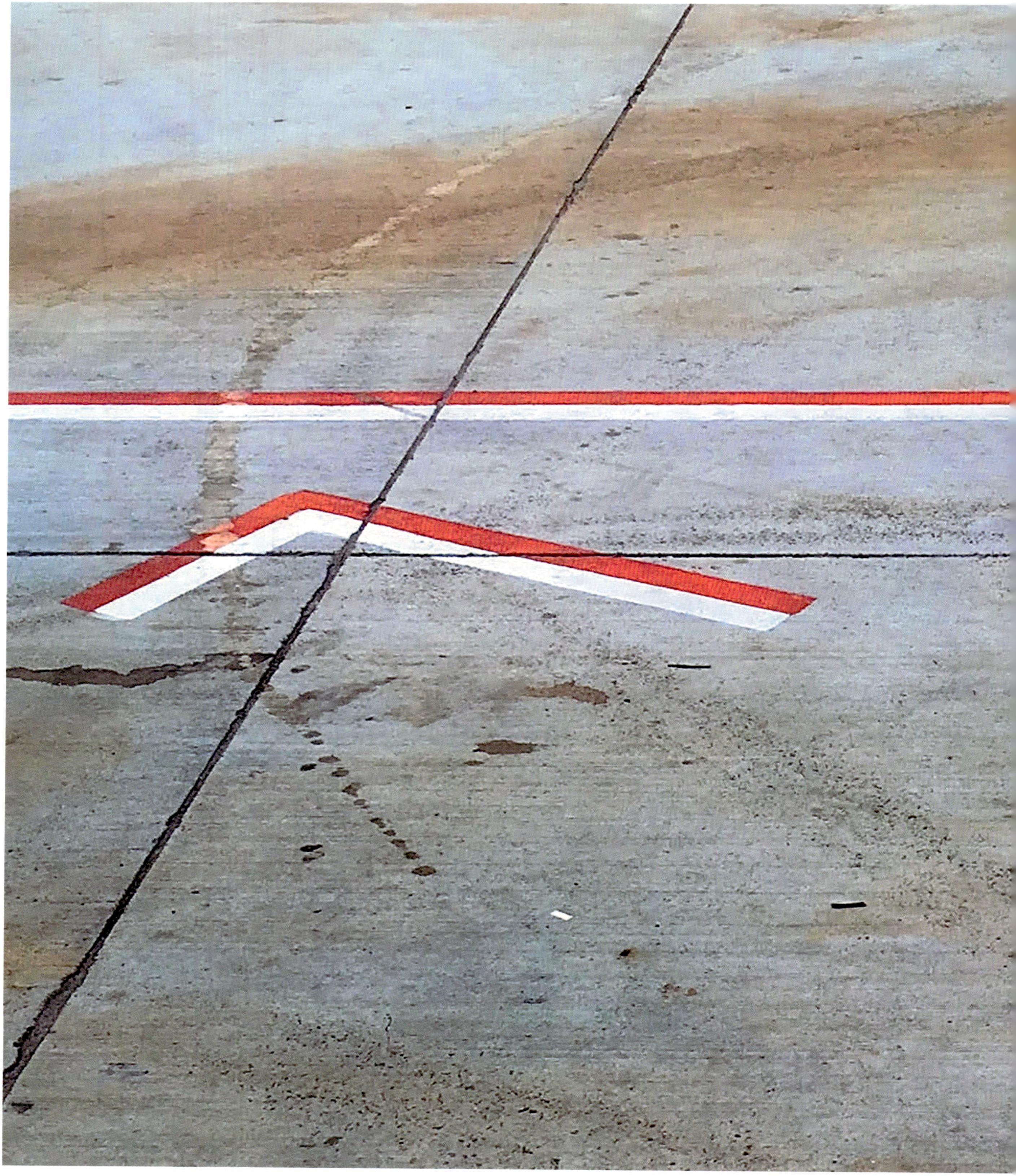

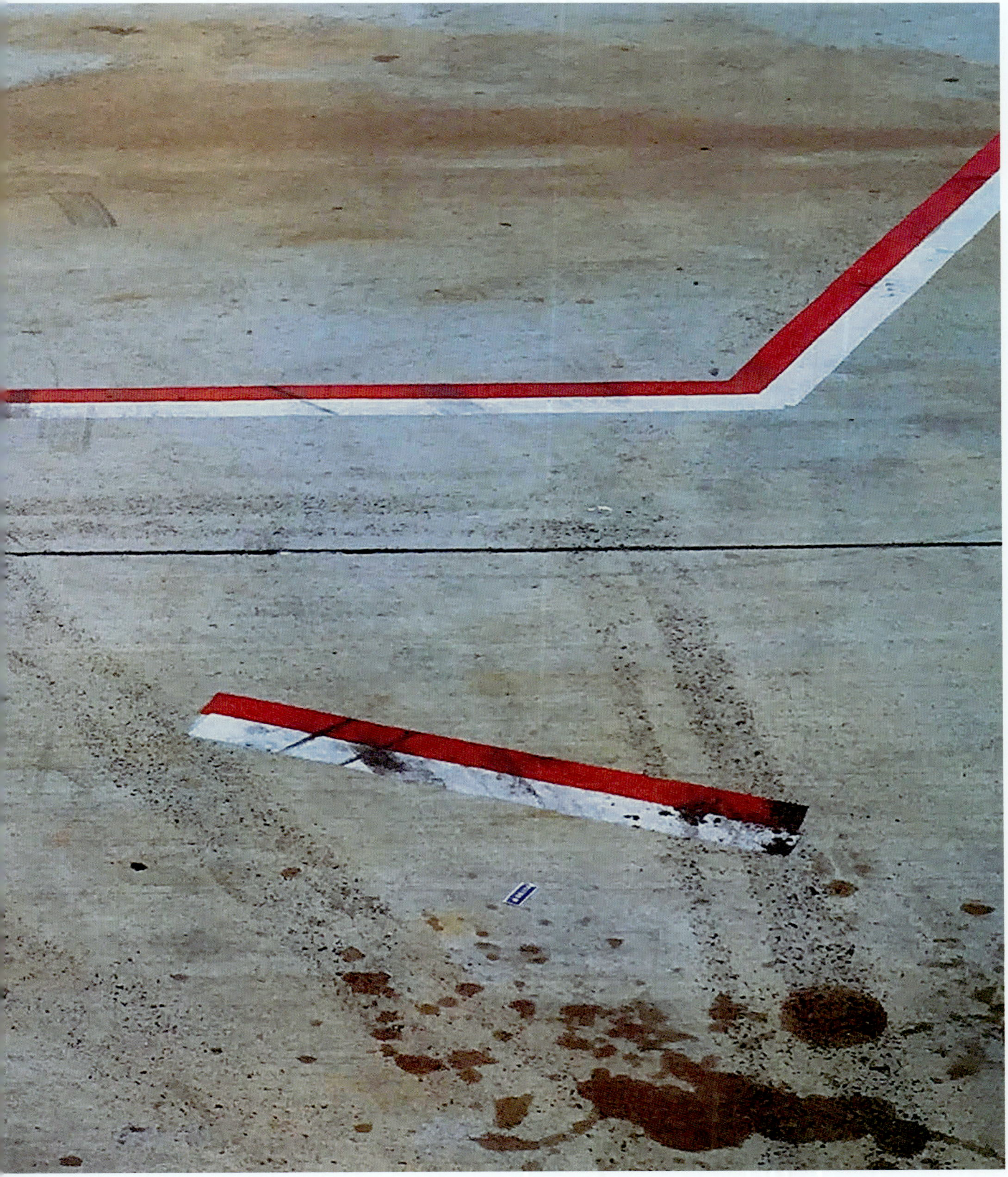

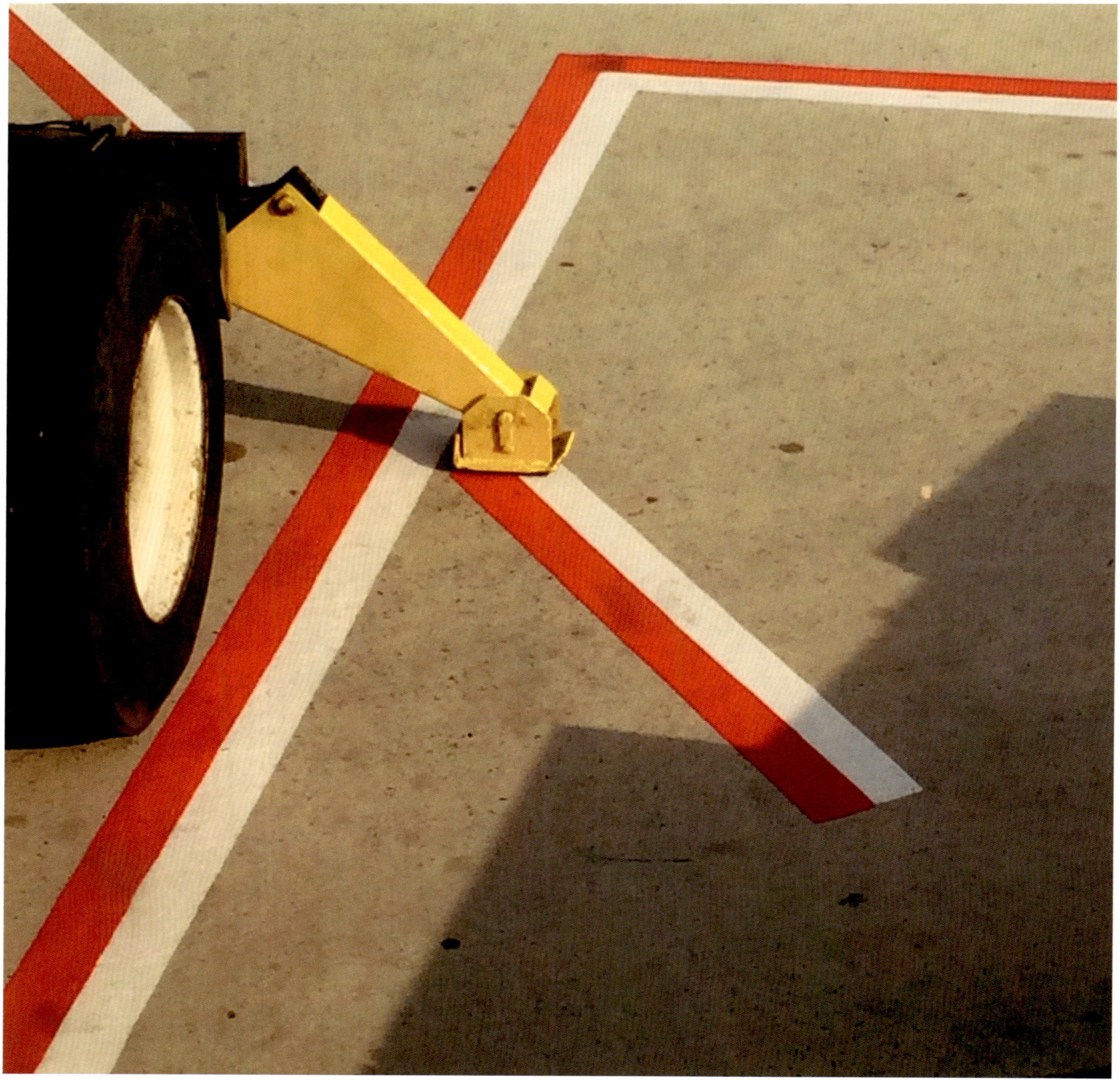

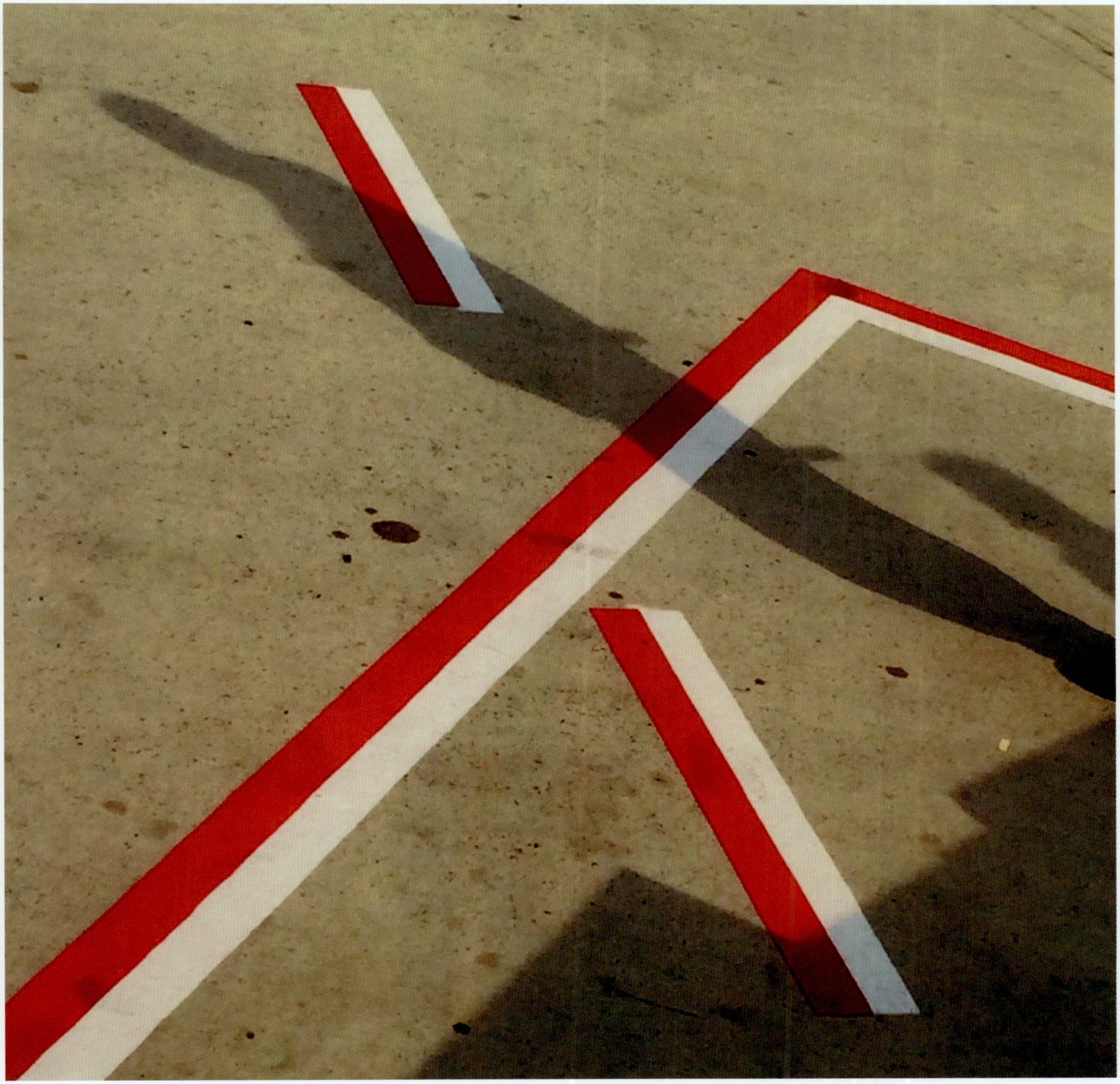

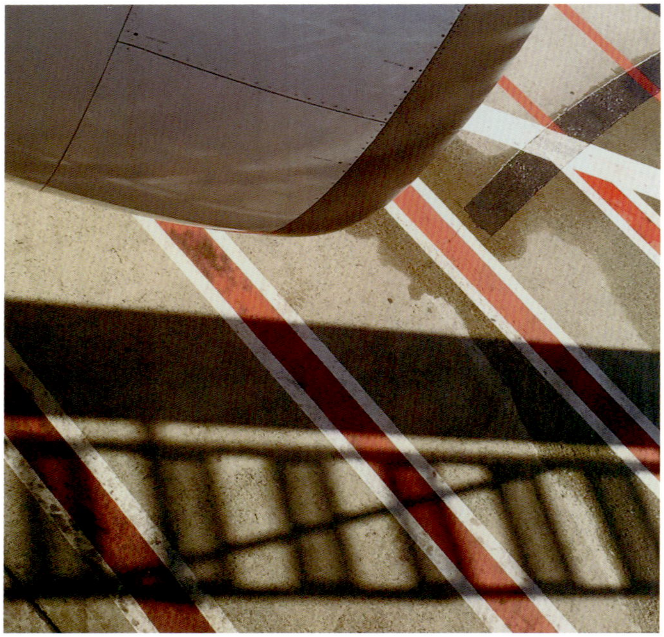

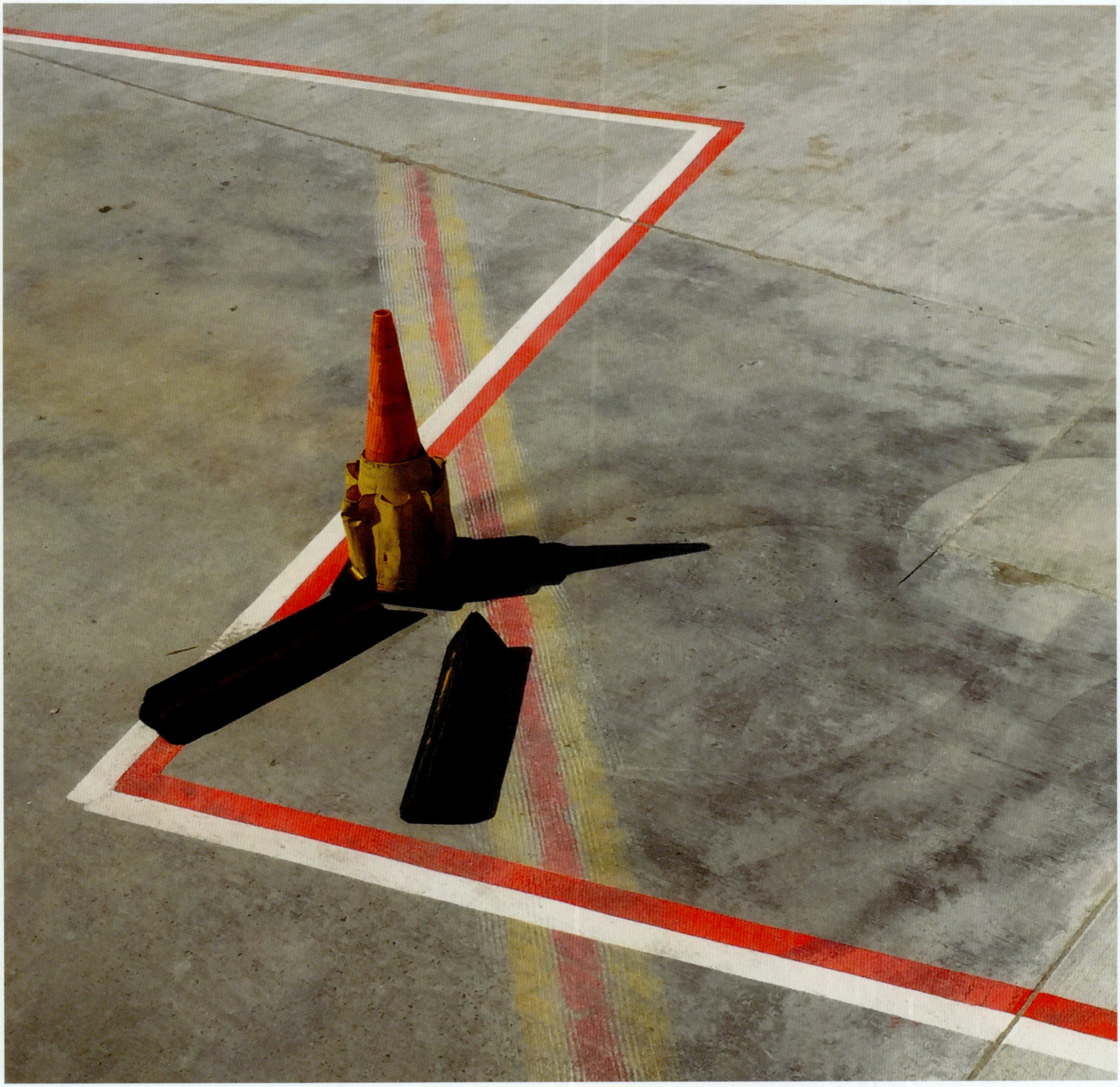

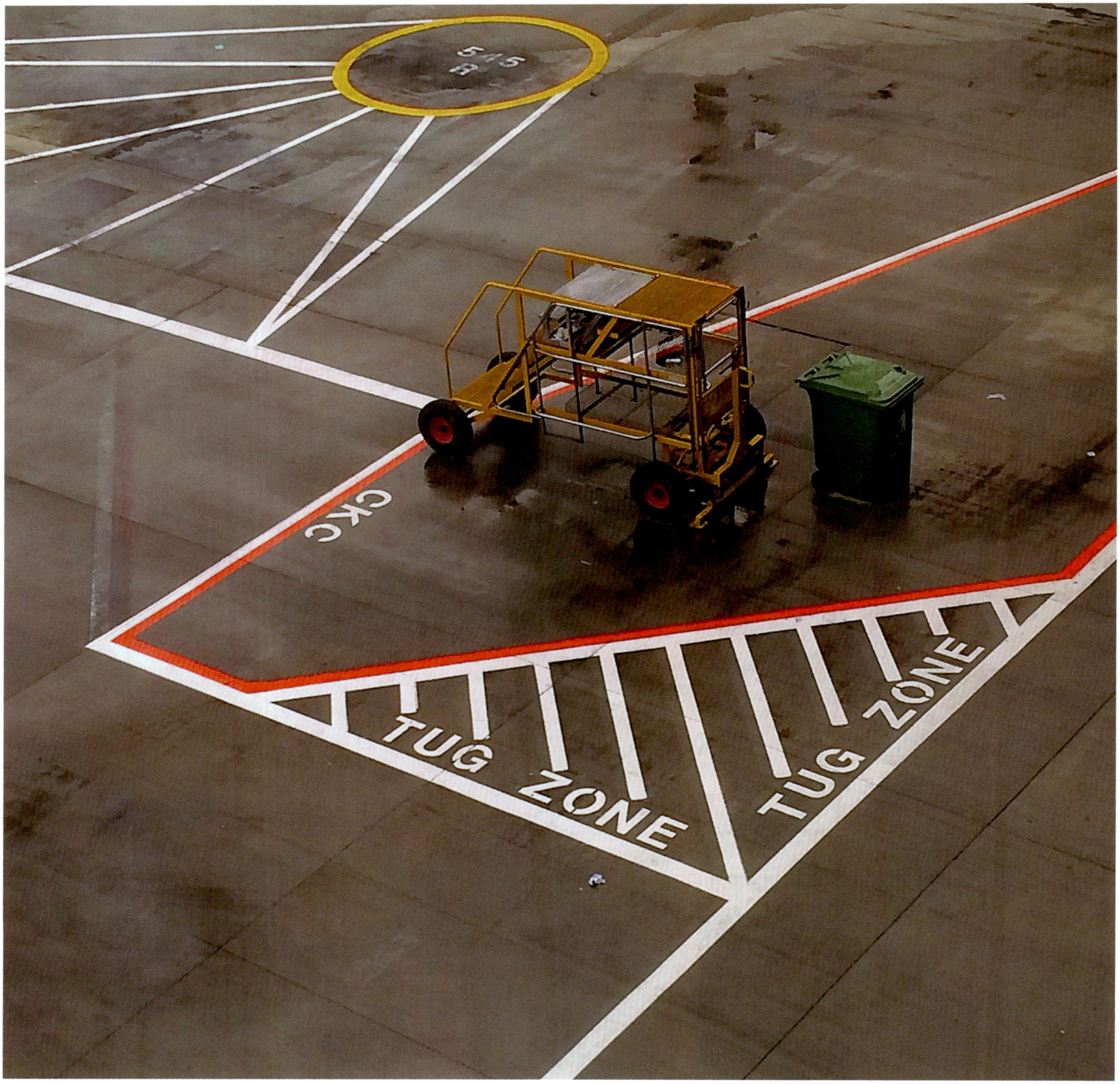
TUG ZONE
TUG ZONE
CKC

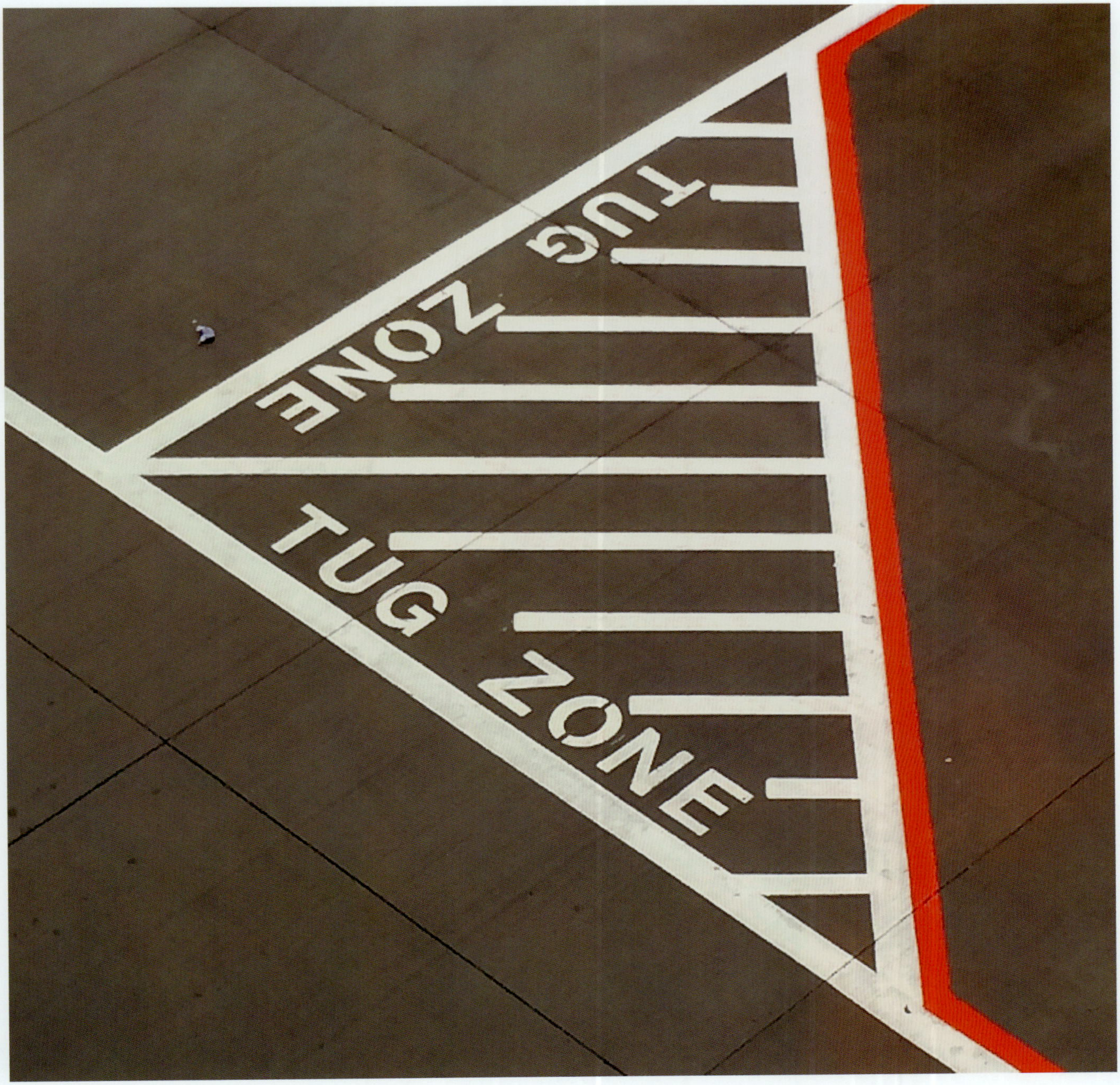
TUG ZONE
TUG ZONE

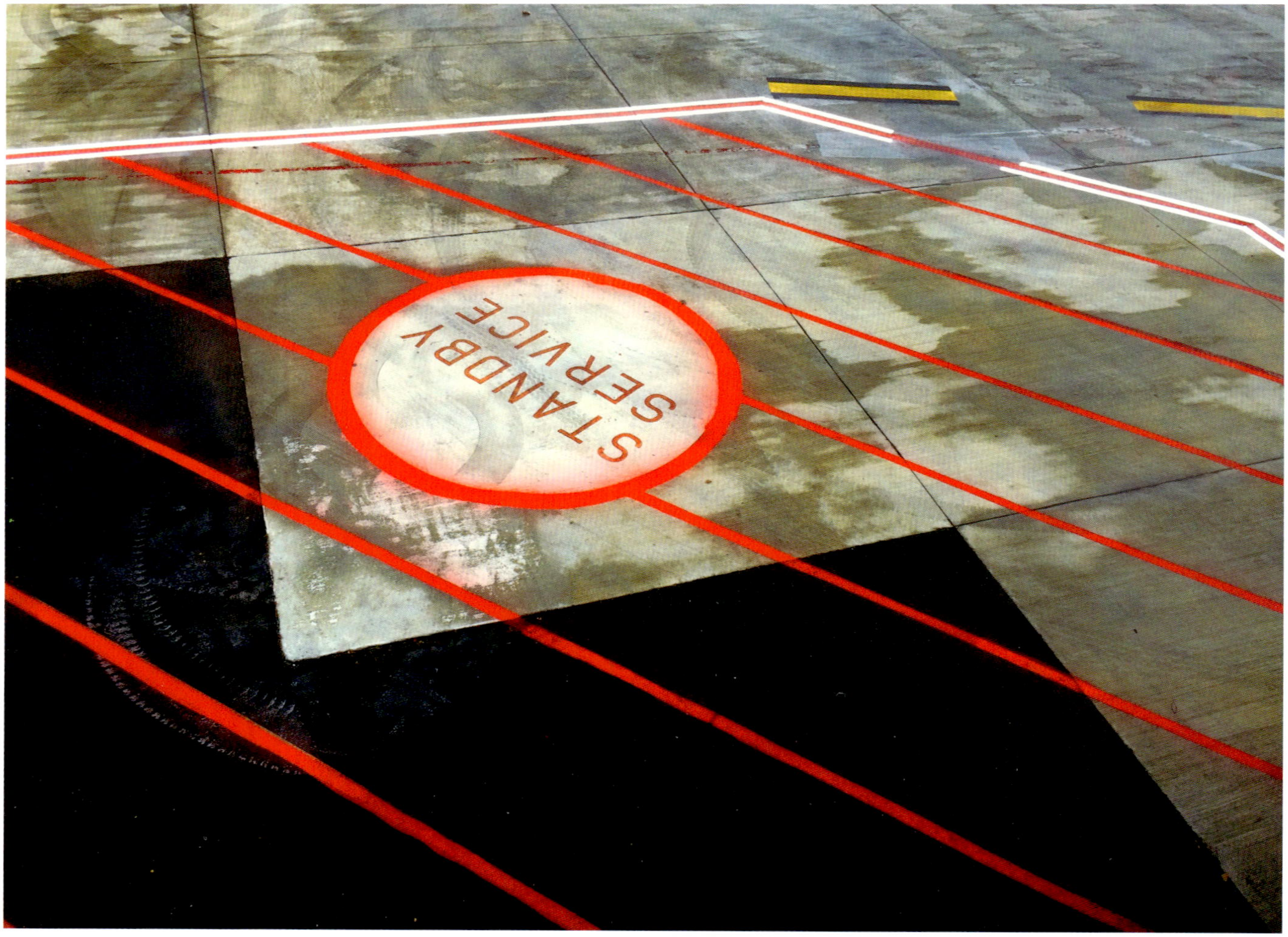
STANDBY
SERVICE

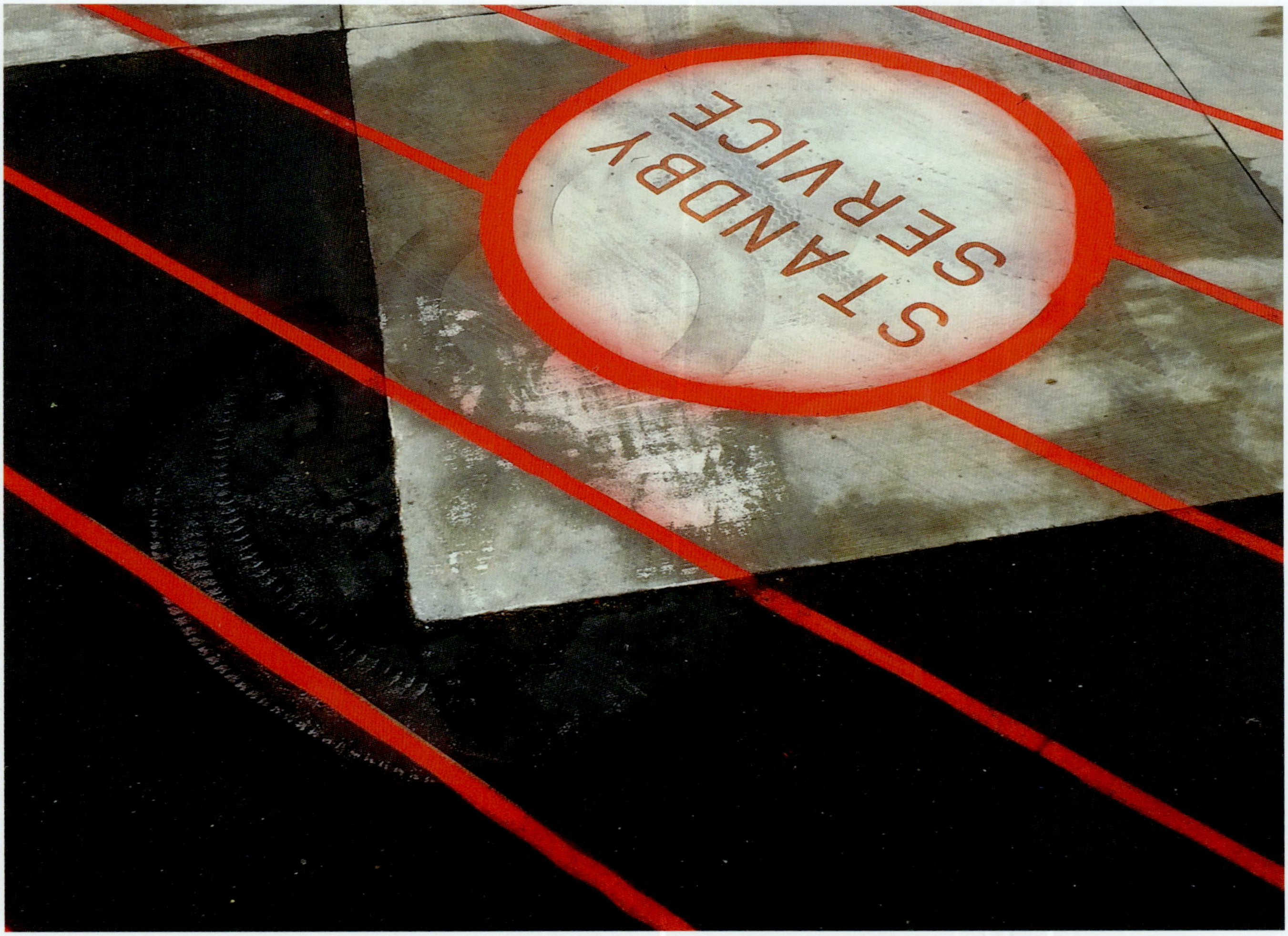
STANDBY
SERVICE

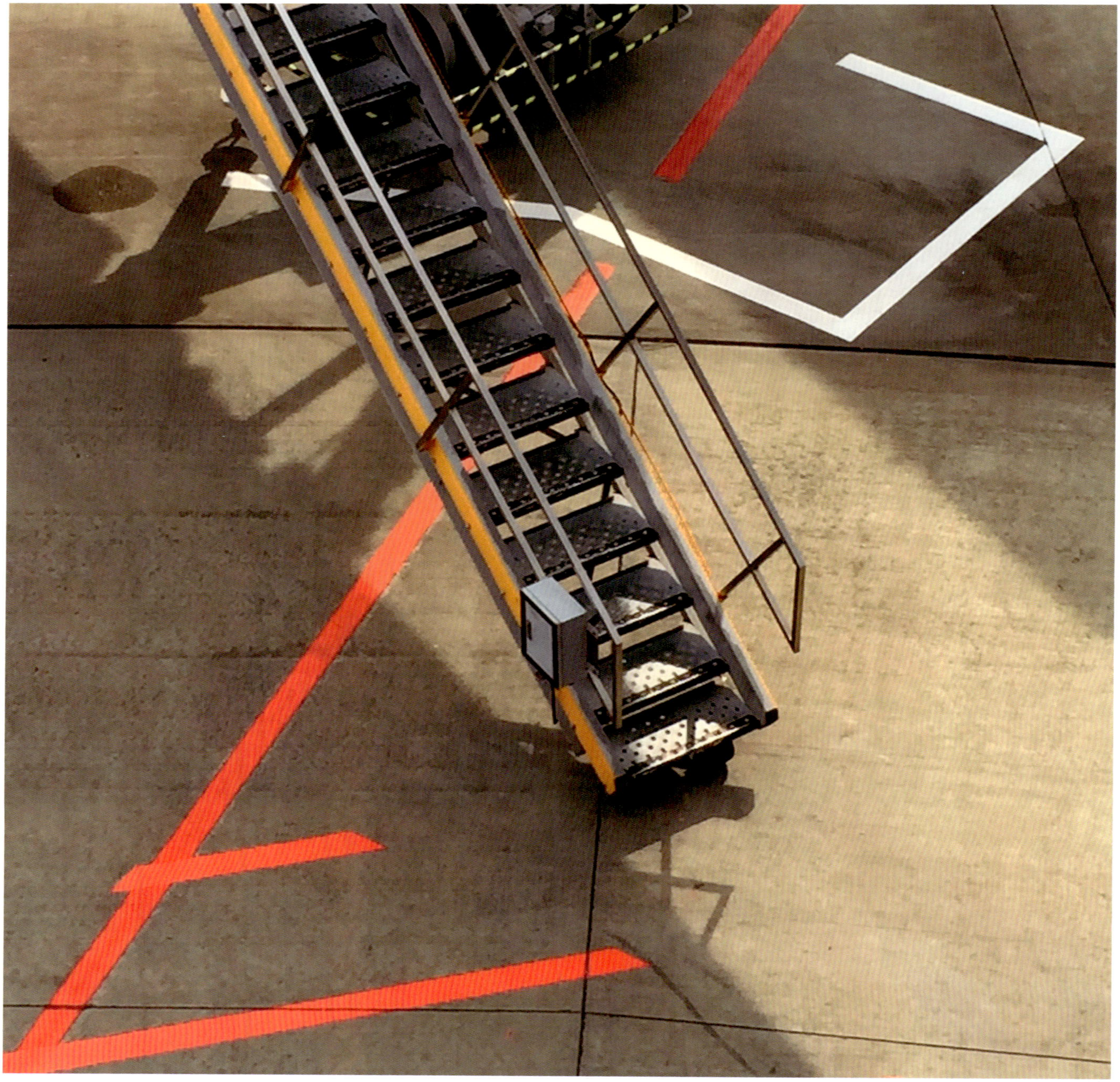

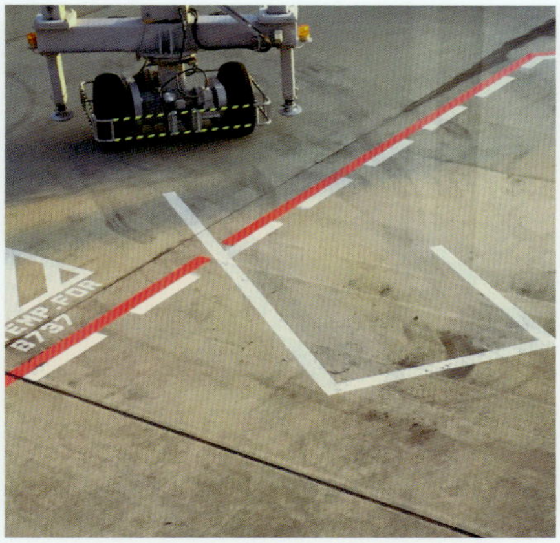
TEMP.FOR
B737
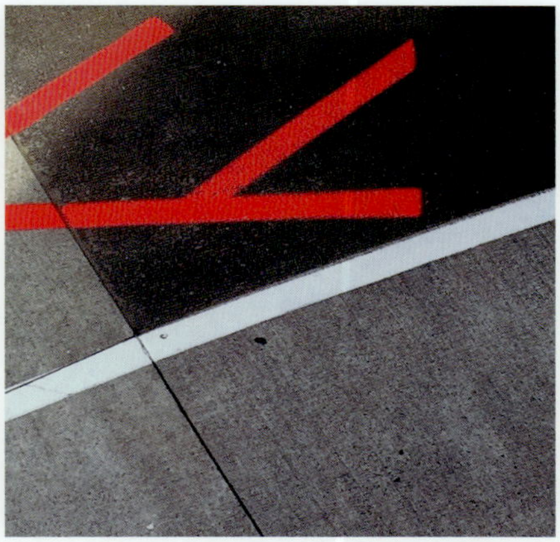
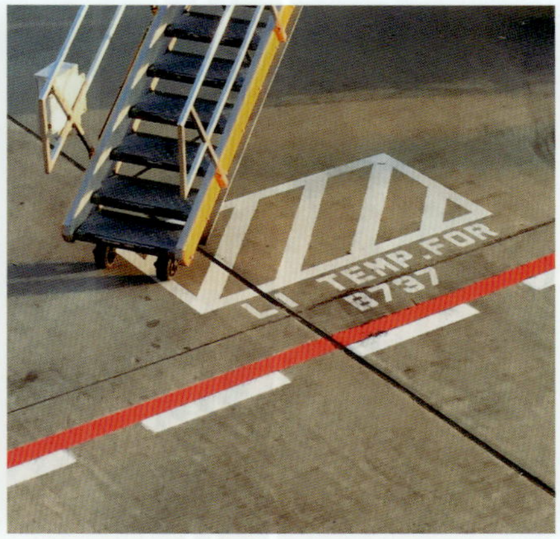
L1 TEMP.FOR
B737
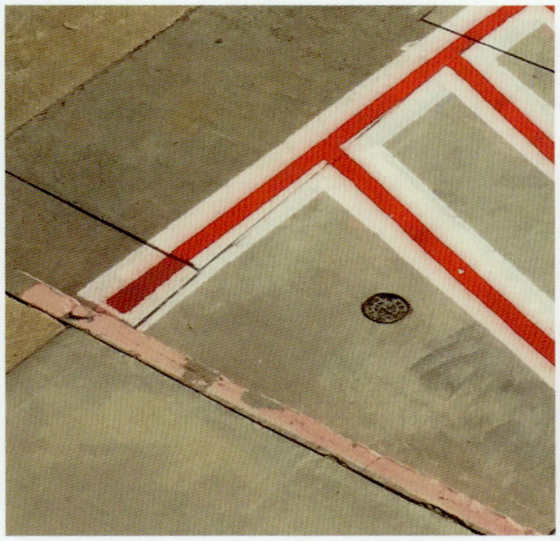
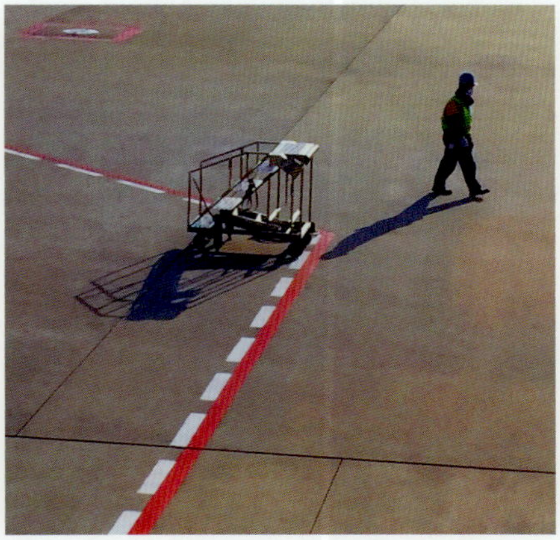
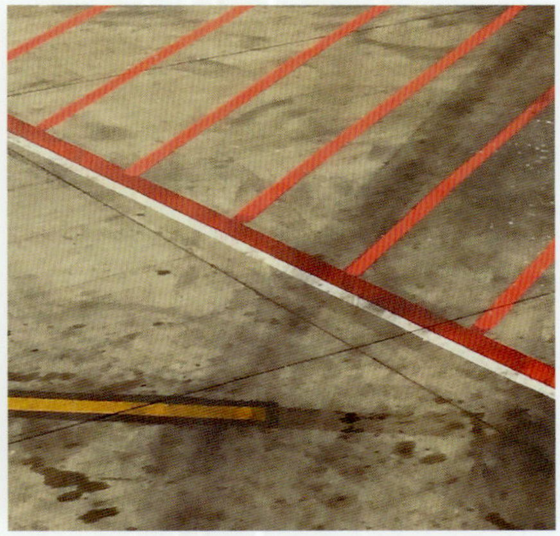
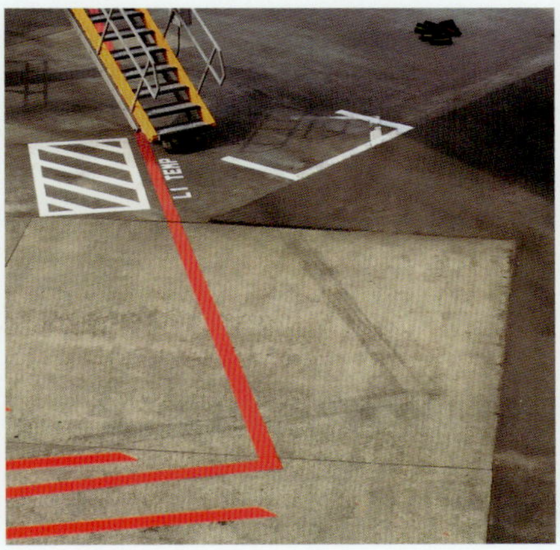
L1 TEMP
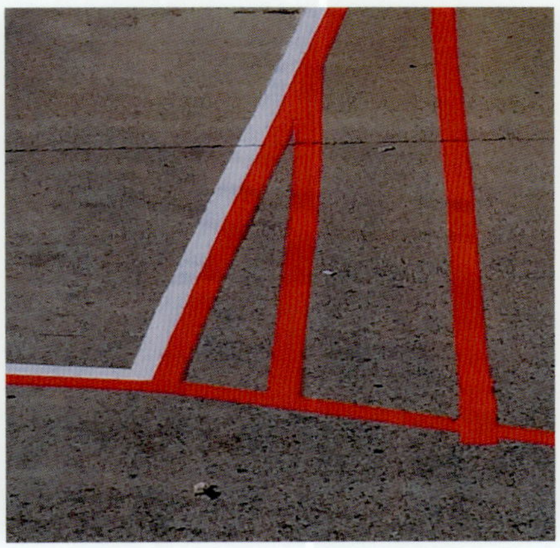
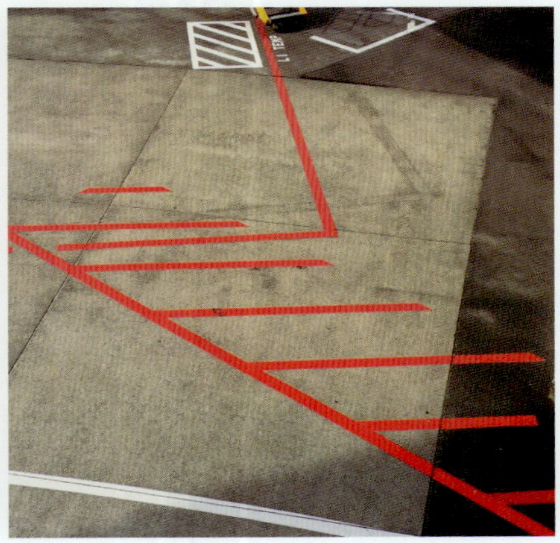

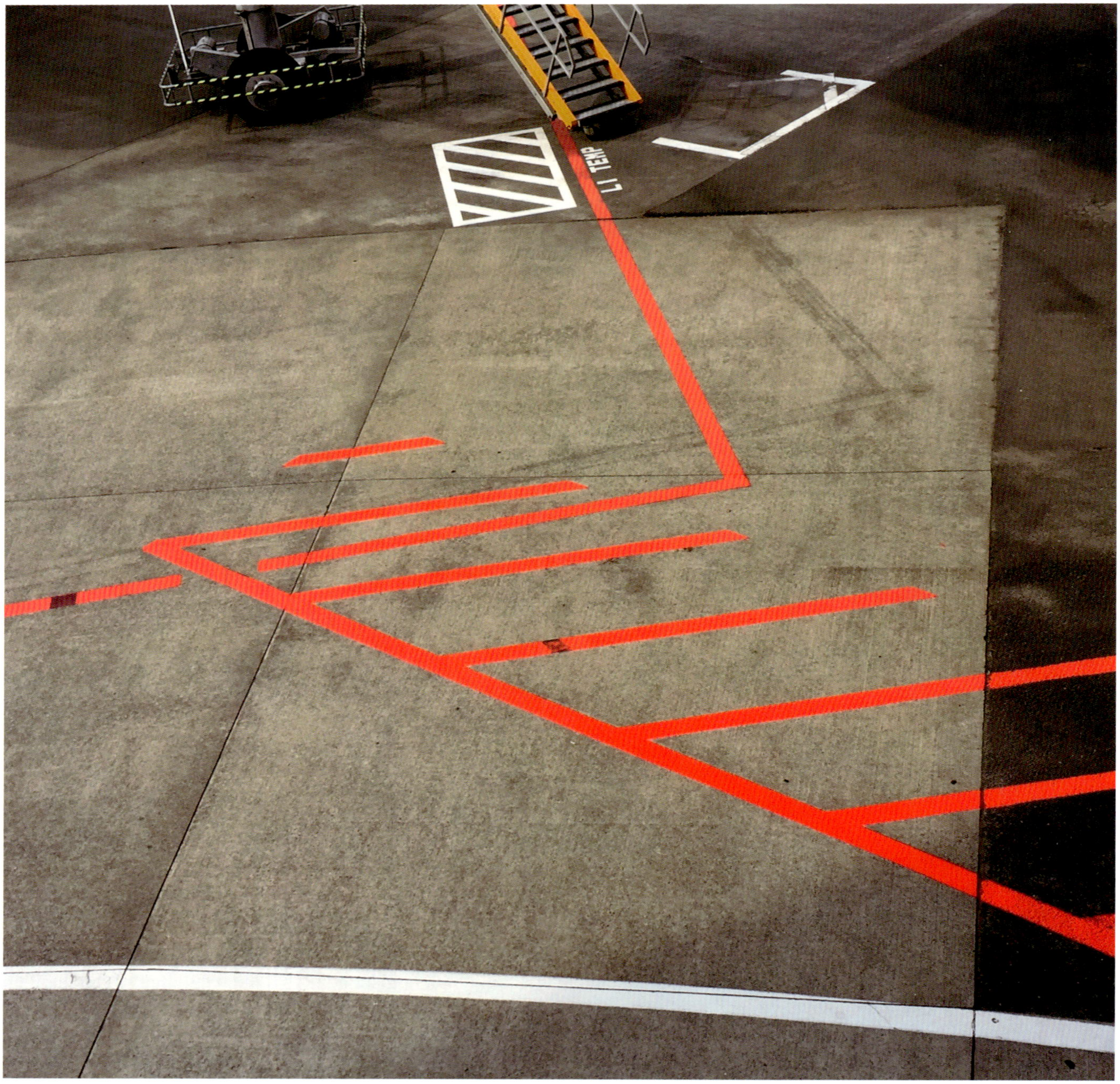
L1 TEMP

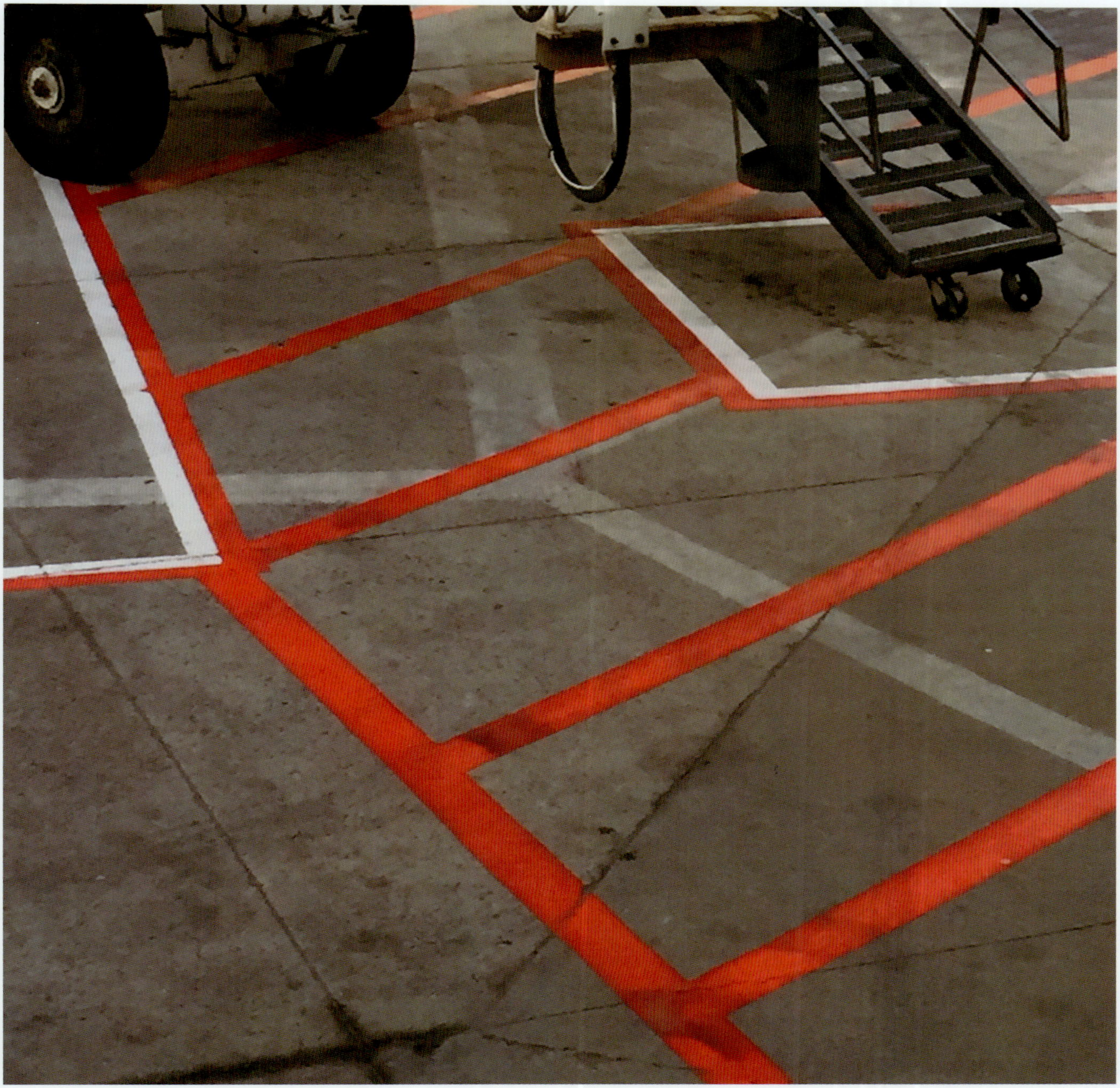

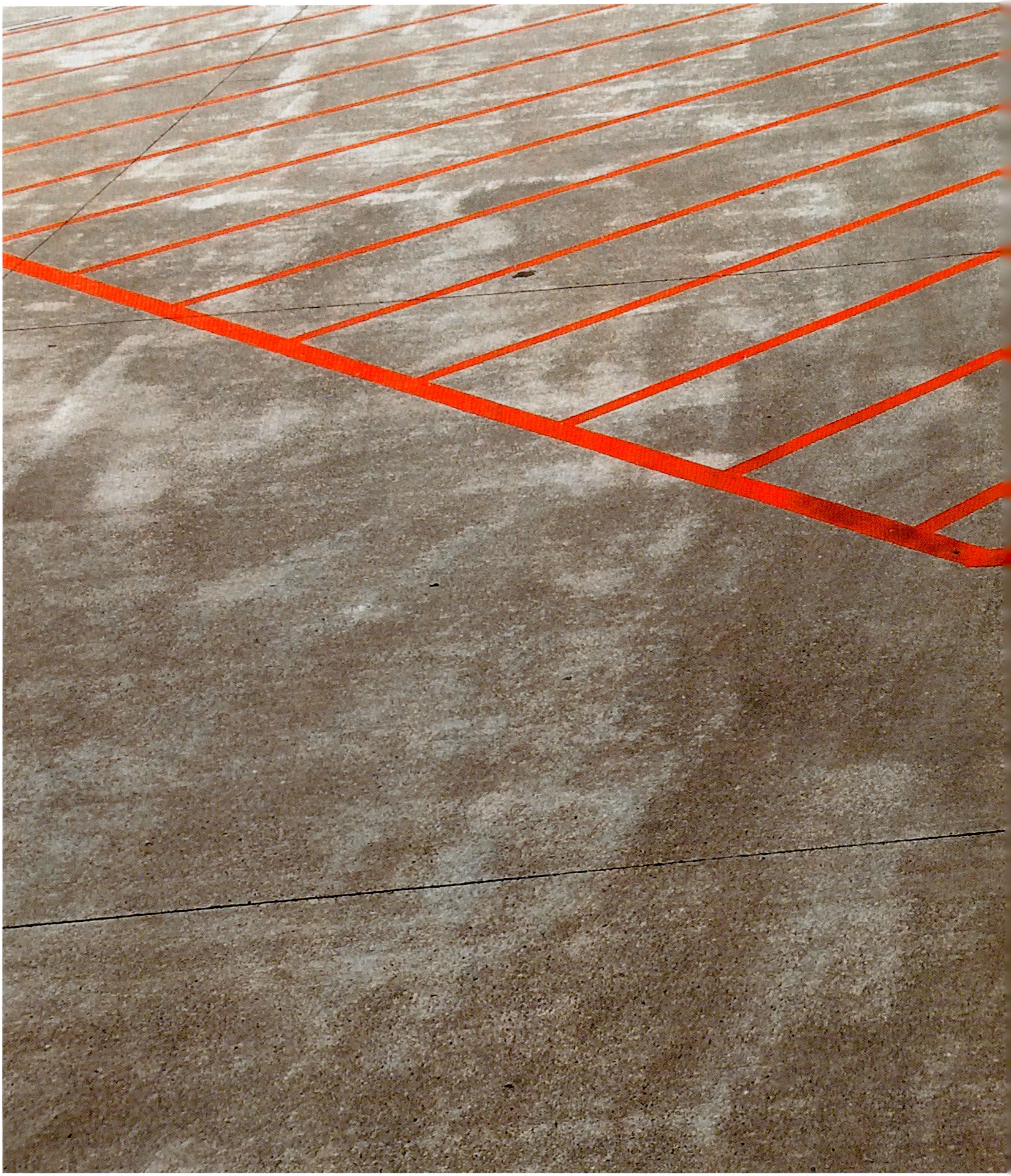

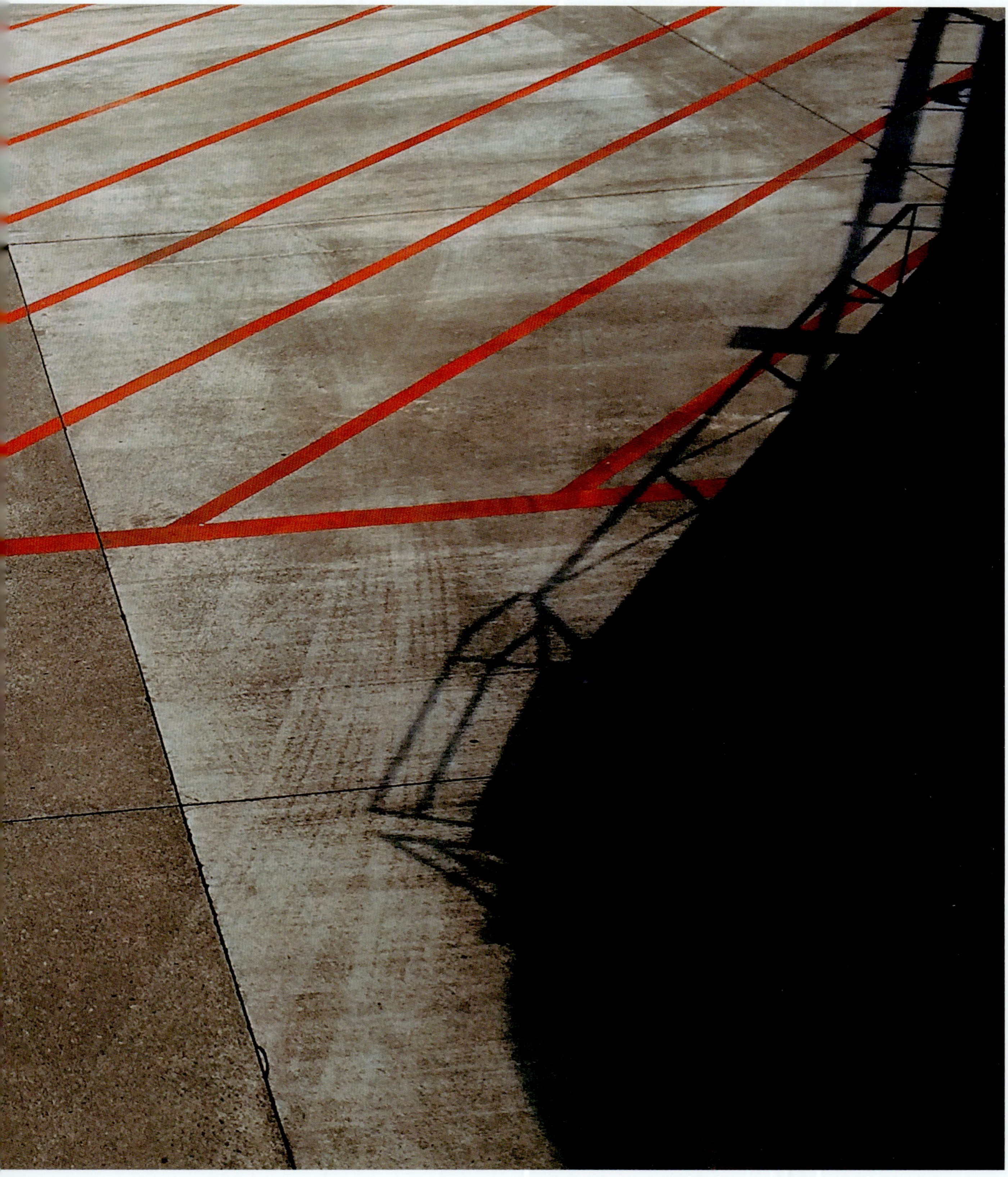

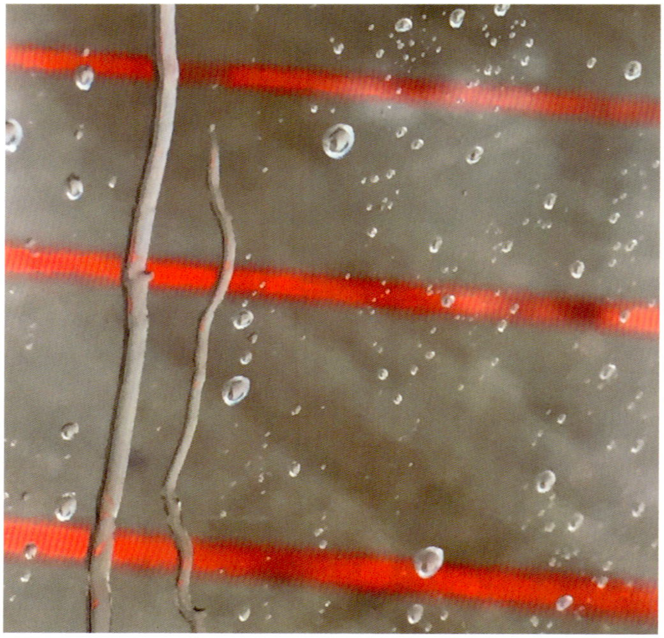

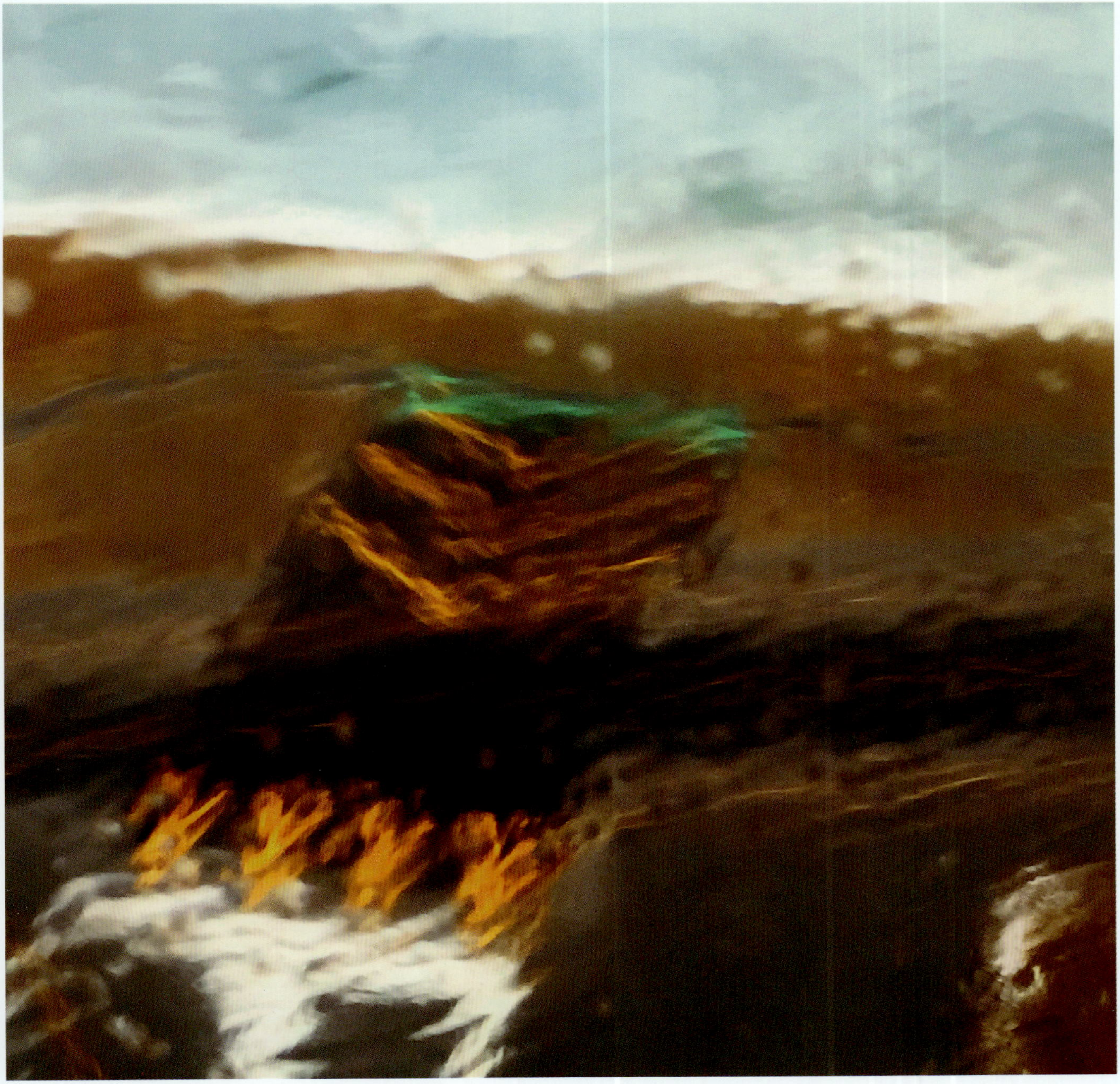

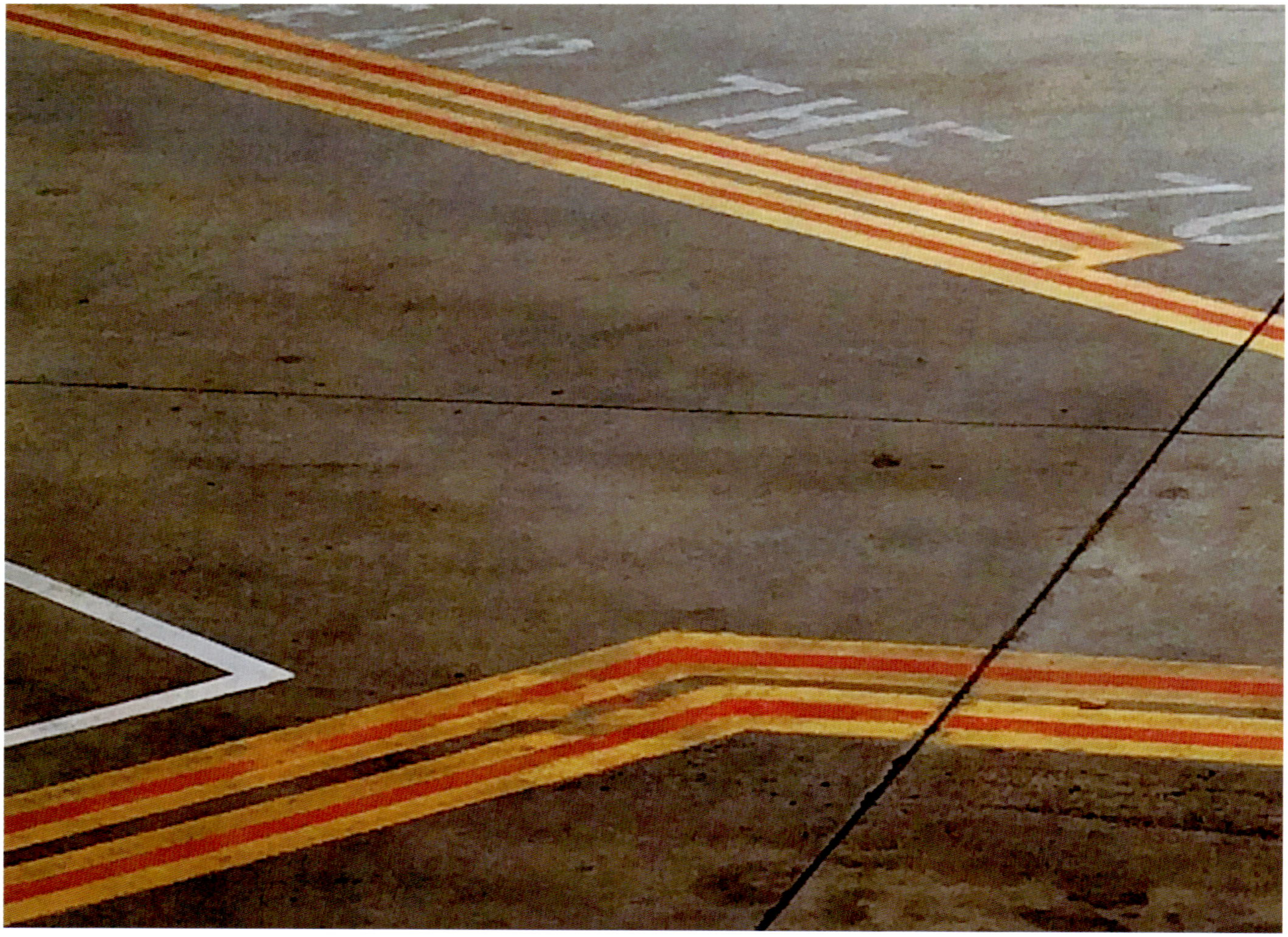

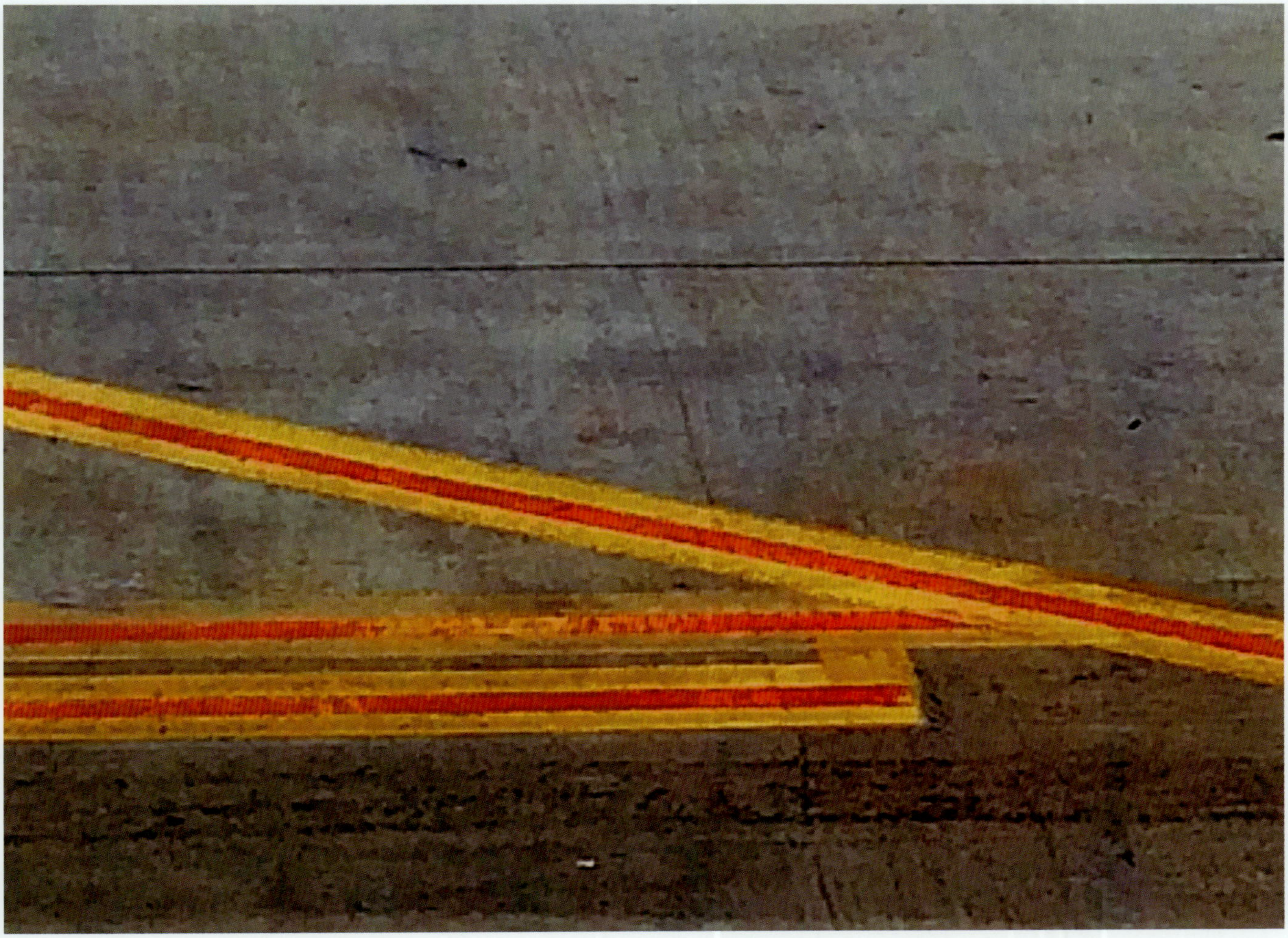

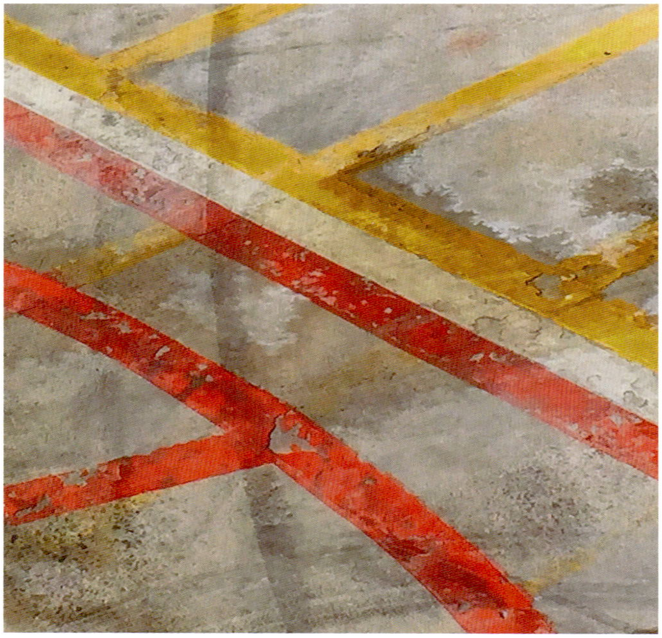

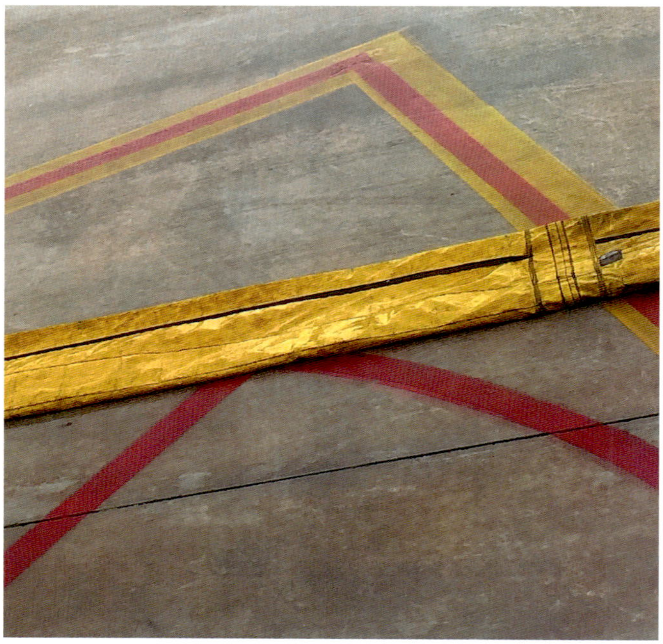

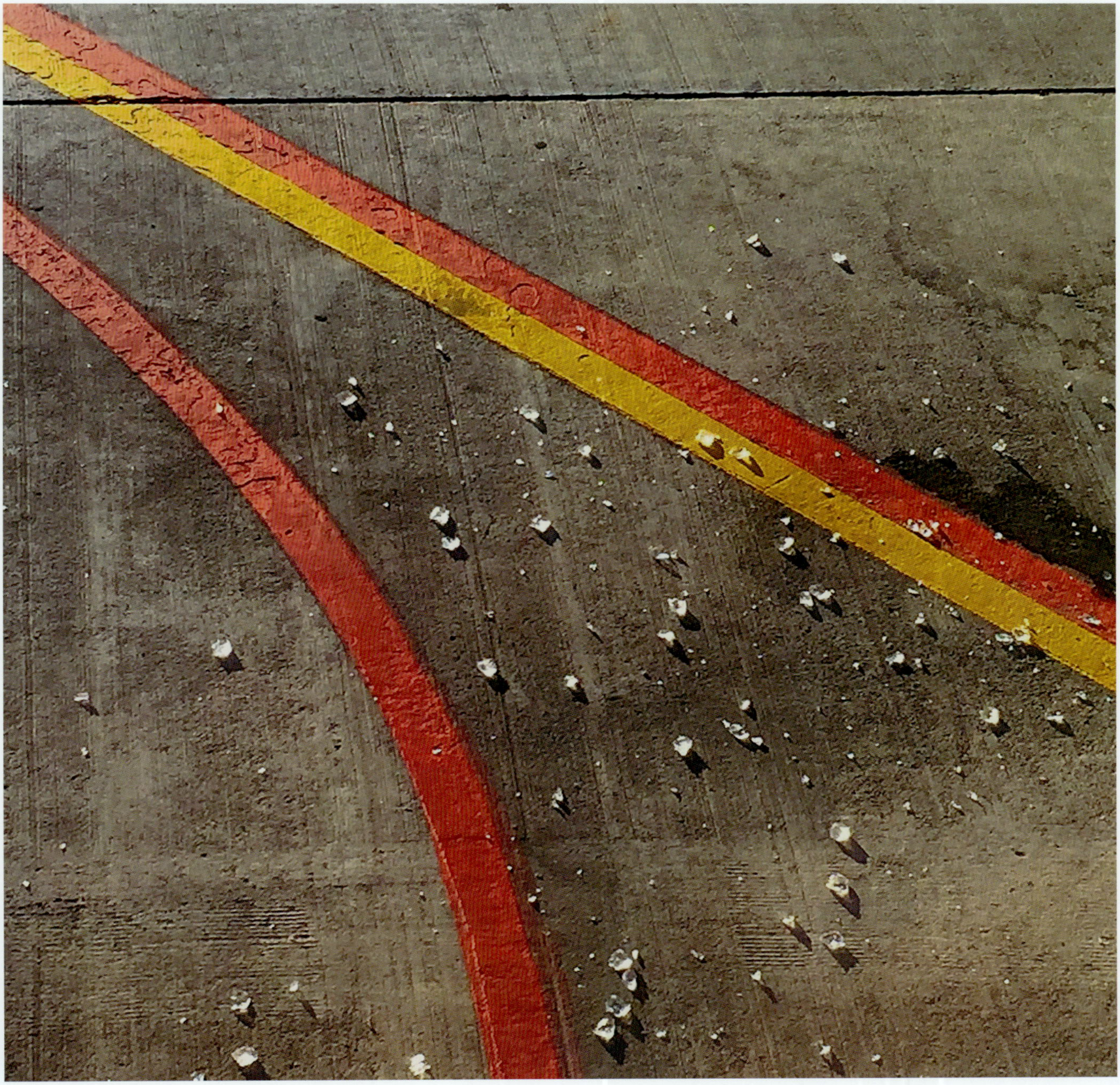

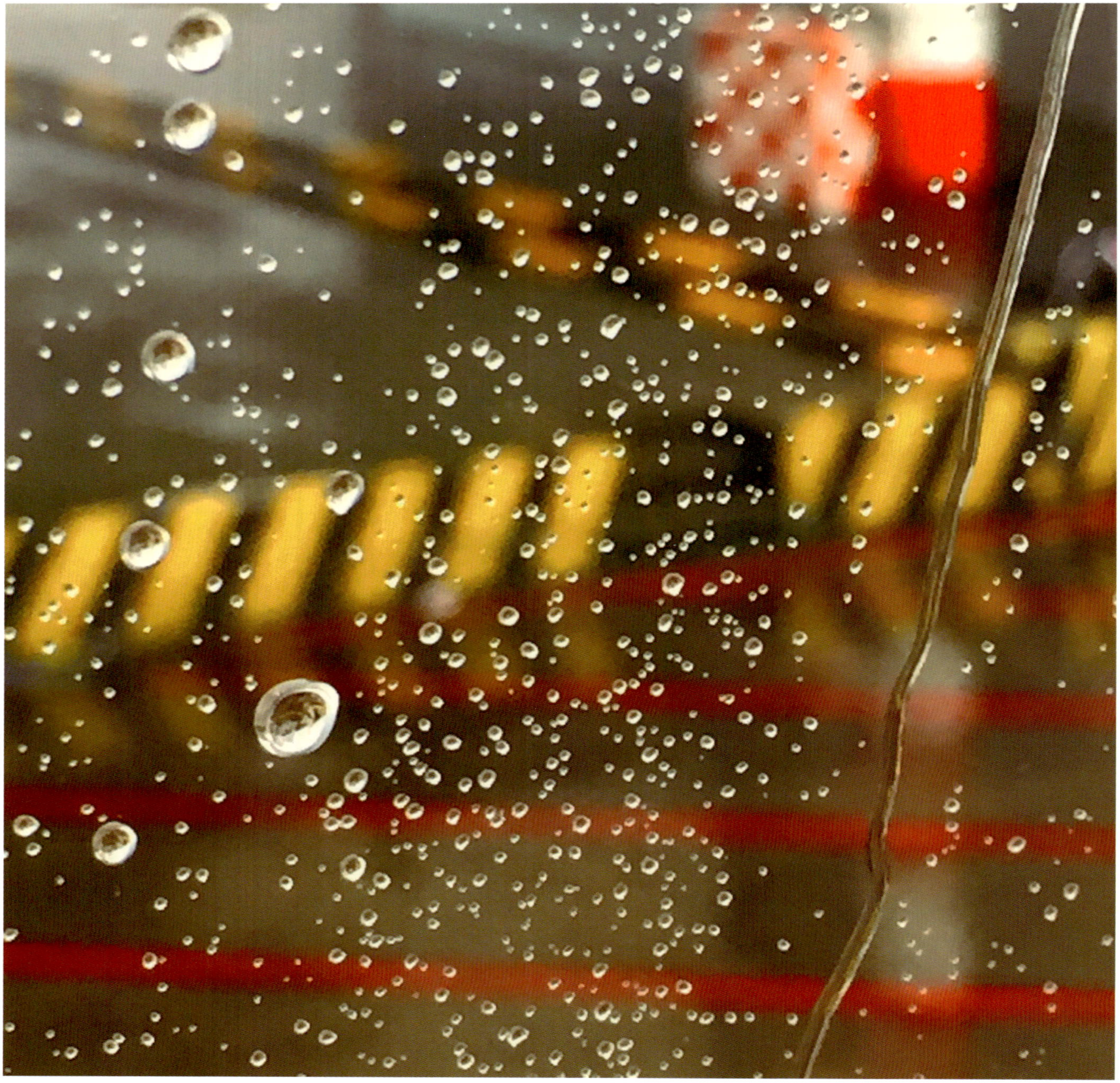

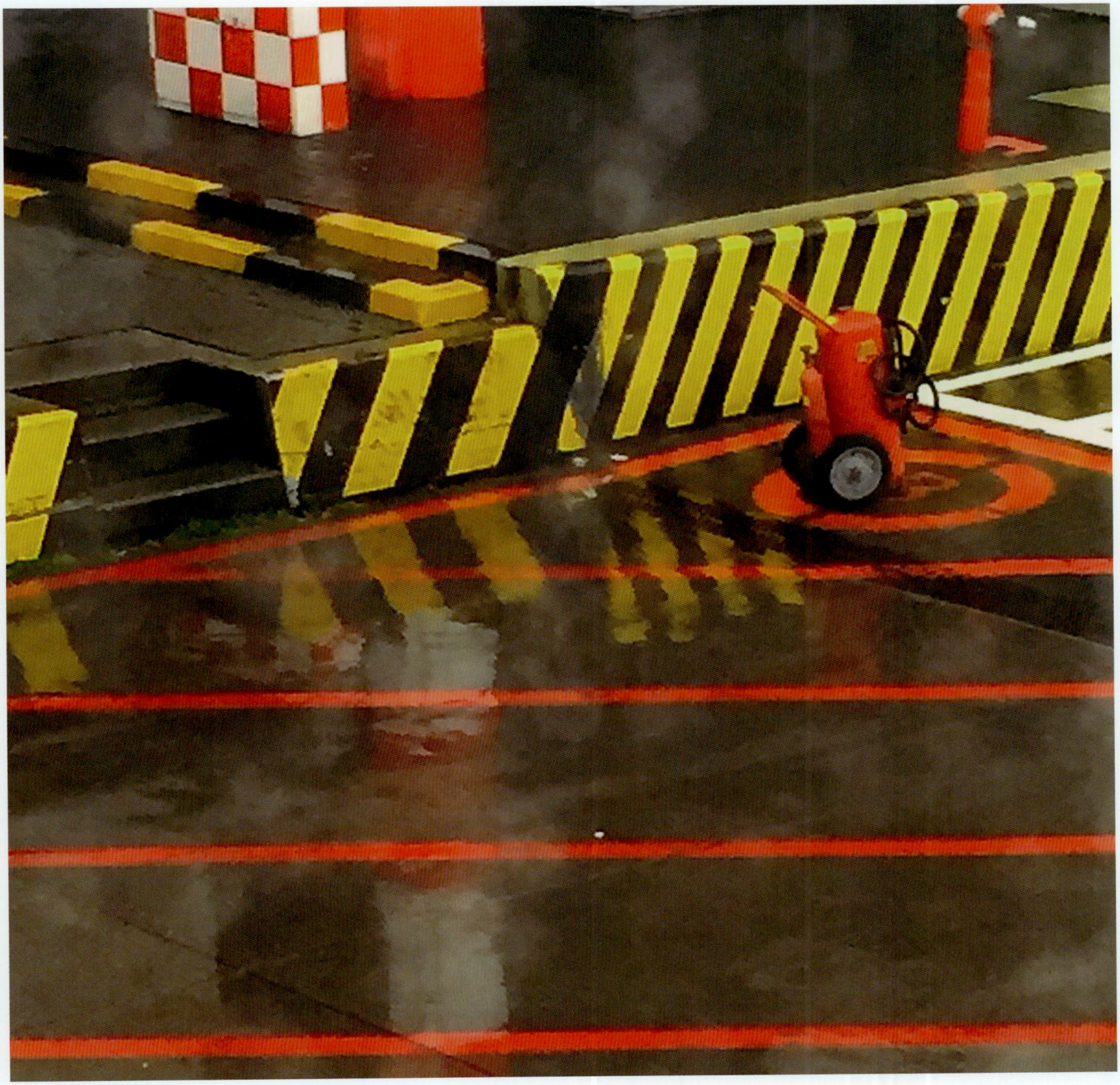

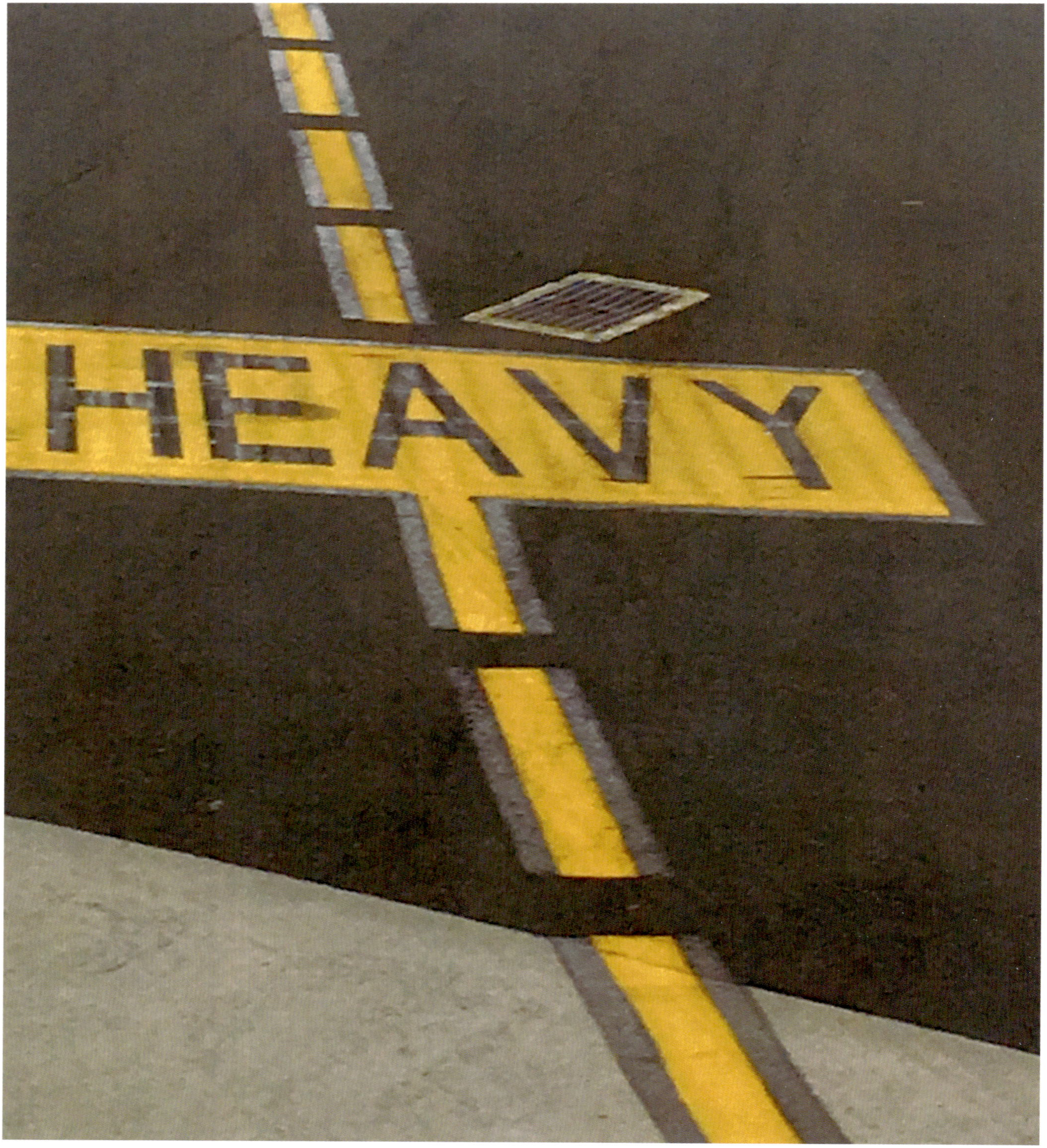
HEAVY

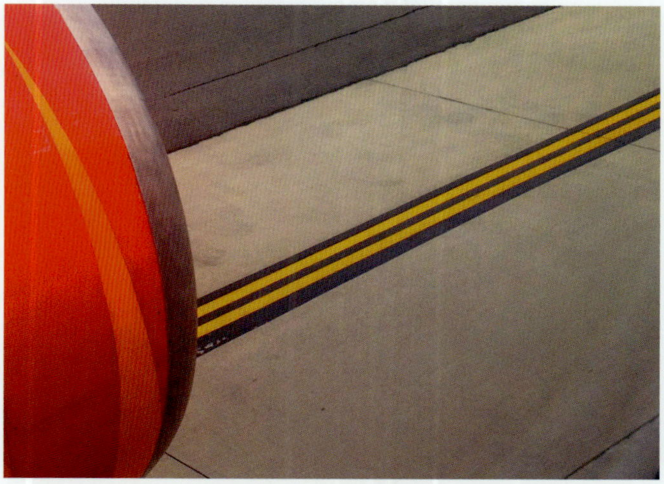

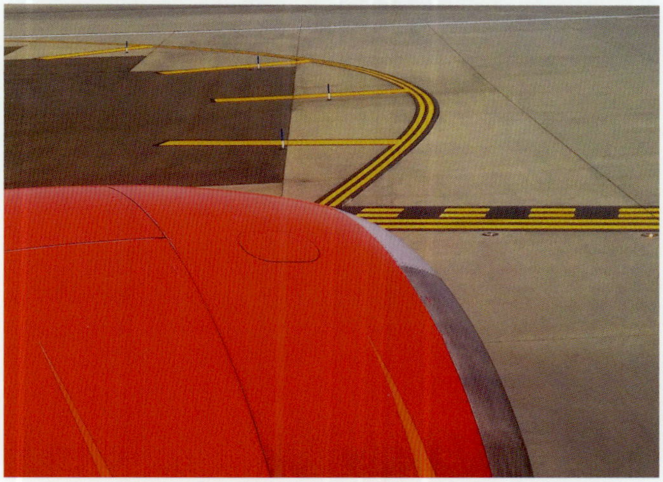

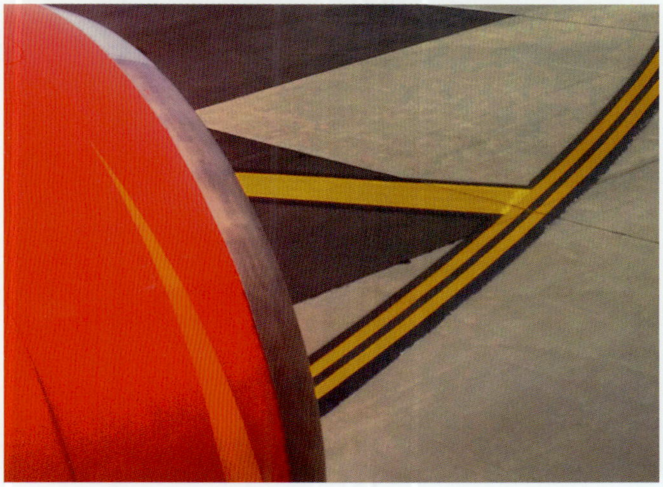

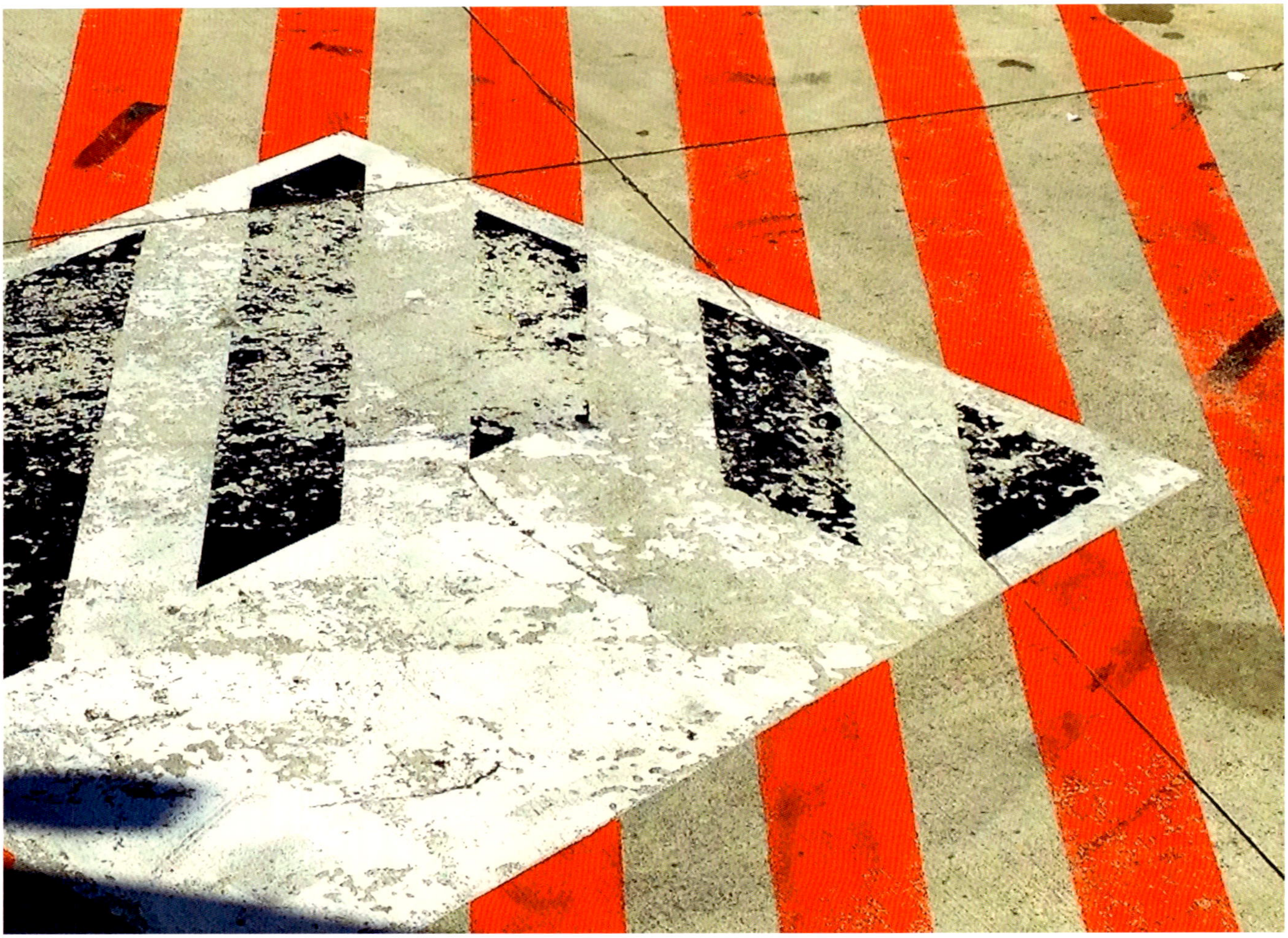

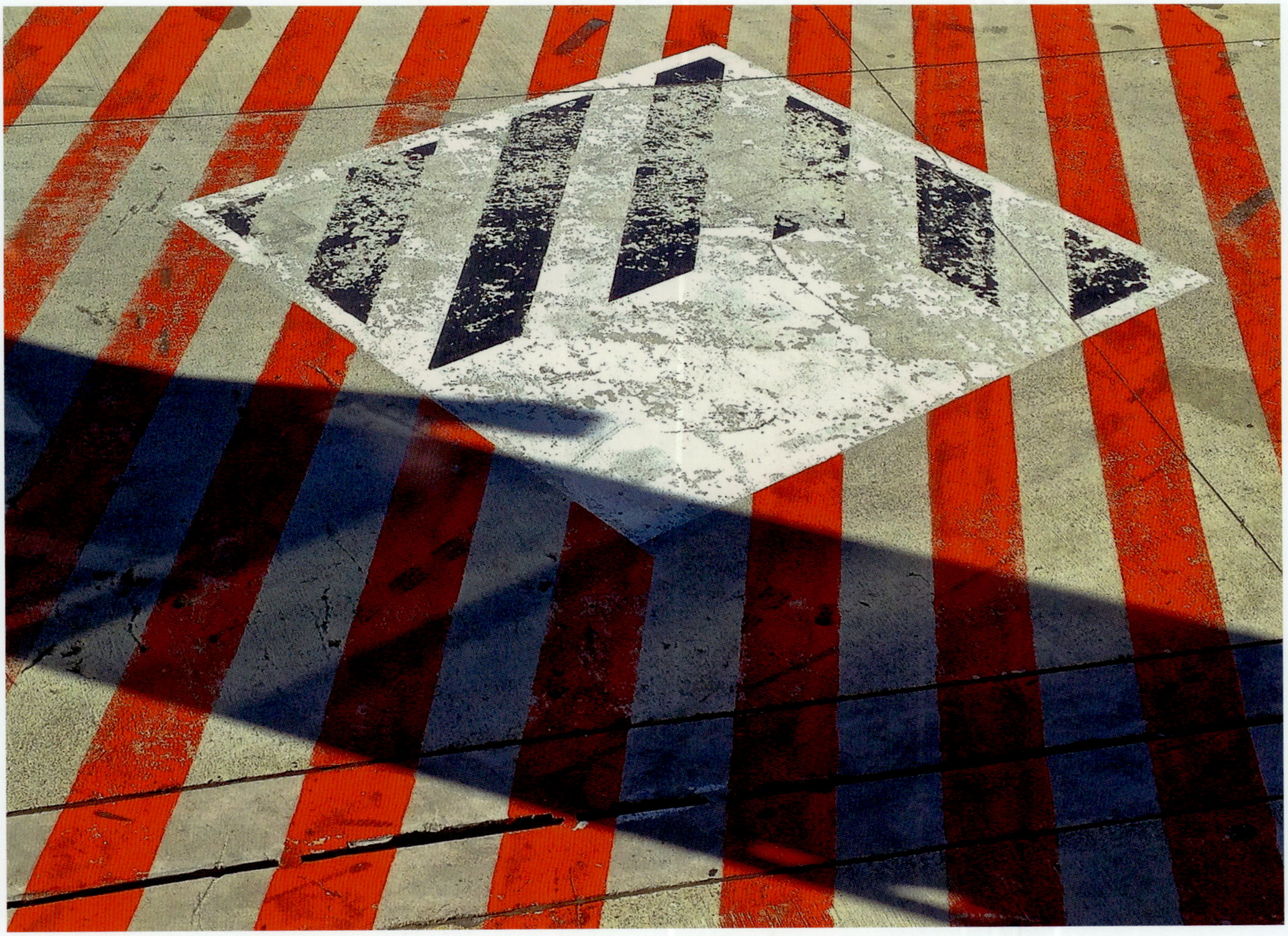

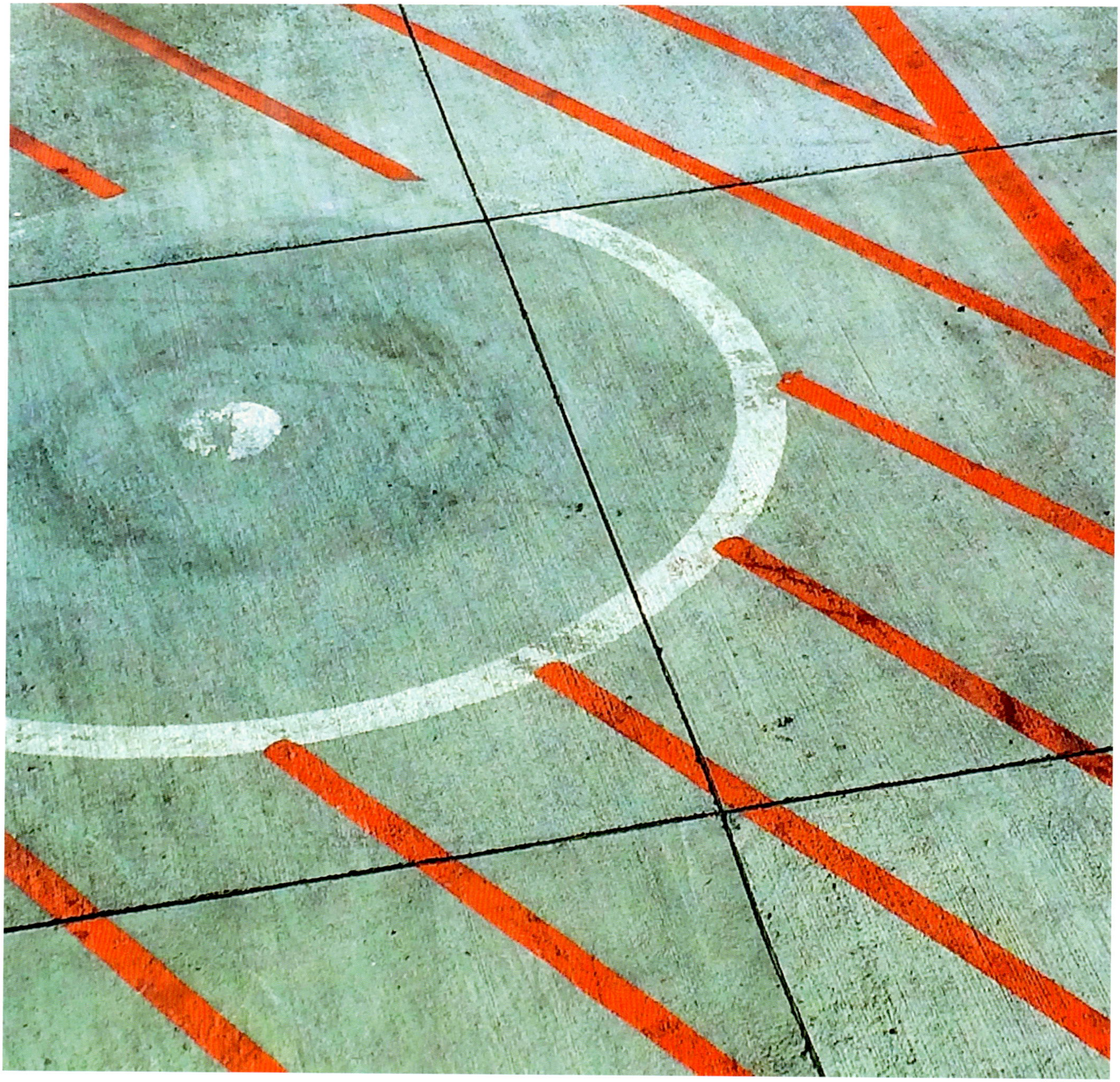

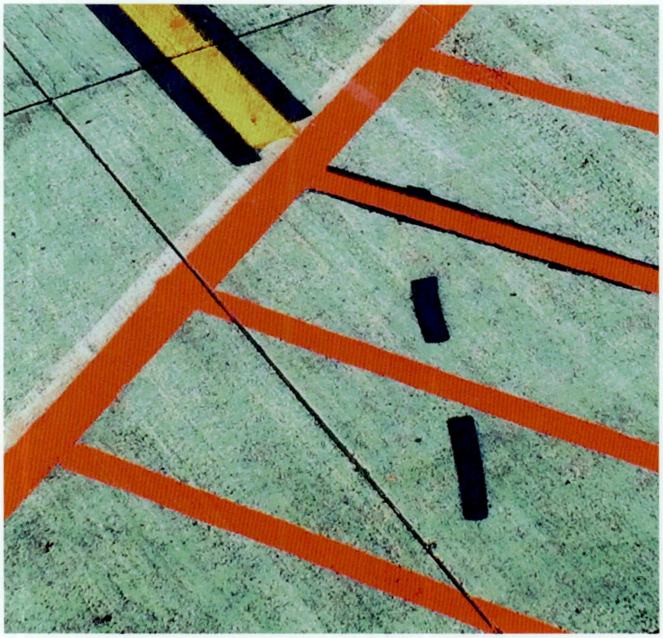

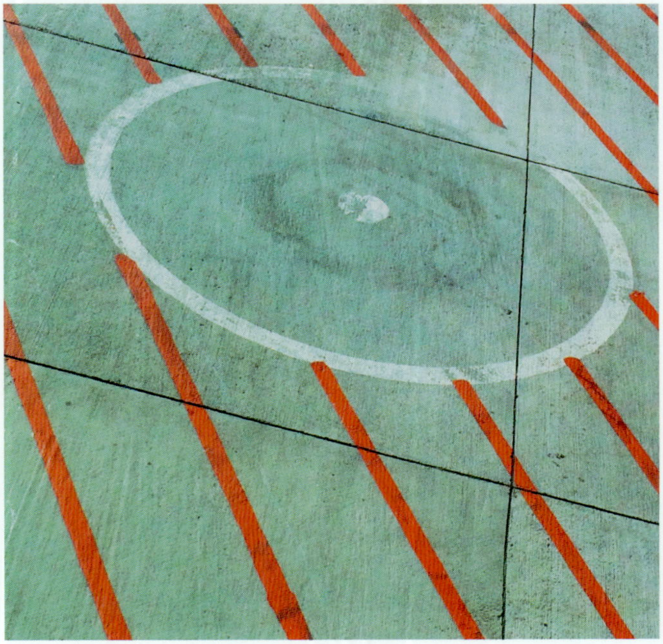

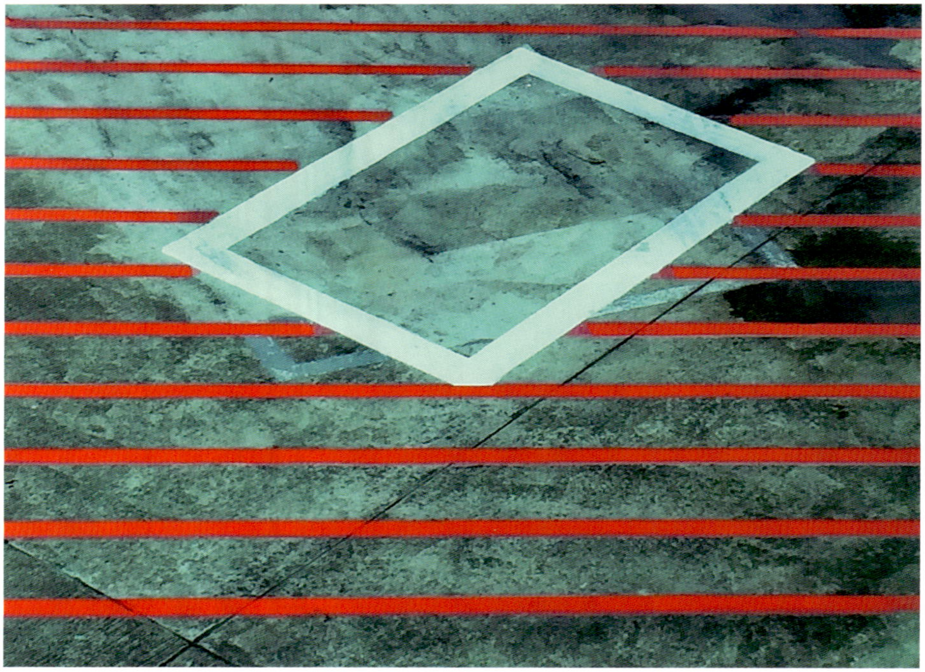

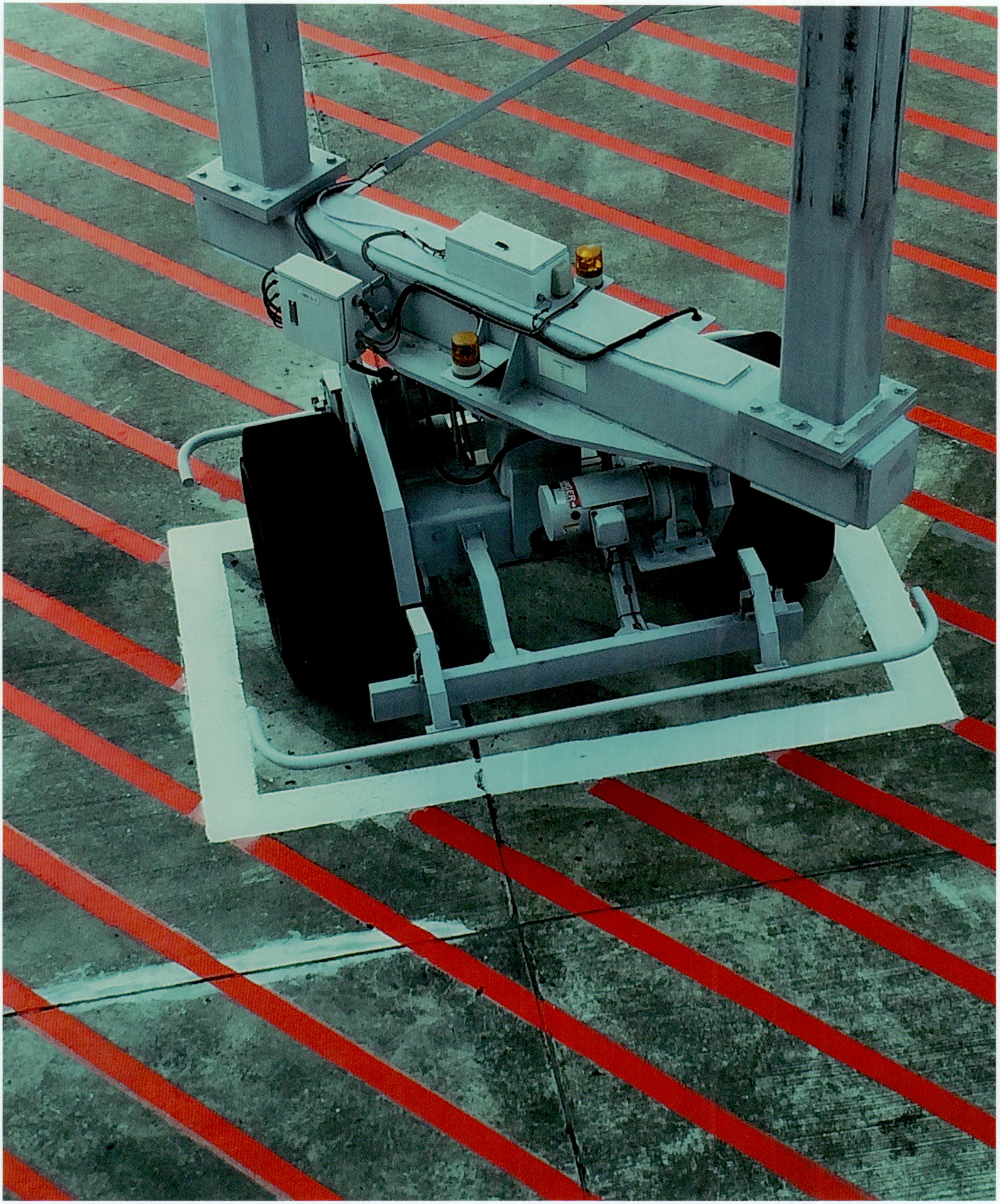

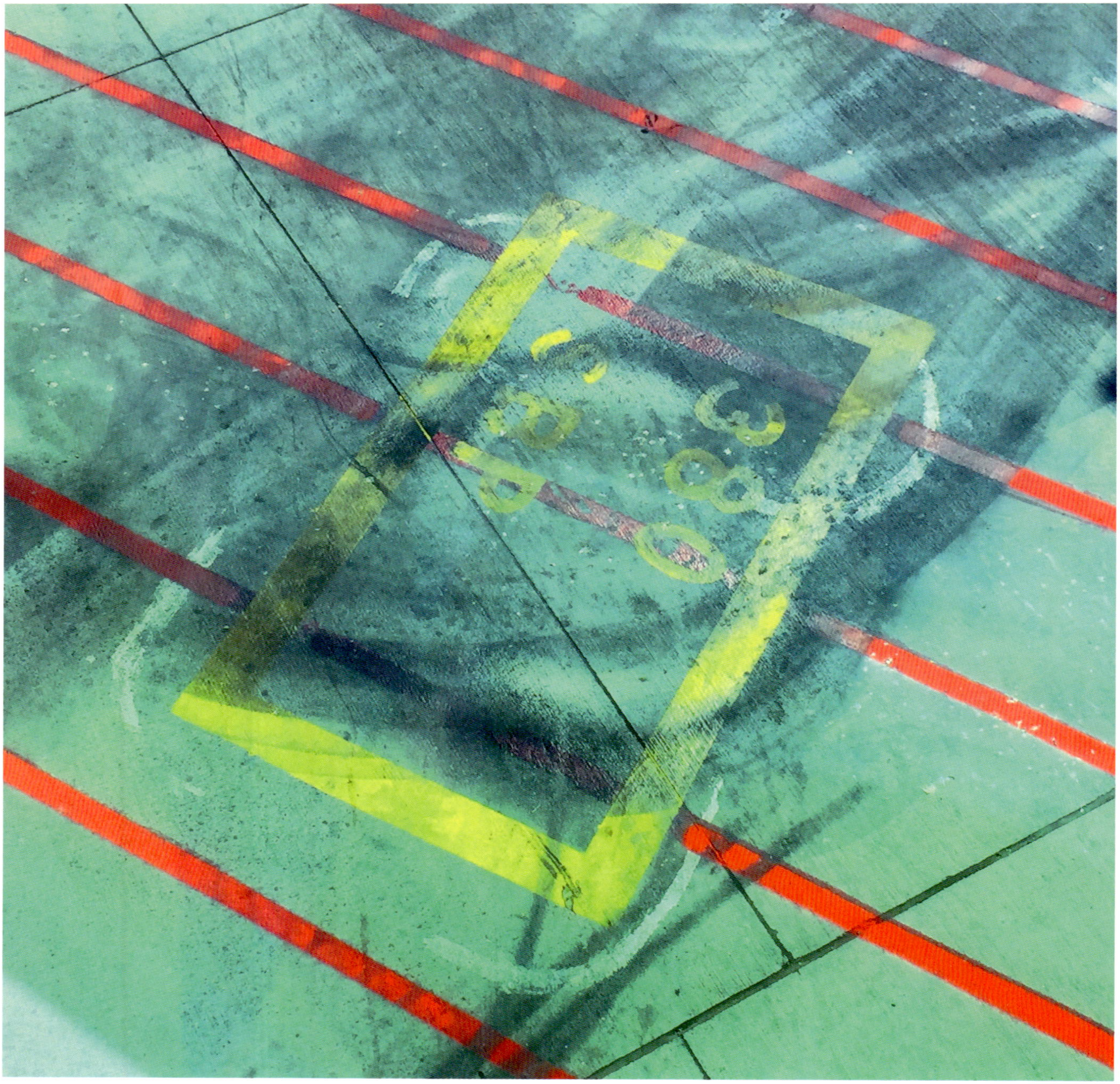

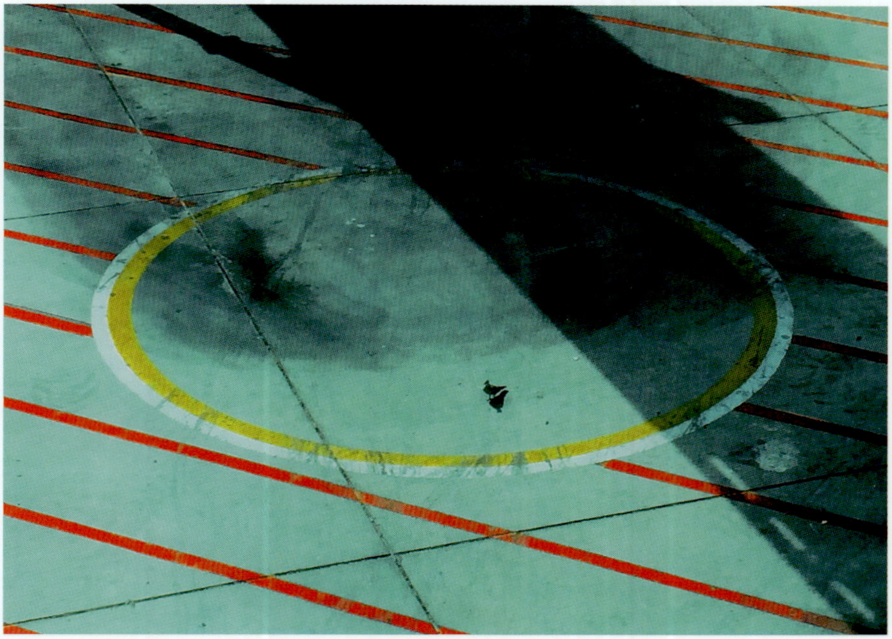

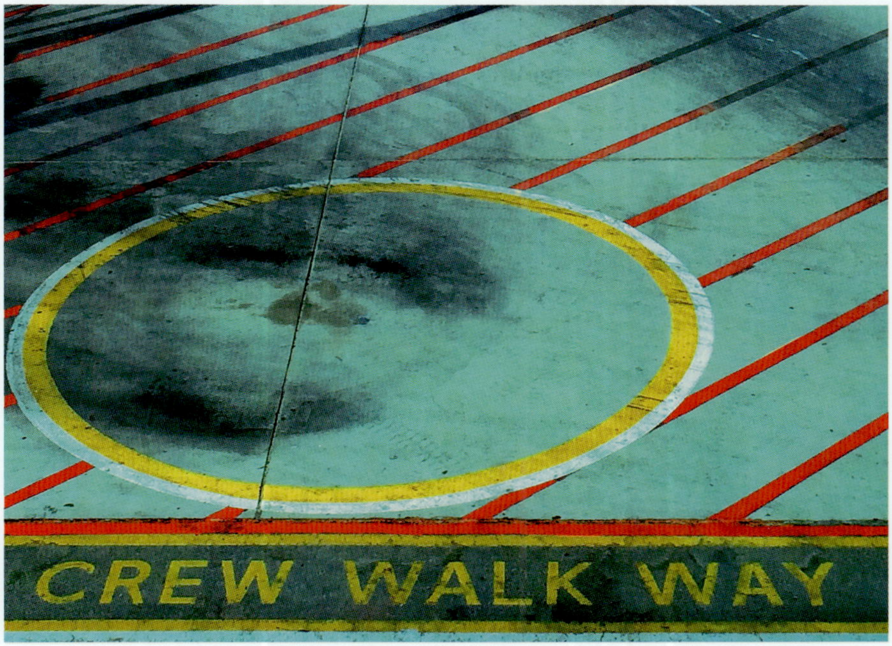
CREW WALK WAY

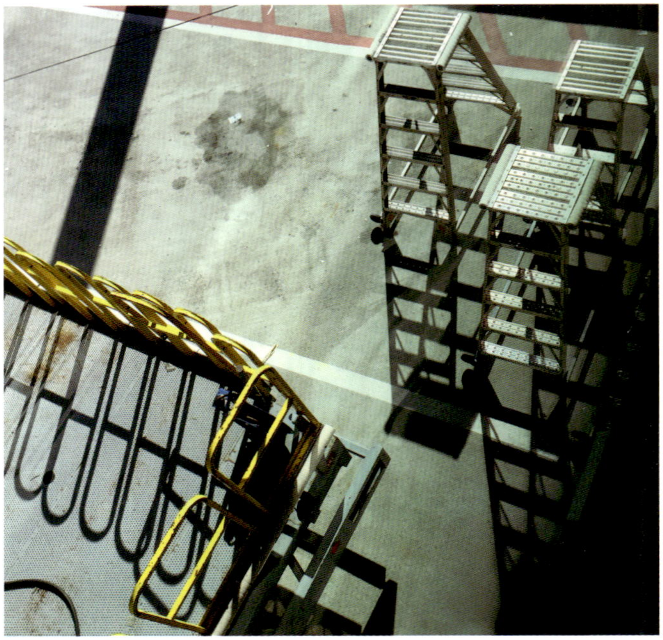

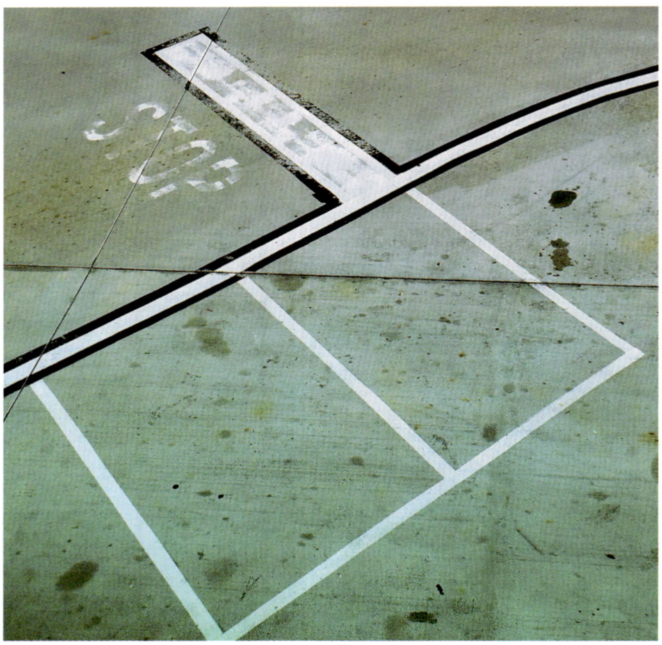
STOP

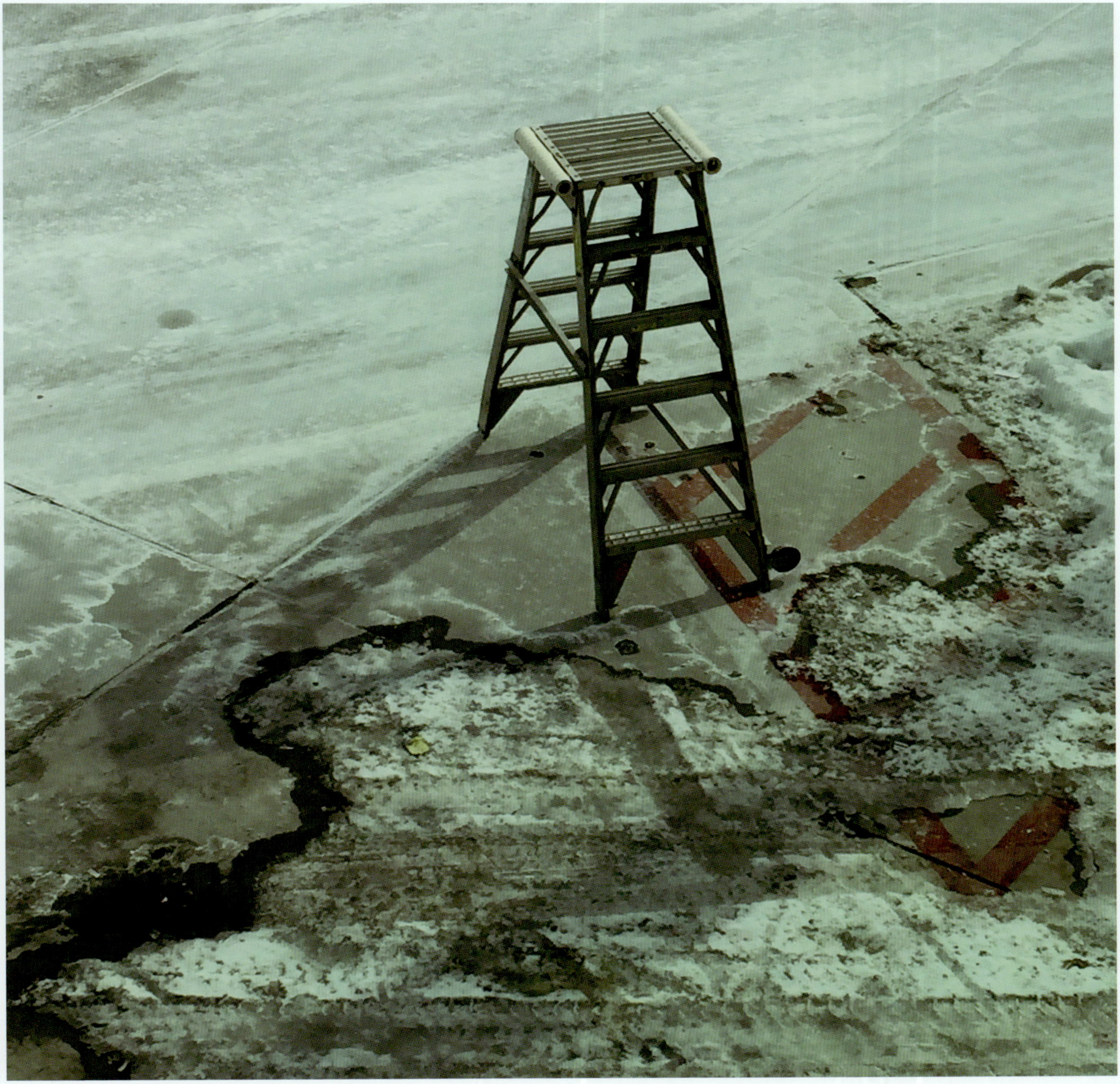

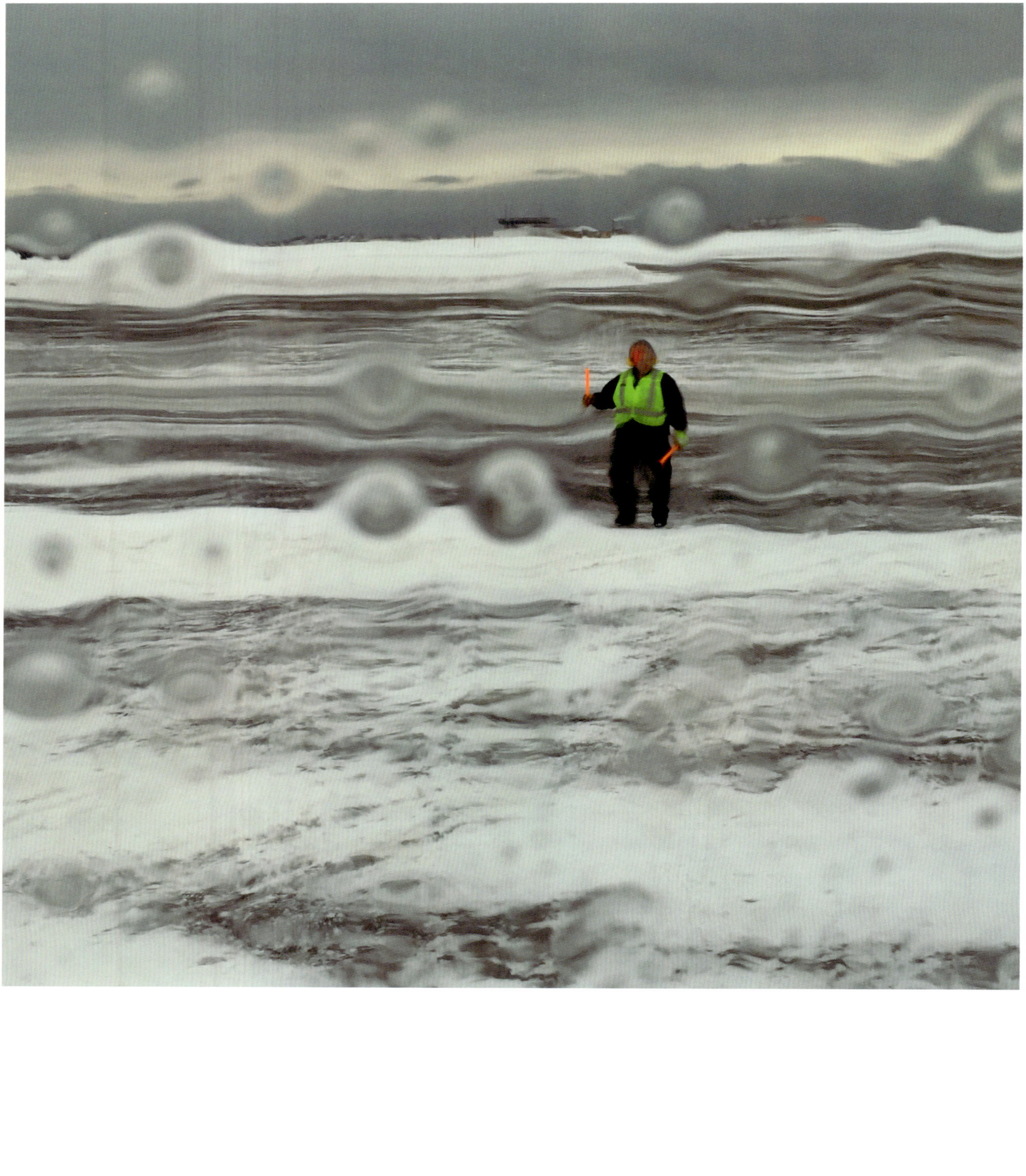

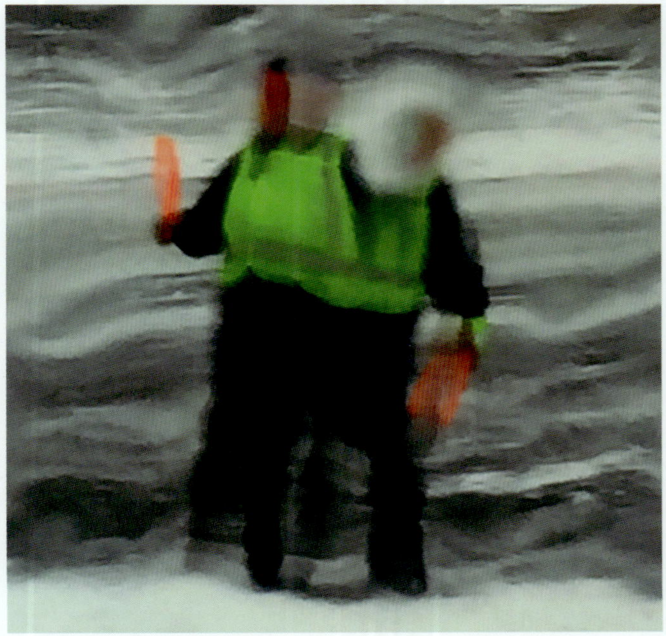

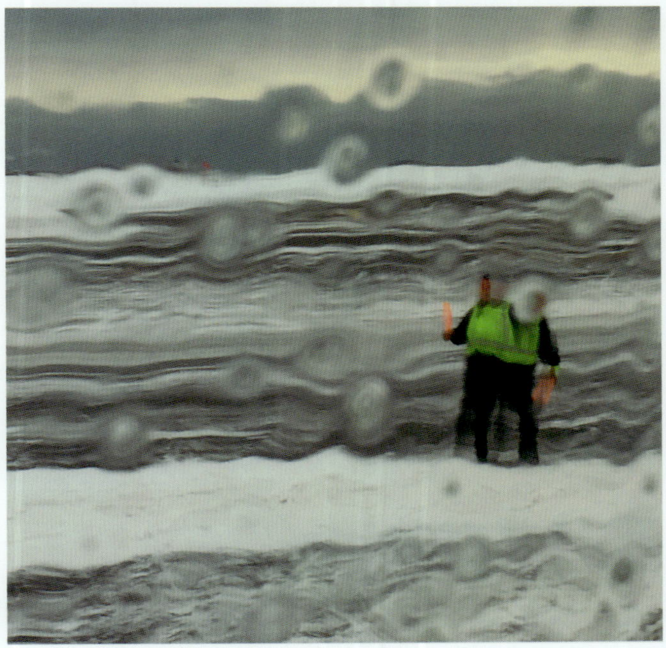

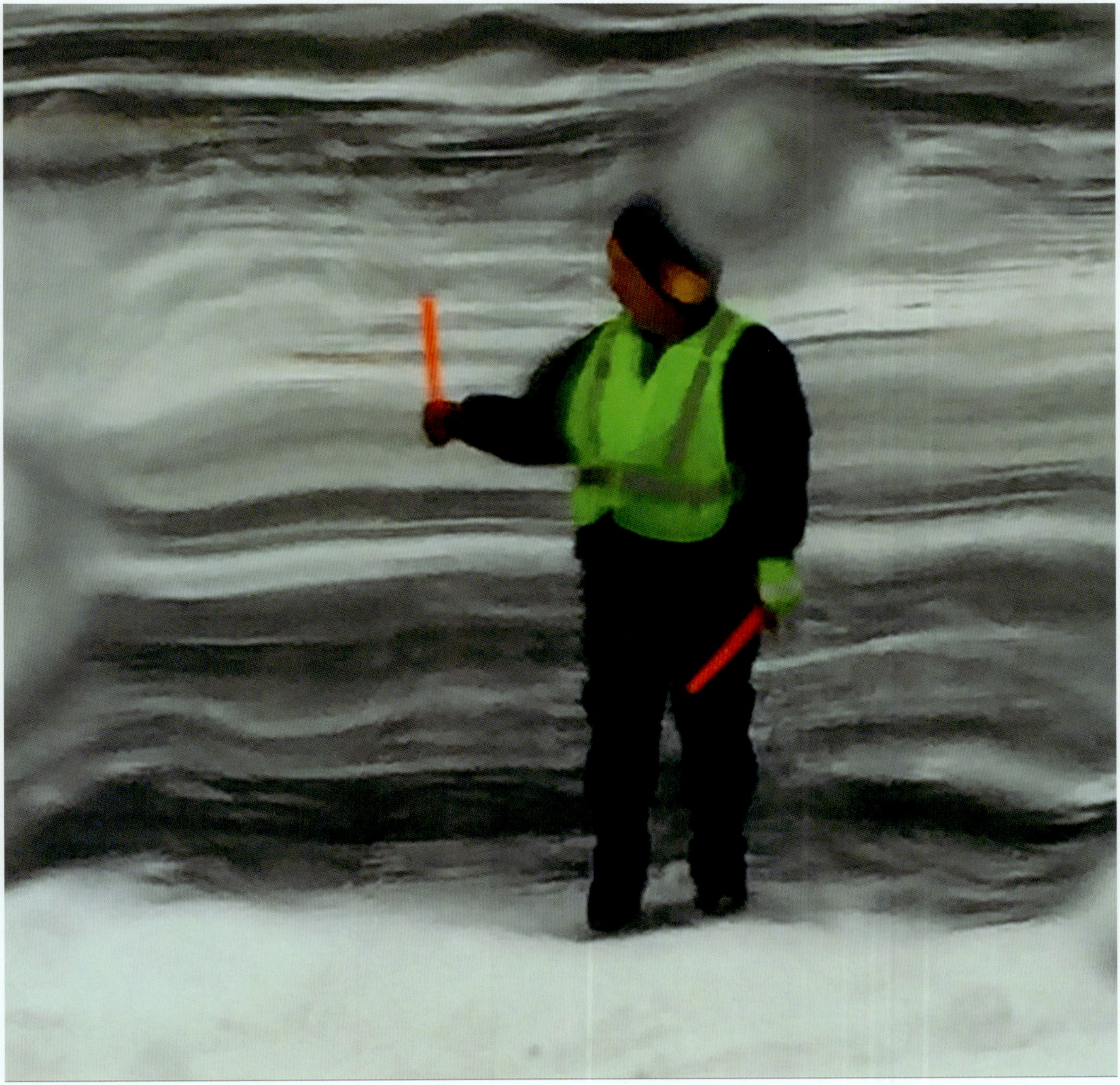

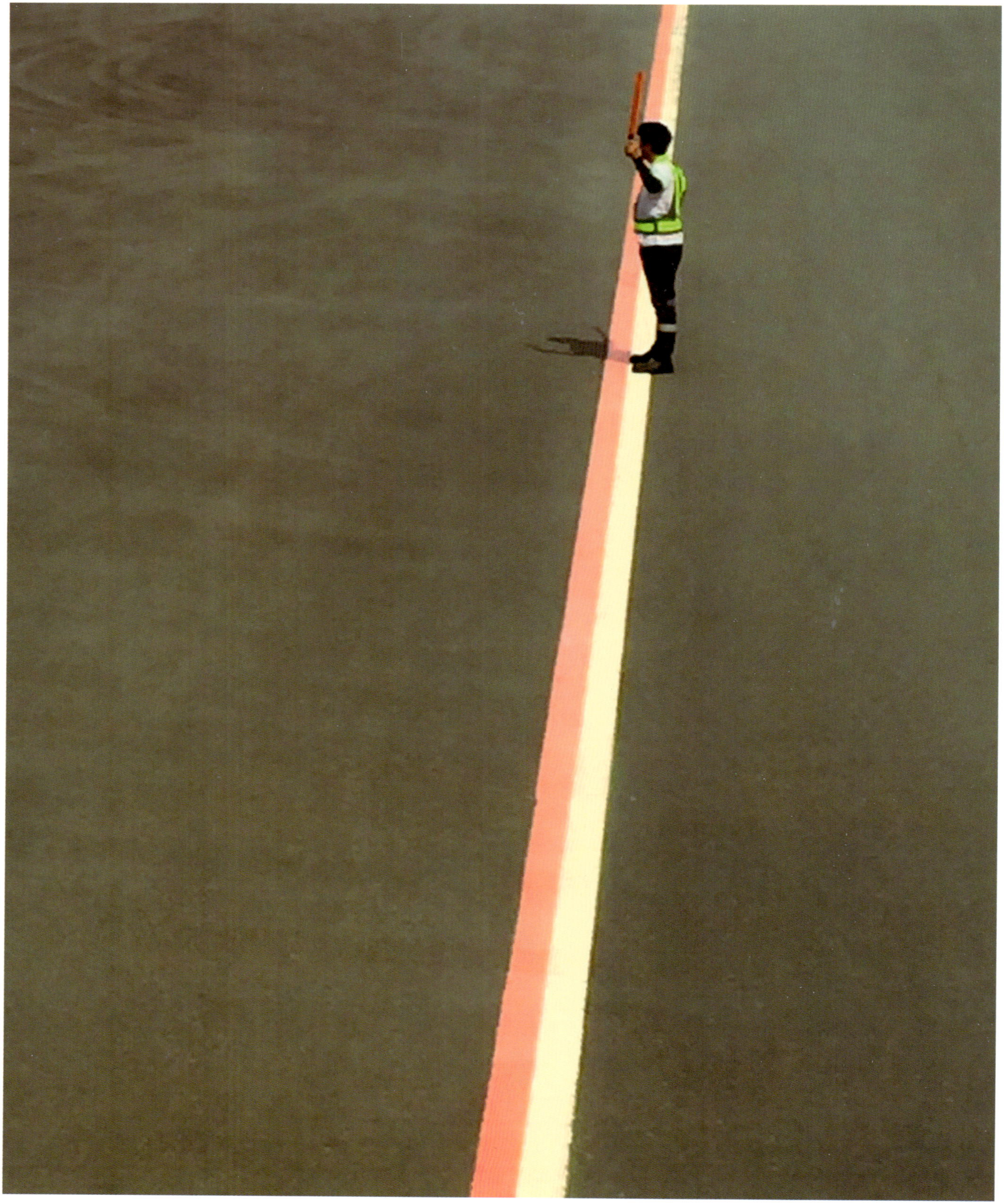

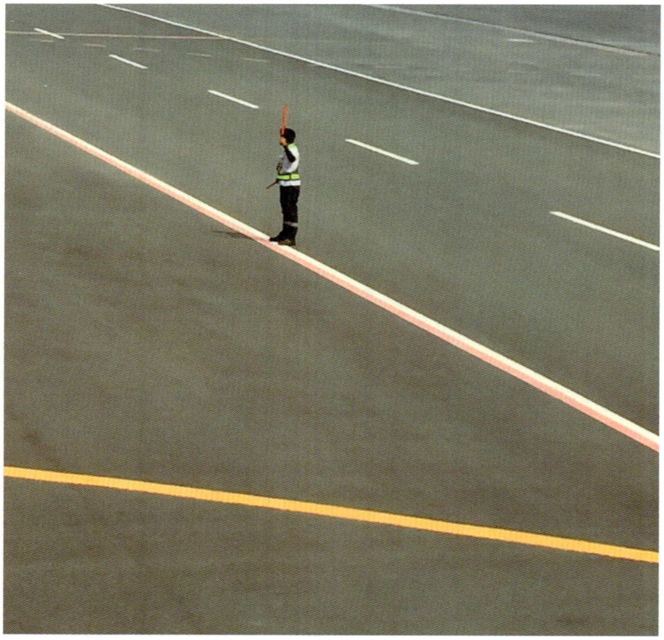

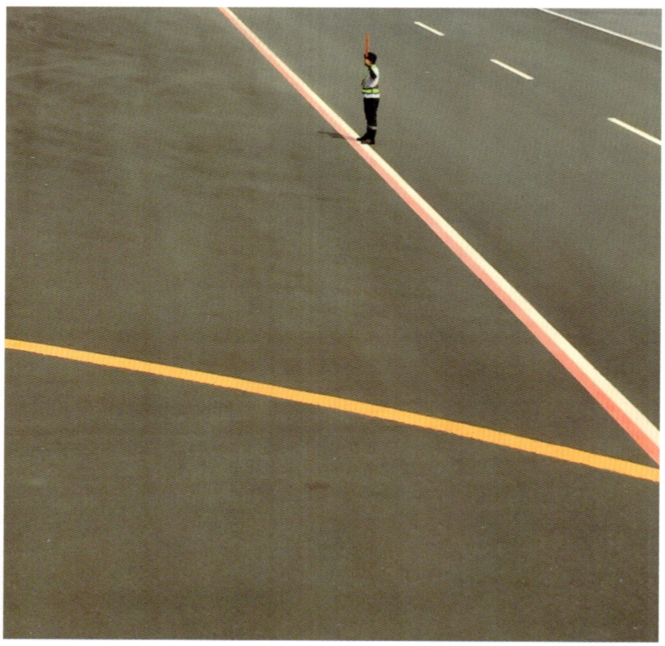

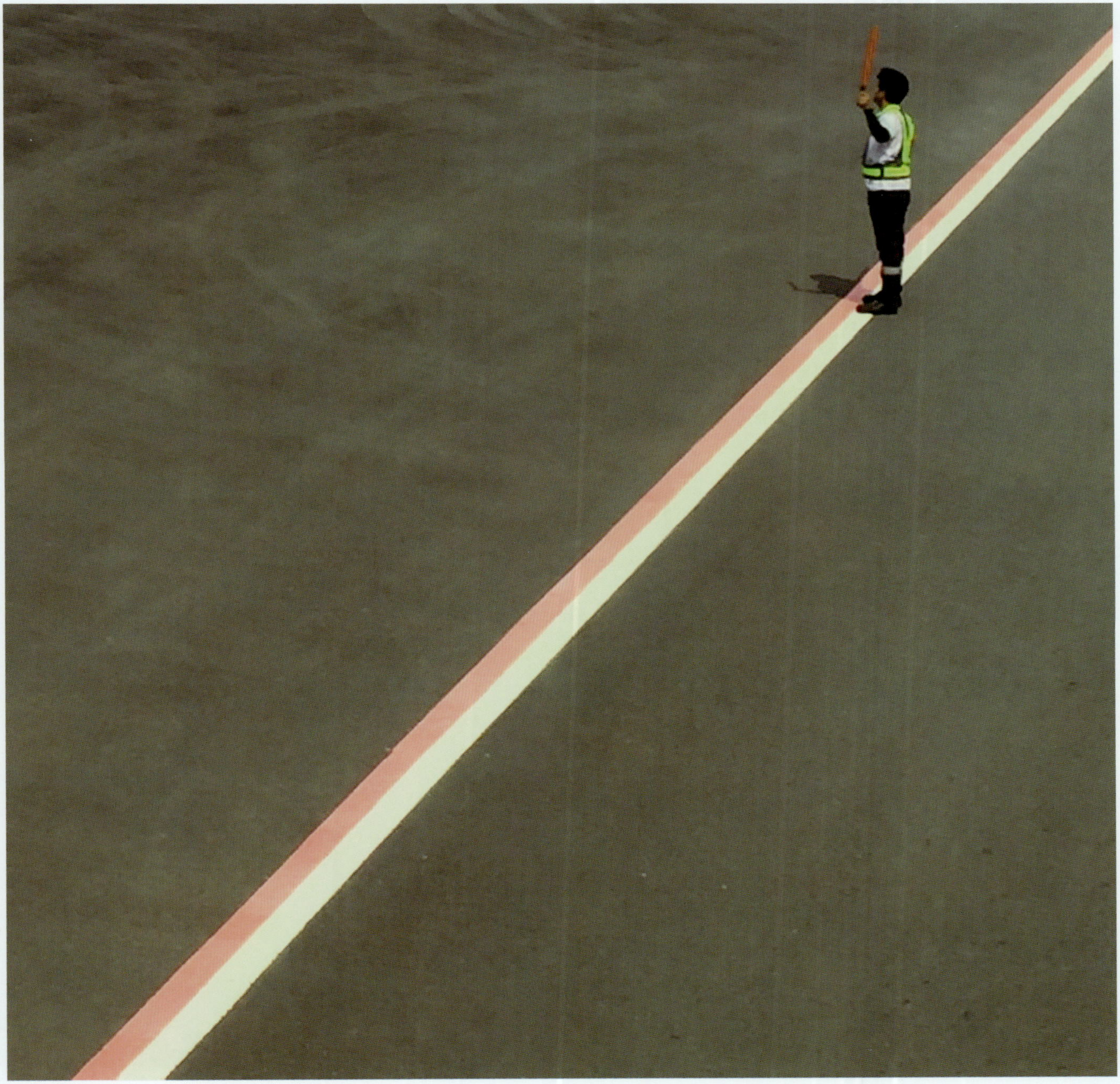

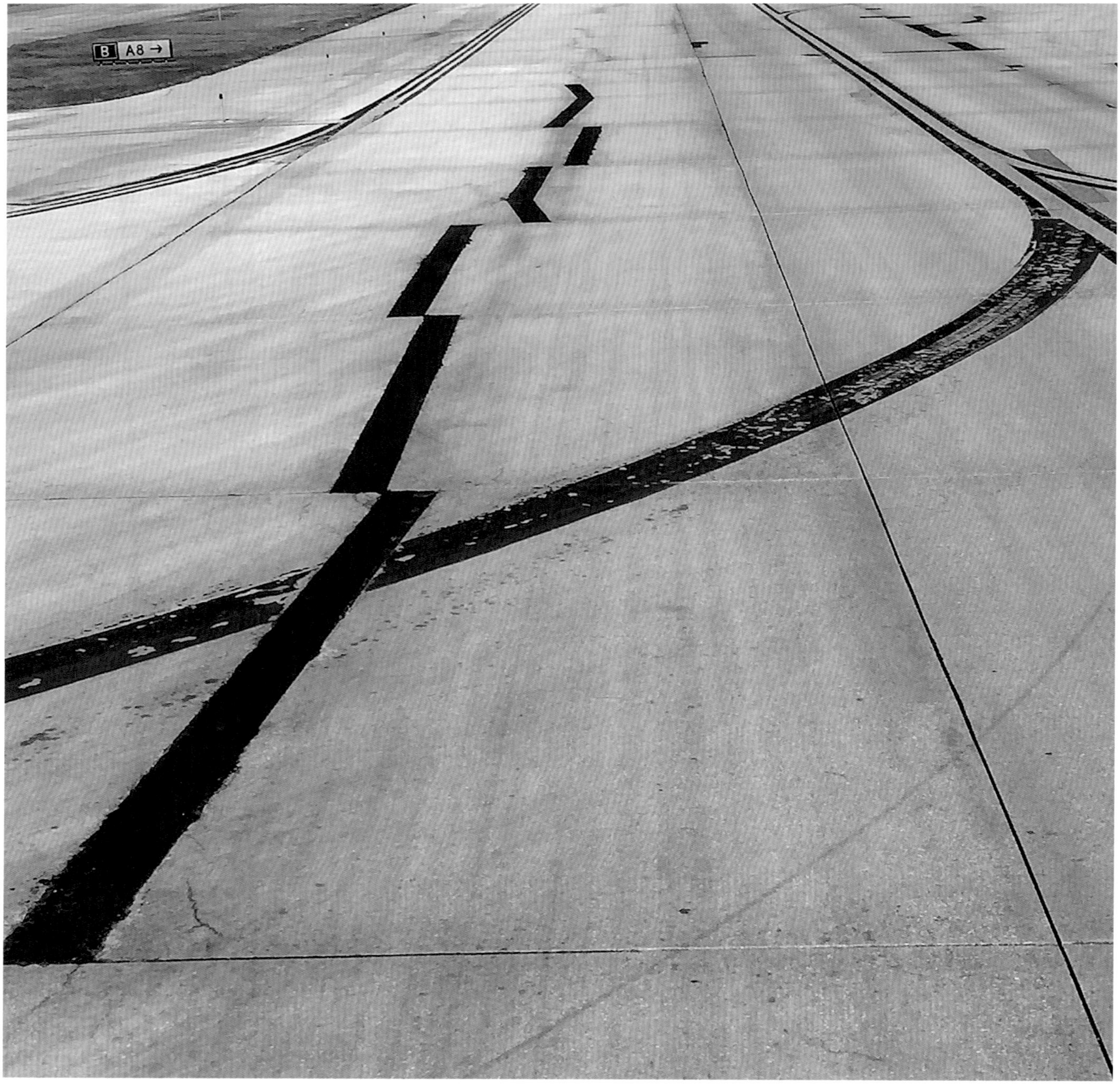
B A8 →

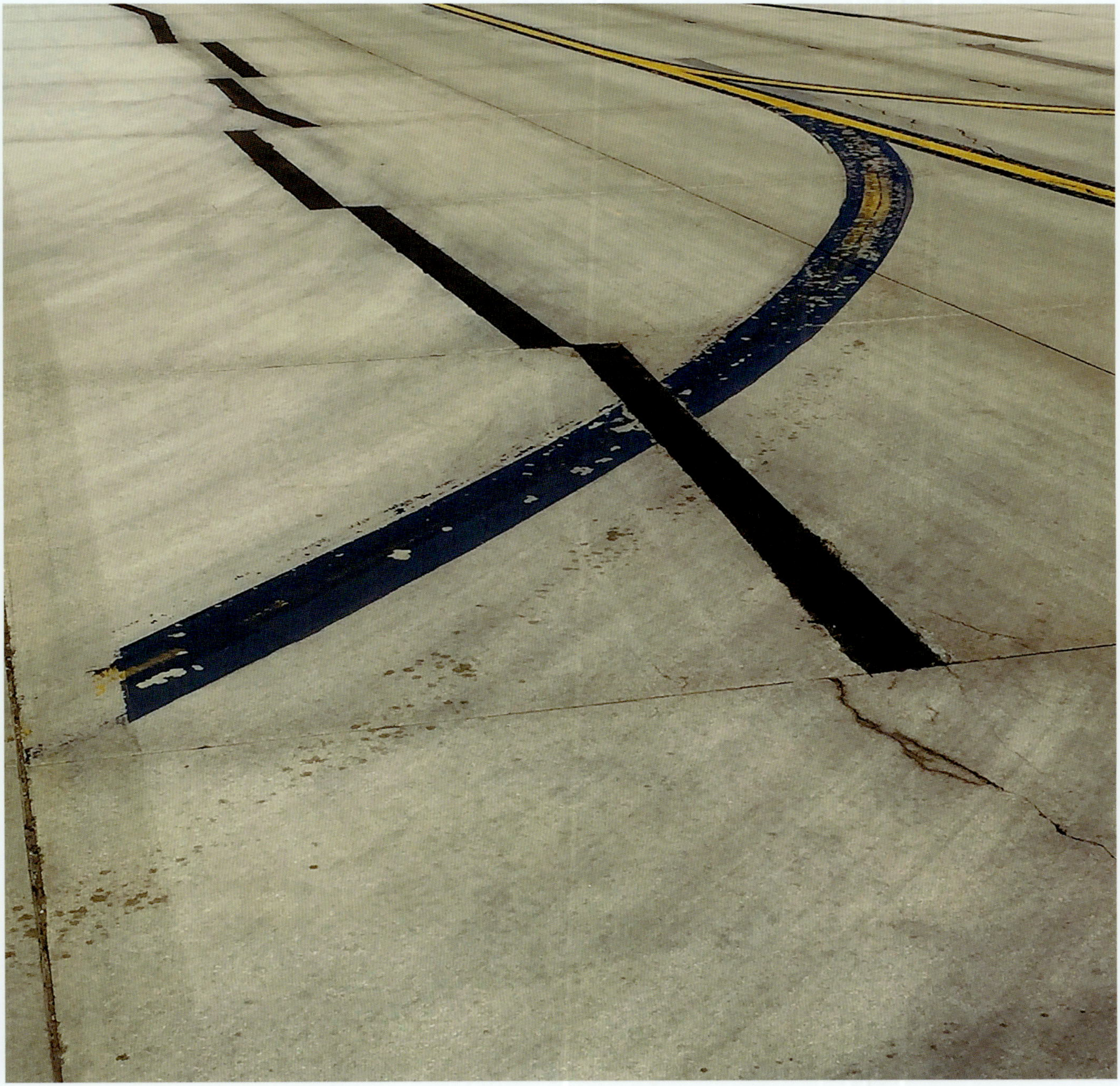

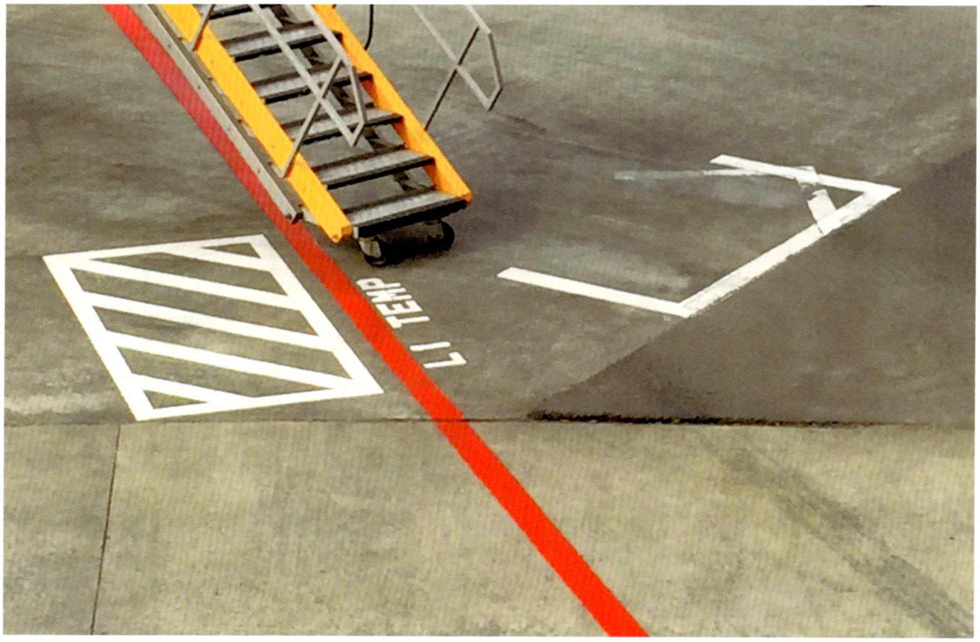
L1 TEMP

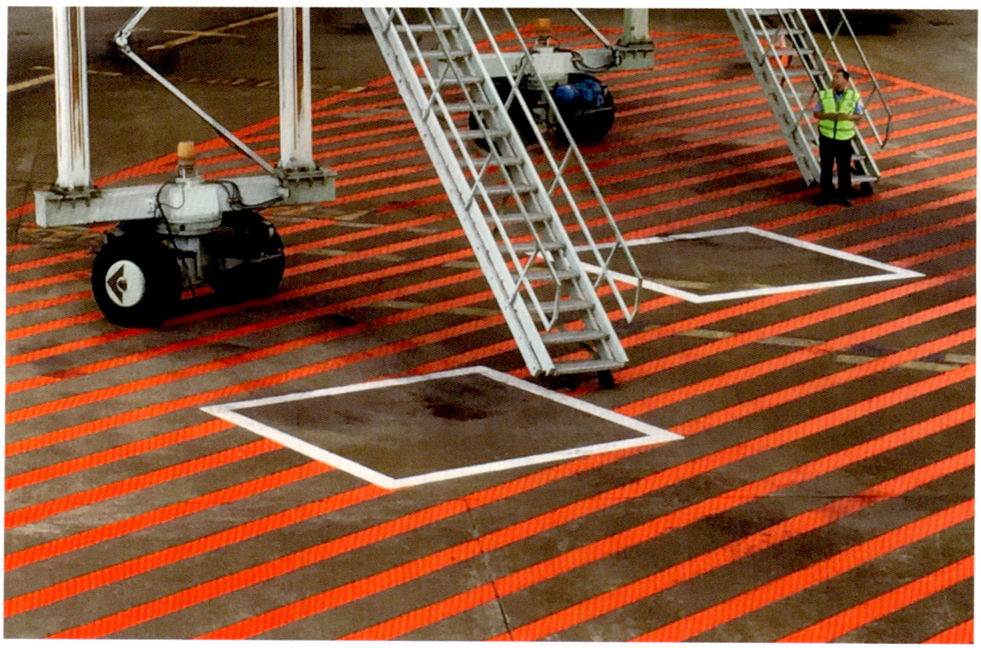

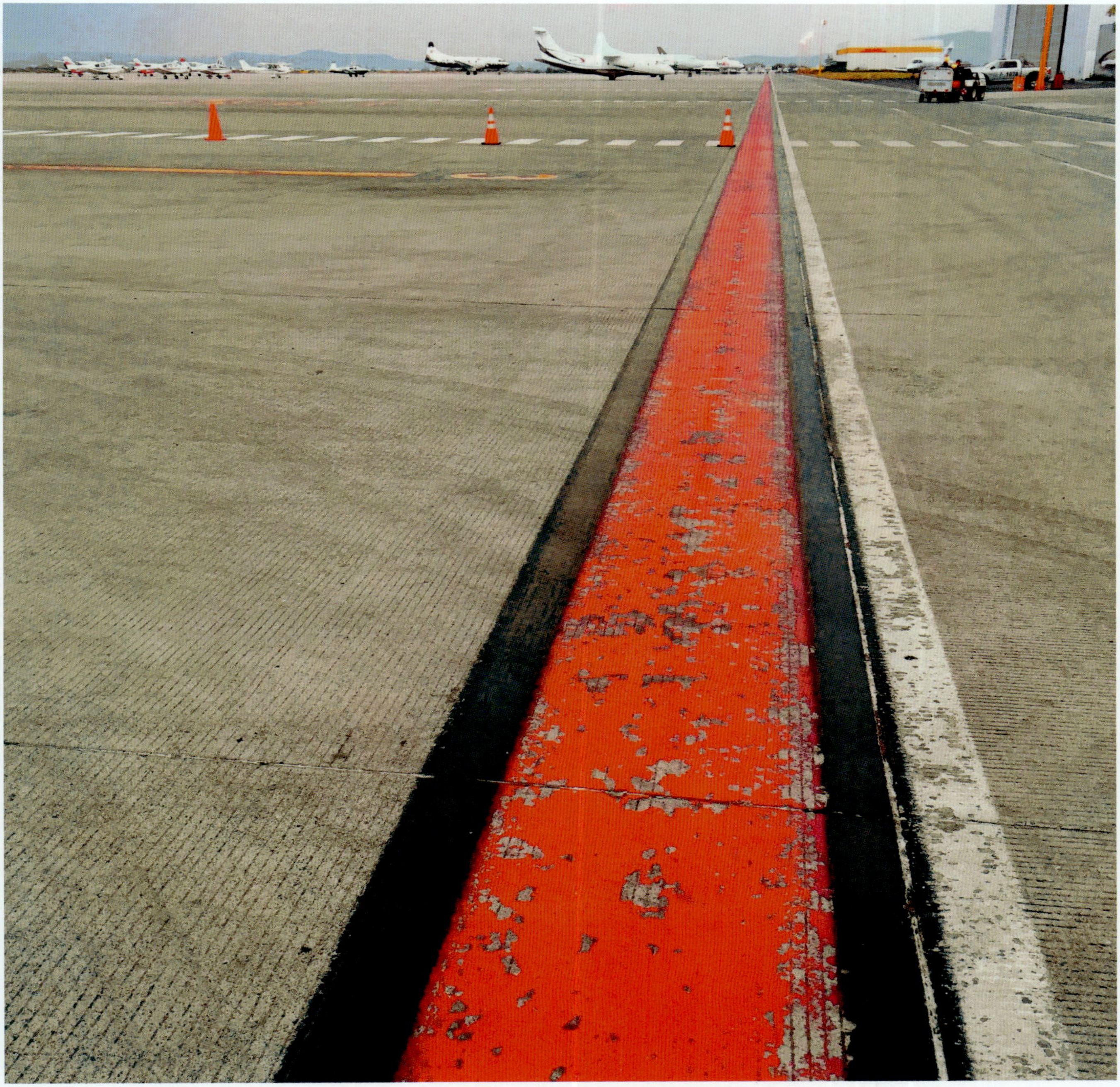

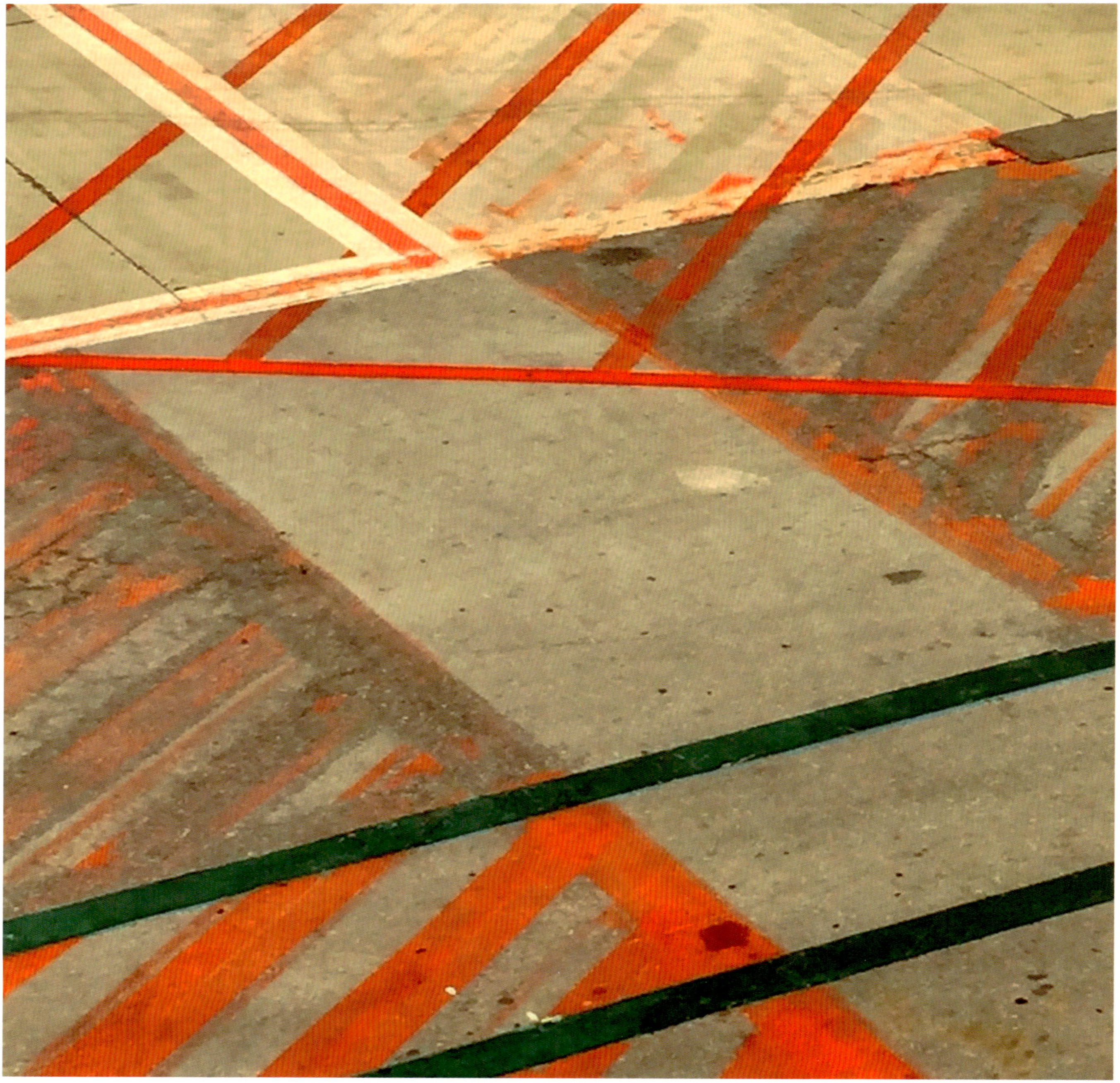

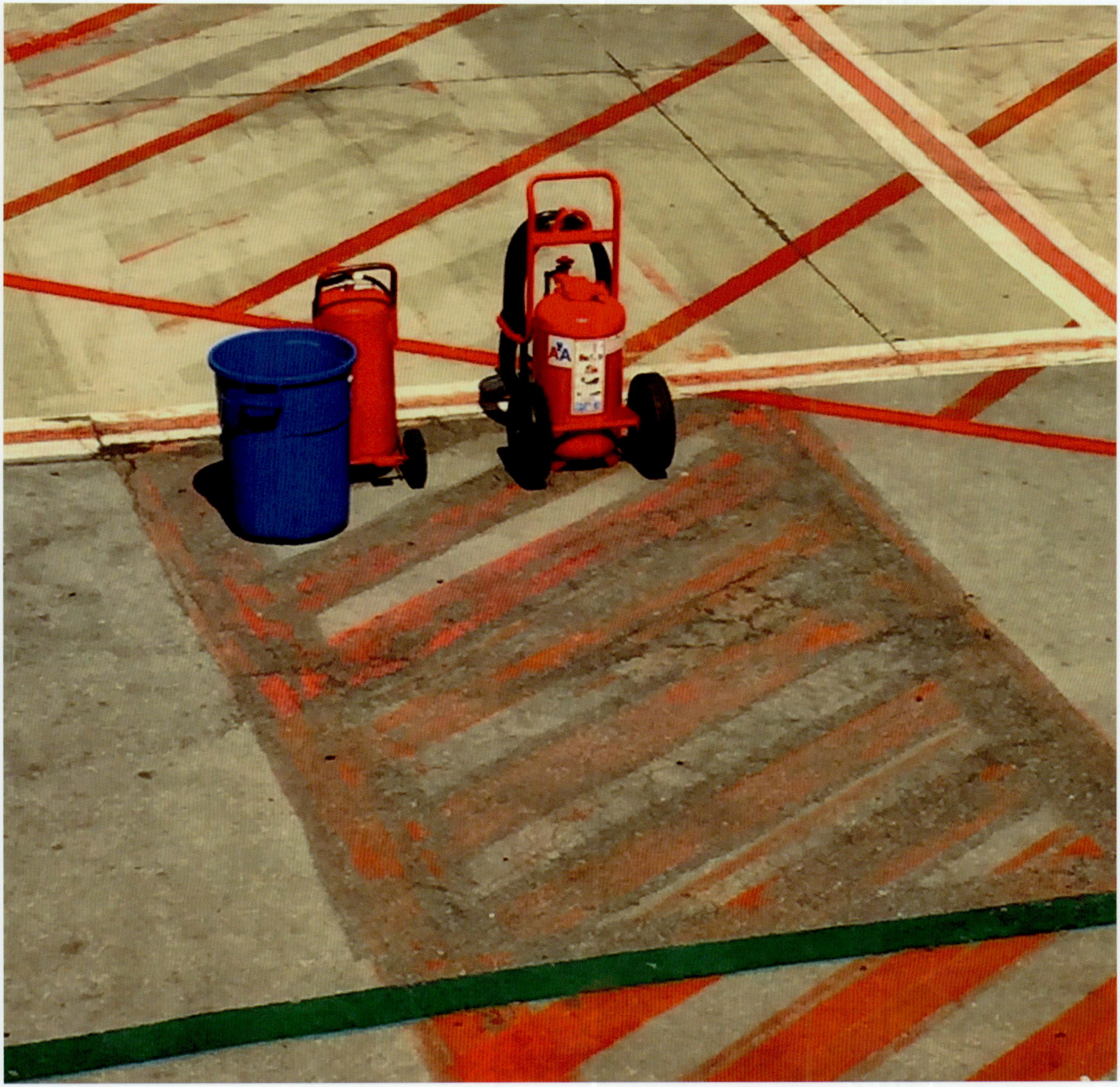

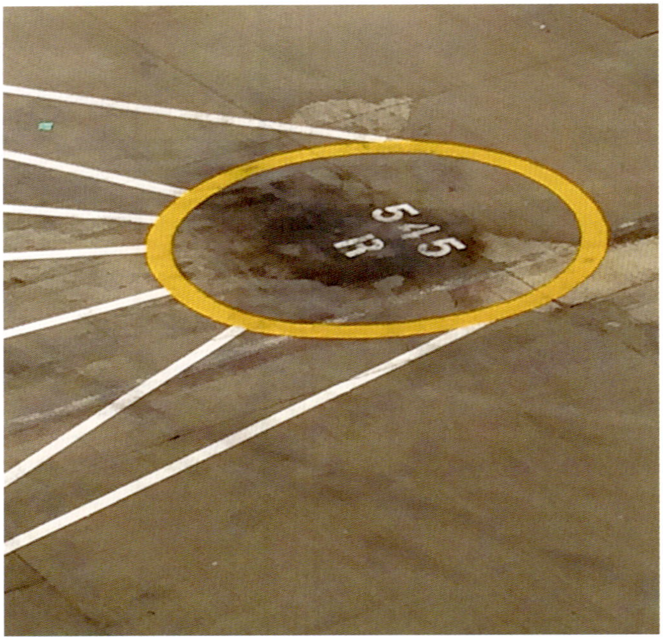
545
R

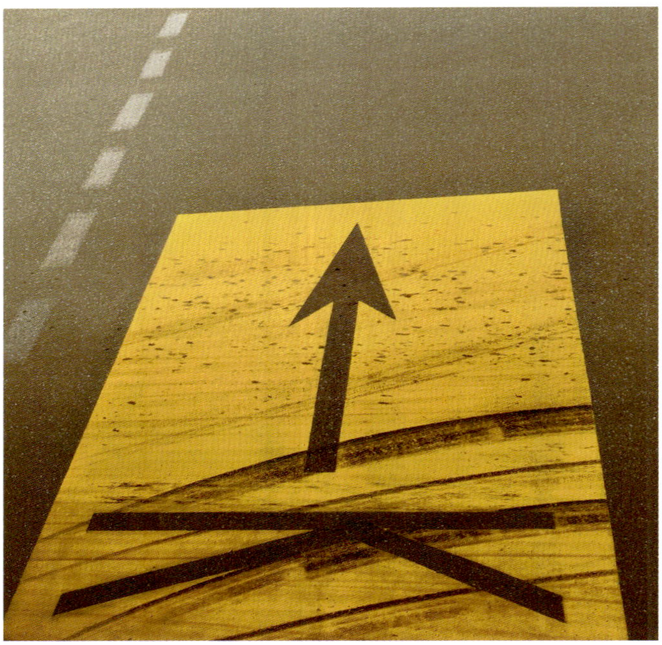

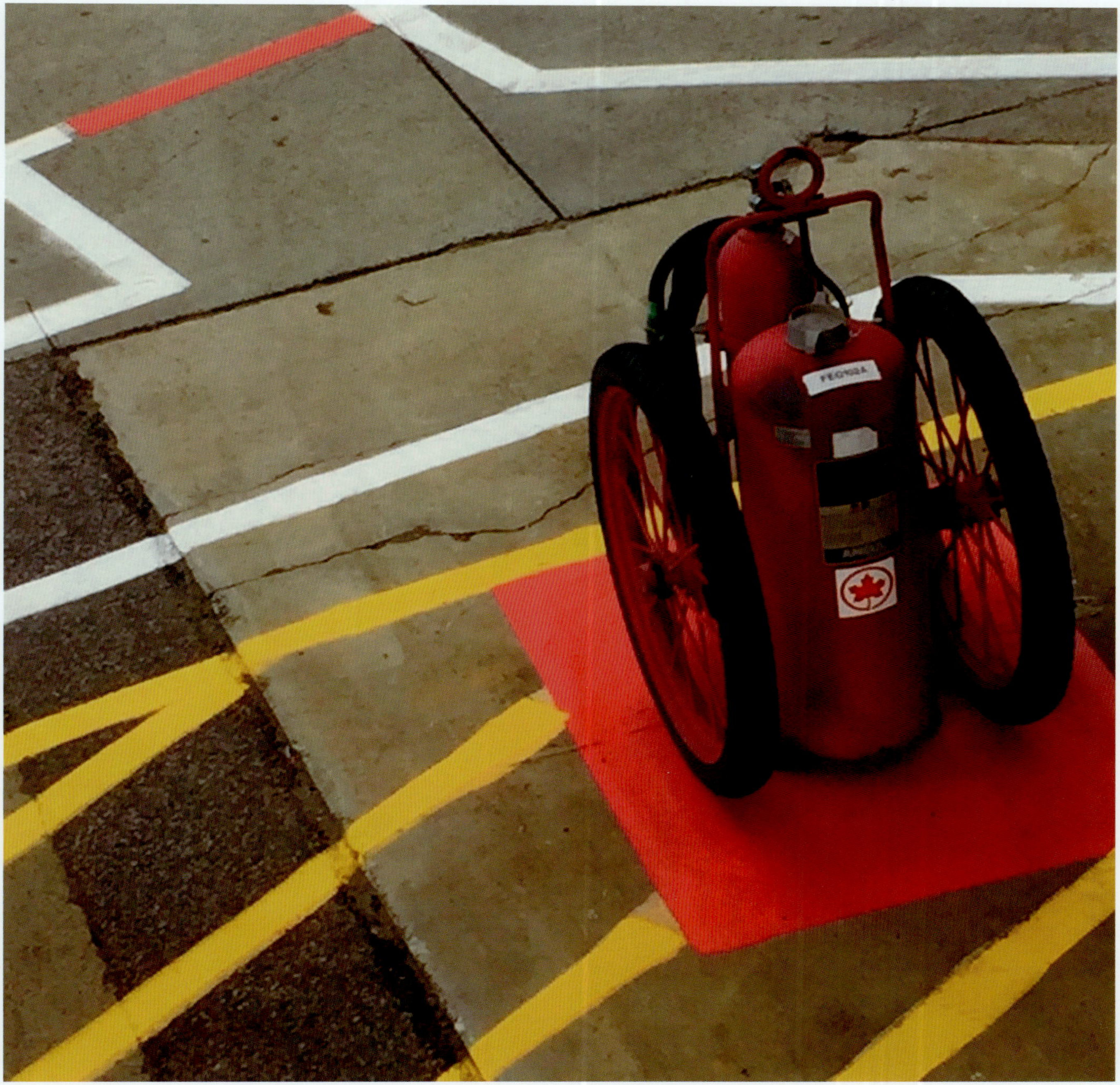

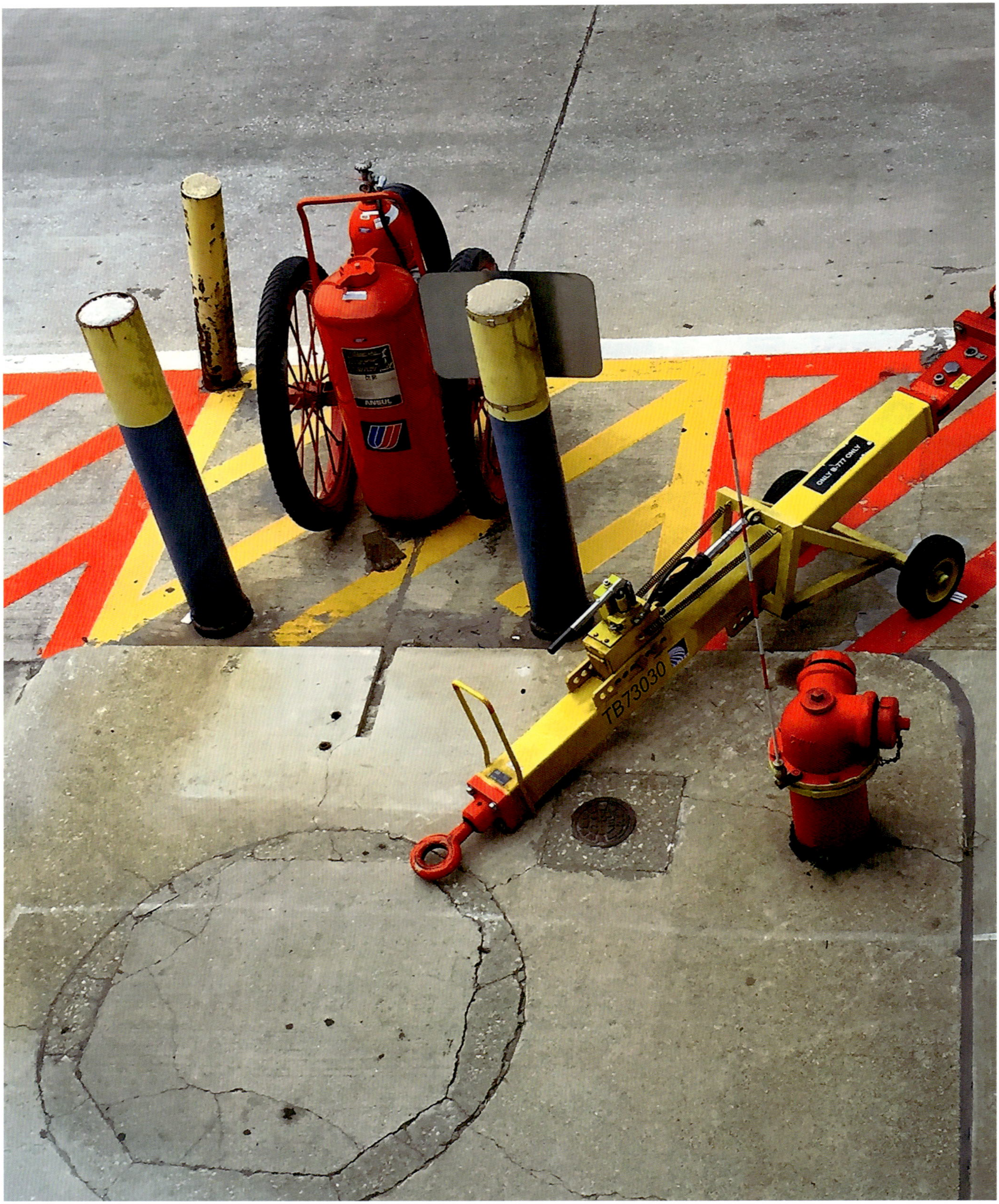
ANSUL
TB73030

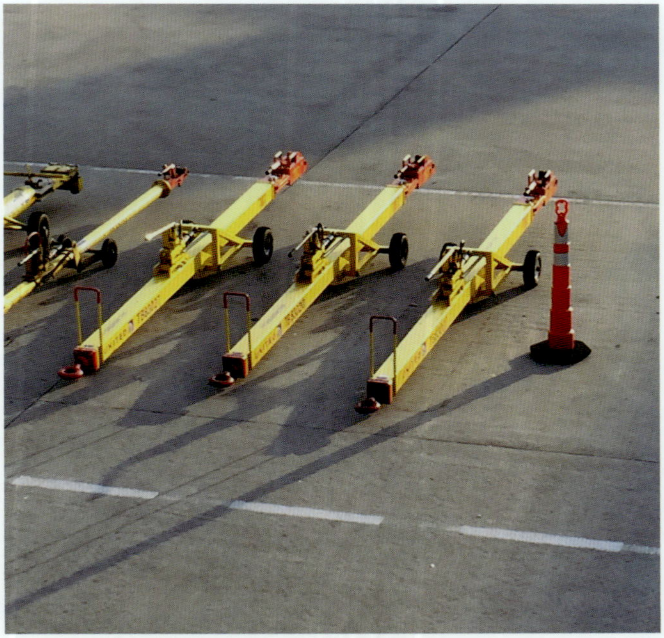

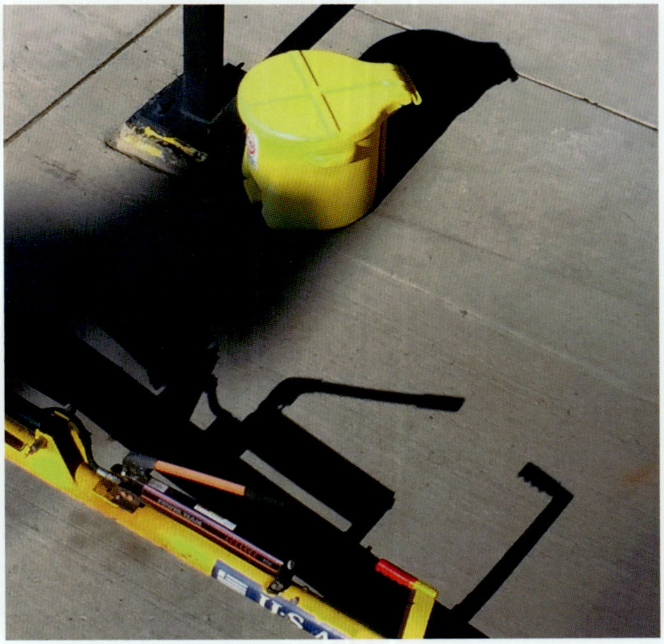

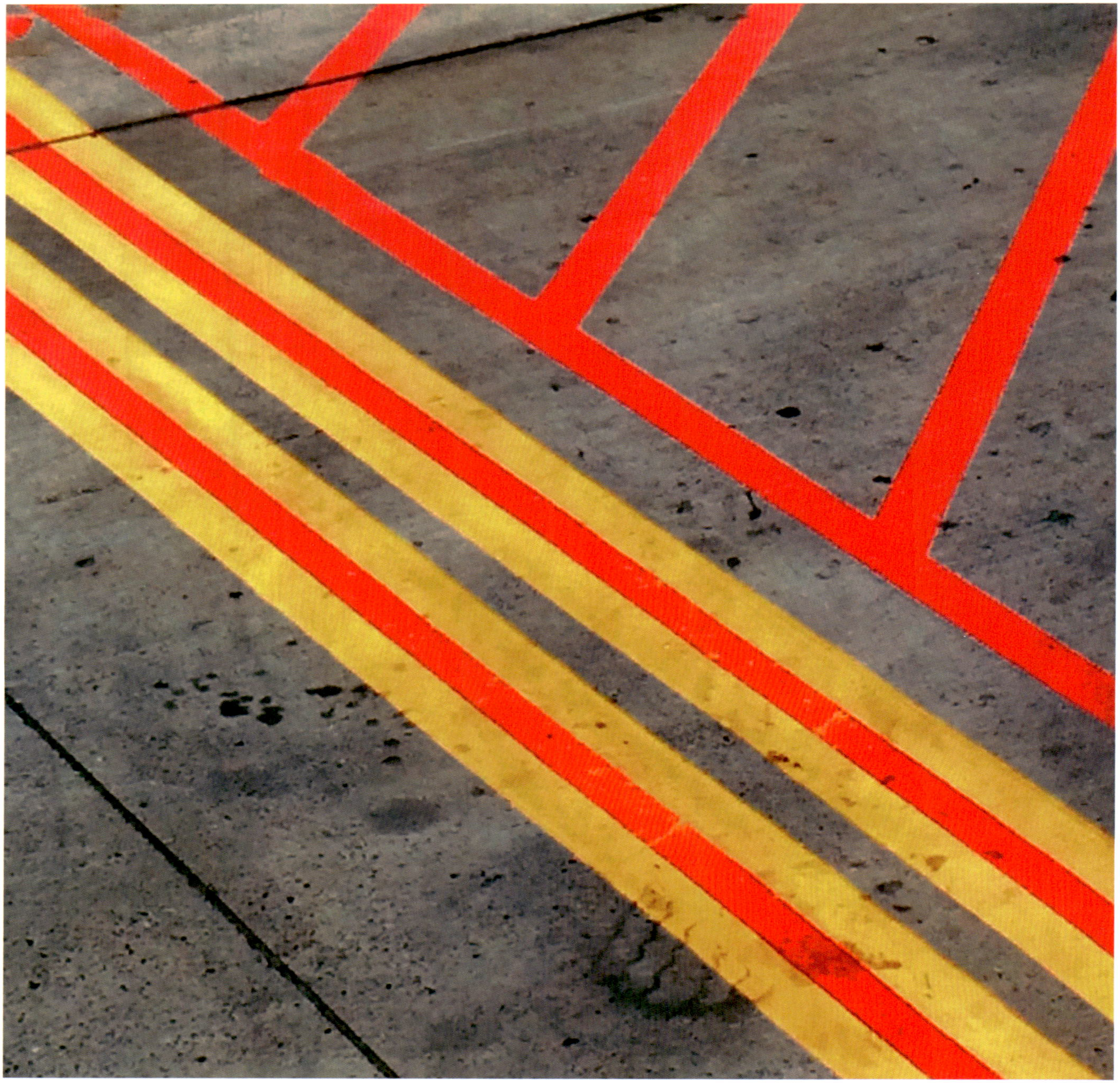

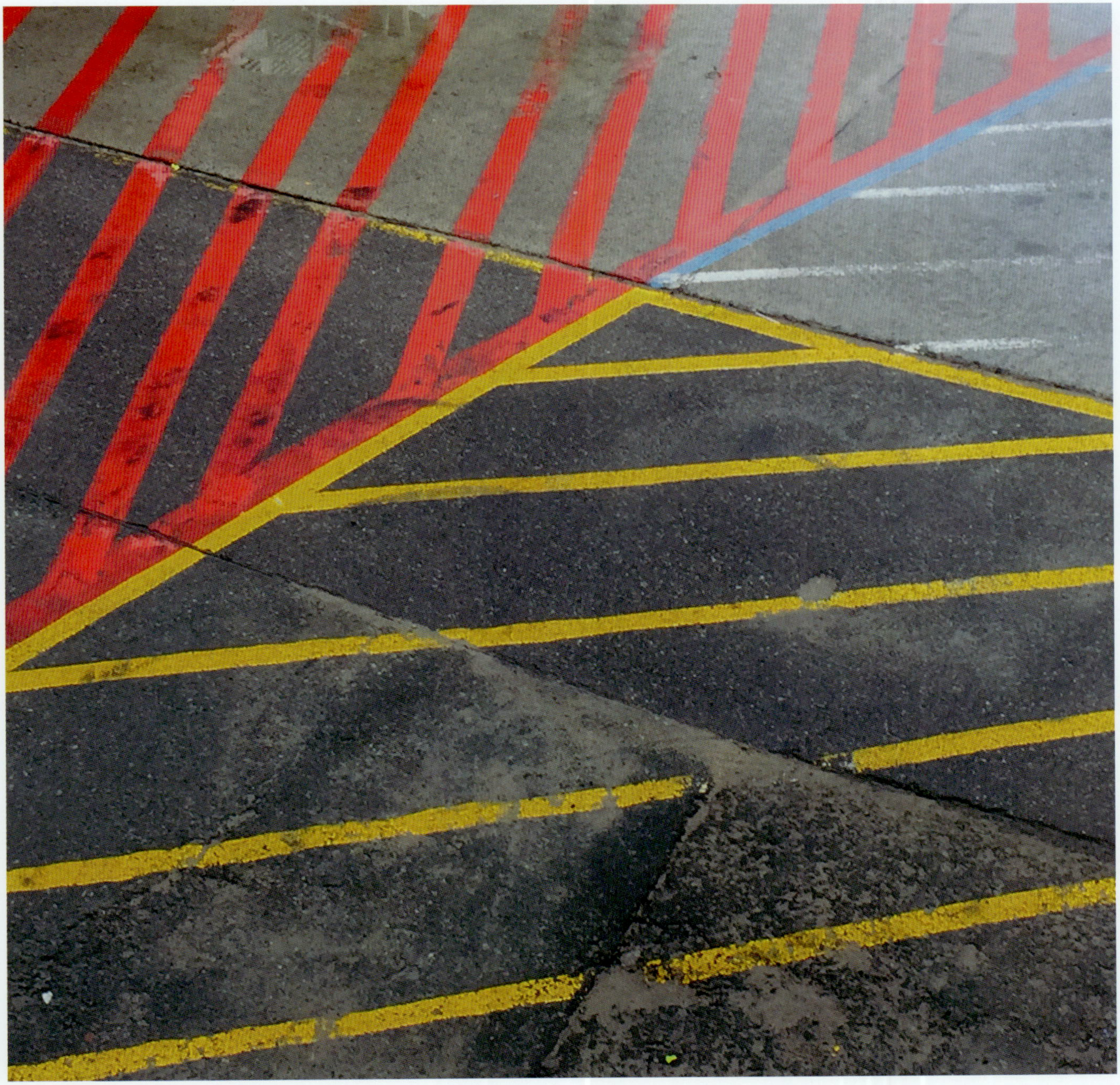

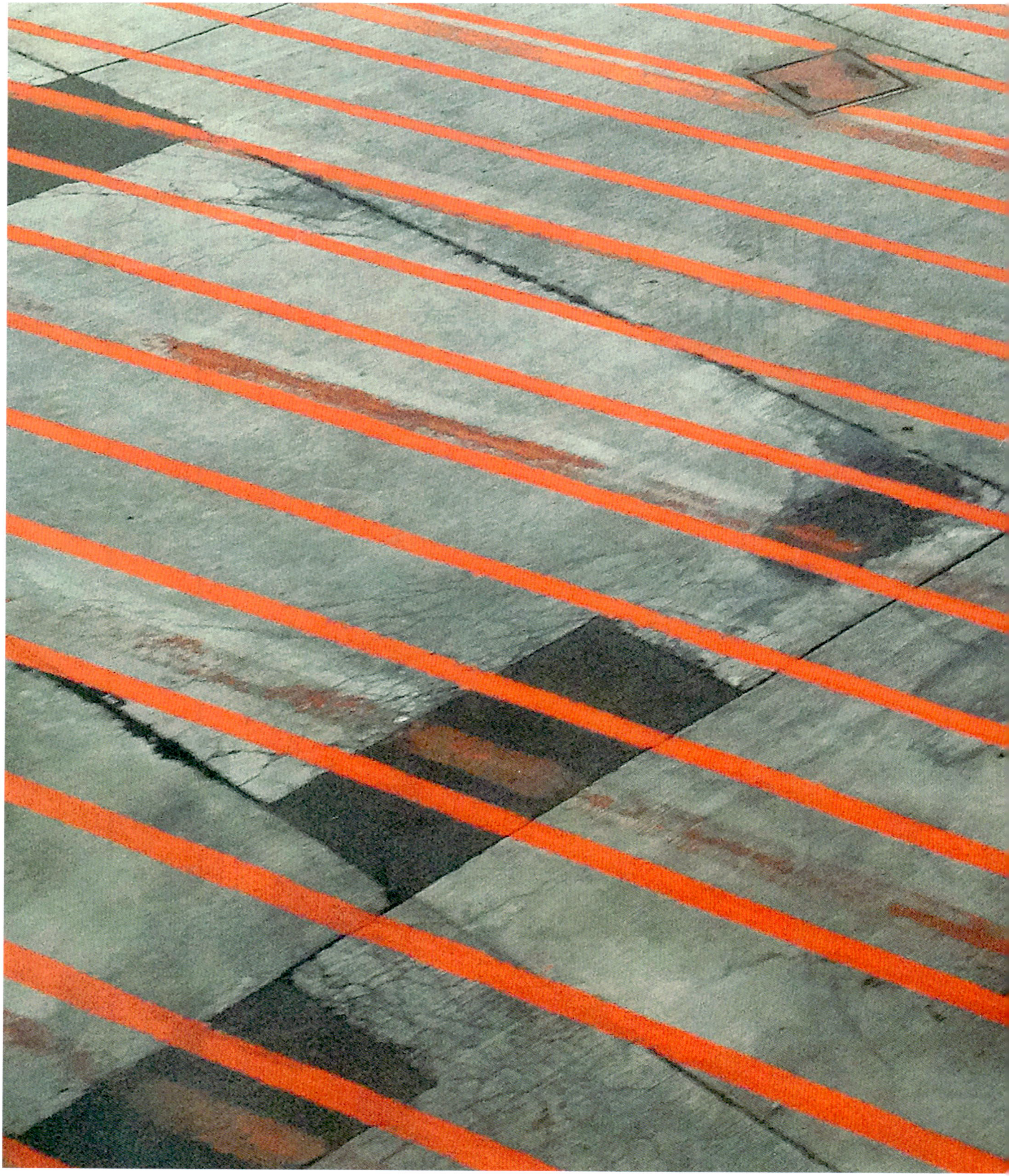

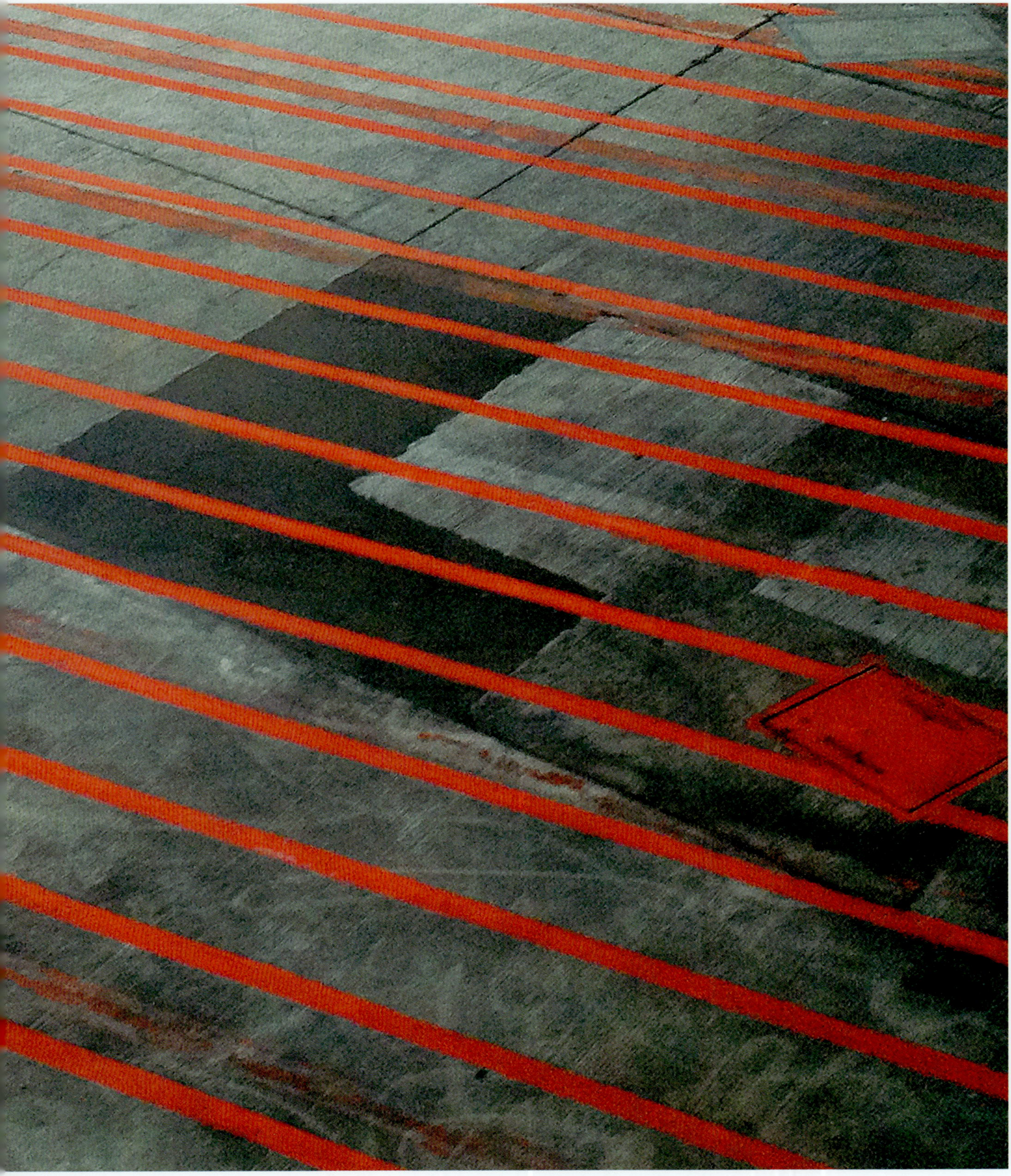

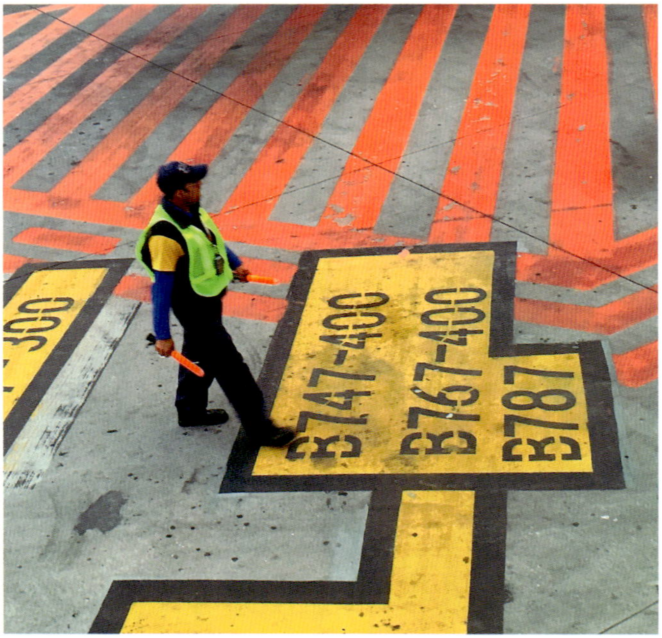
B747-400
B767-400
B787

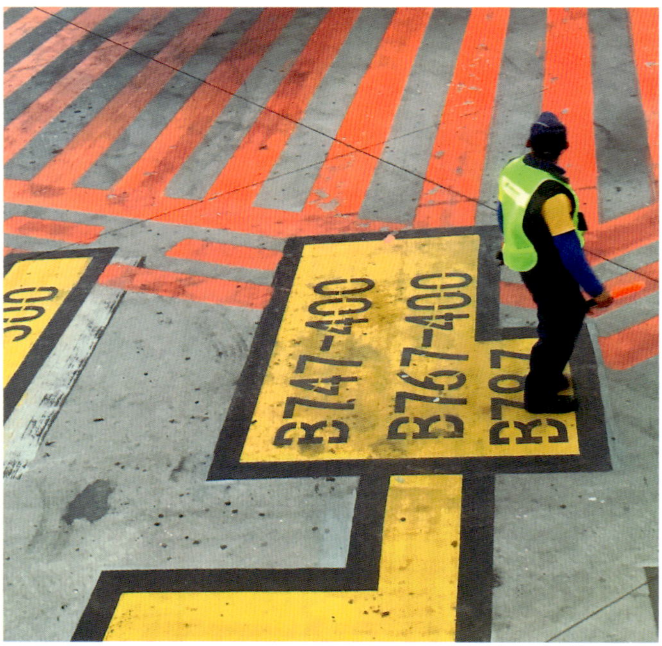
B747-400
B767-400

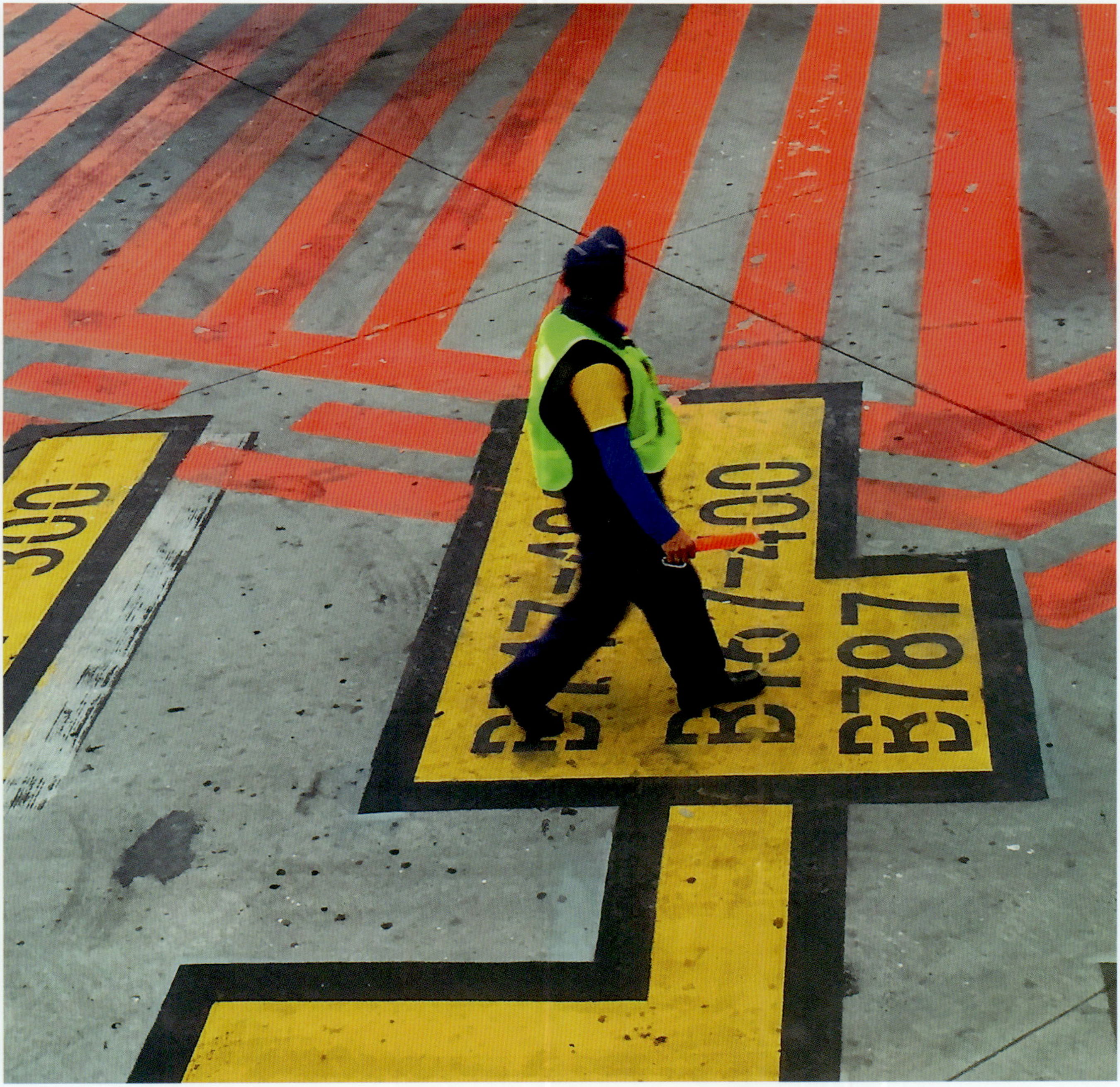
B767-400
B787

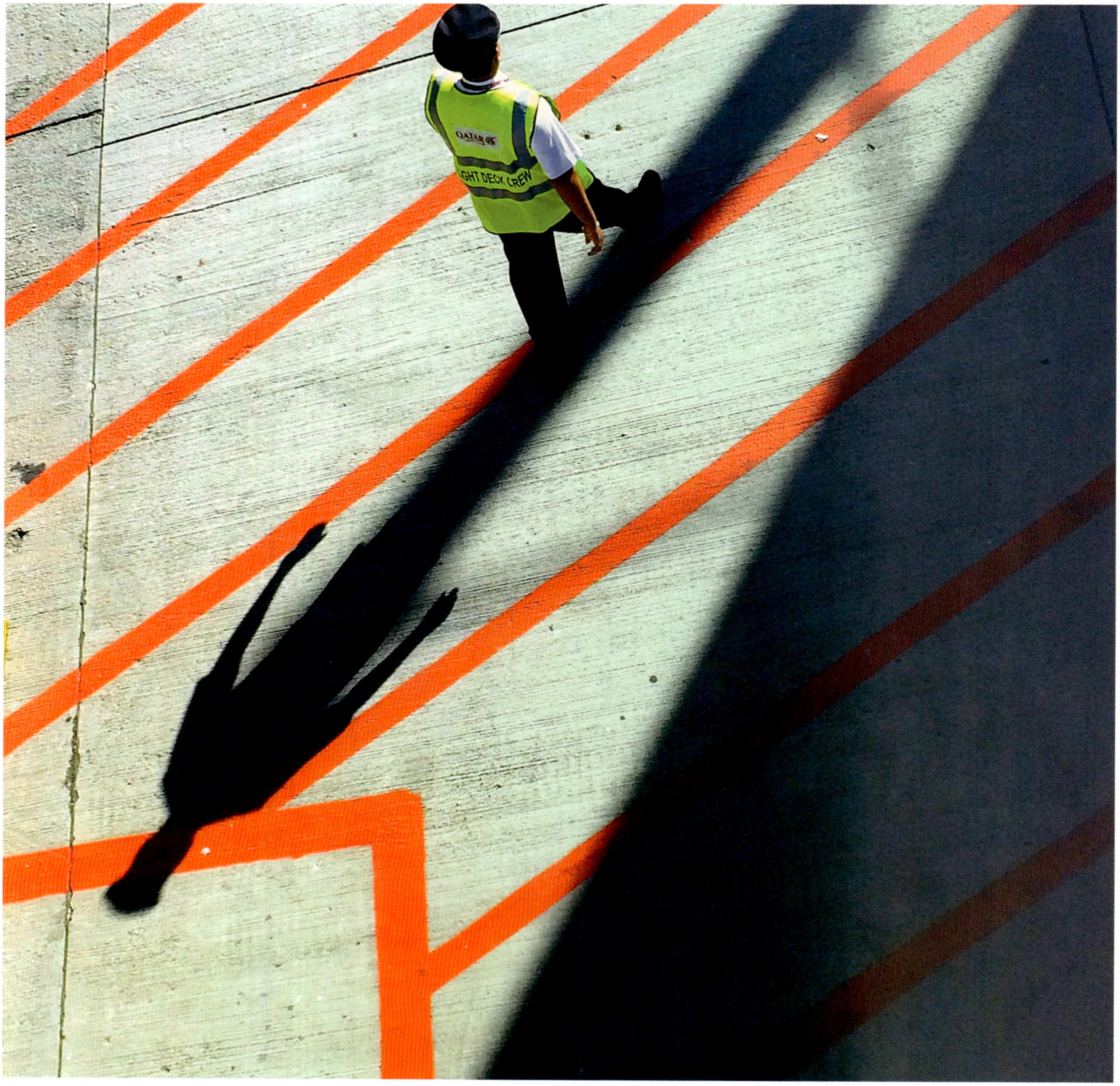
QATAR
FLIGHT DECK CREW

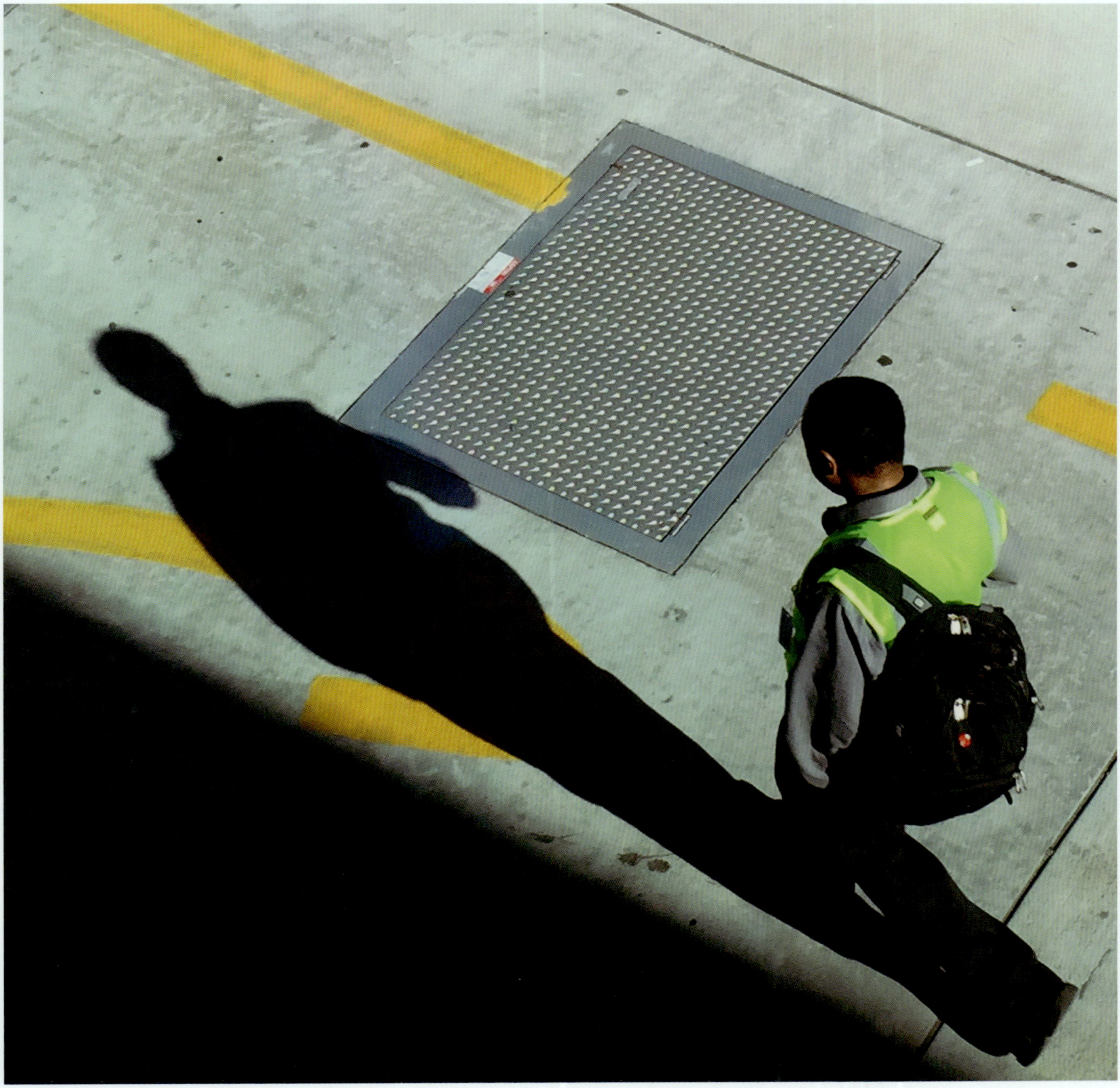

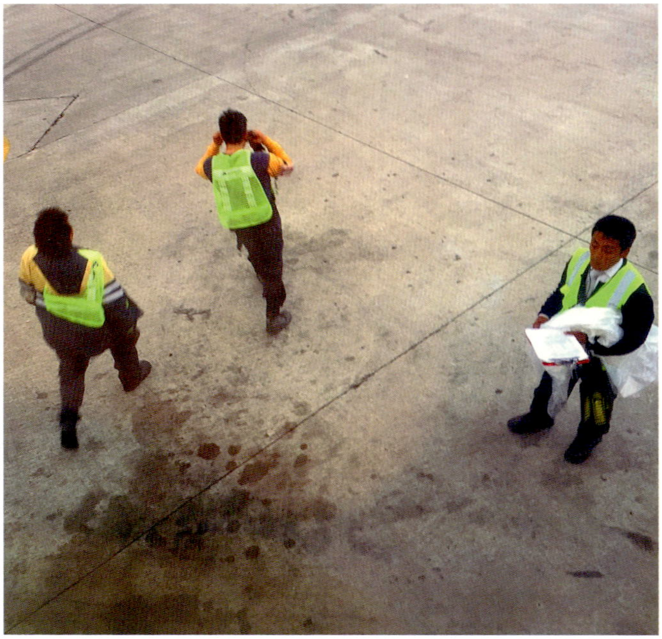

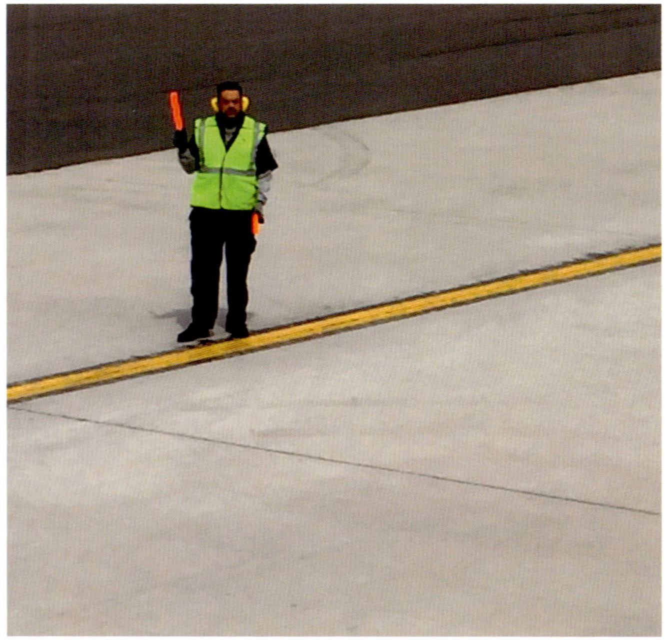

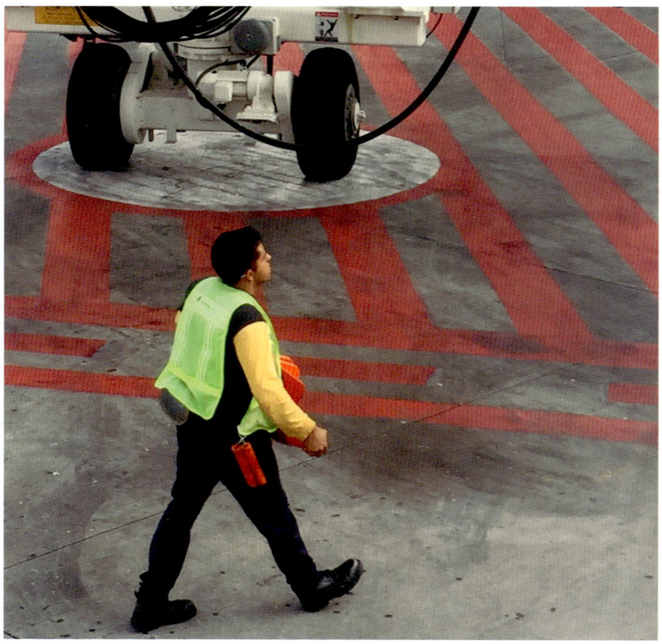

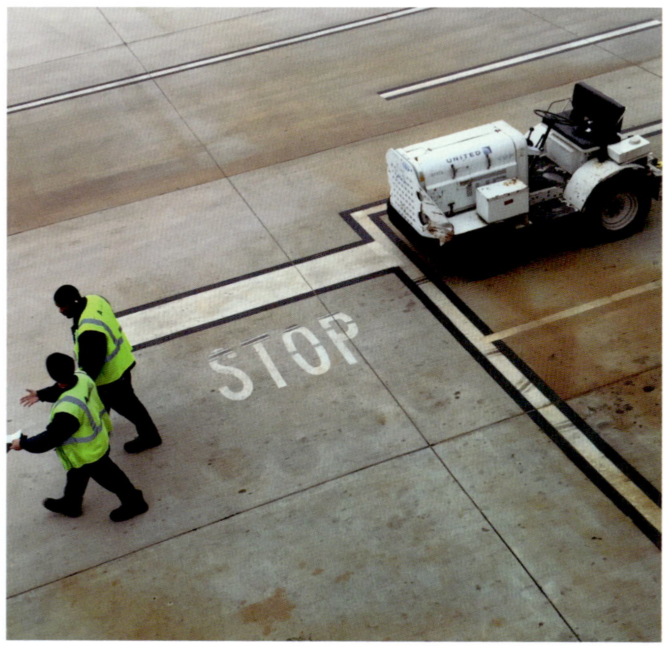
STOP

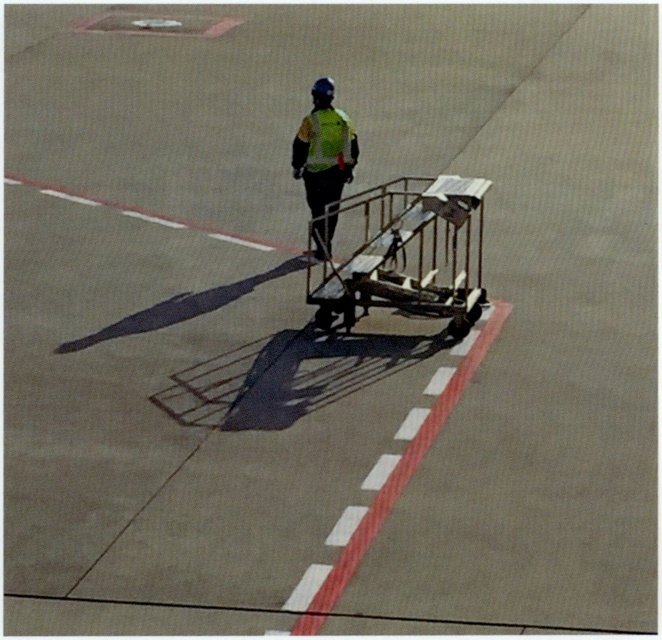
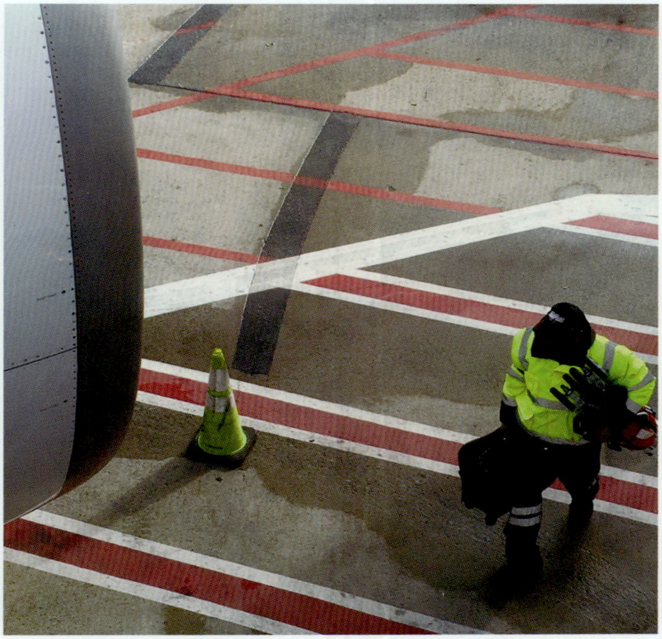
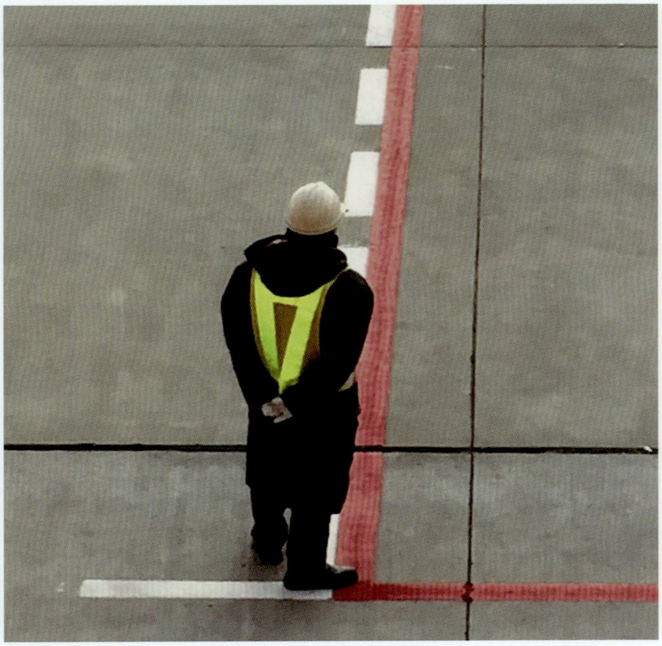
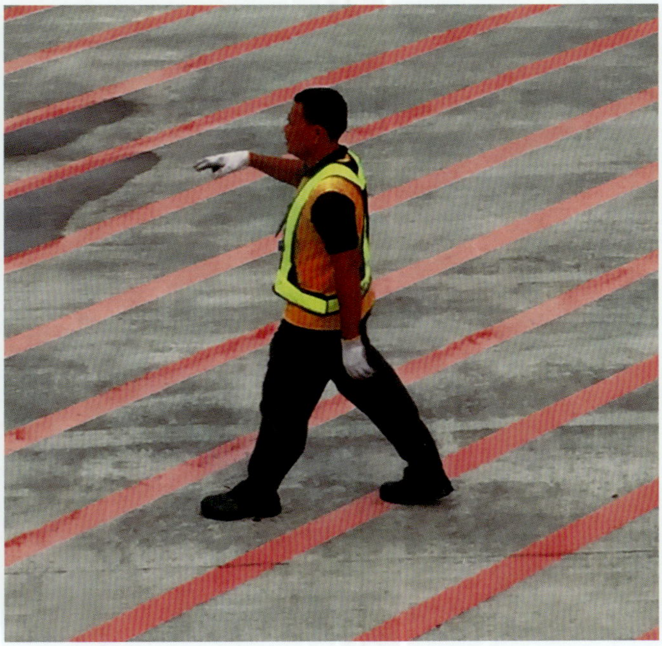

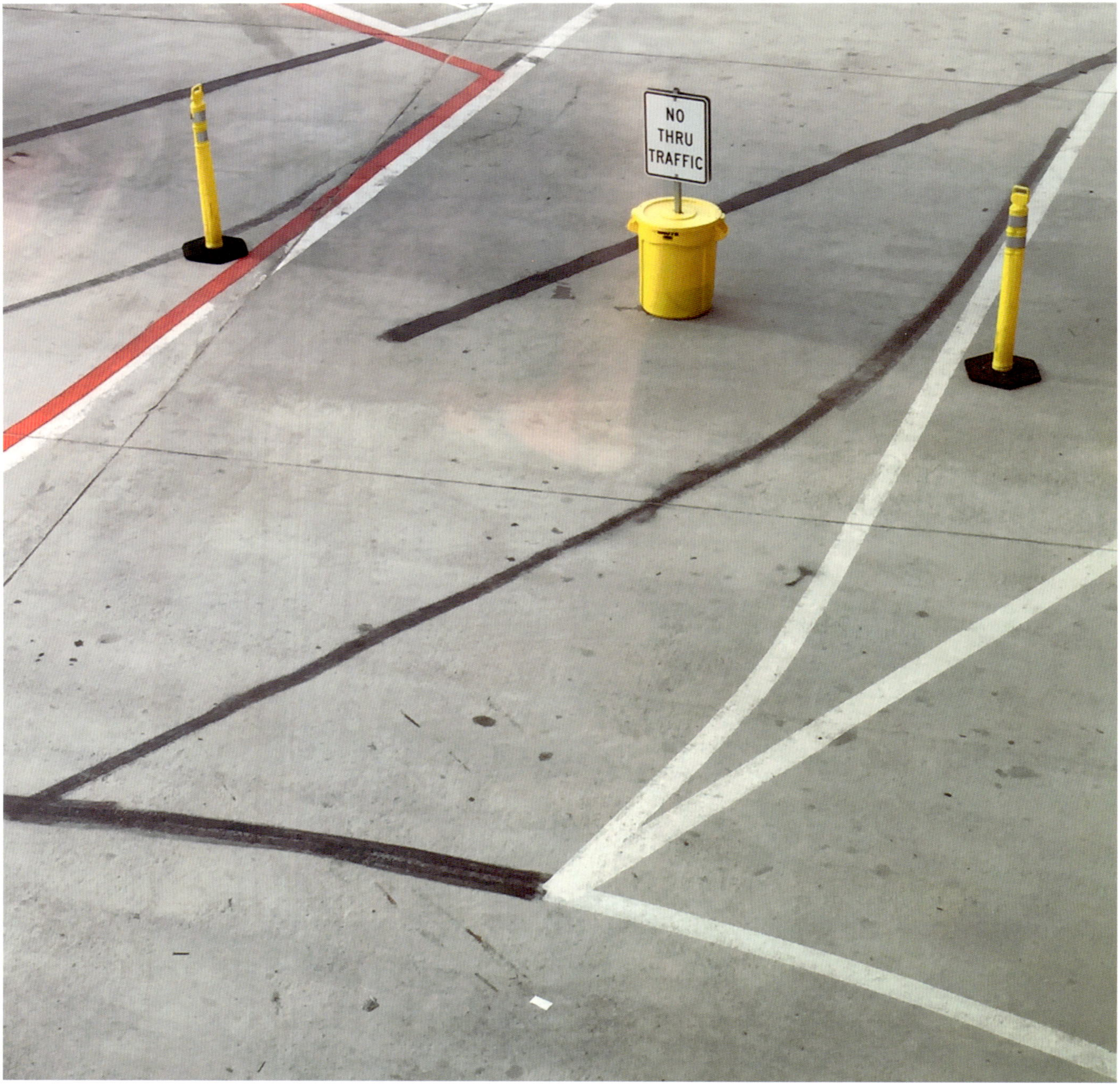
NO
THRU
TRAFFIC

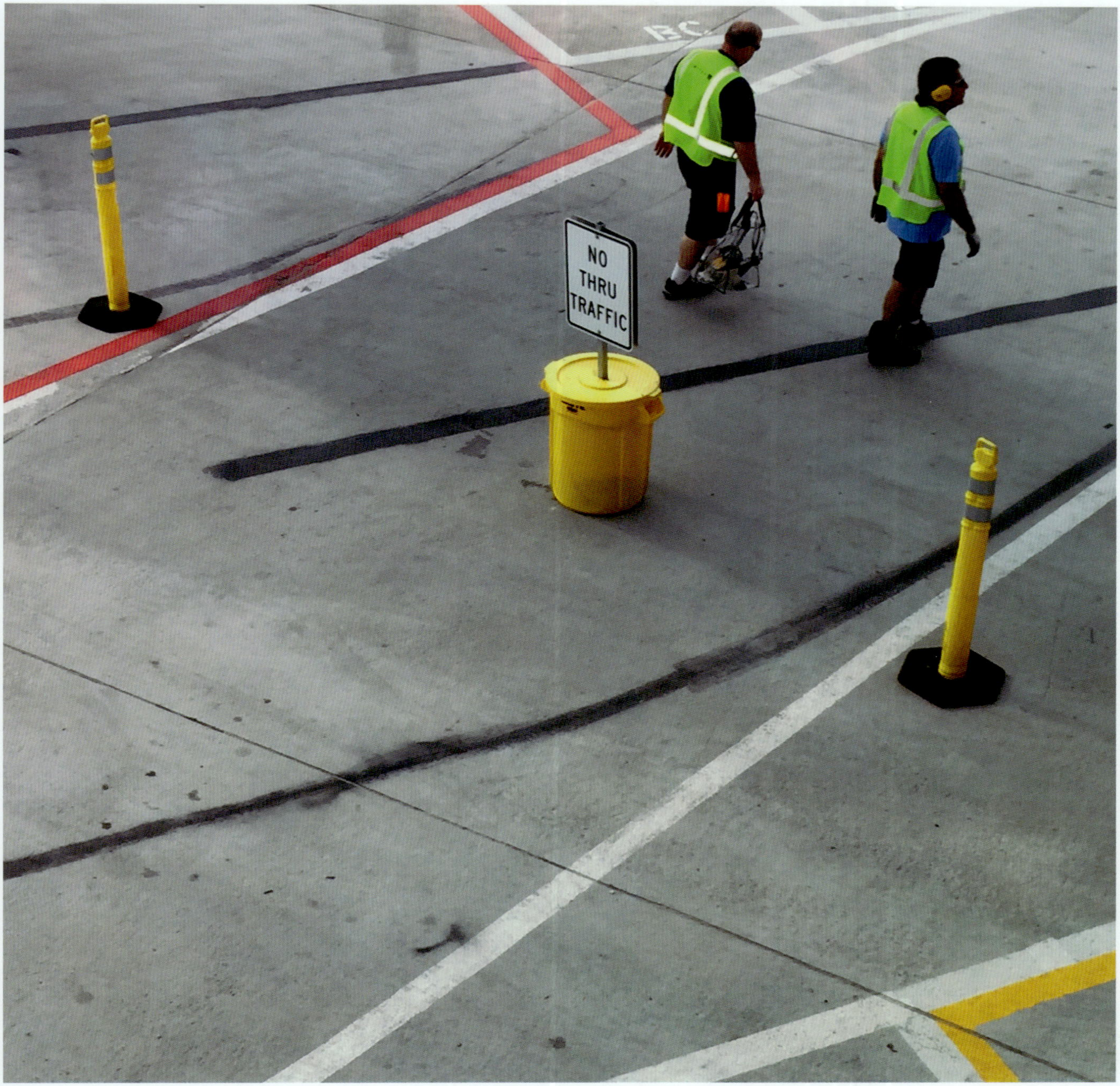
NO
THRU
TRAFFIC

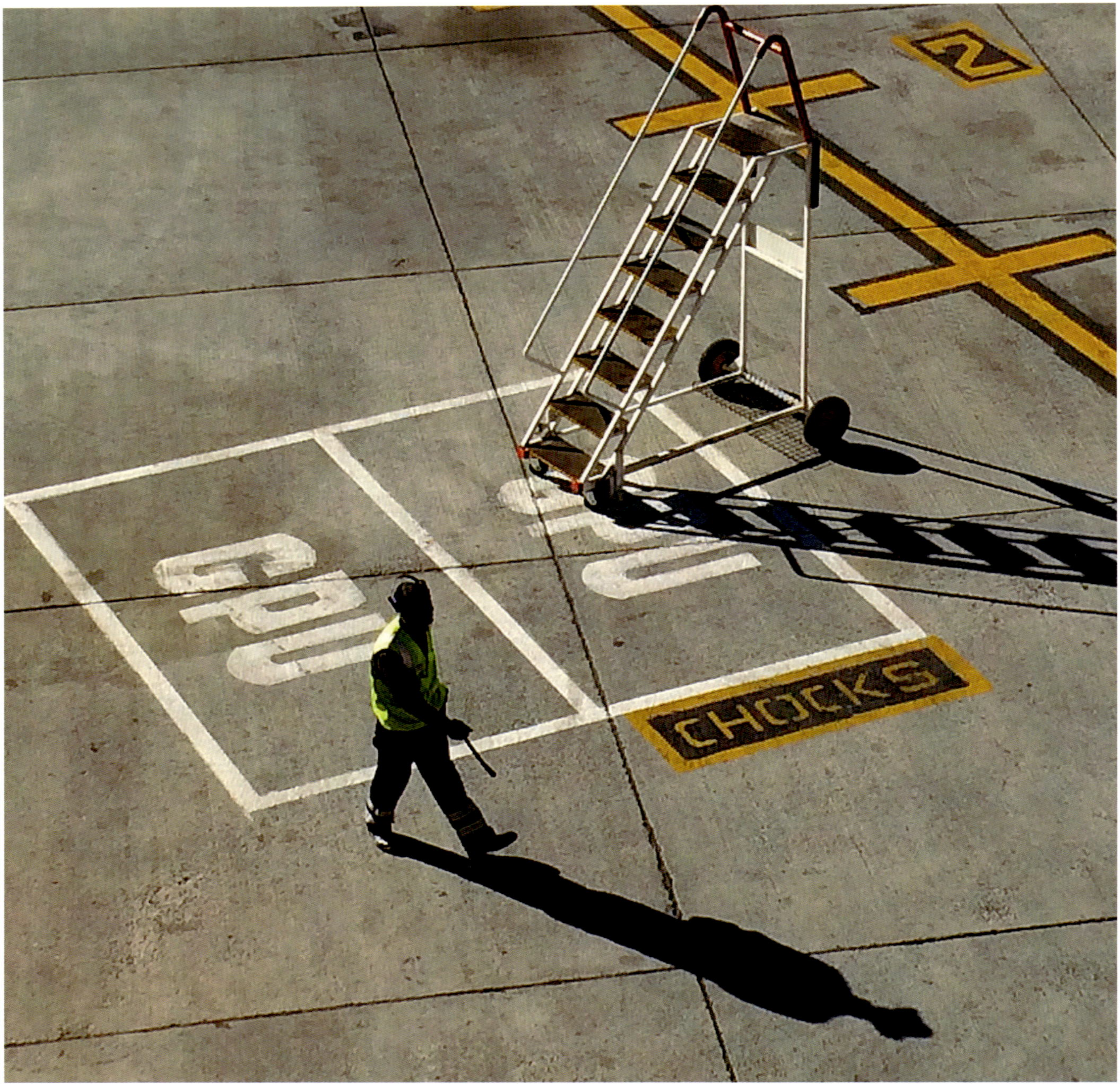
GPU
GPU
CHOCKS
2

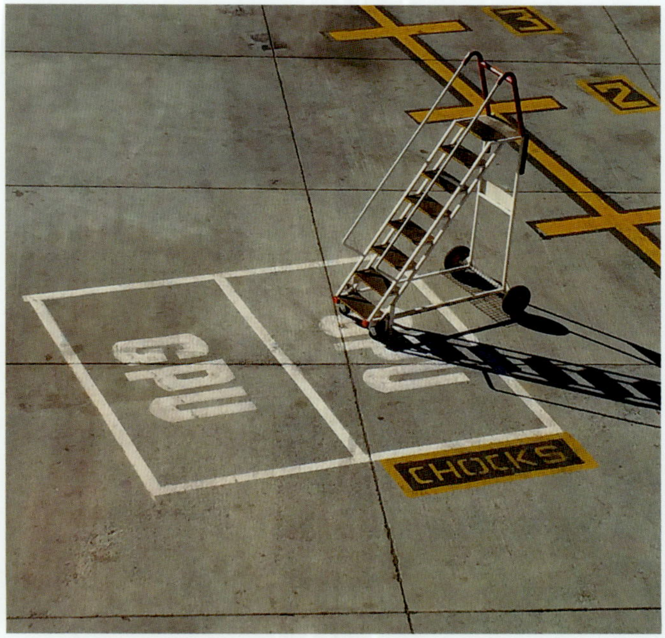
GPU
CHOCKS

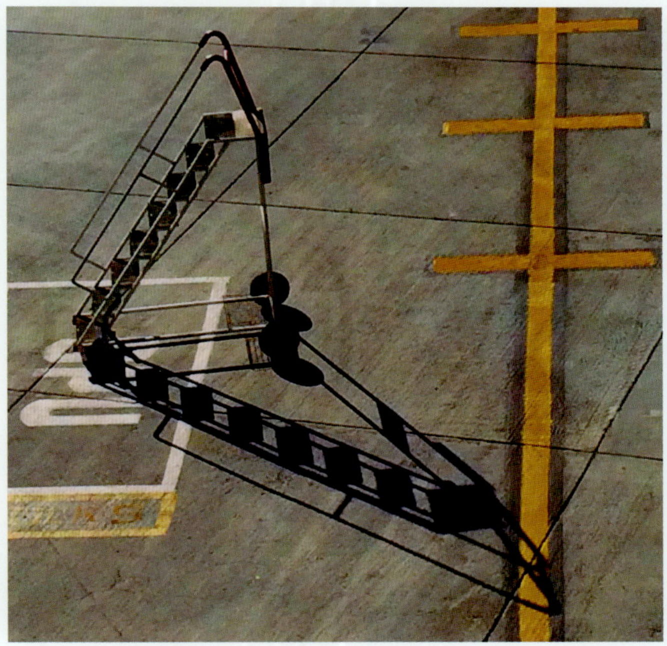

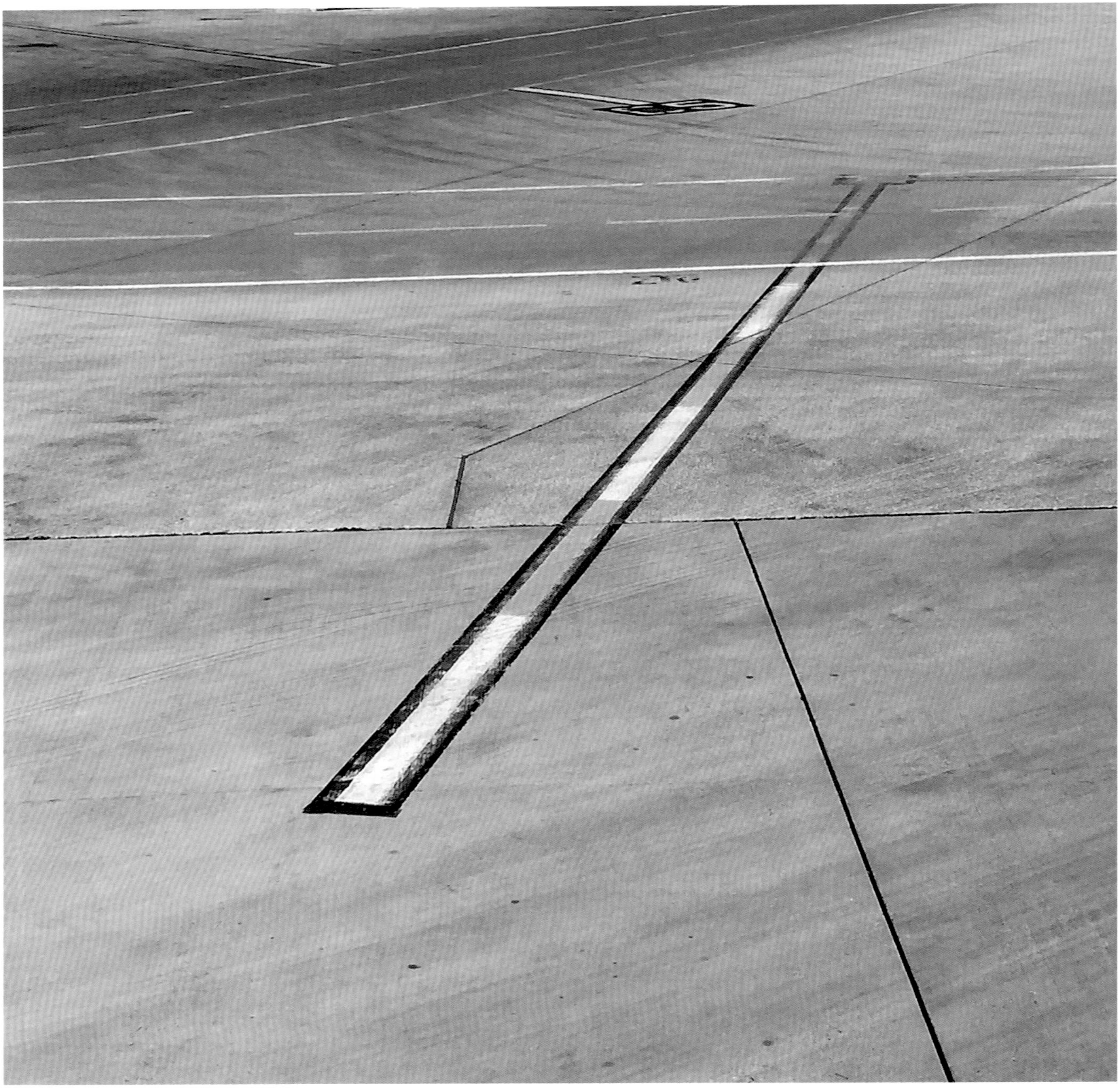

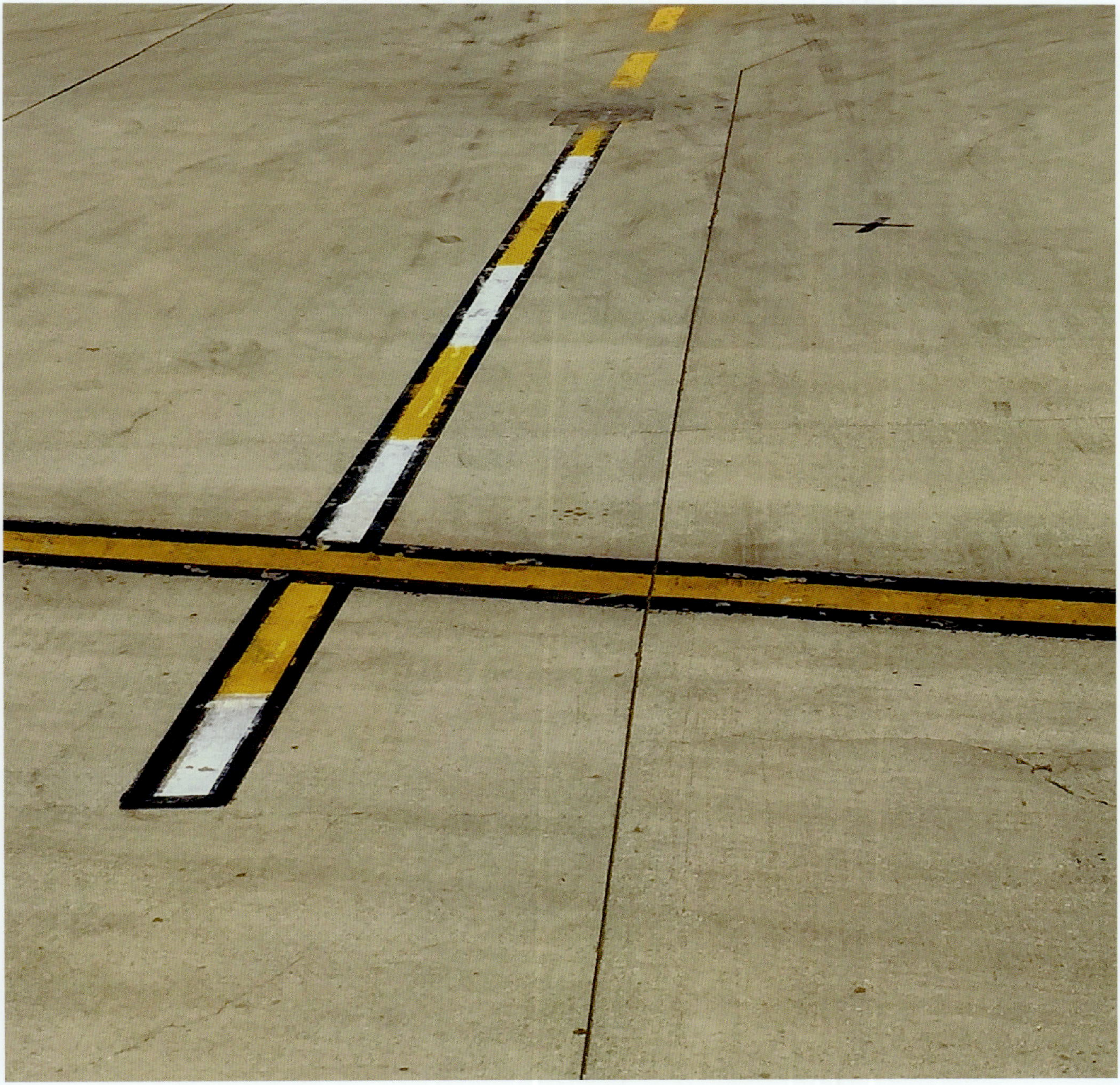

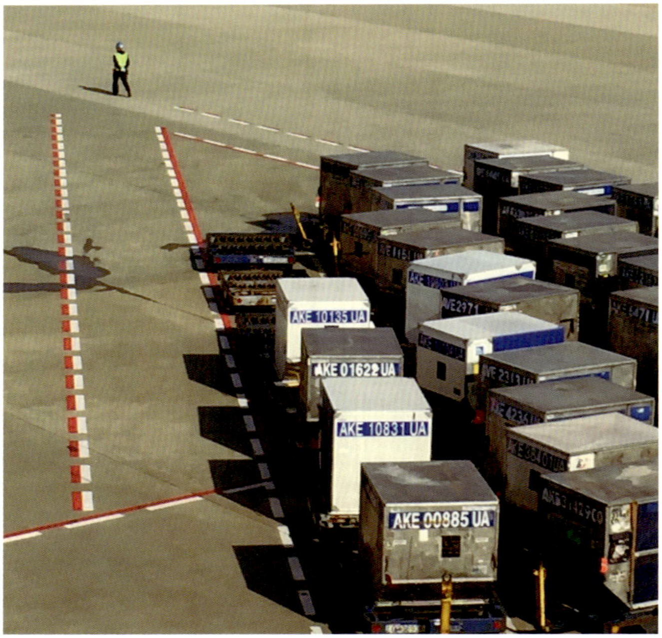
AKE 10135 UA
AKE 01622 UA
AKE 10831 UA
AKE 00885 UA

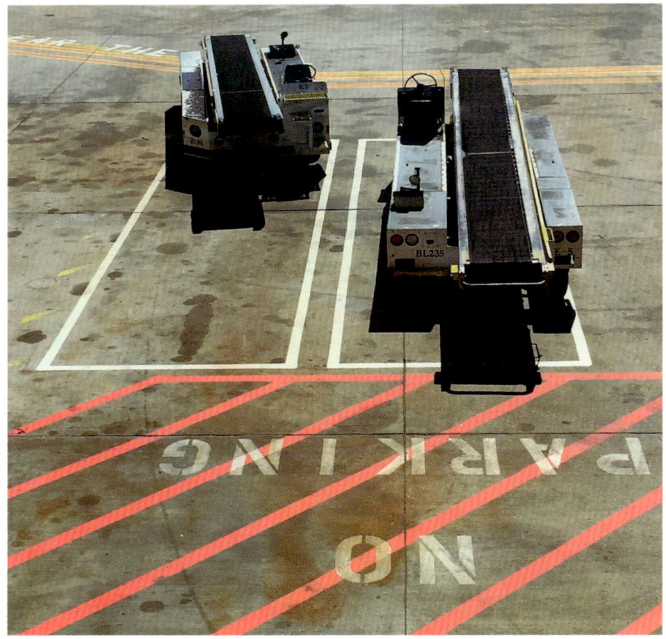
BL235
NO
PARKING

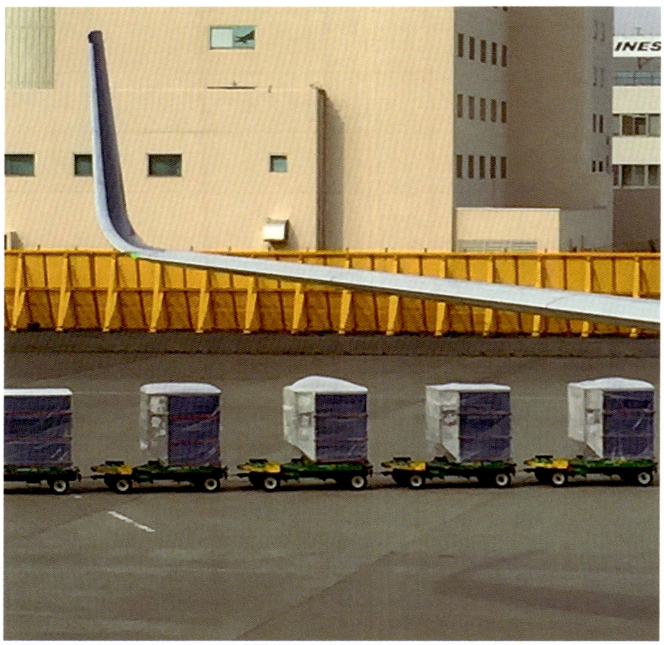

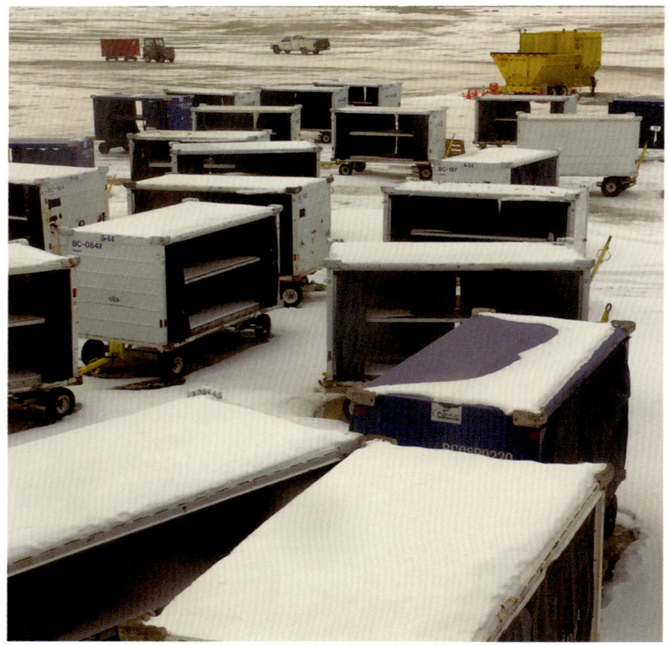

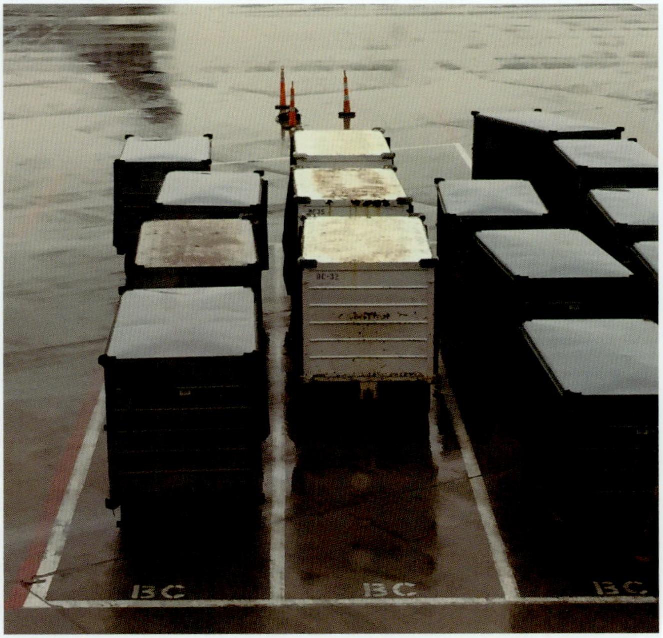
BC
BC
BC
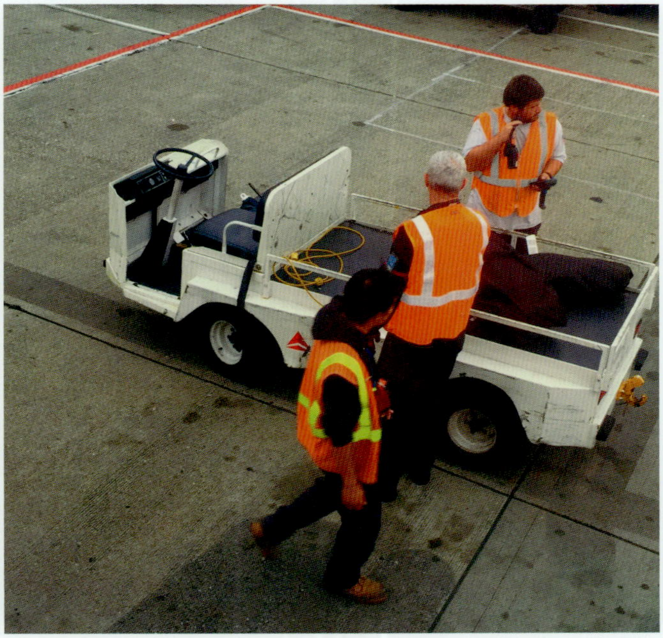
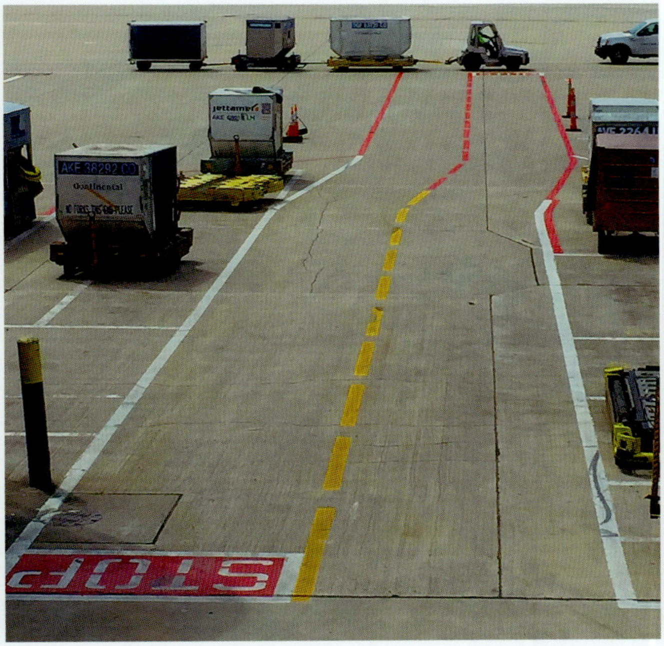
STOP
Continental
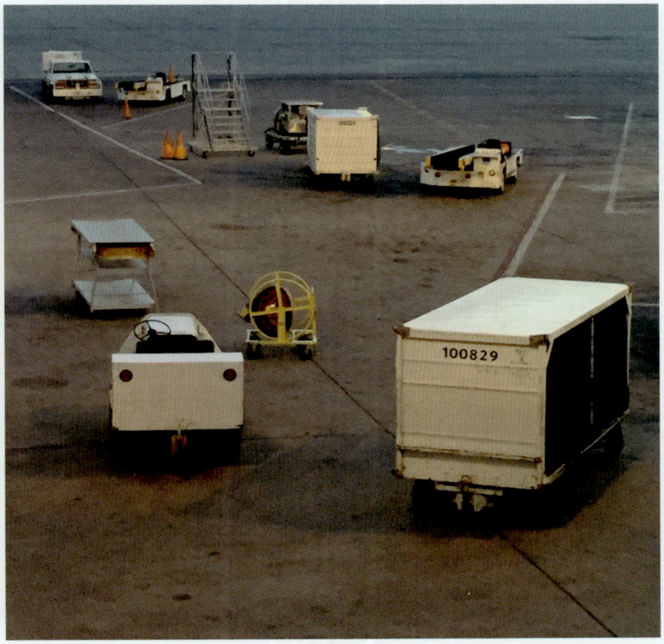
100829

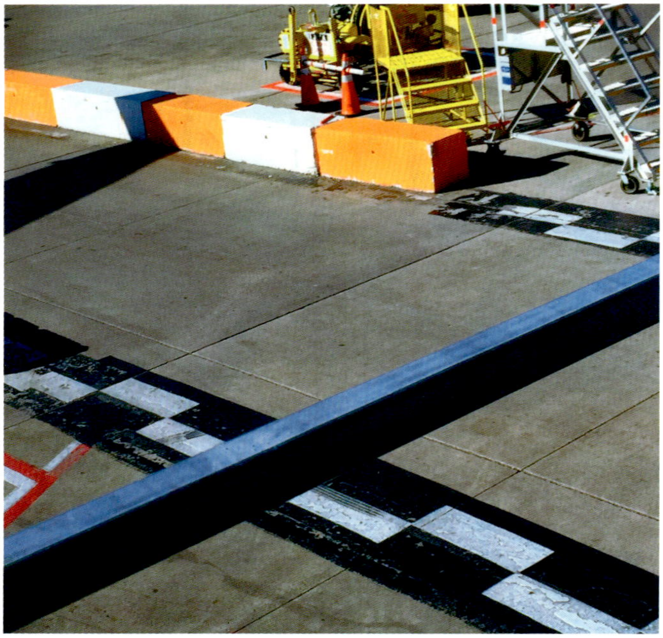

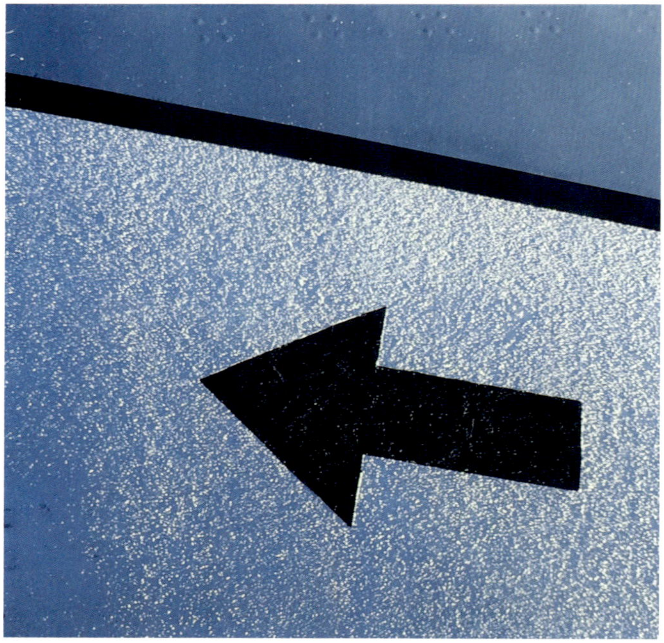

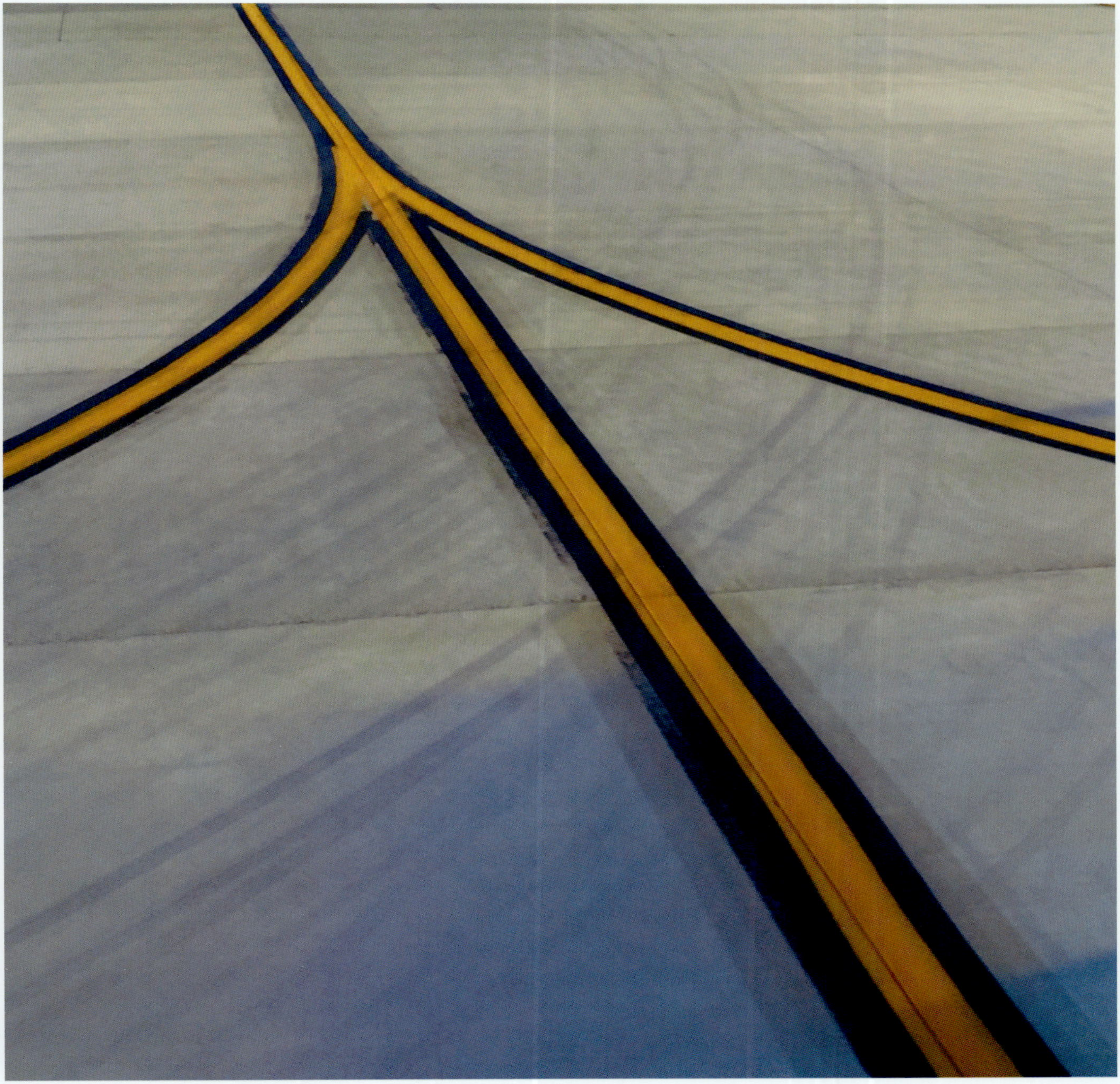

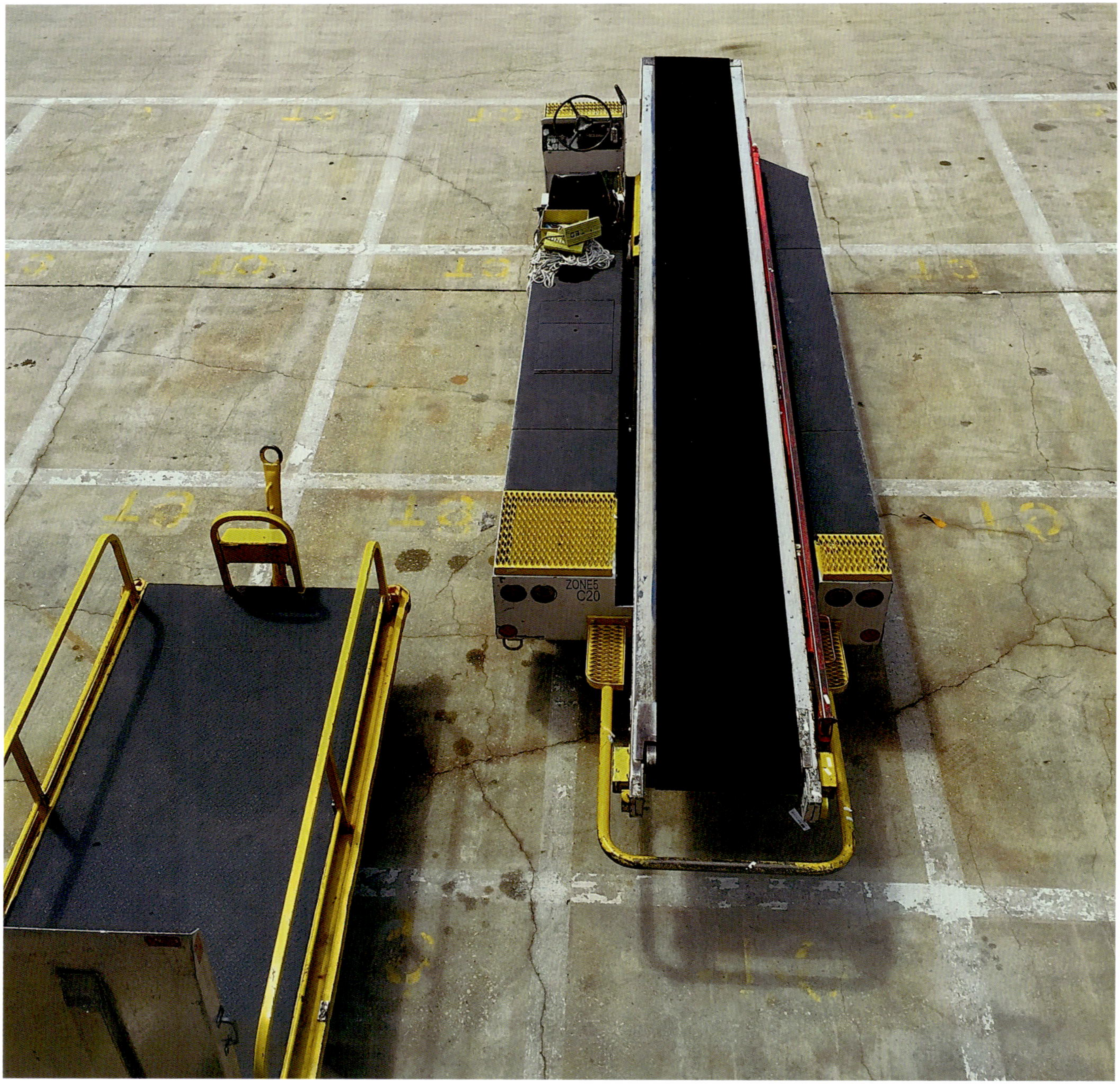
ZONE5
C20

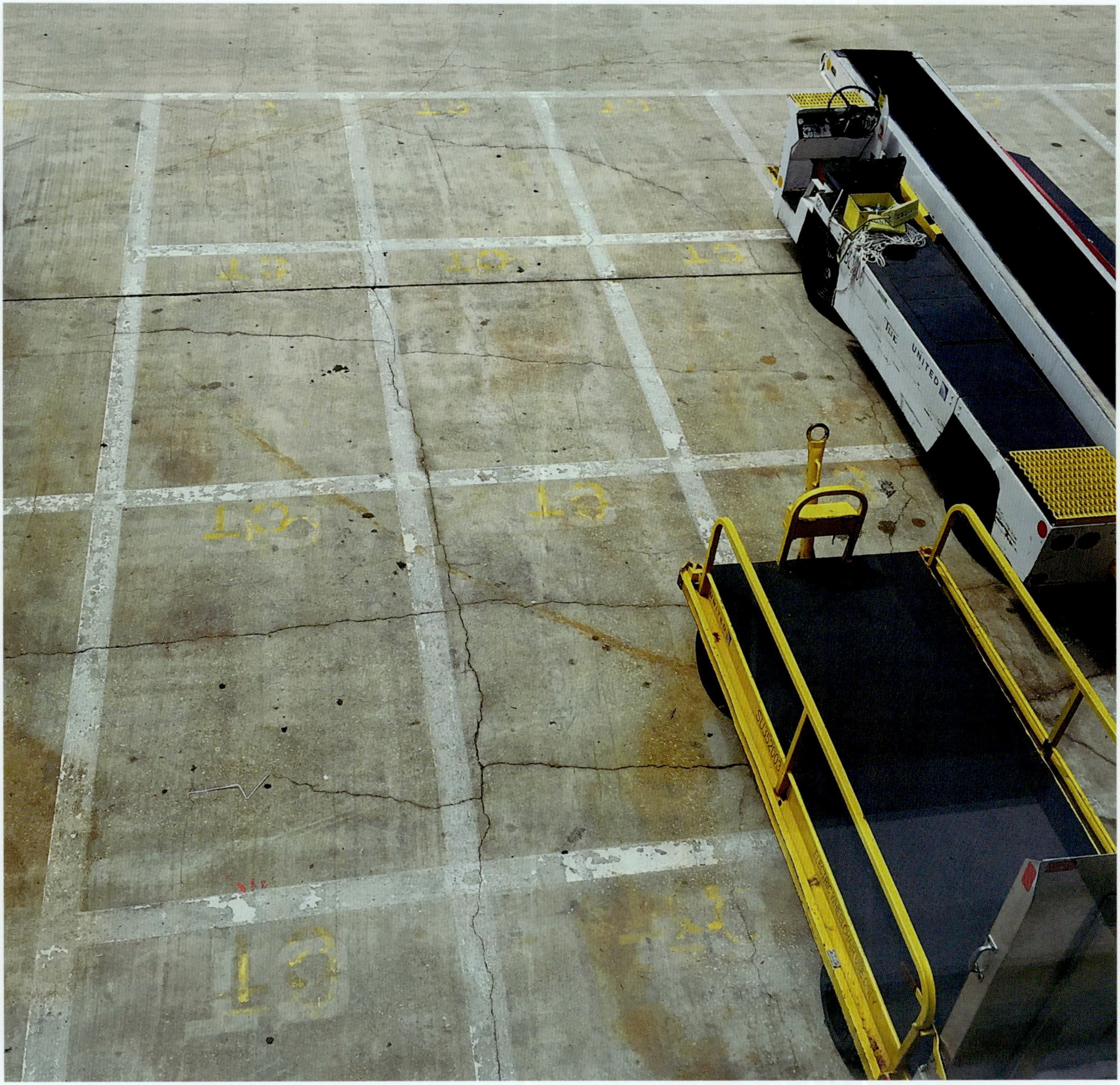

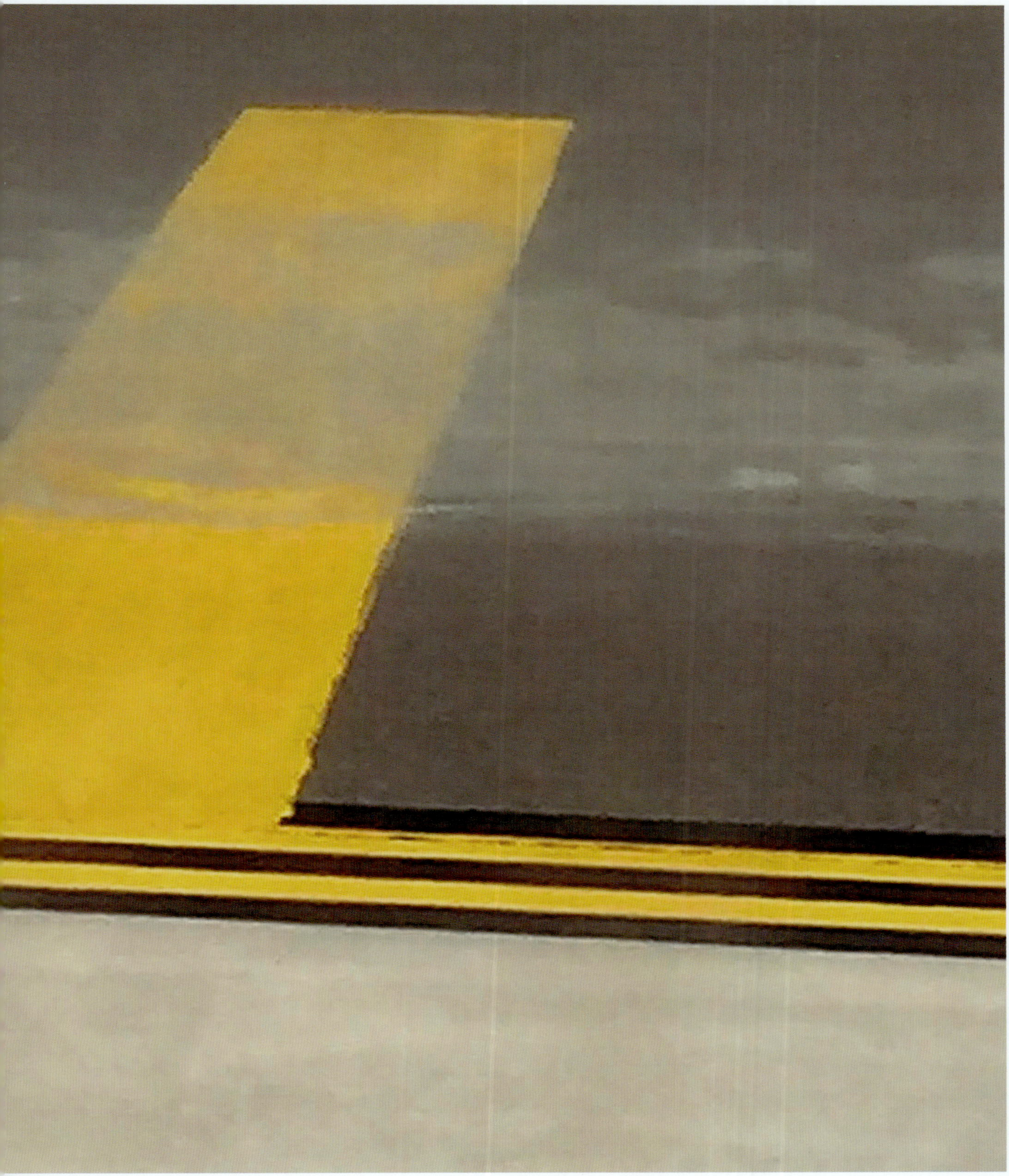

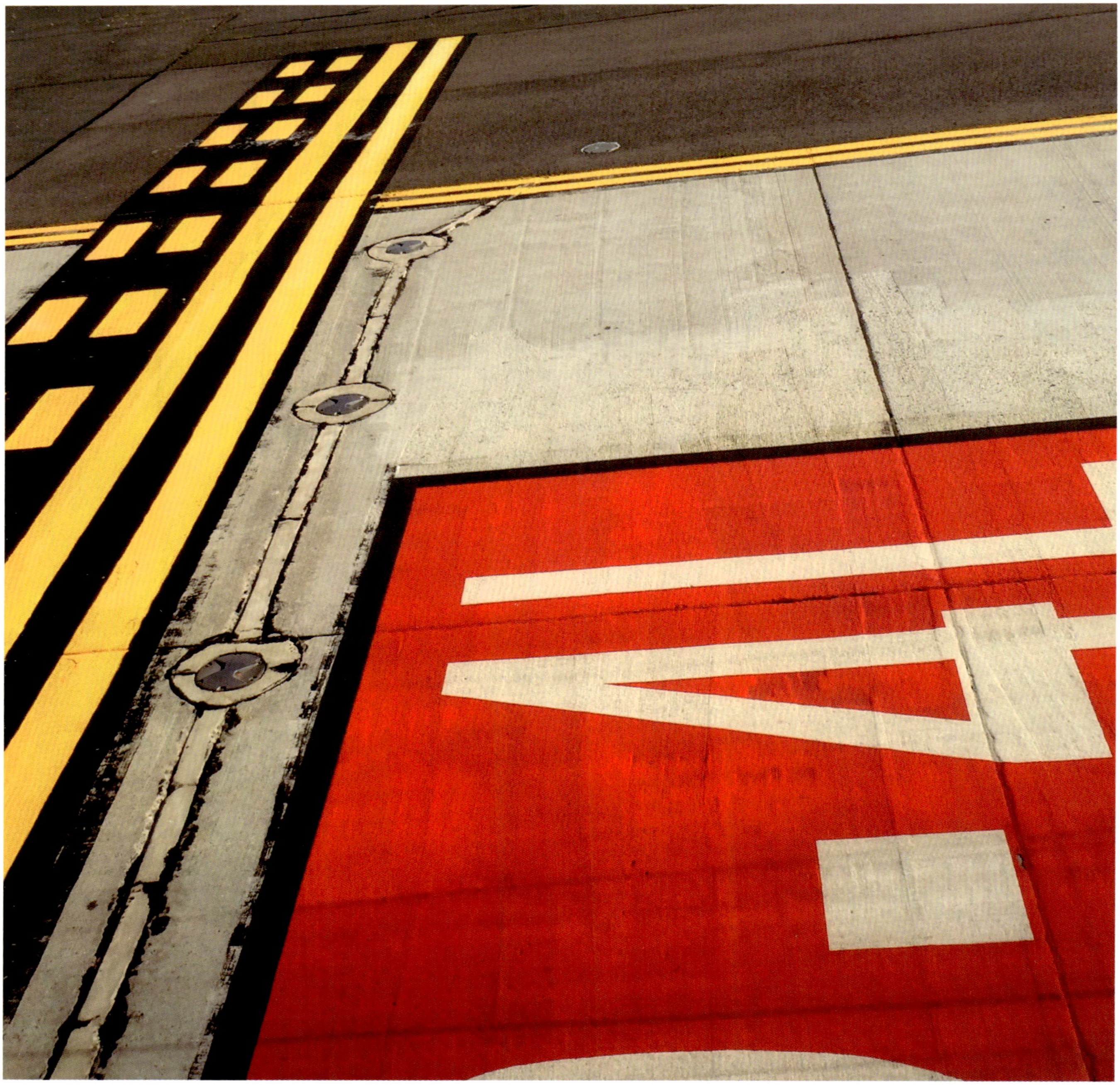

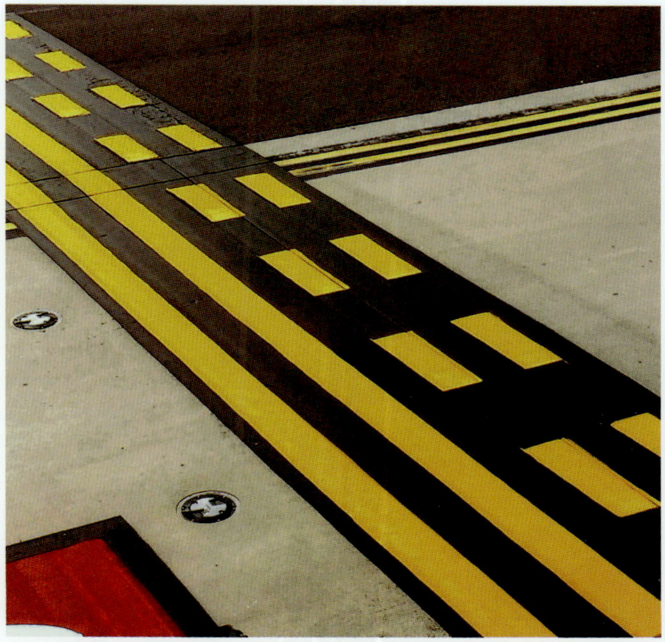

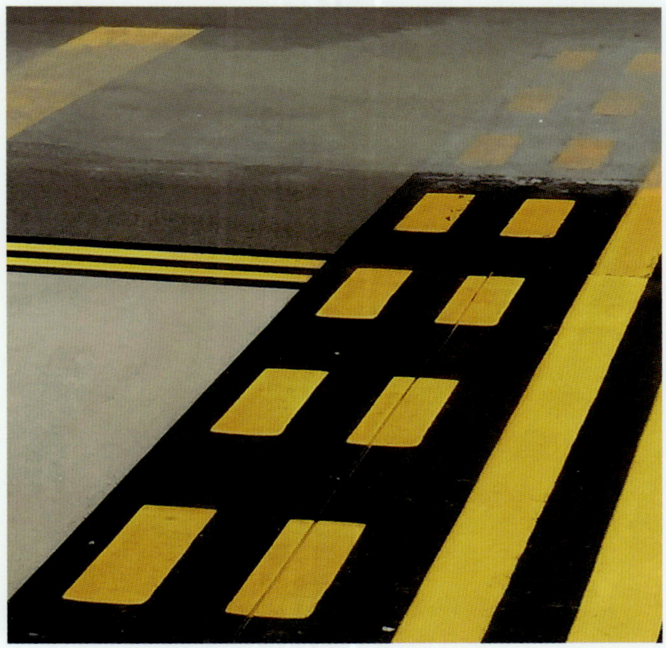

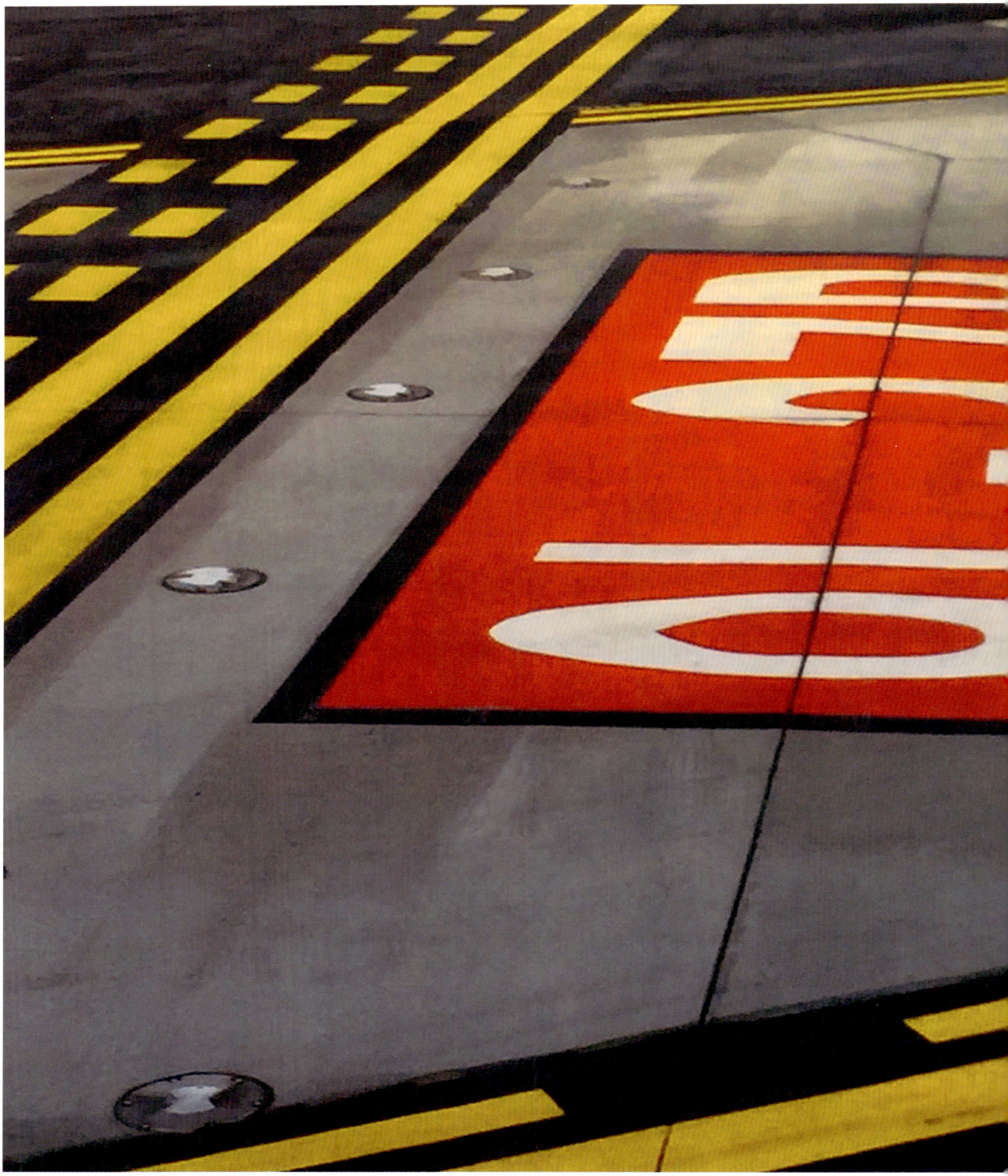

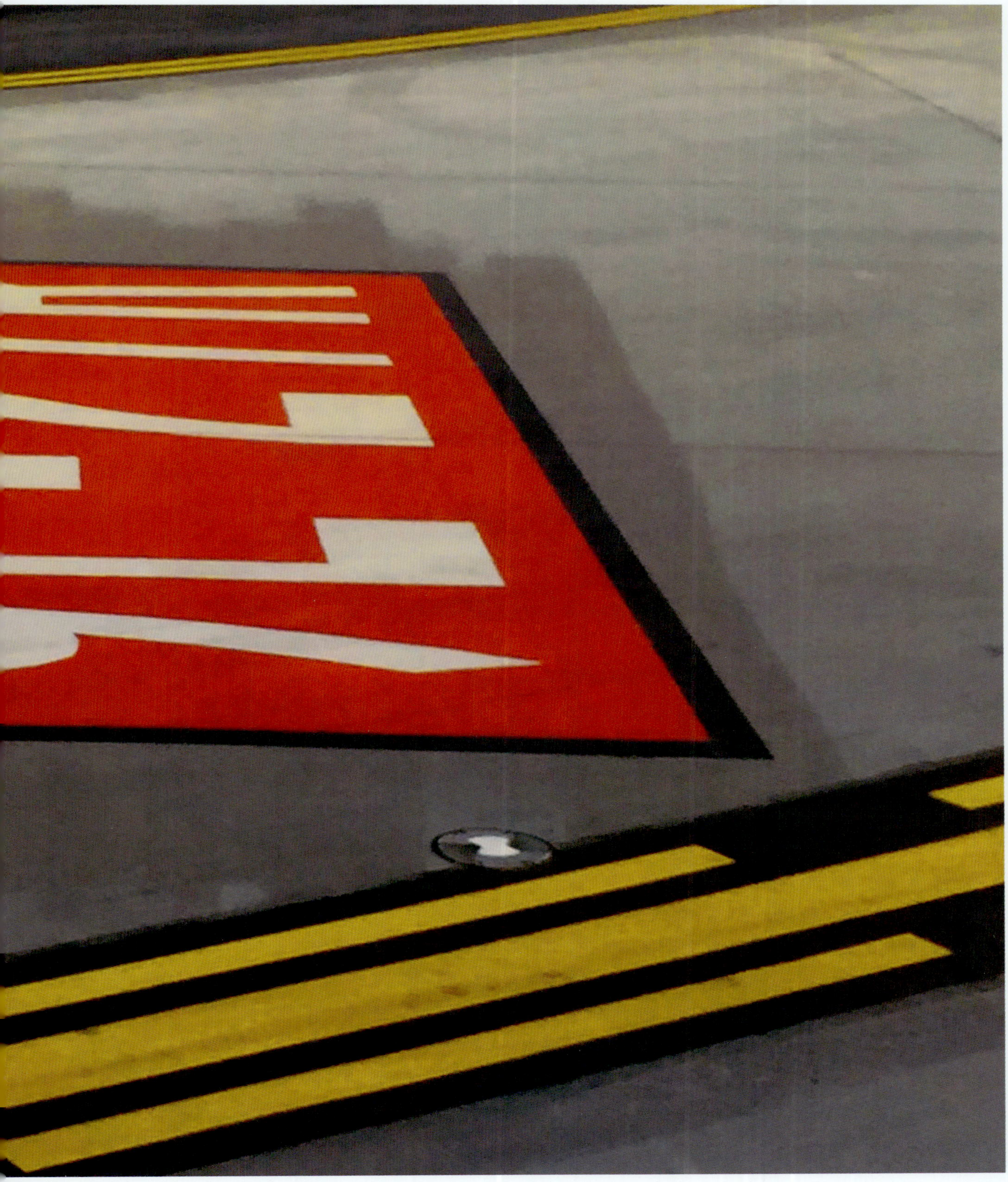

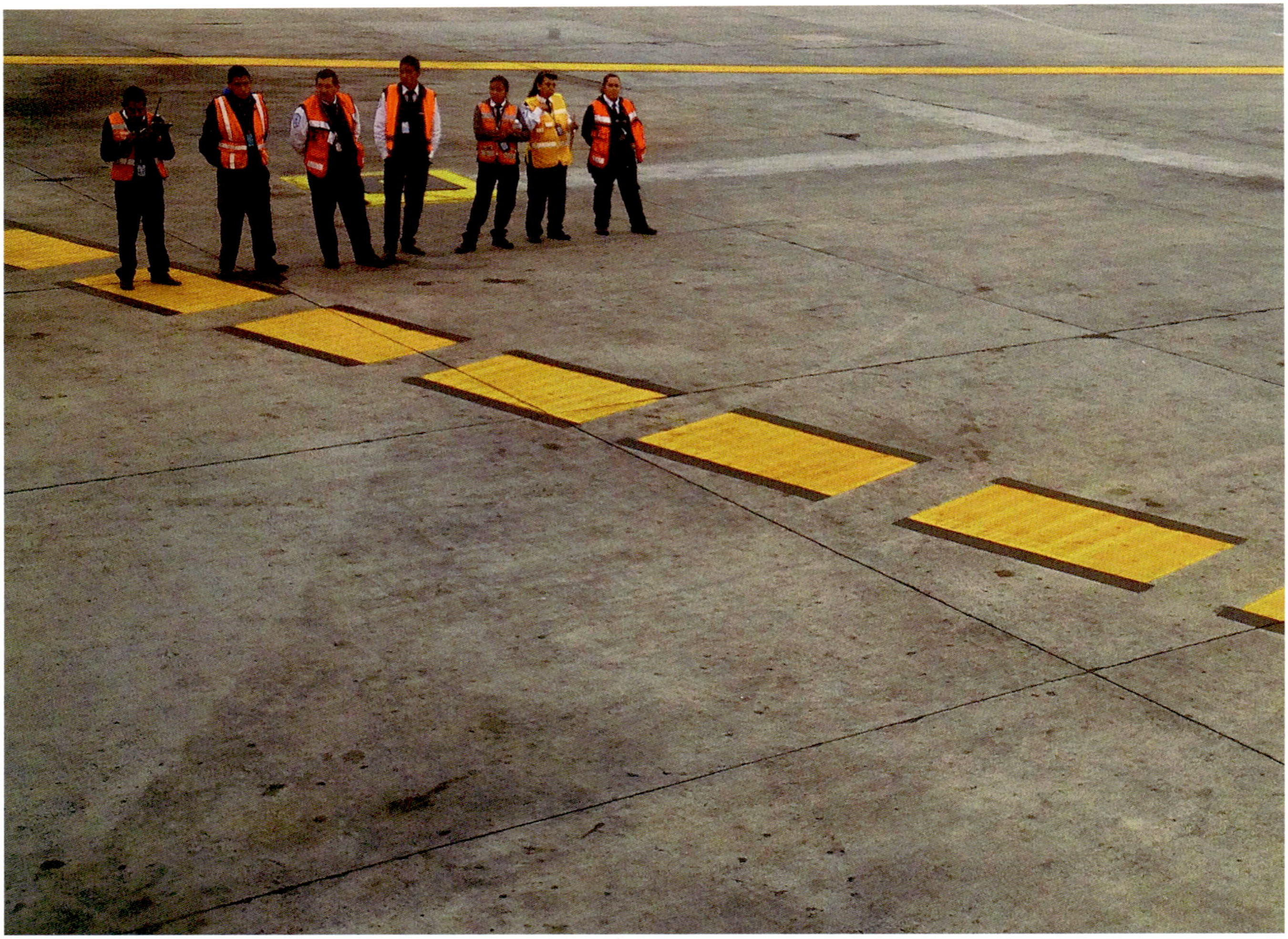

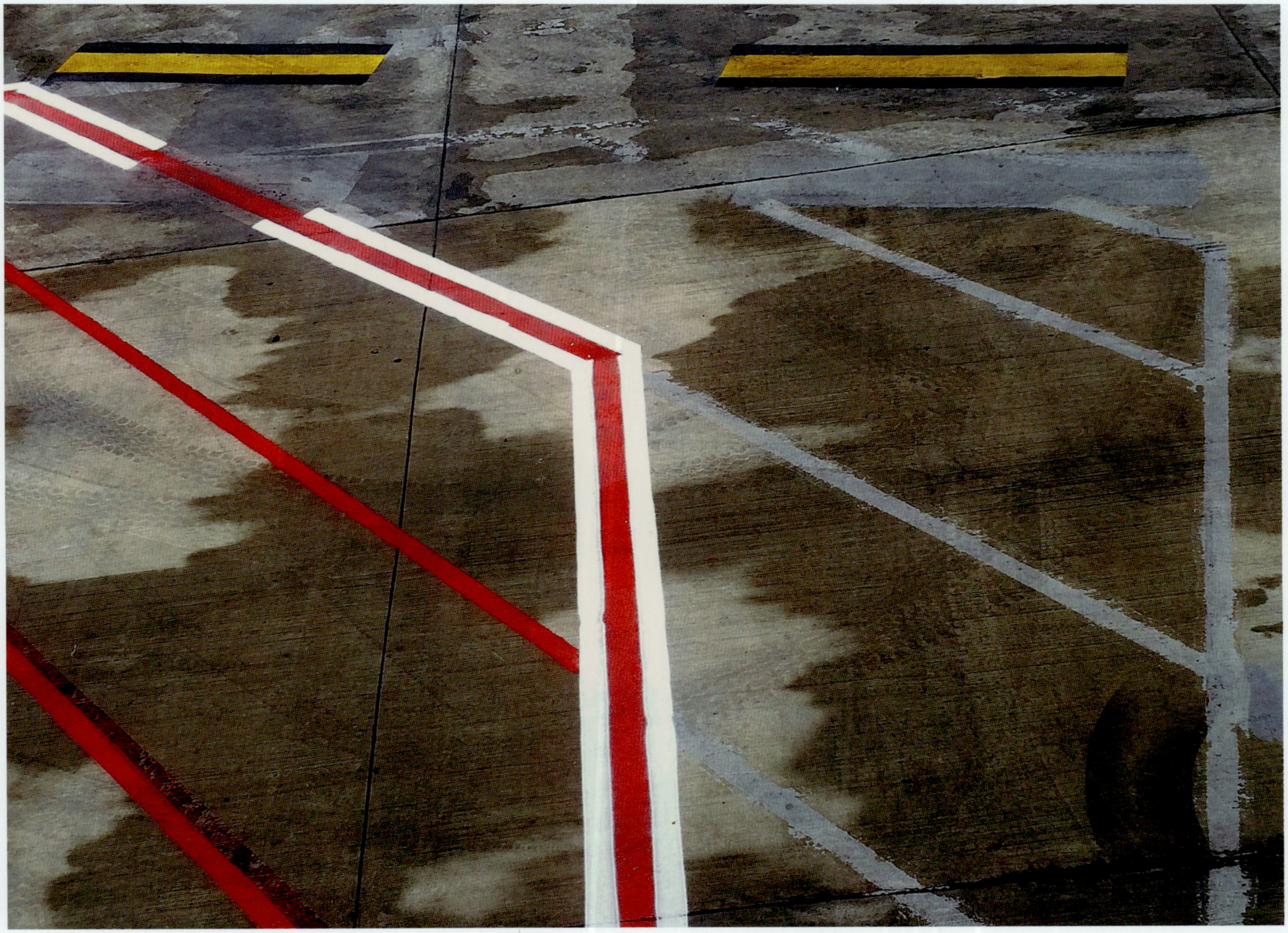

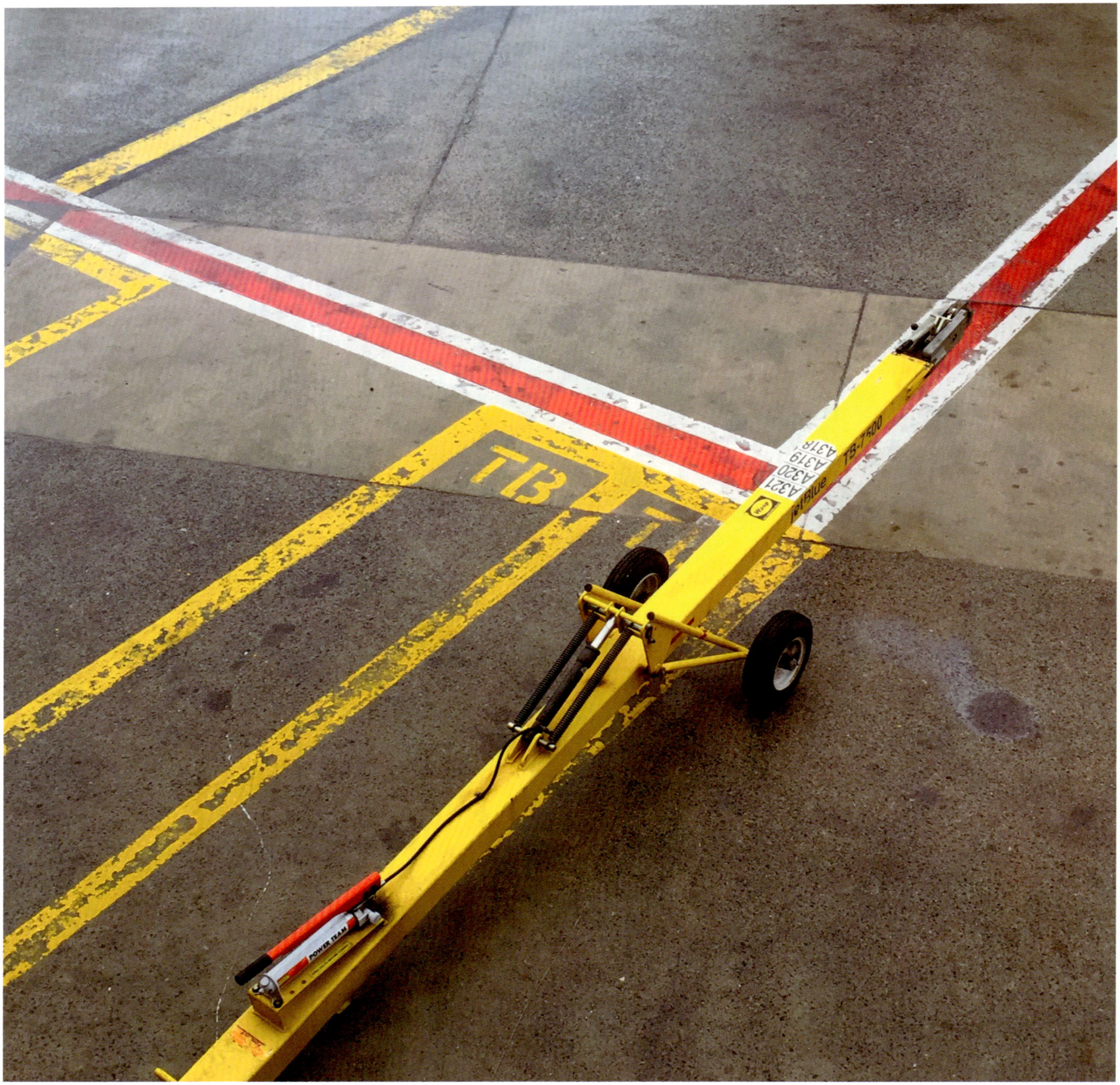
TB
A318
A319
A320
A321
POWER TEAM

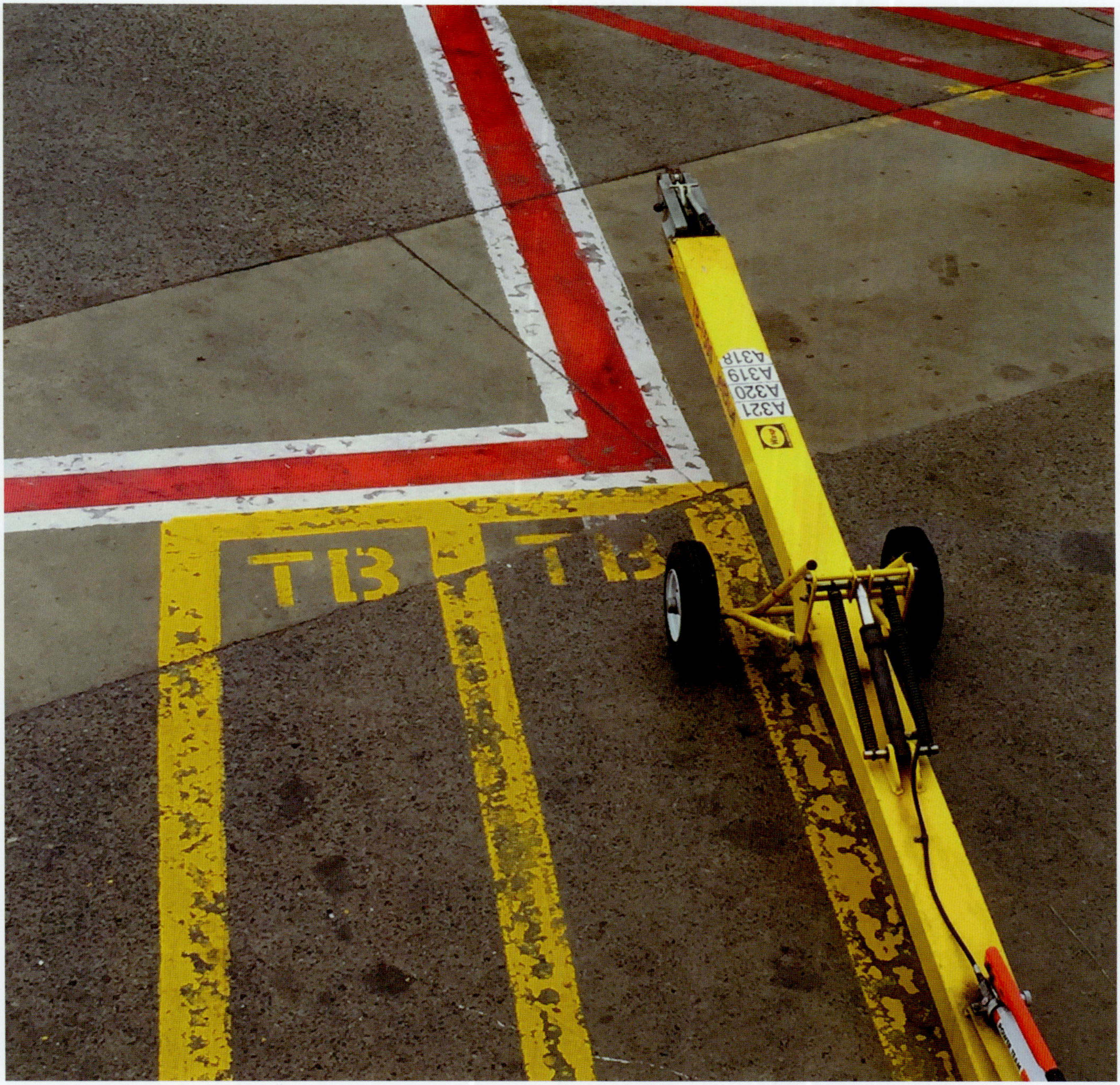
TB
A321
A320
A319
A318

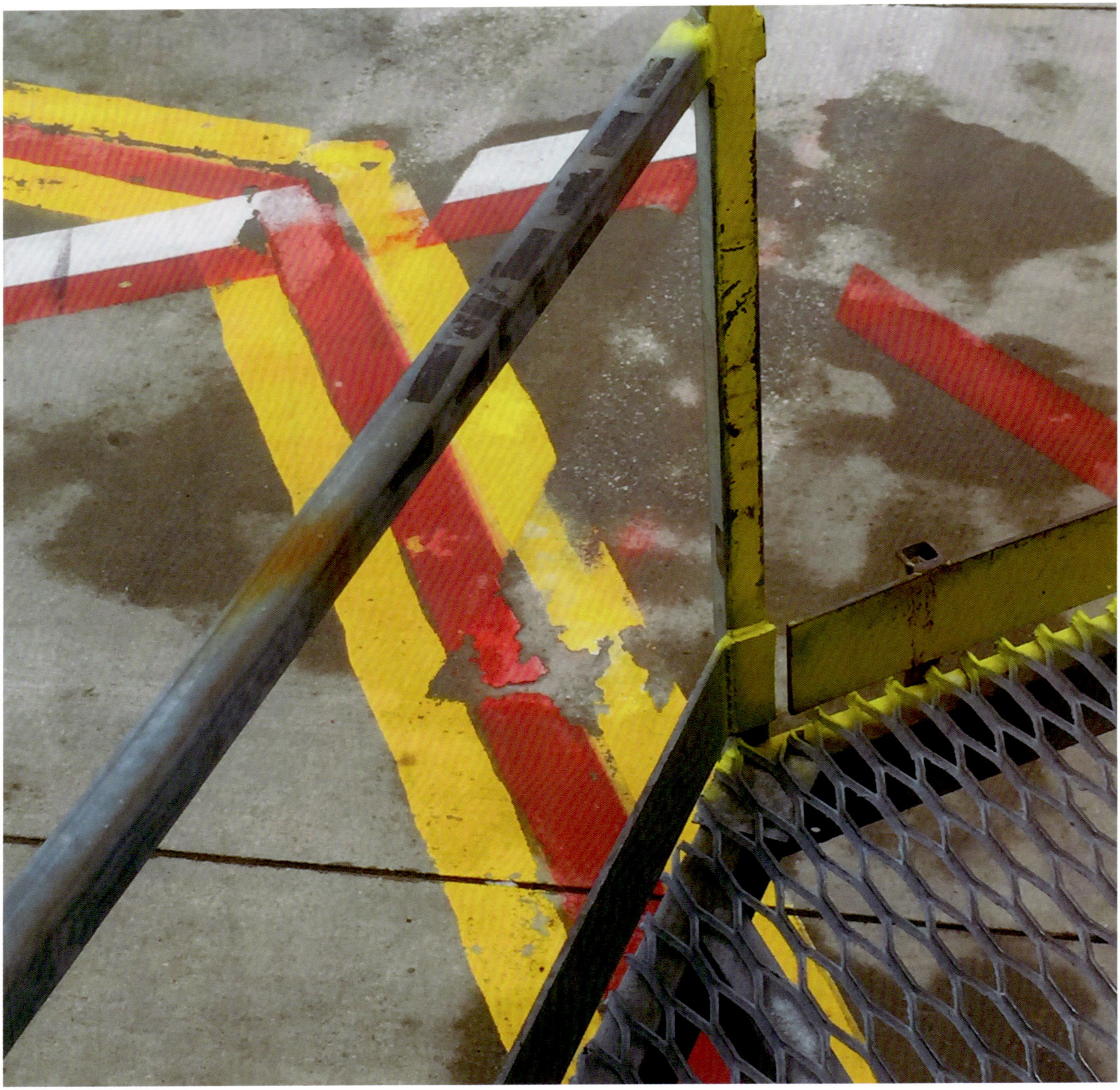

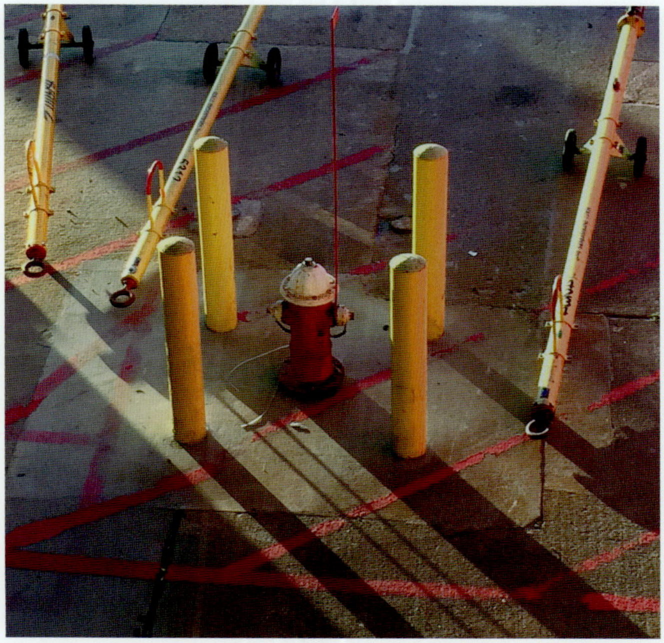

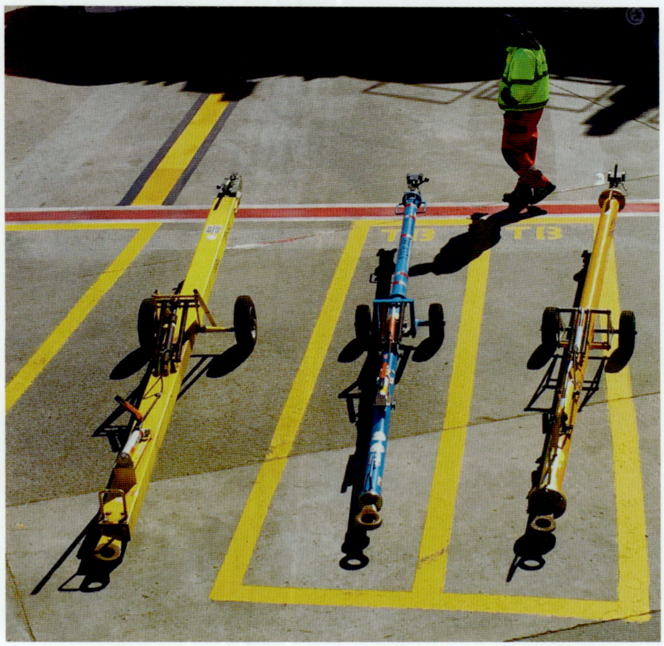
TB
TB

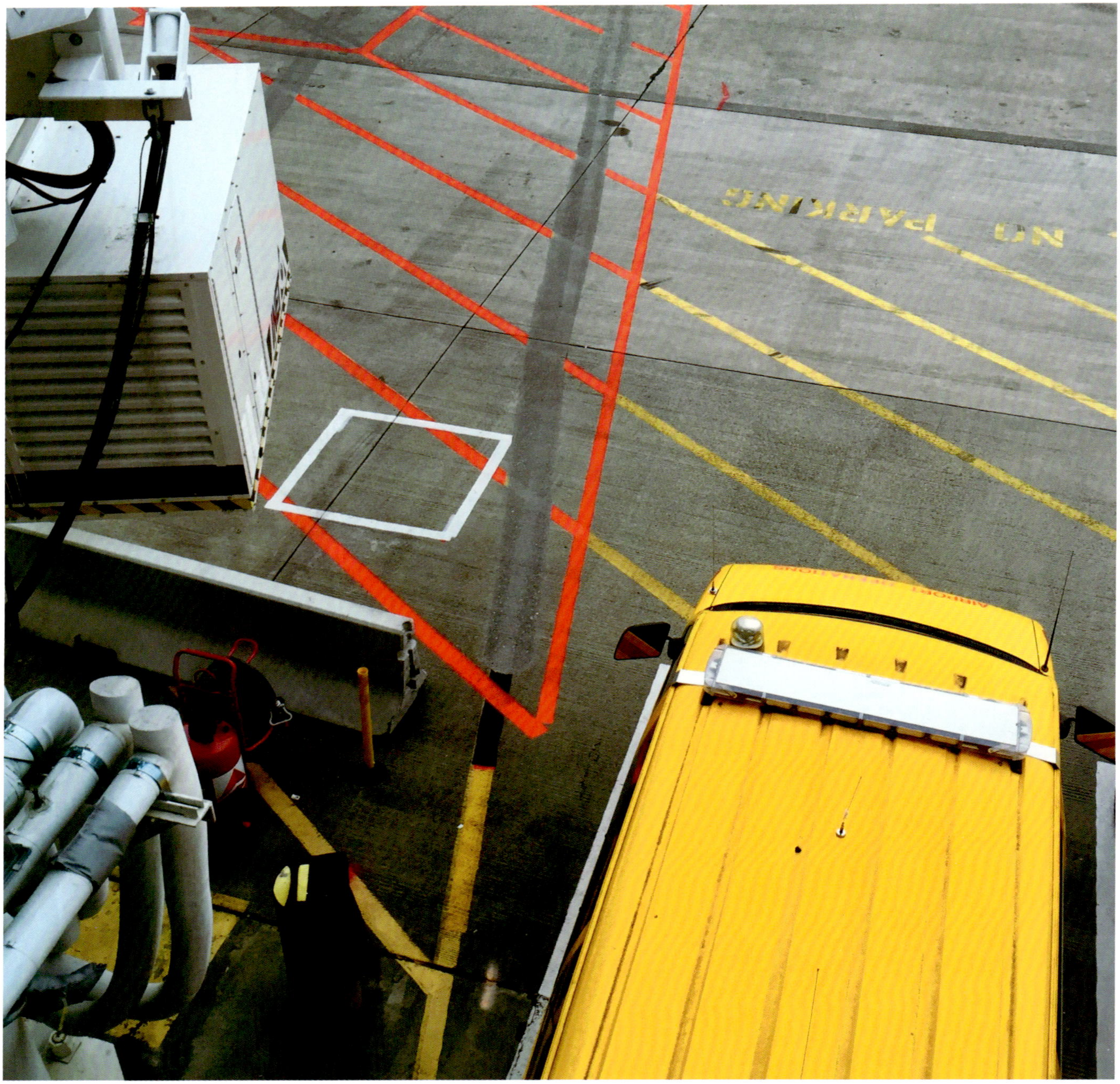
NO PARKING

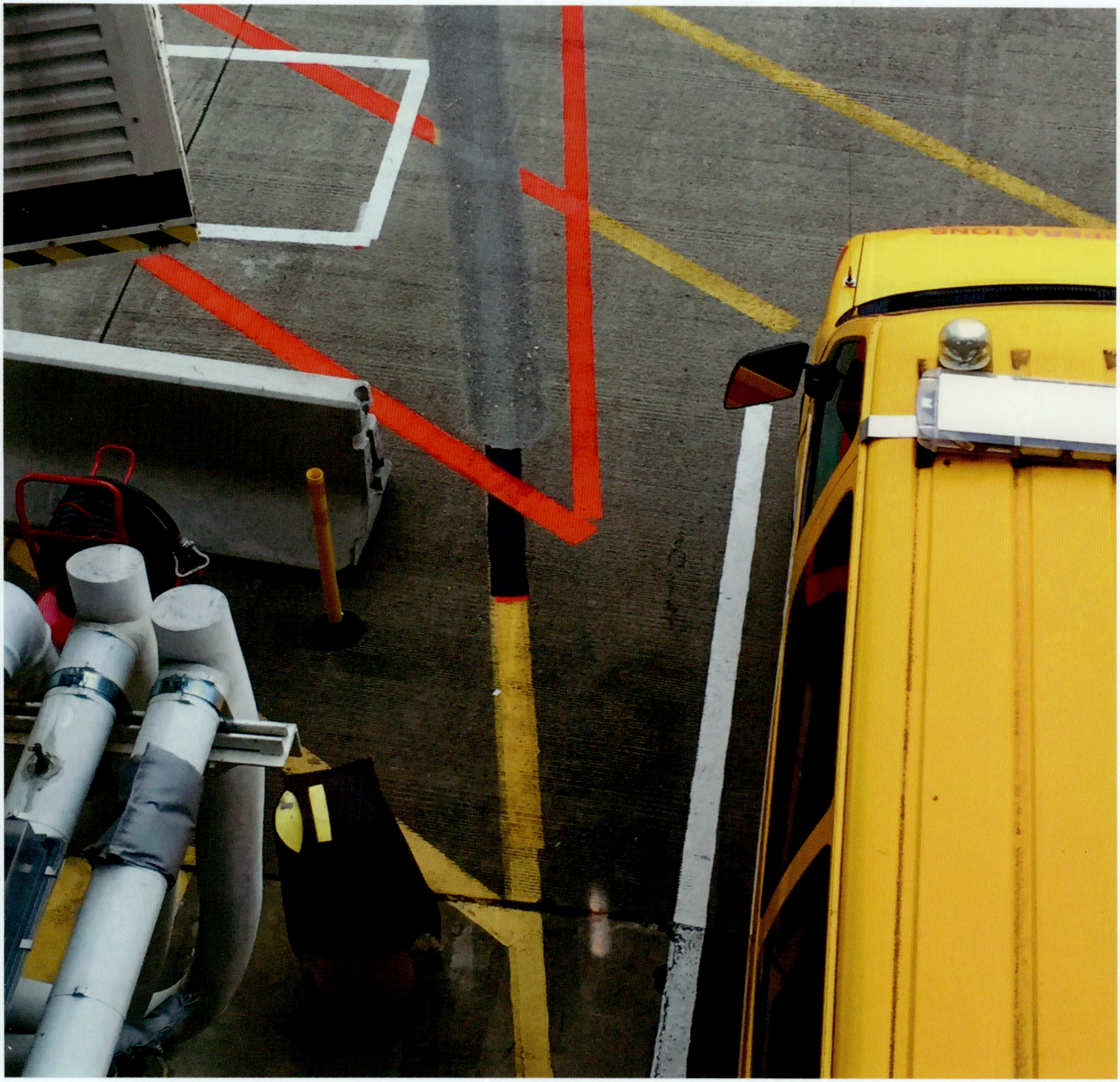

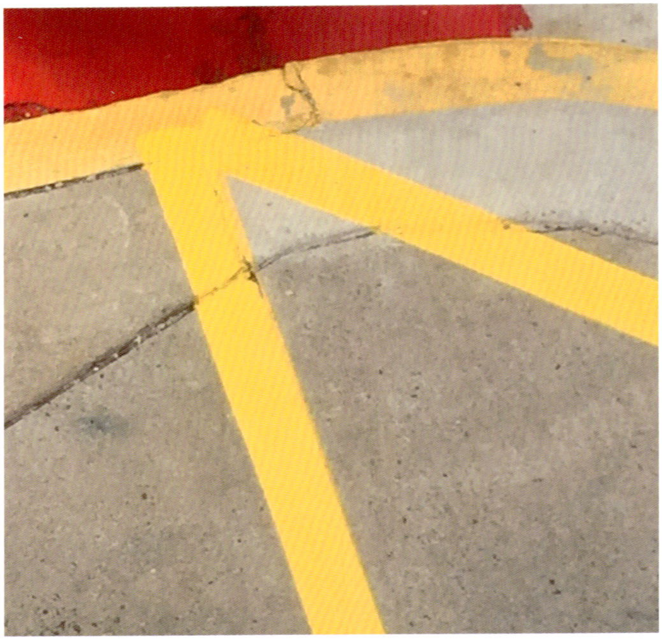

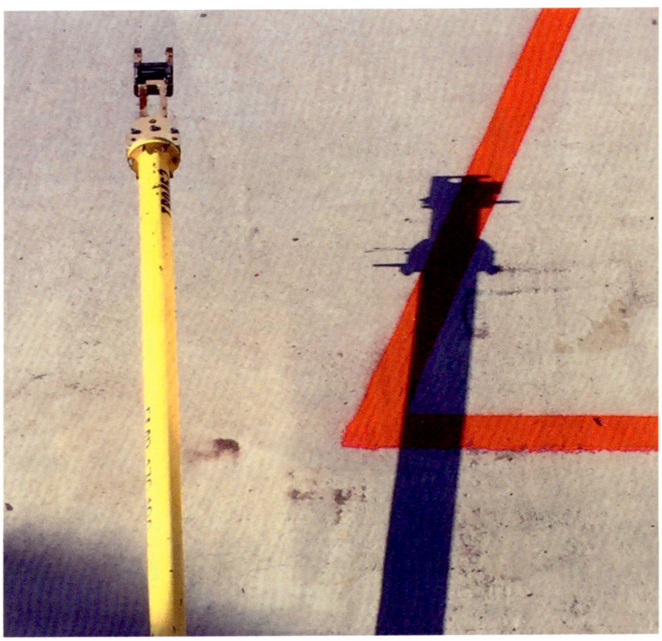

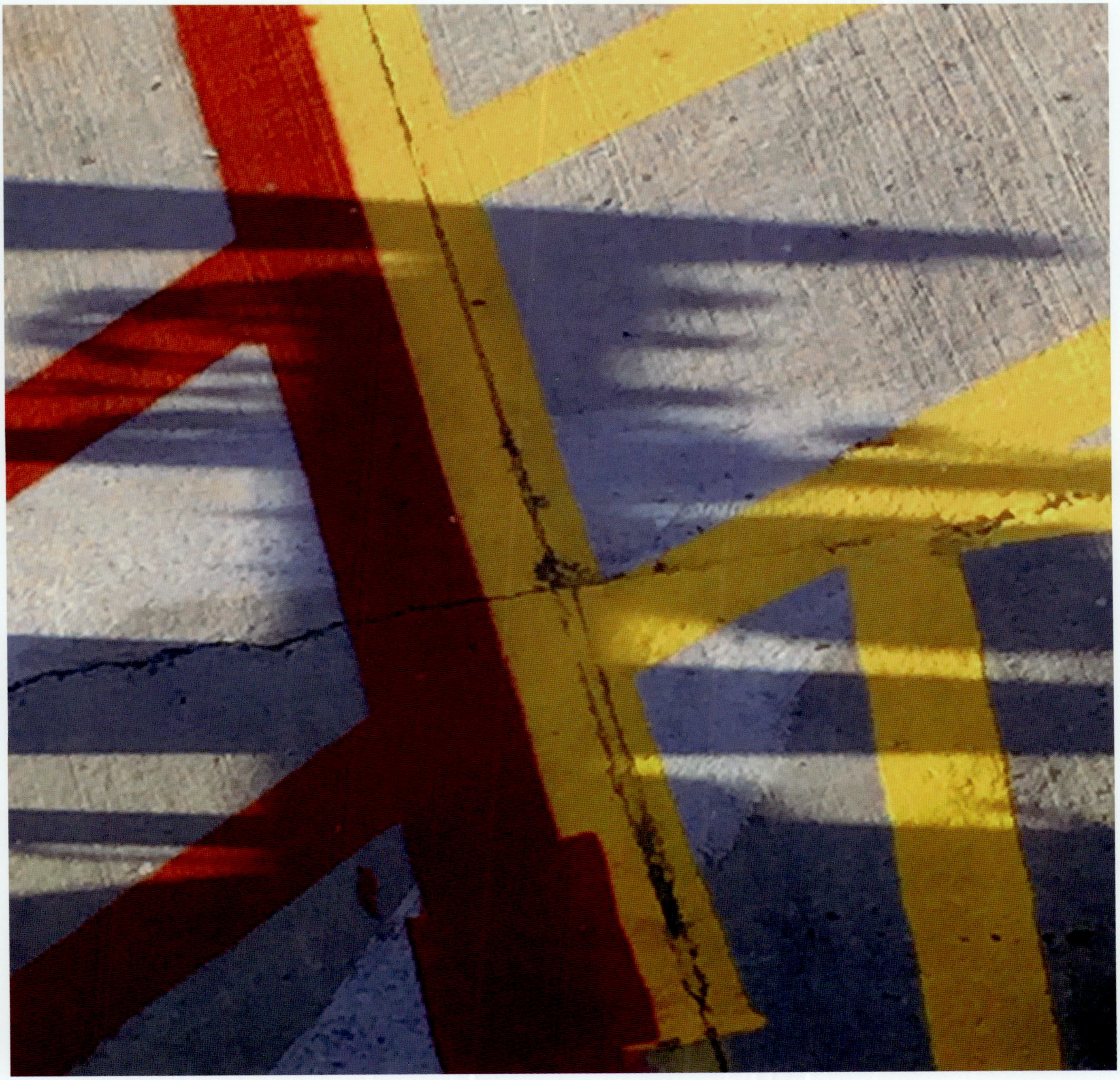

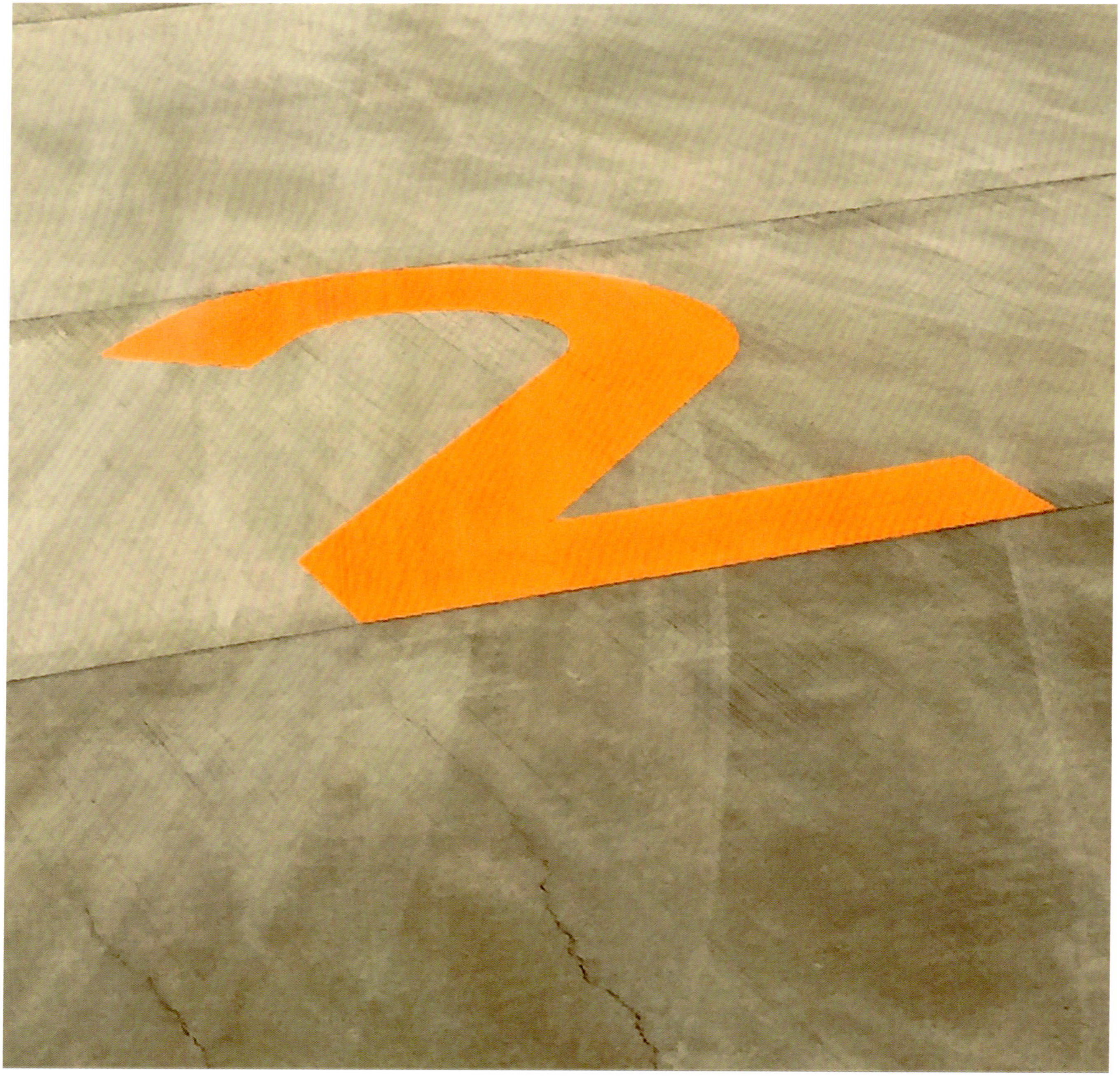

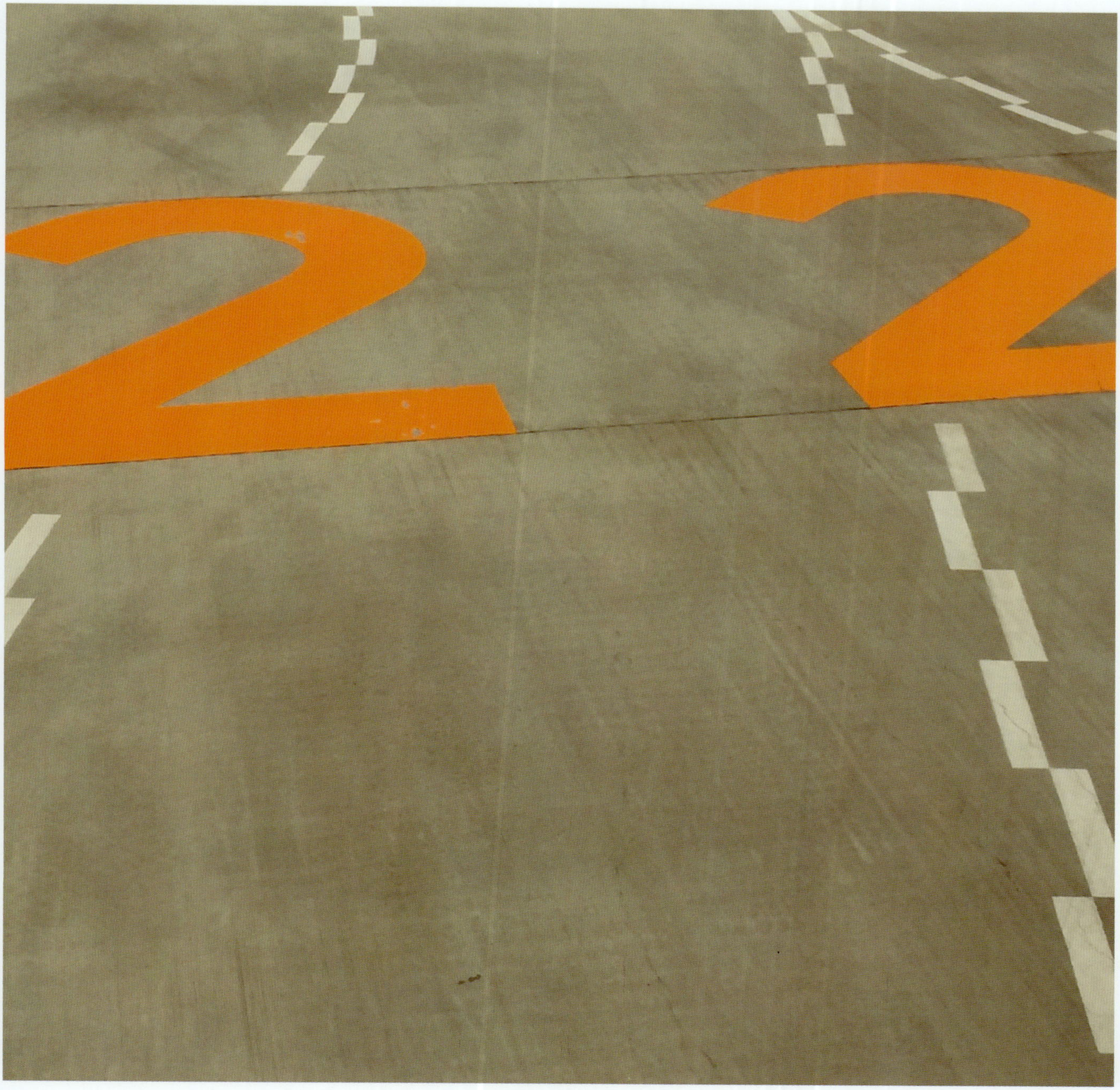

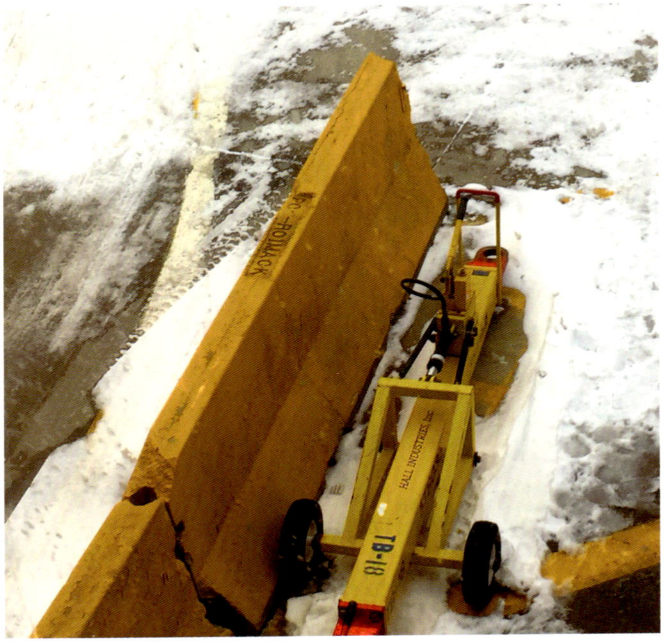
TB-18

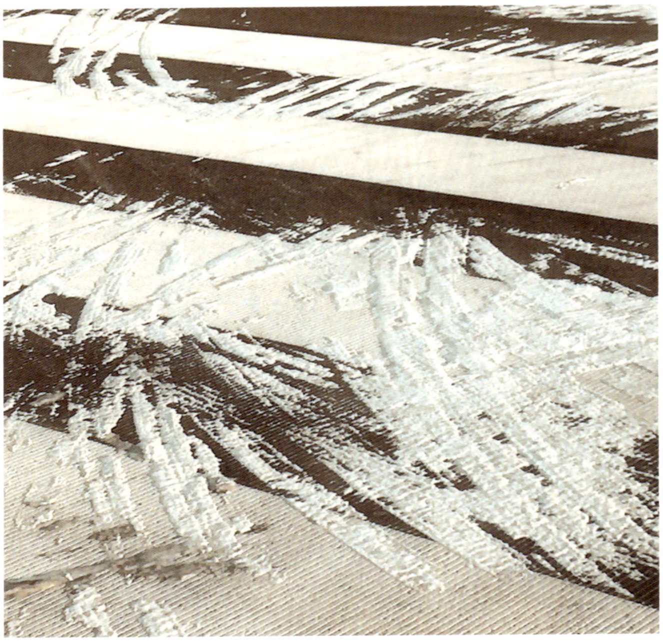

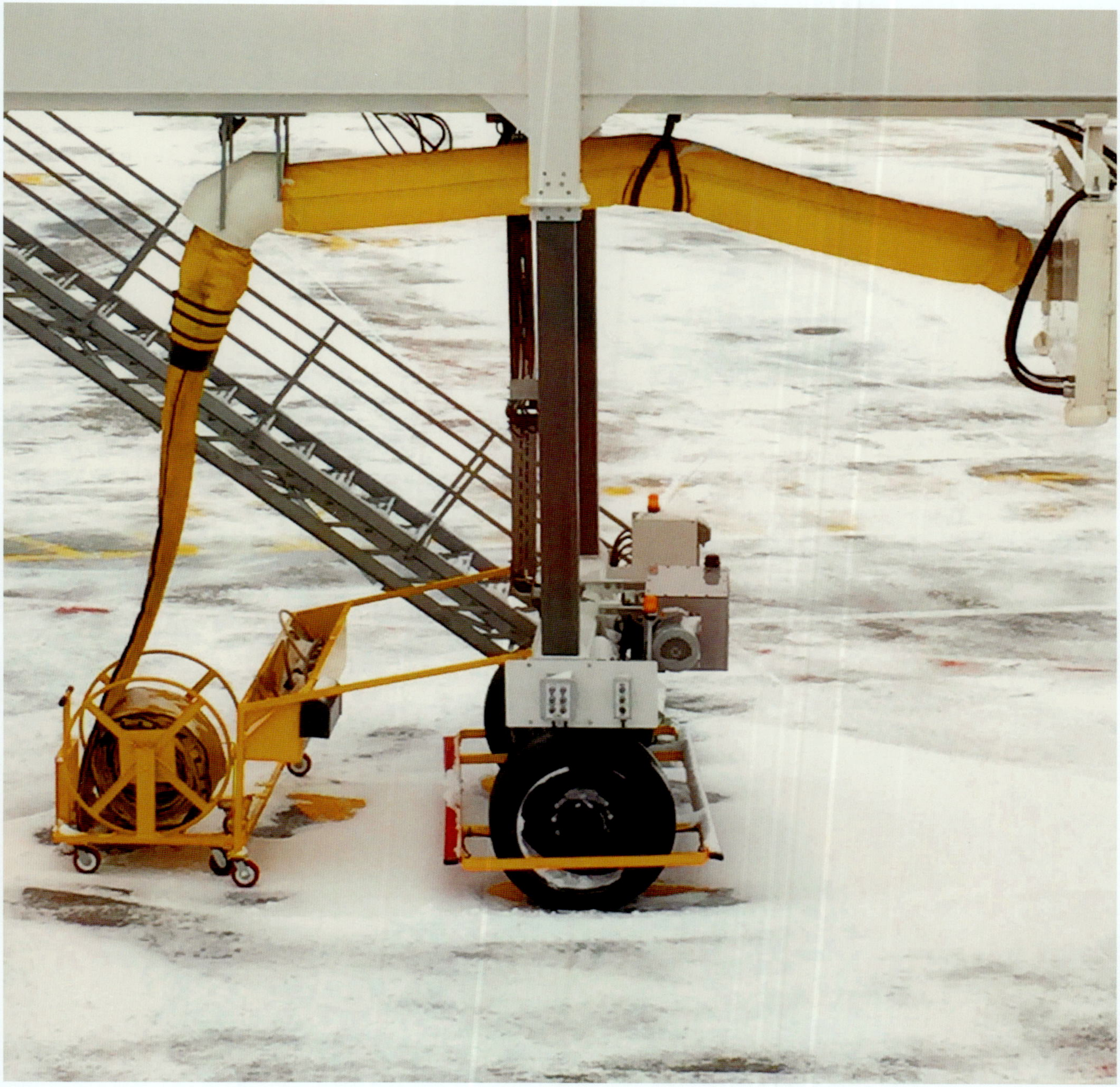

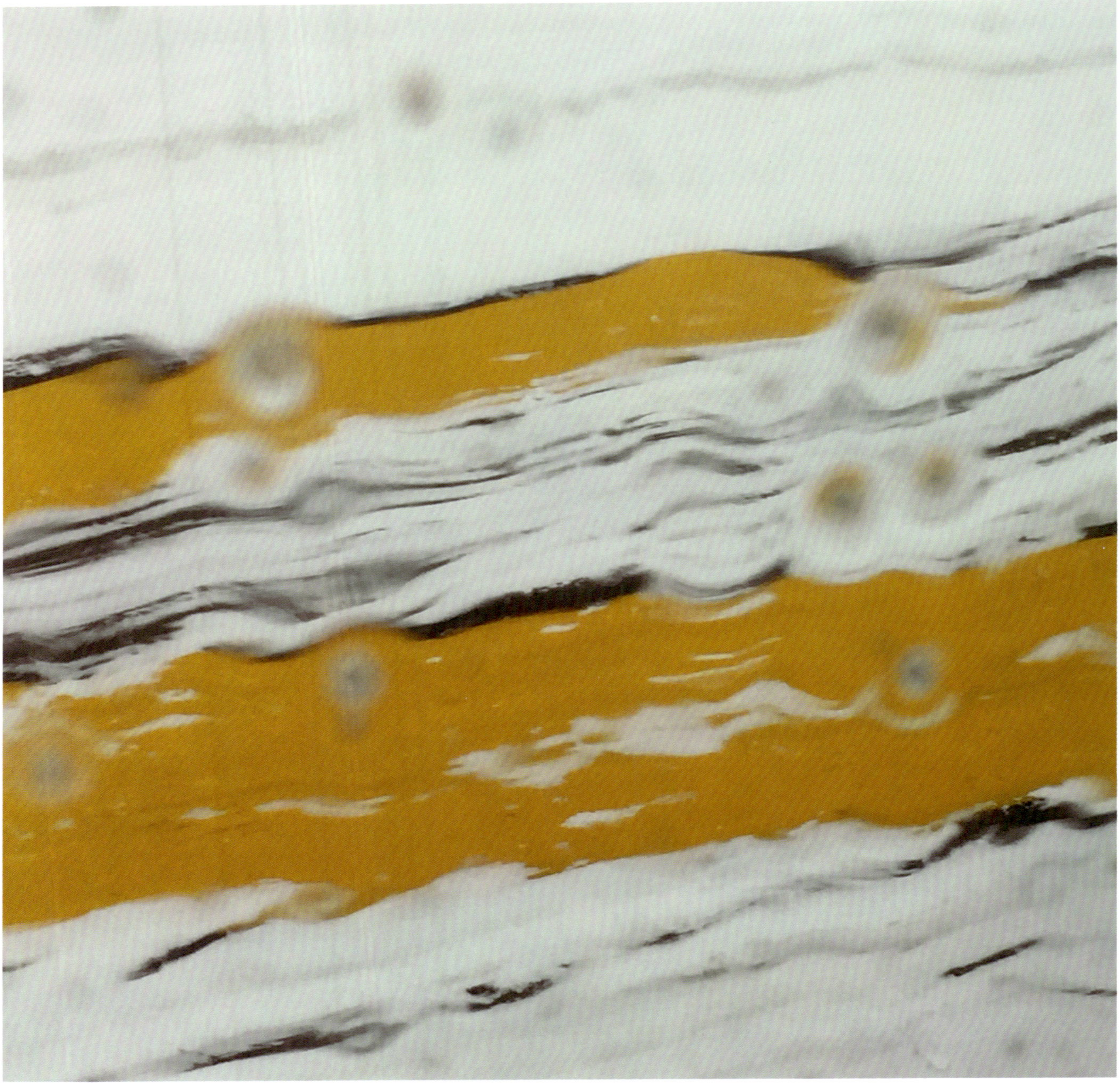

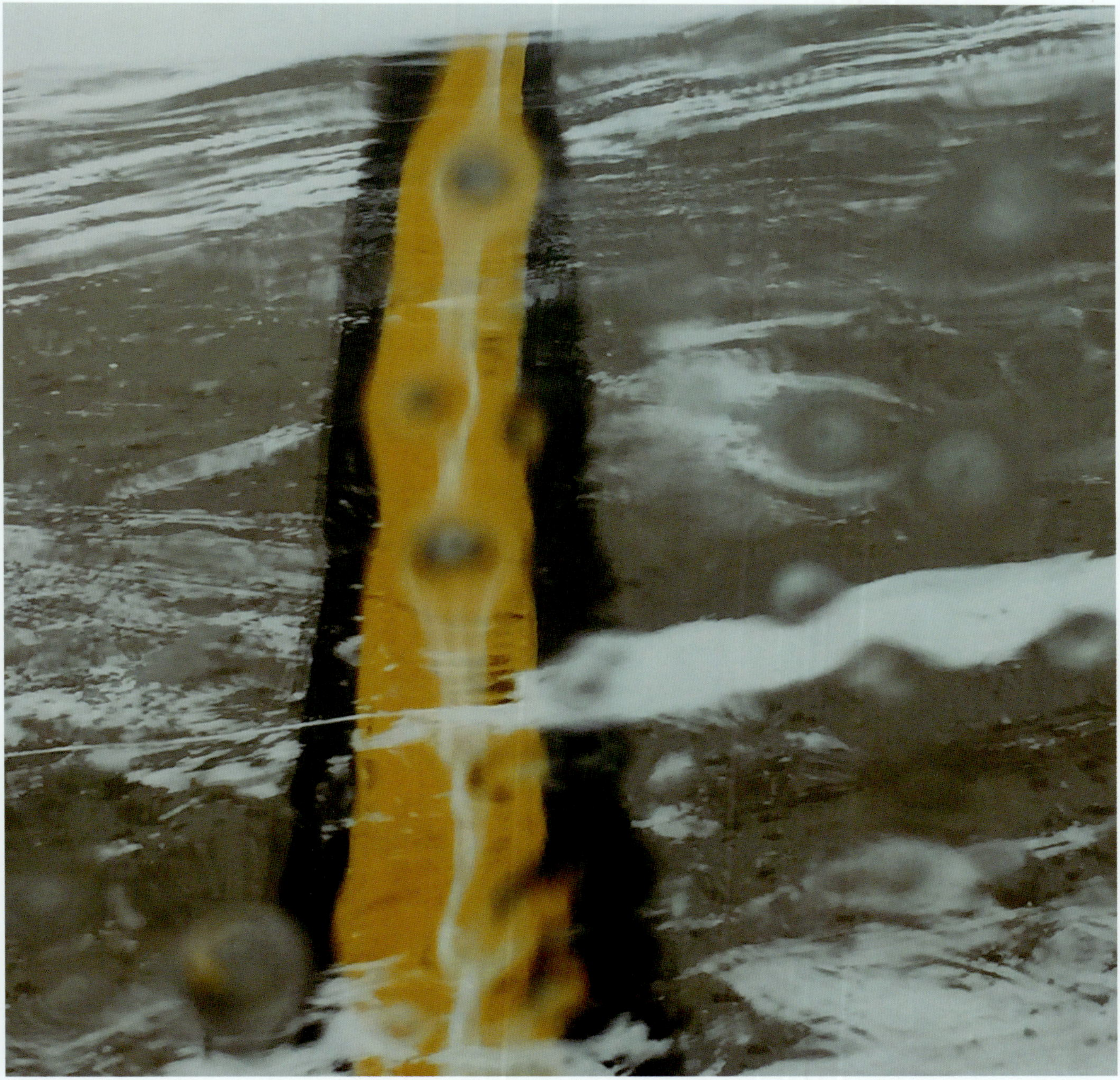

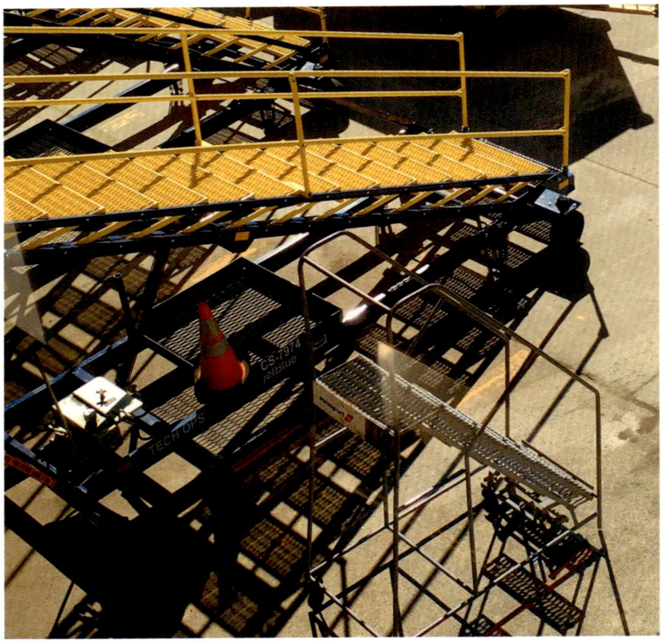
CS-7974
jetBlue
TECH OPS

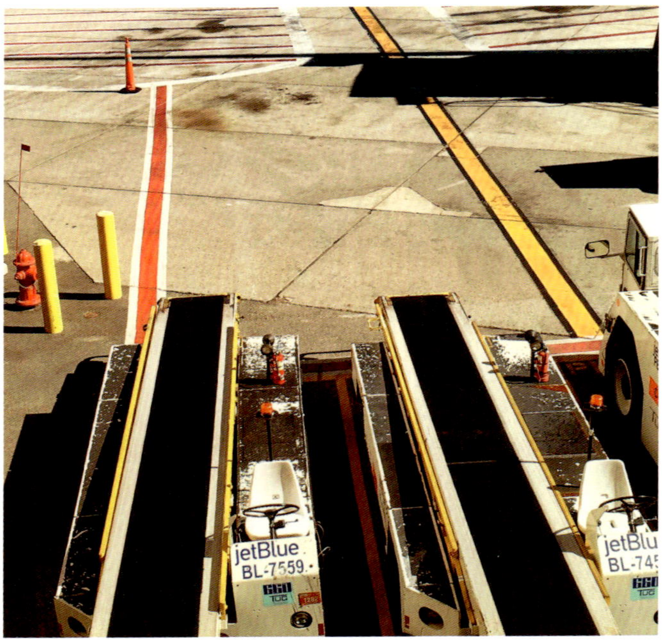
jetBlue
BL-7559

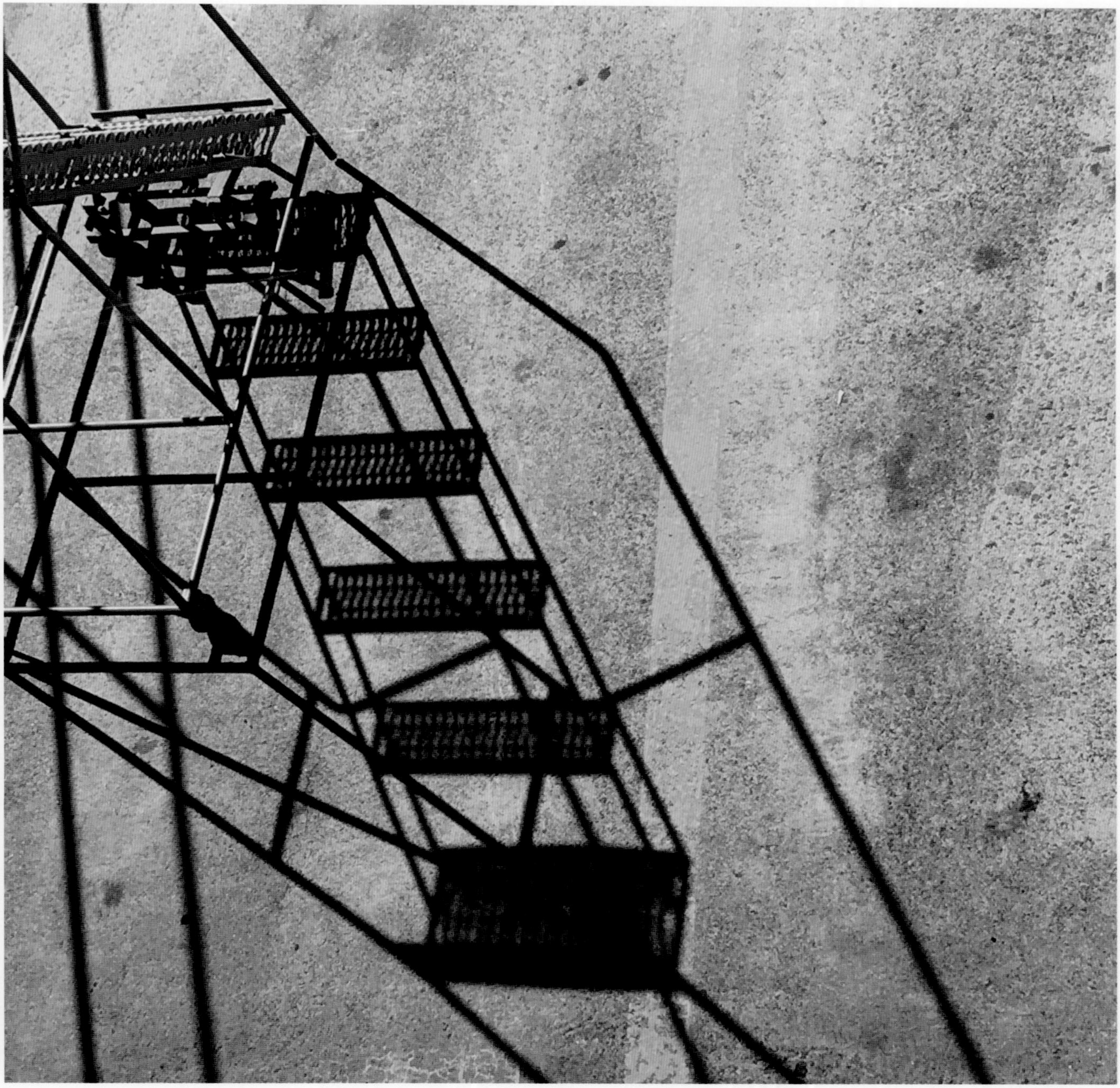

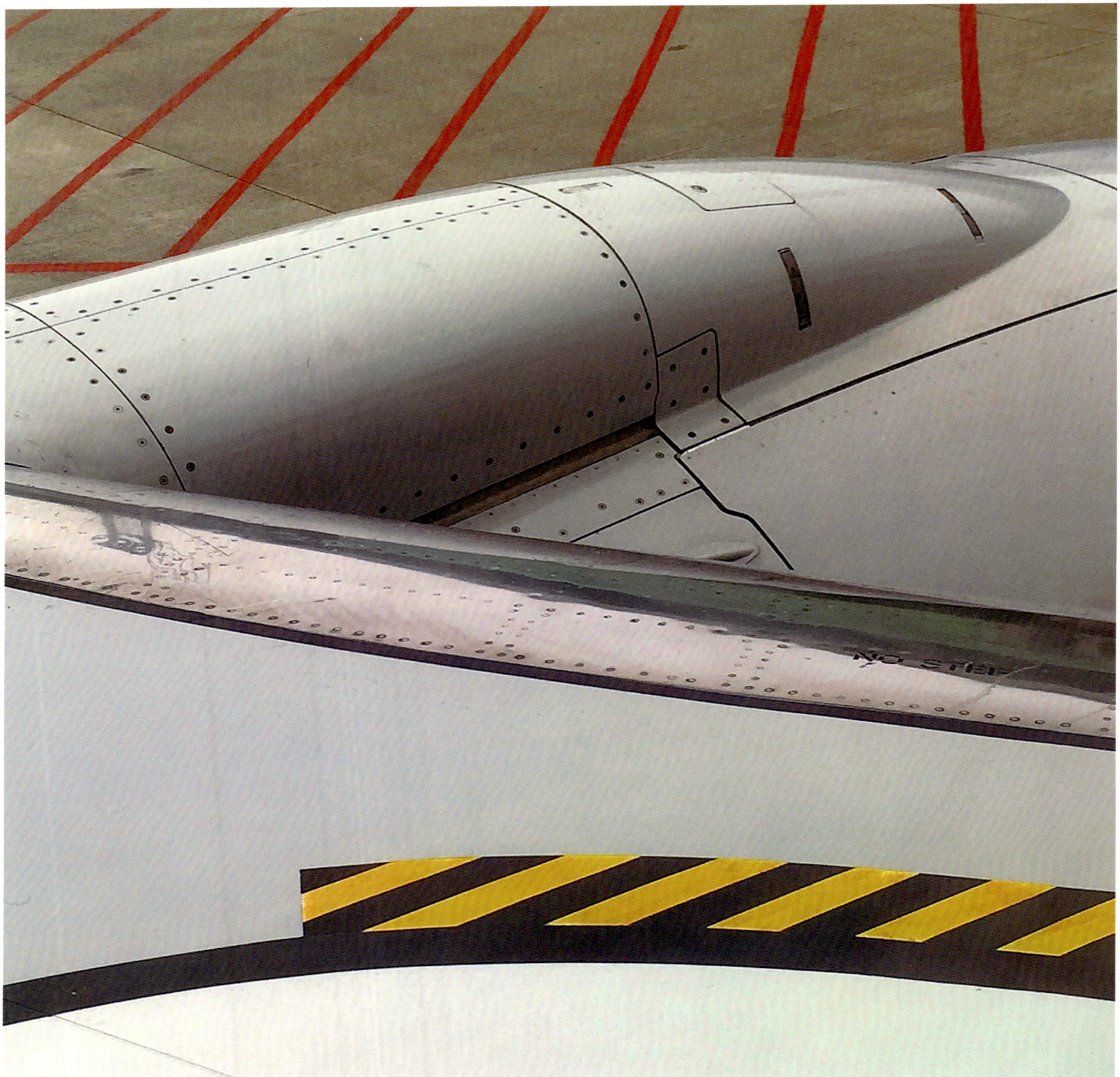

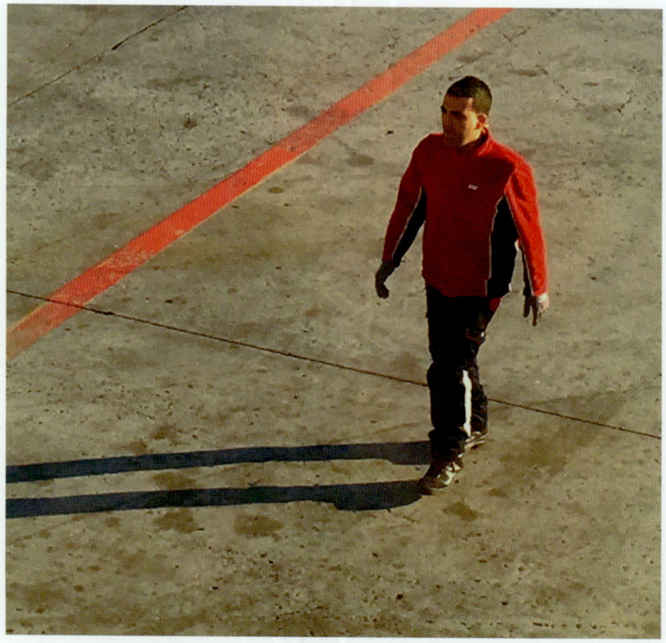

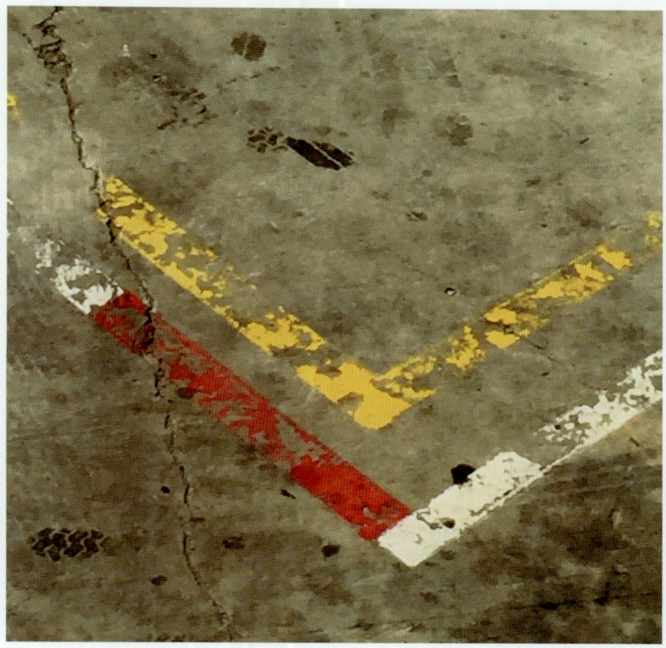

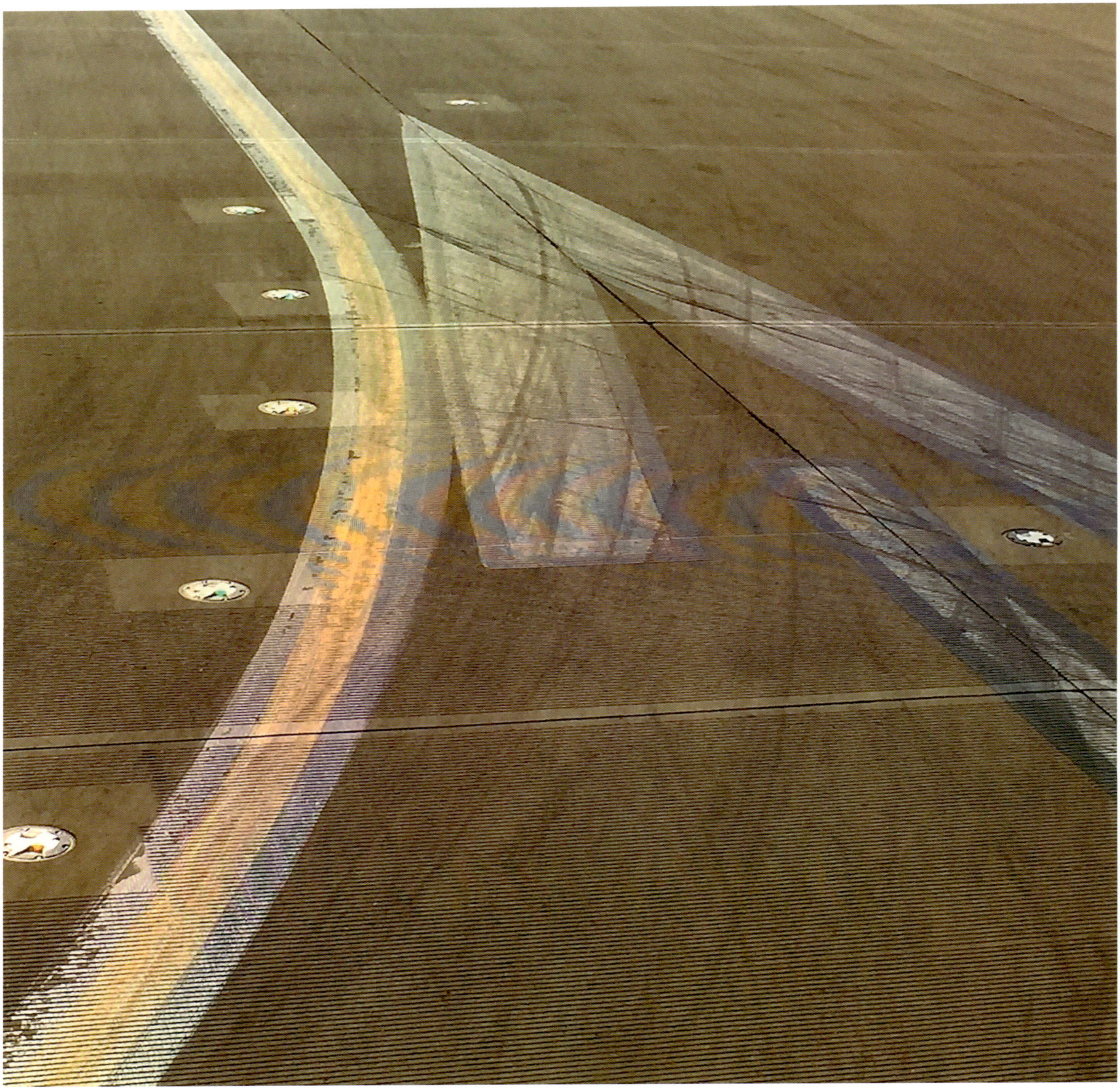

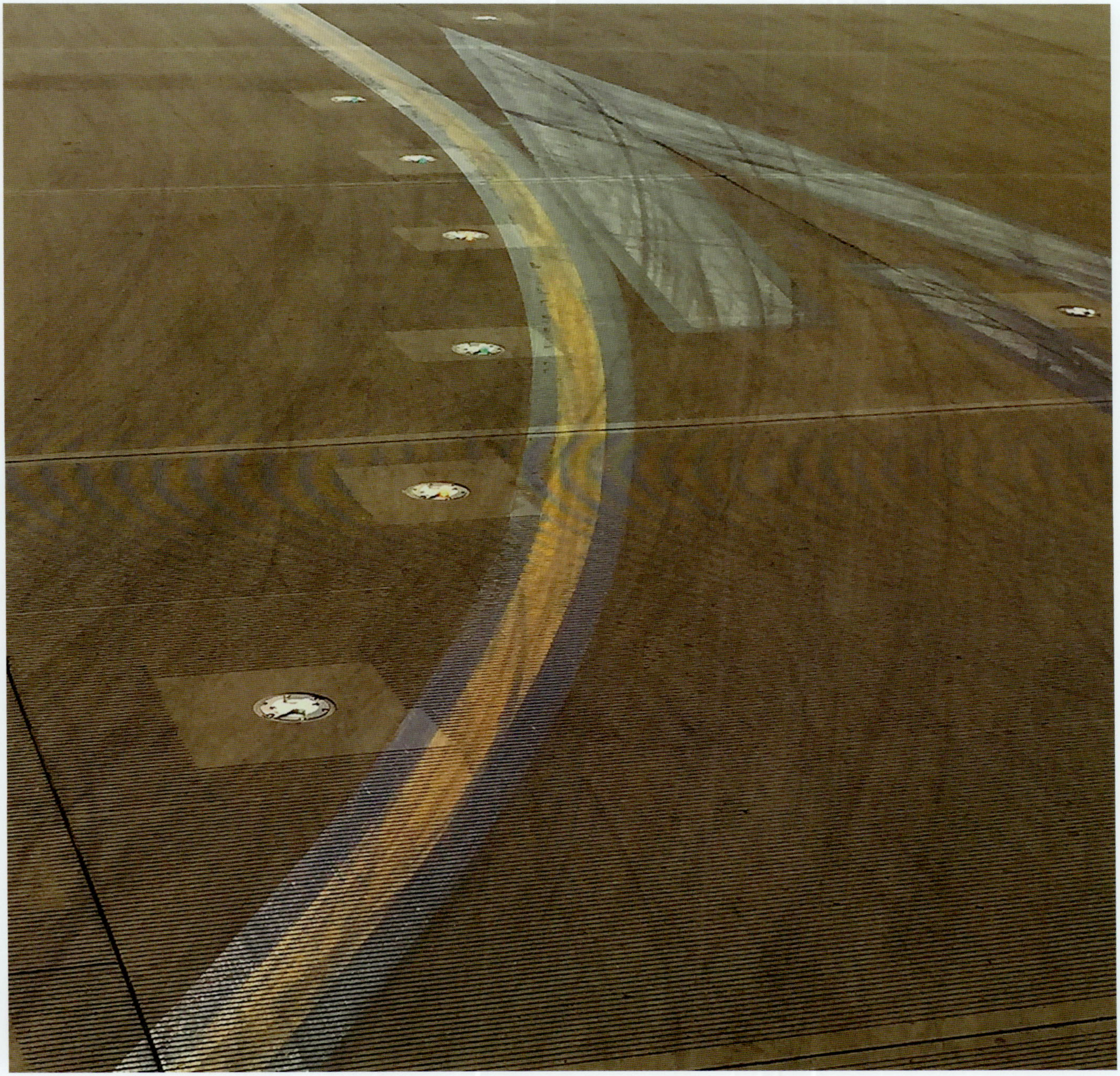

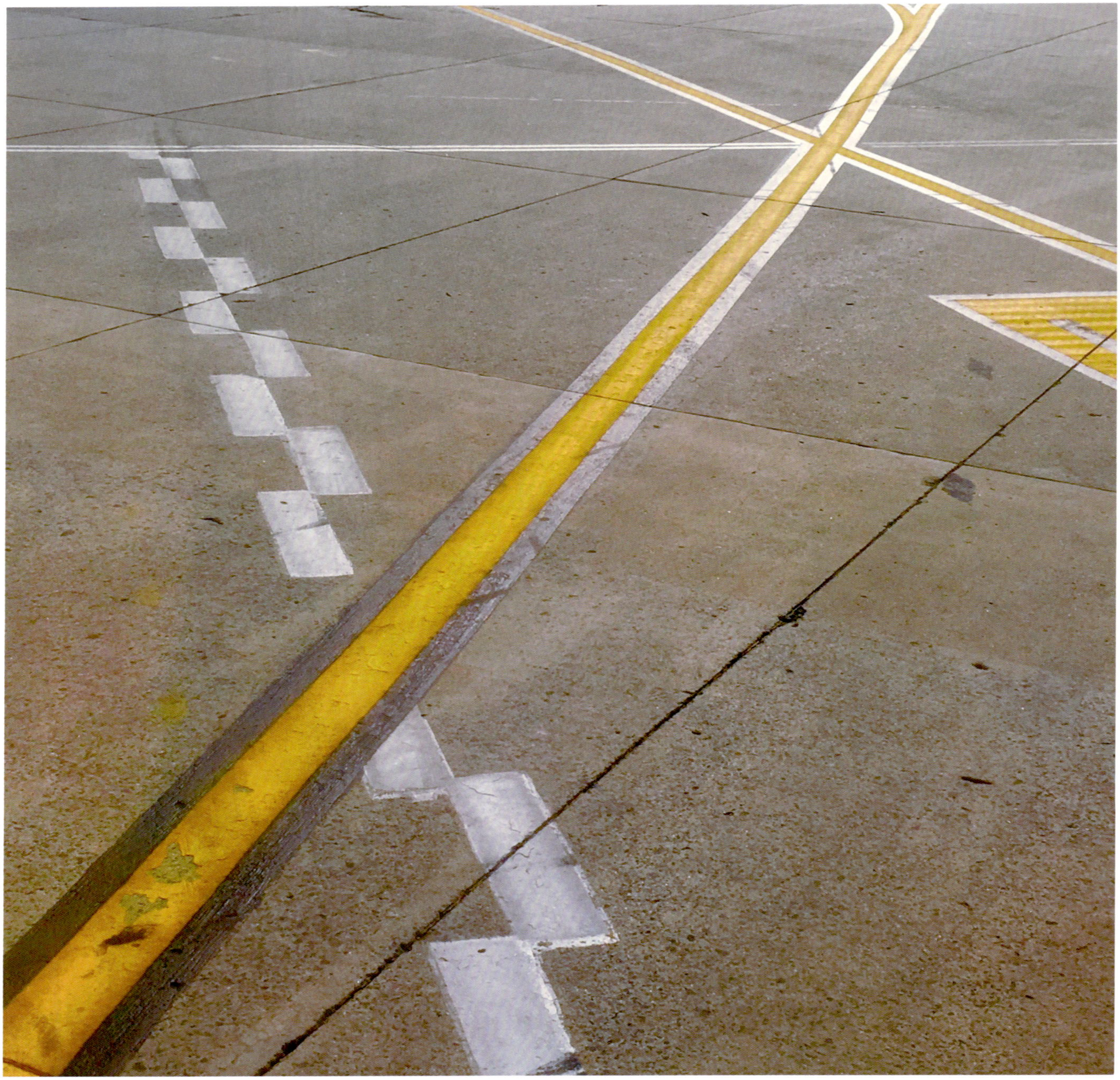

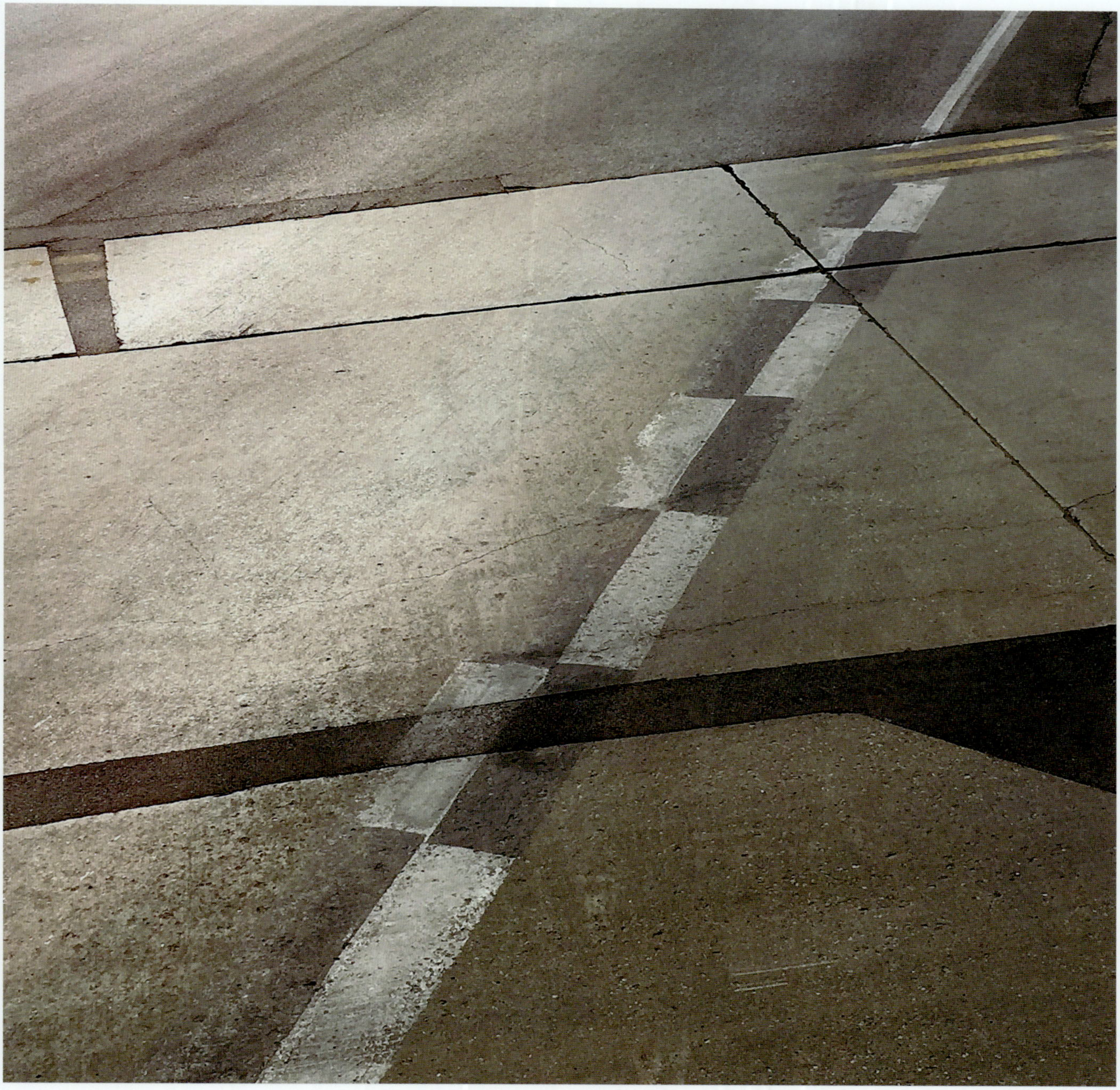

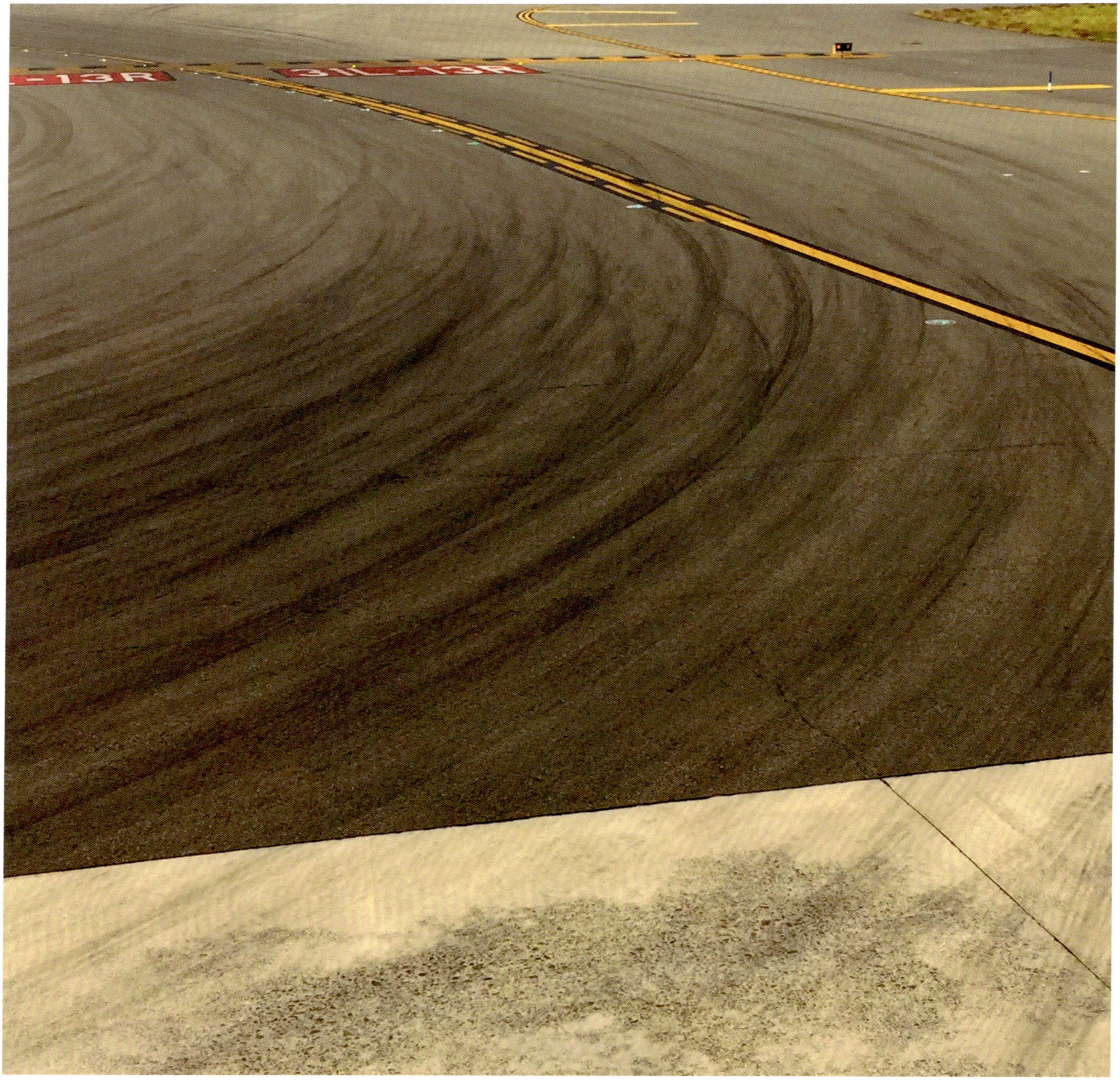
-13R
31L-13R

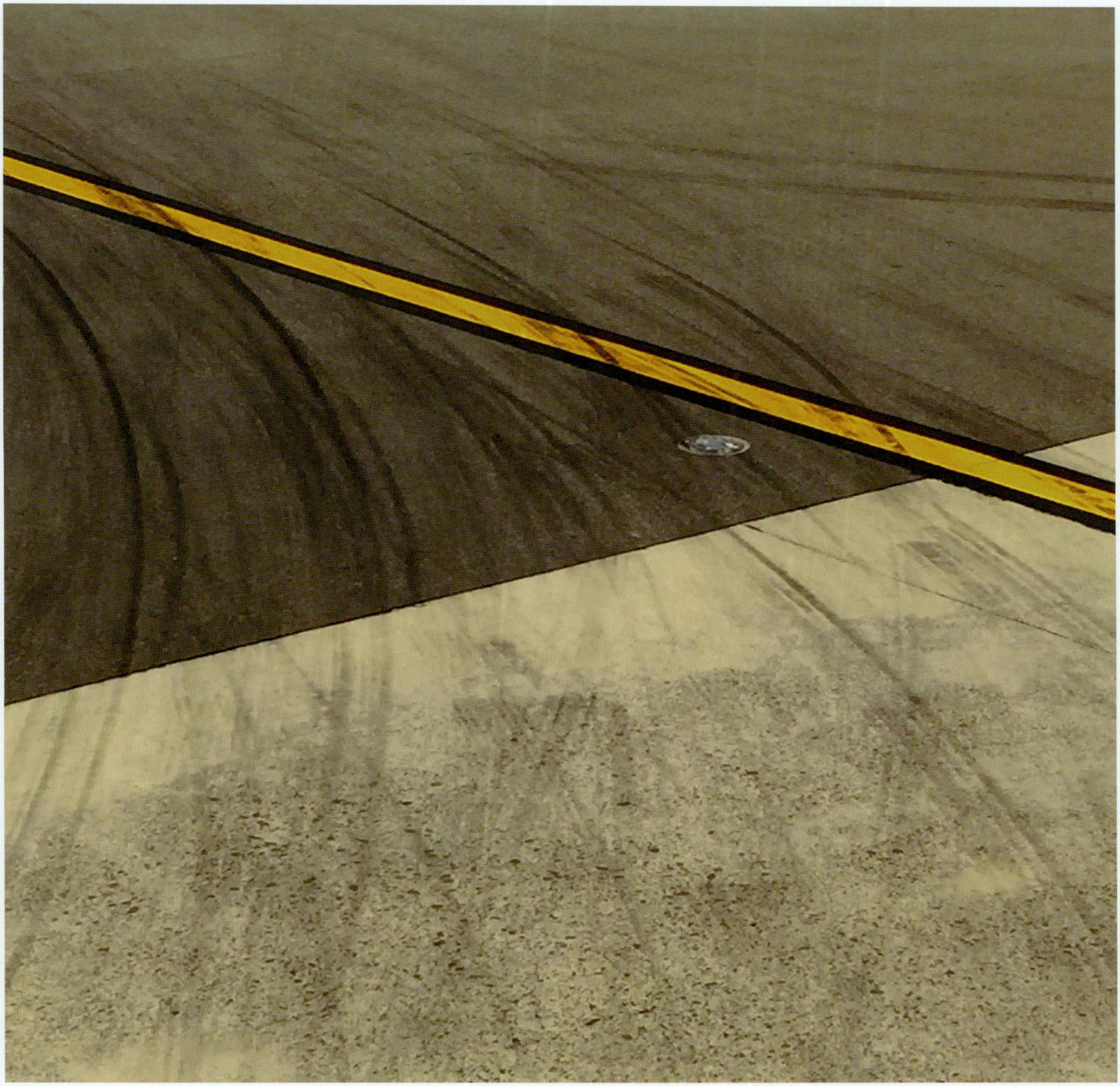

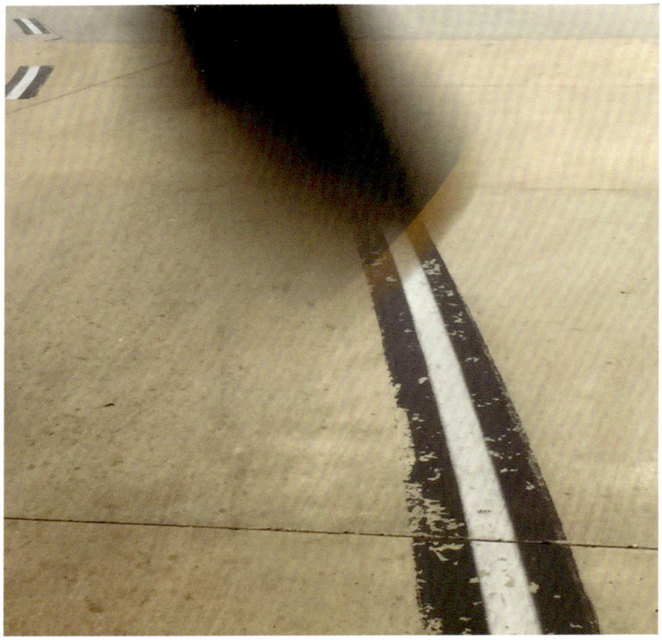

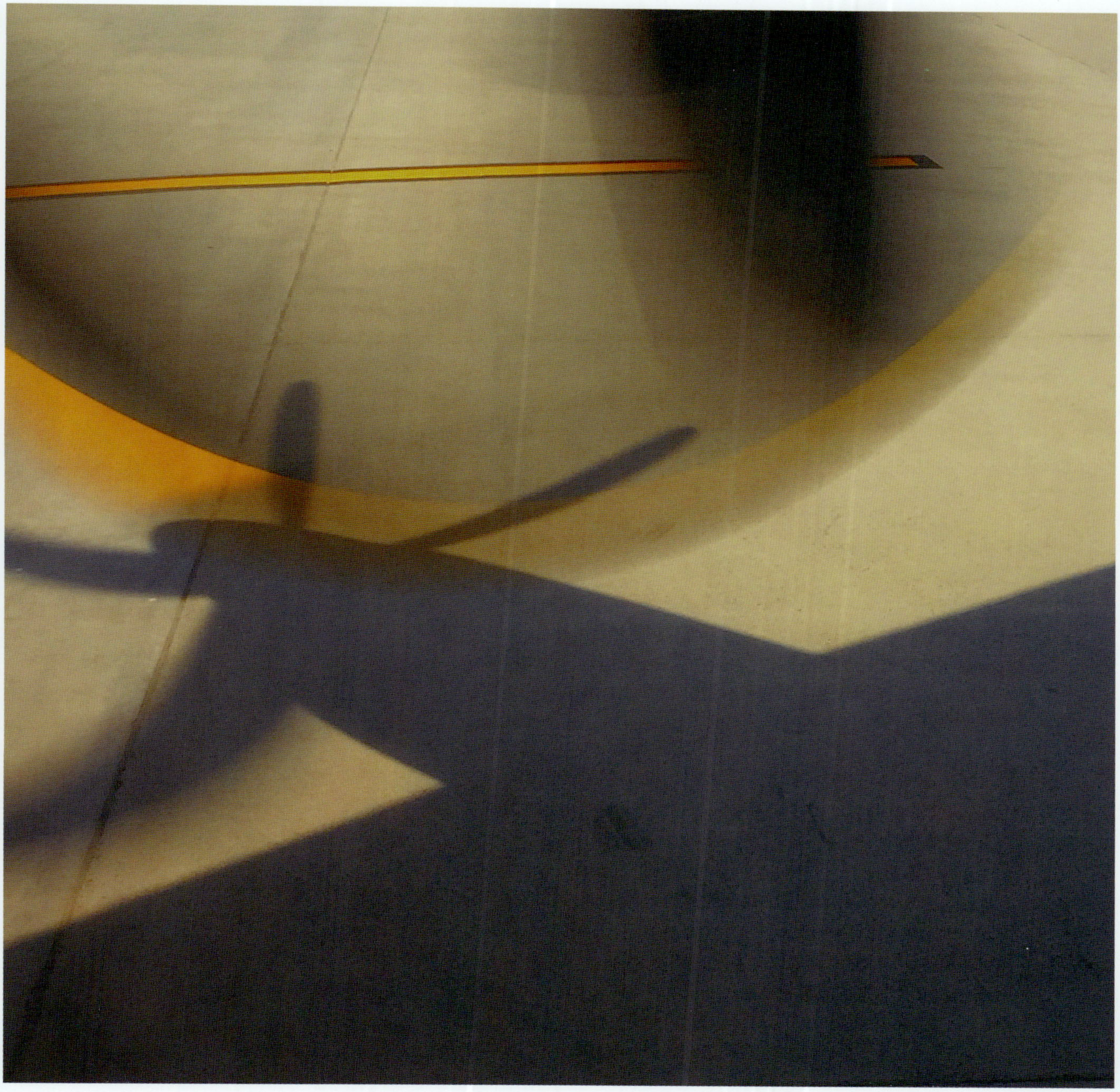

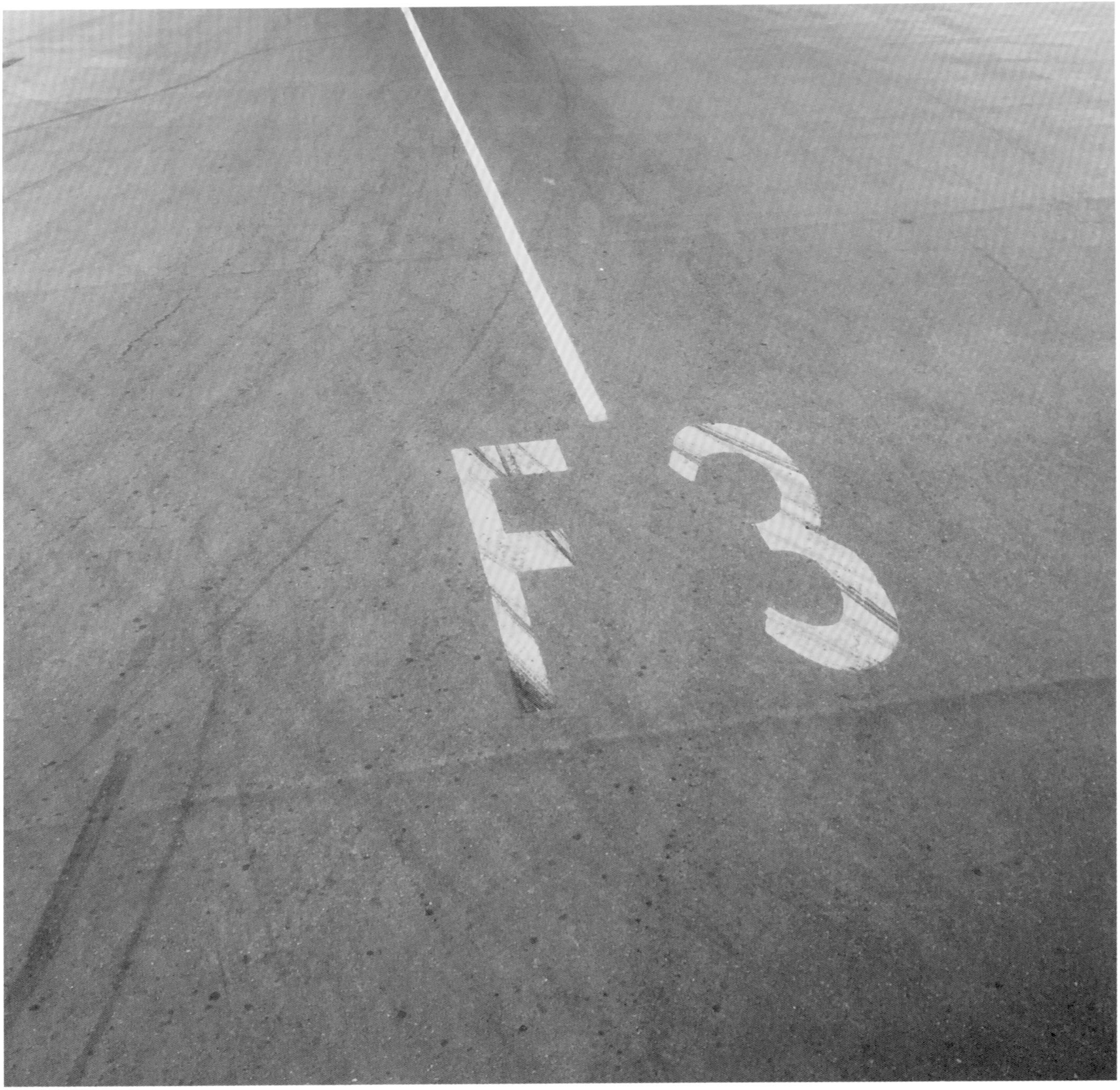
F3

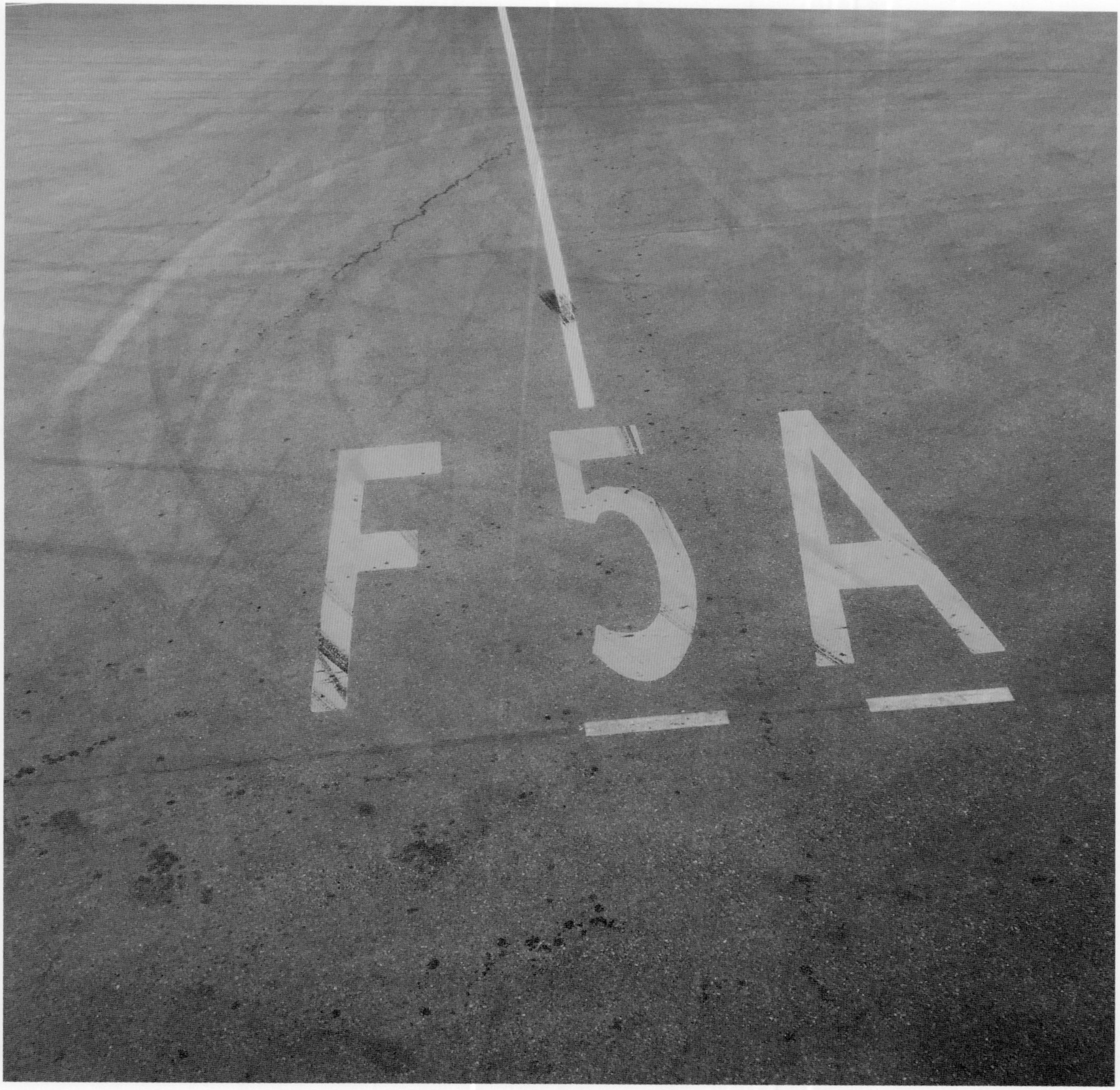
F5A

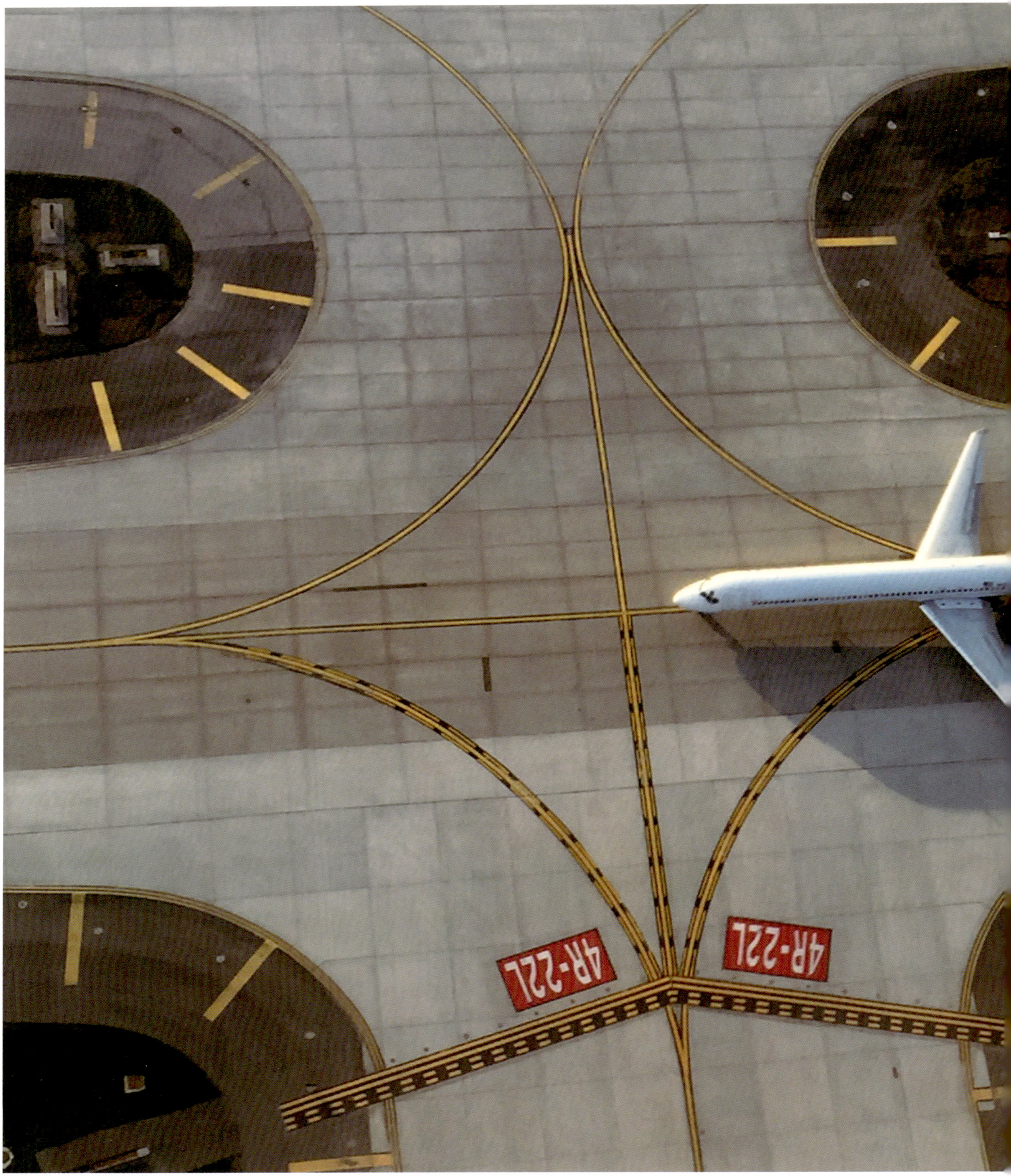
4R-22L
4R-22L

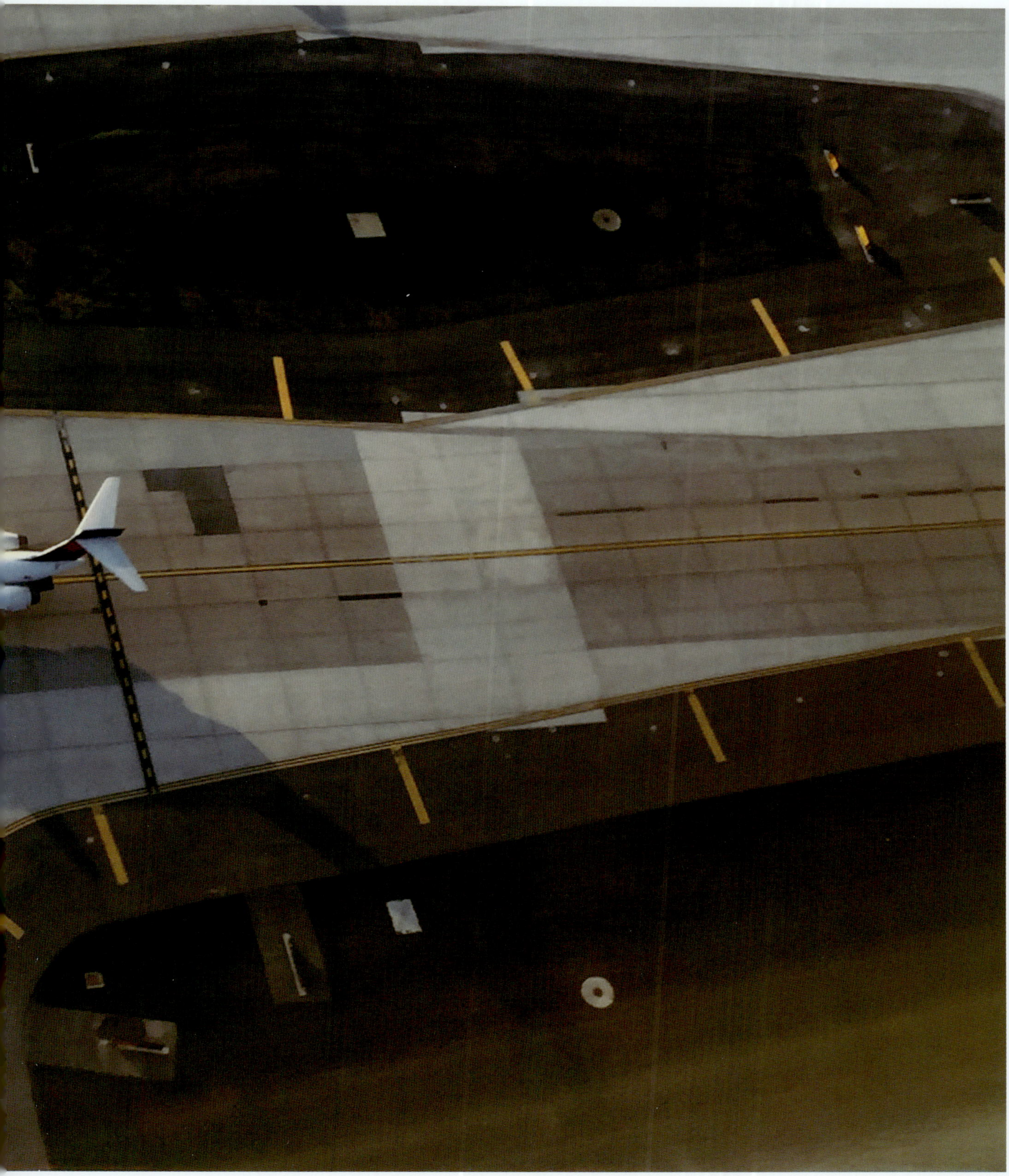

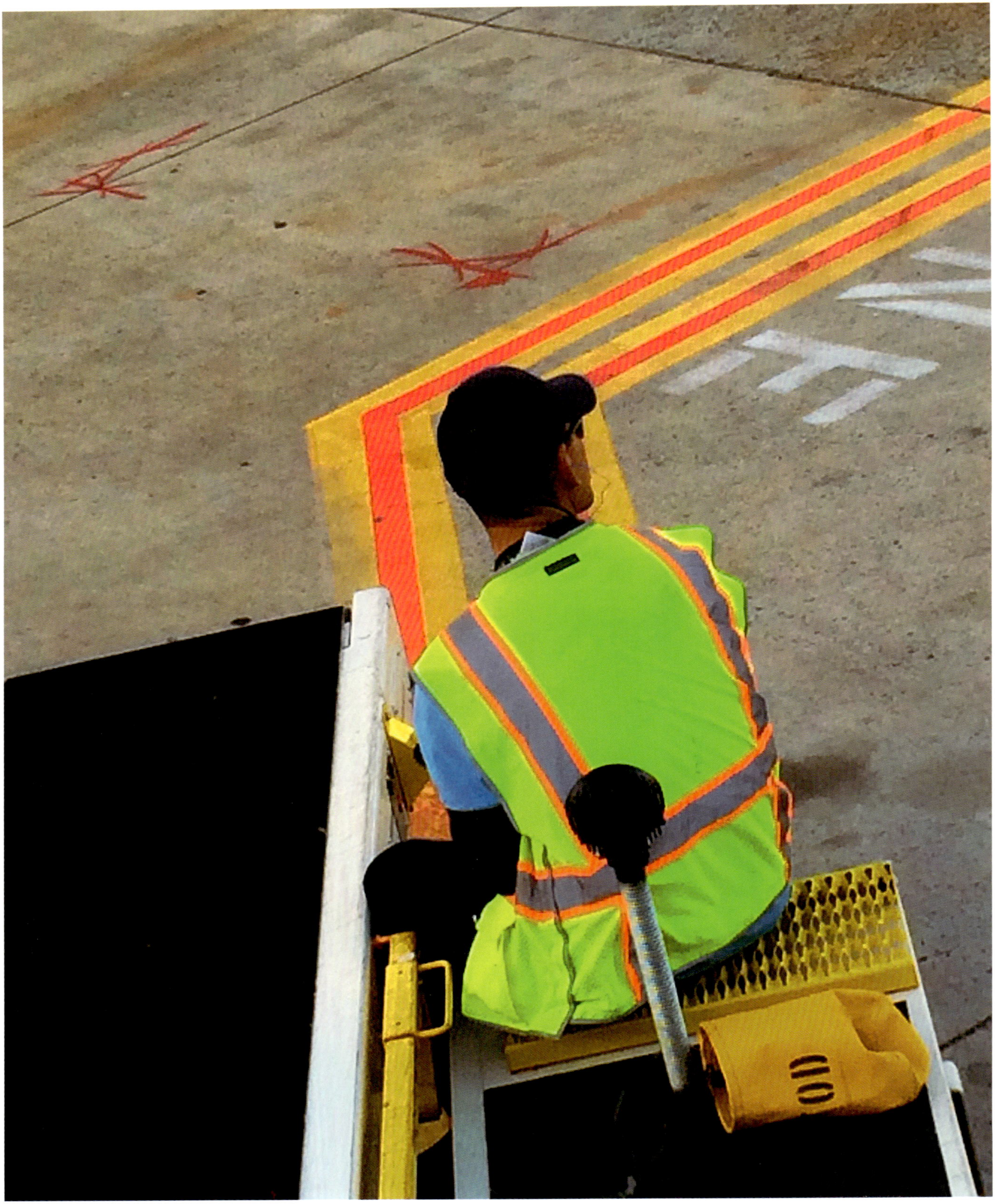

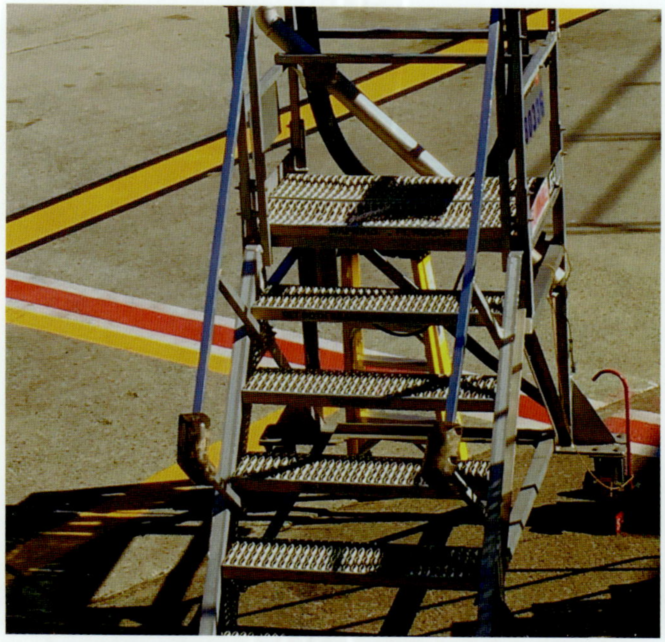

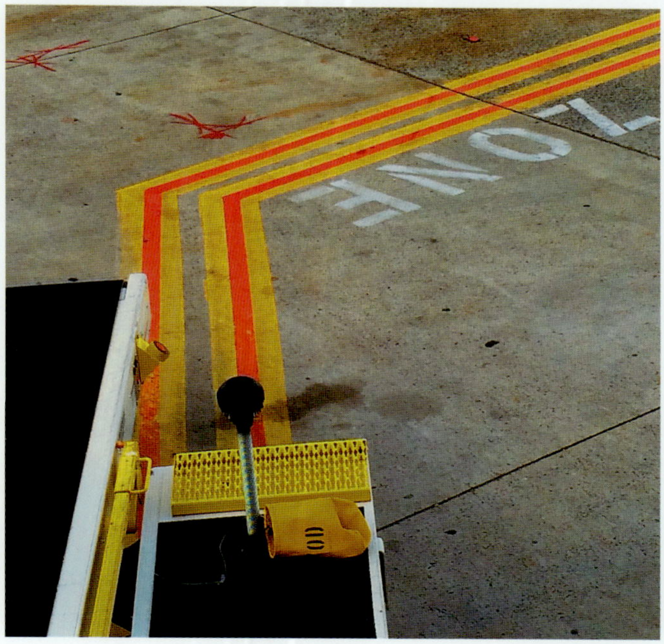
ZONE

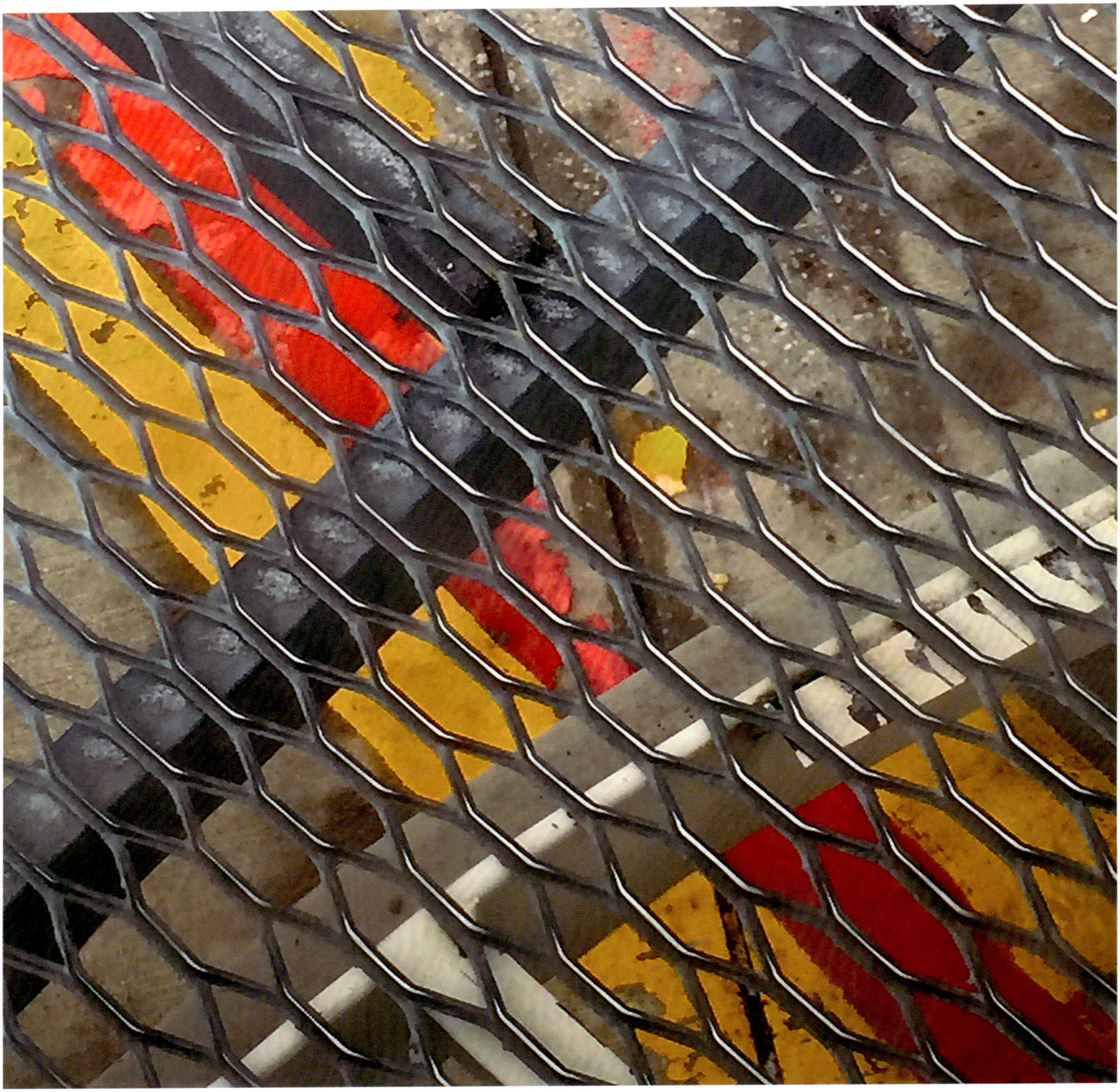

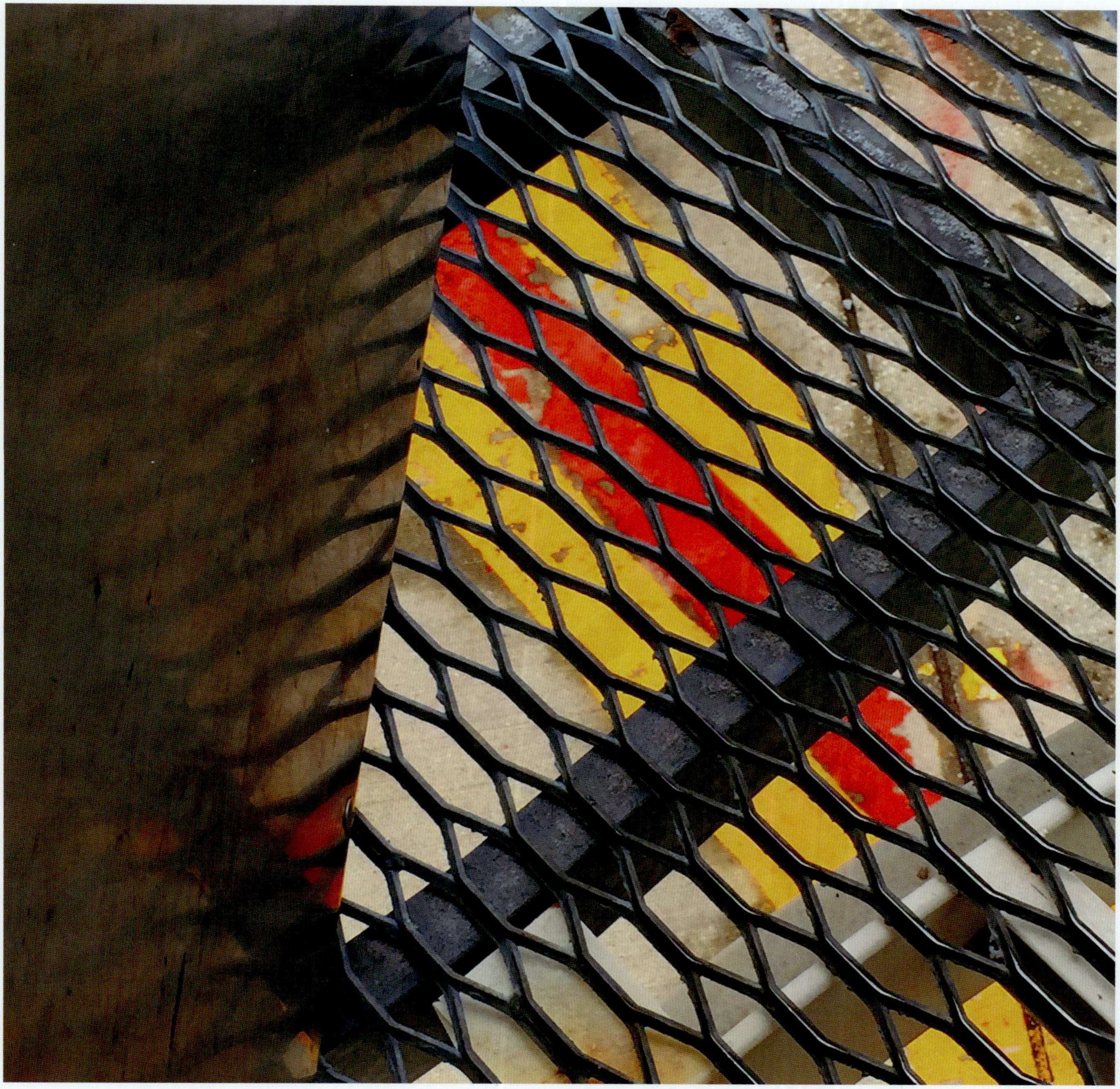

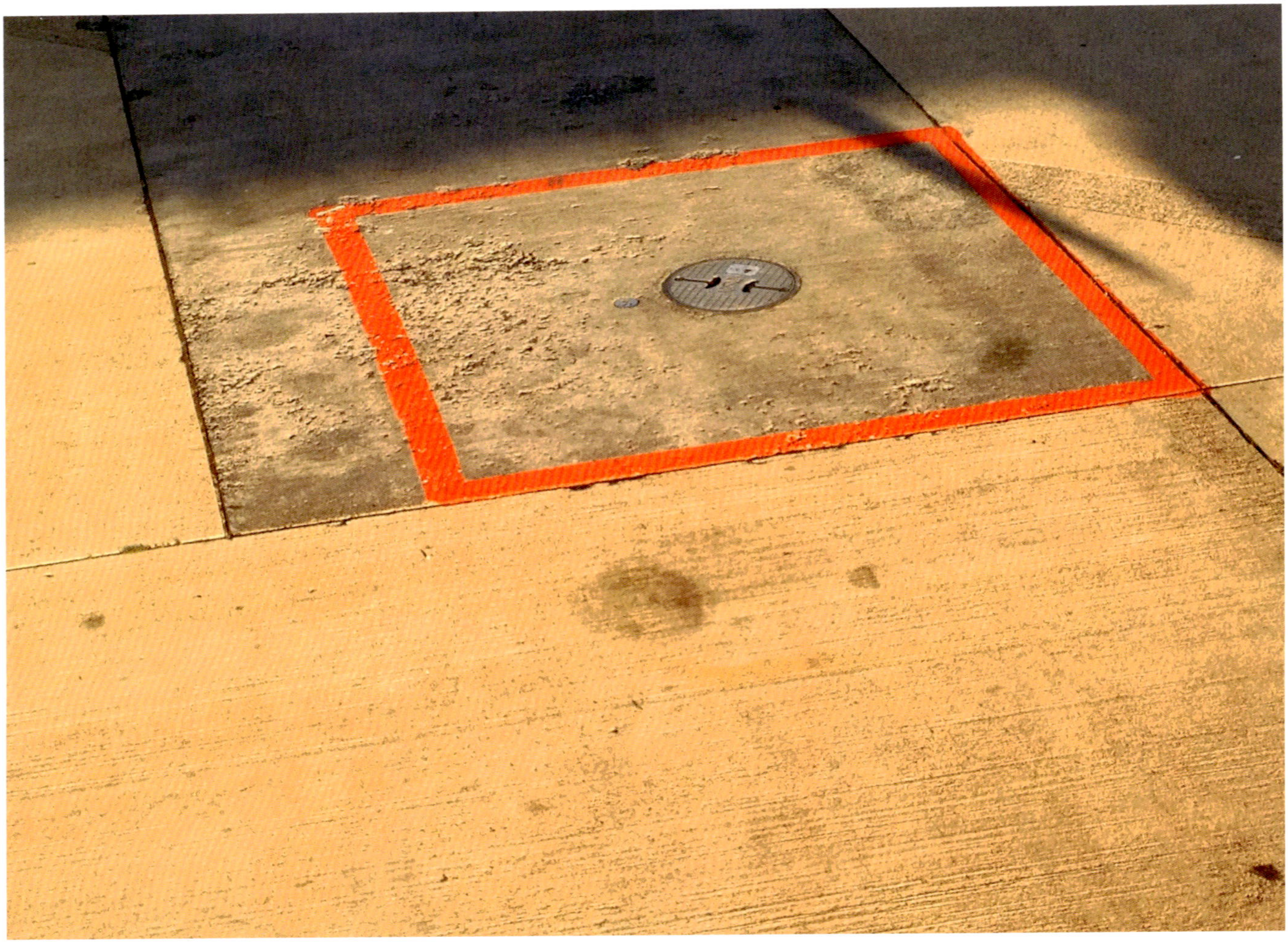

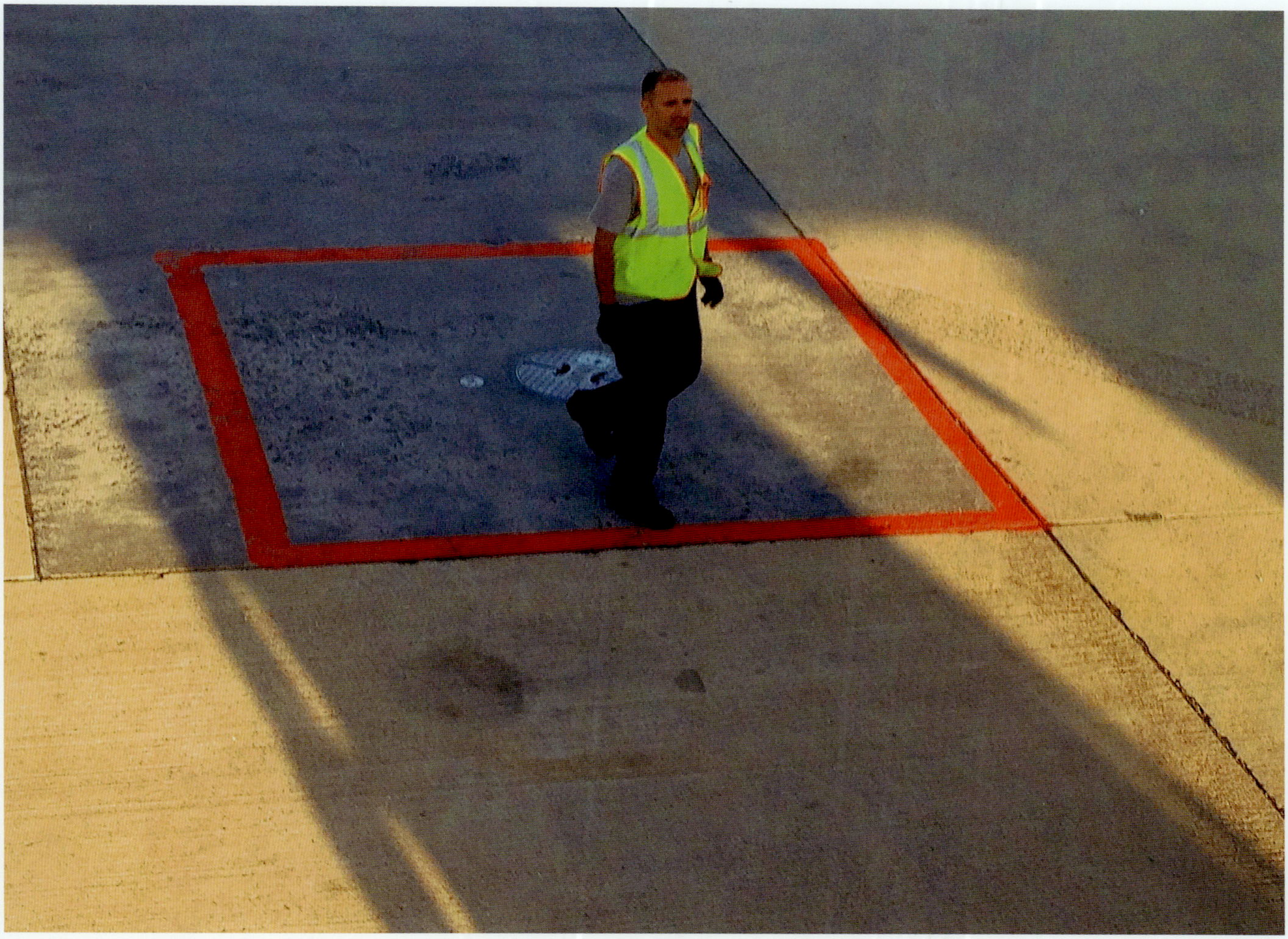

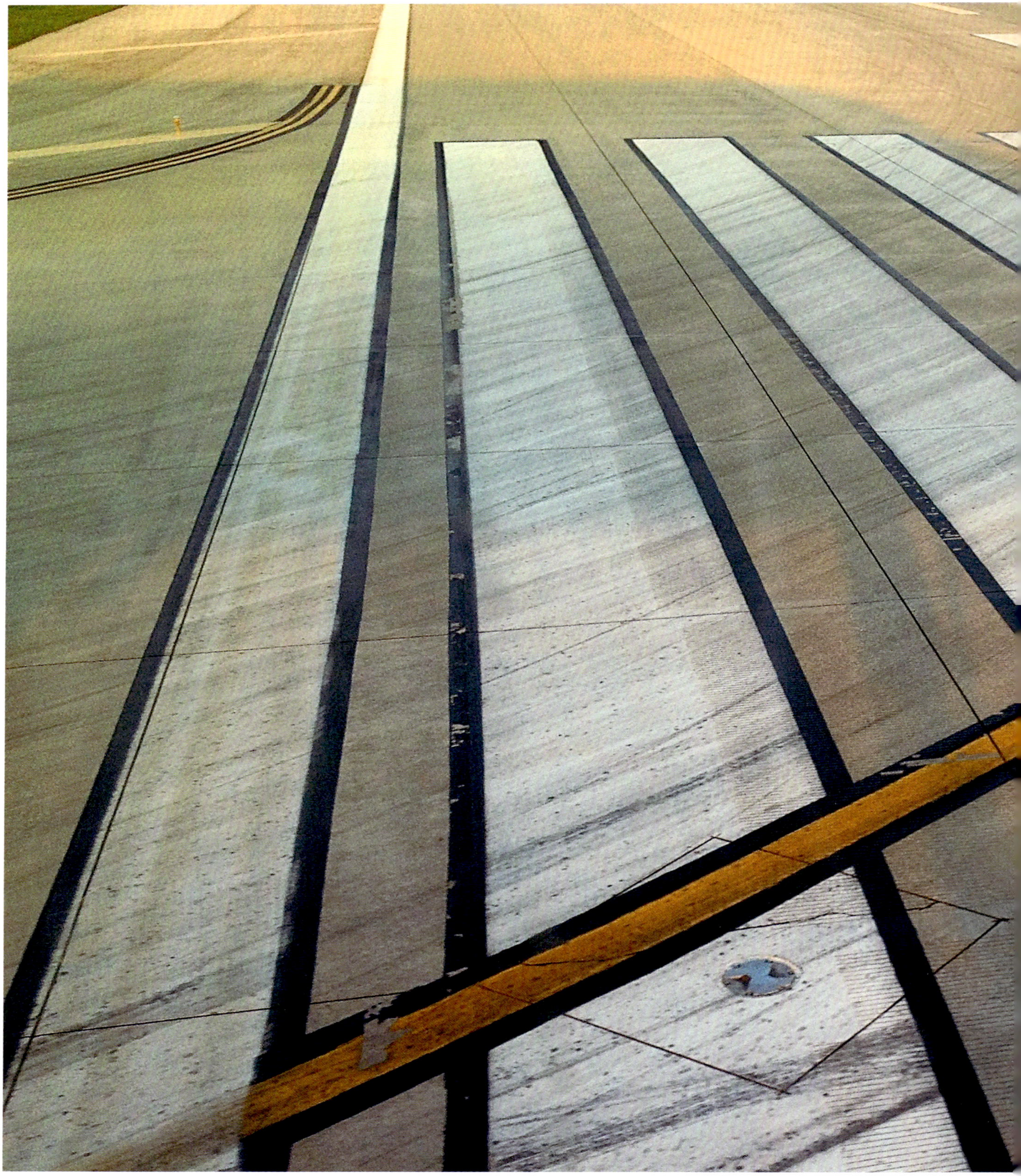

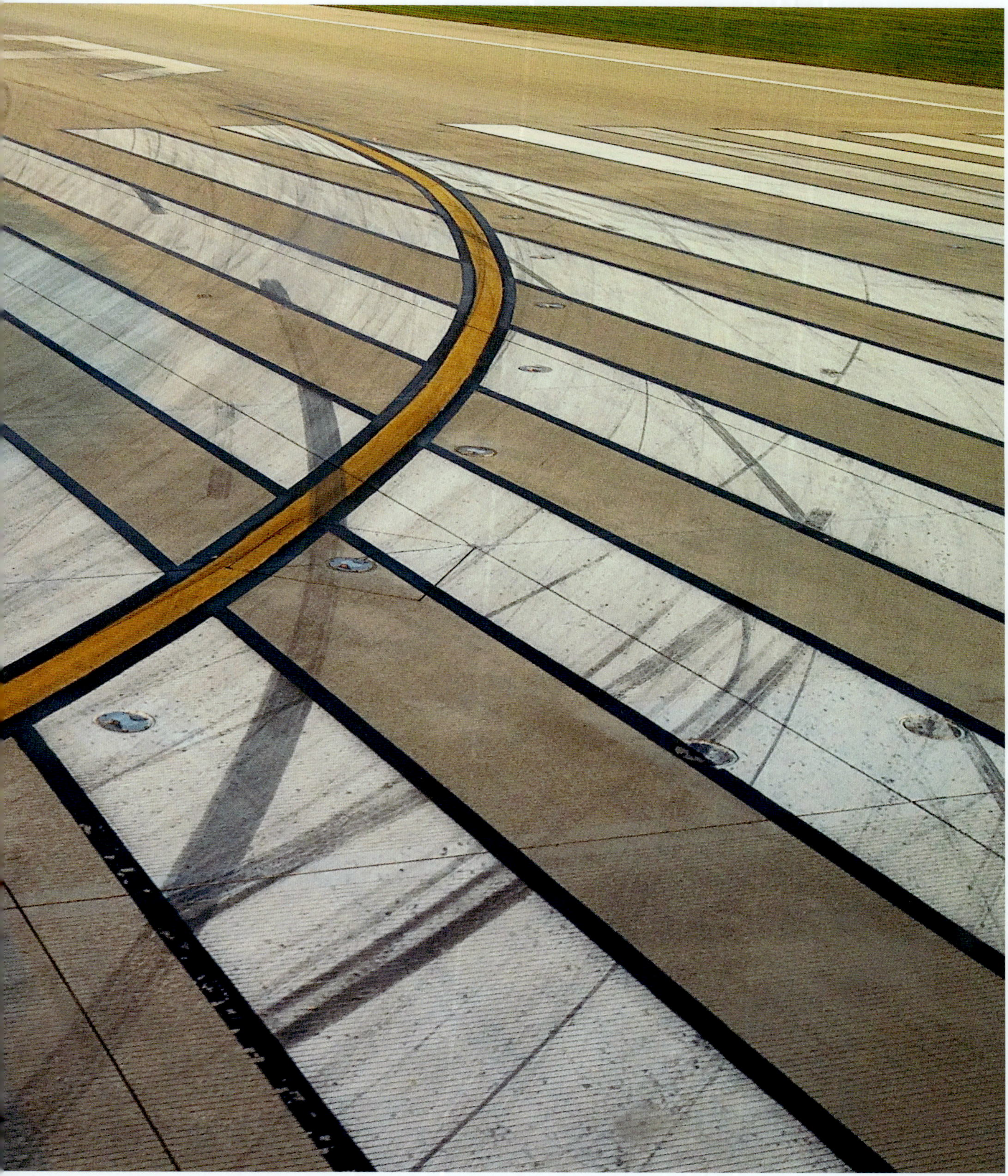

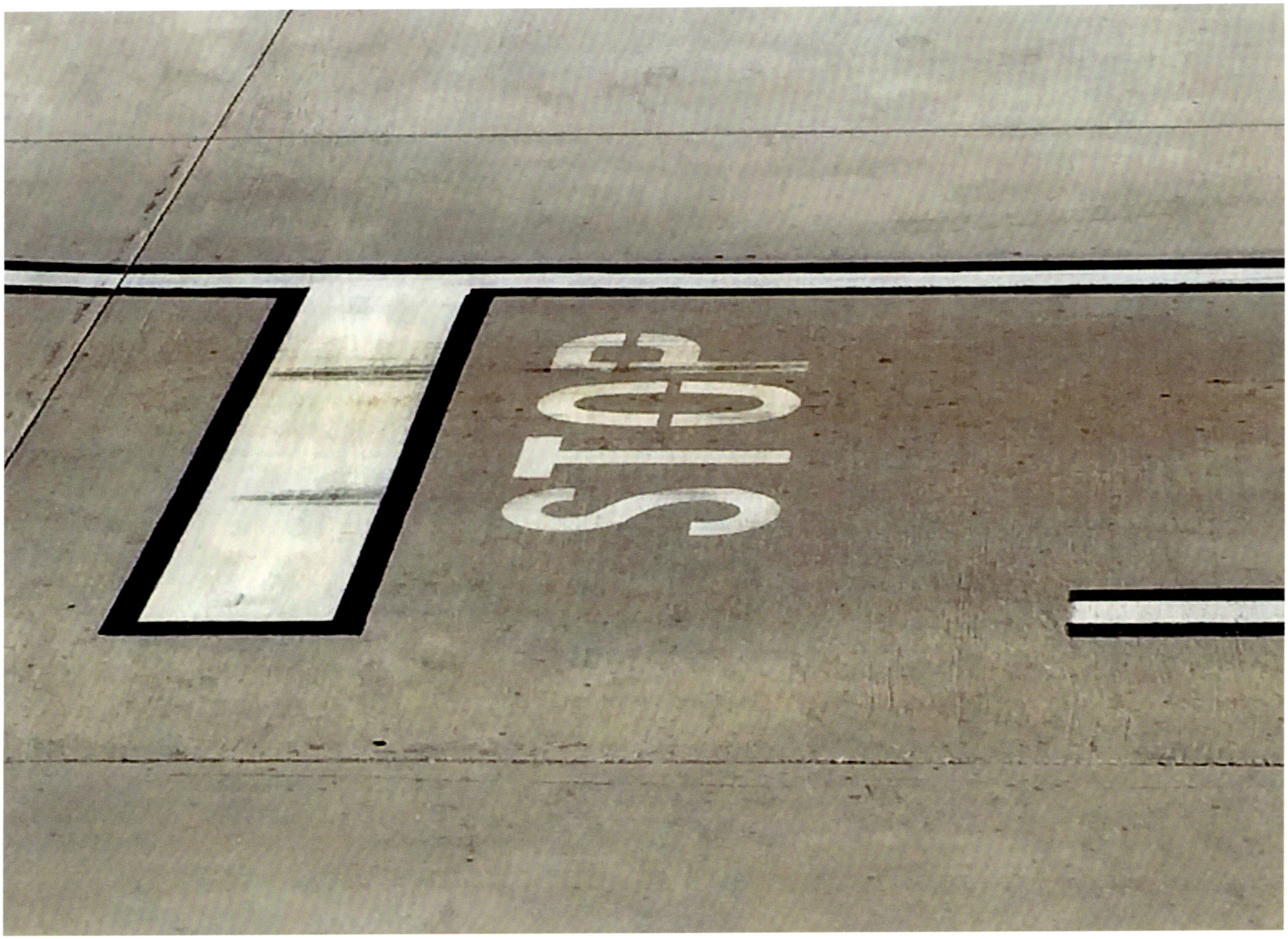
STOP

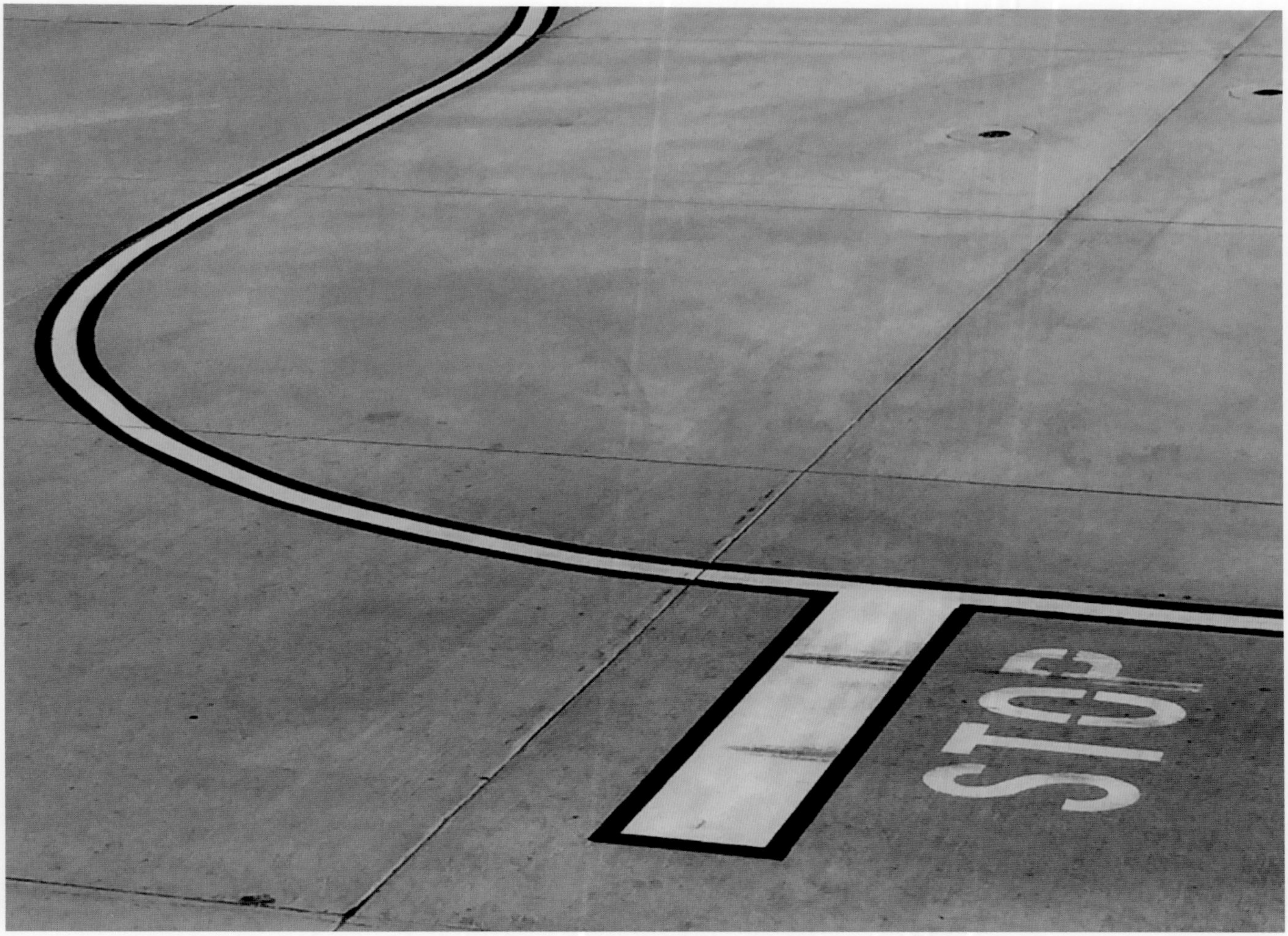
STOP

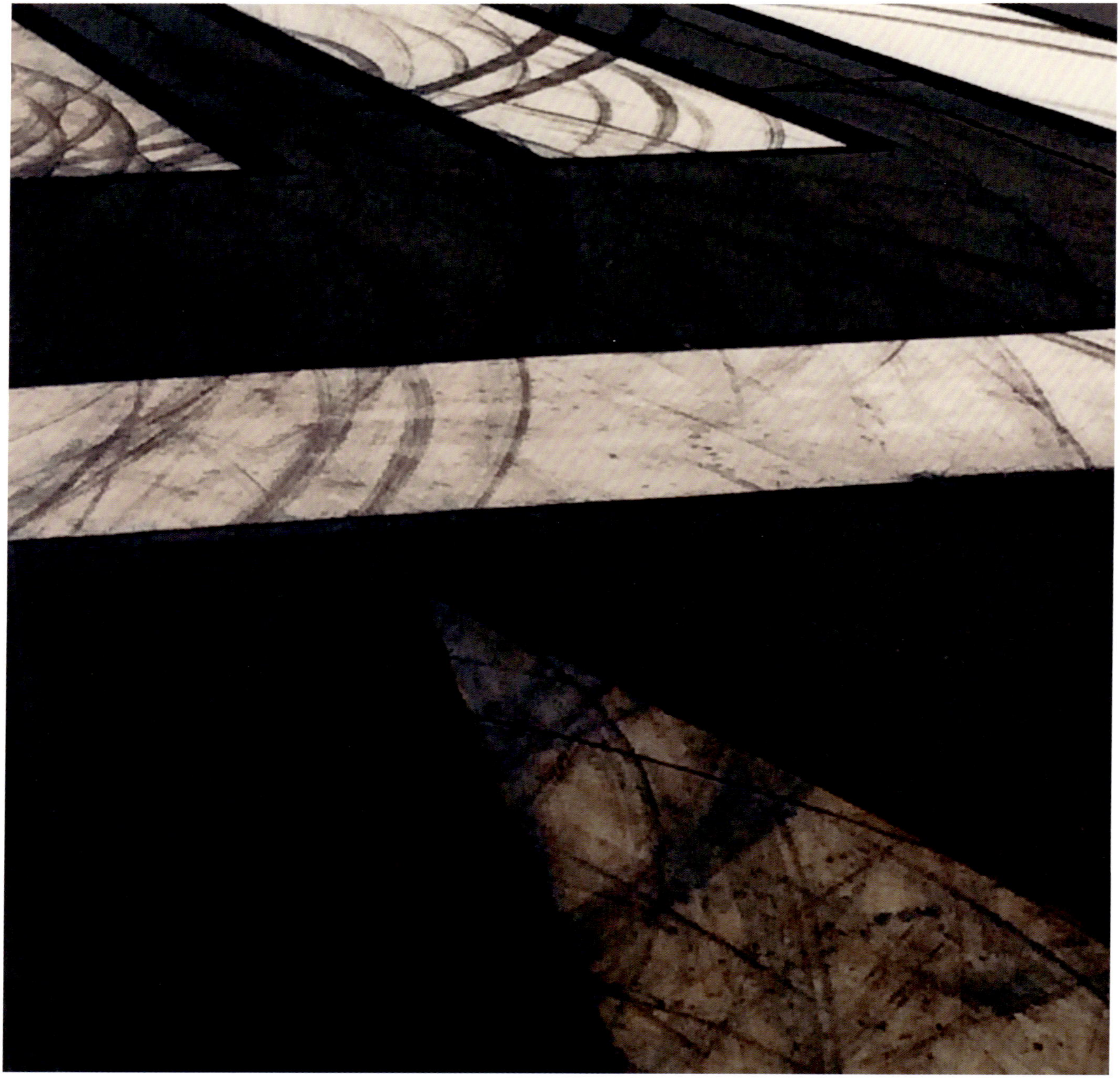

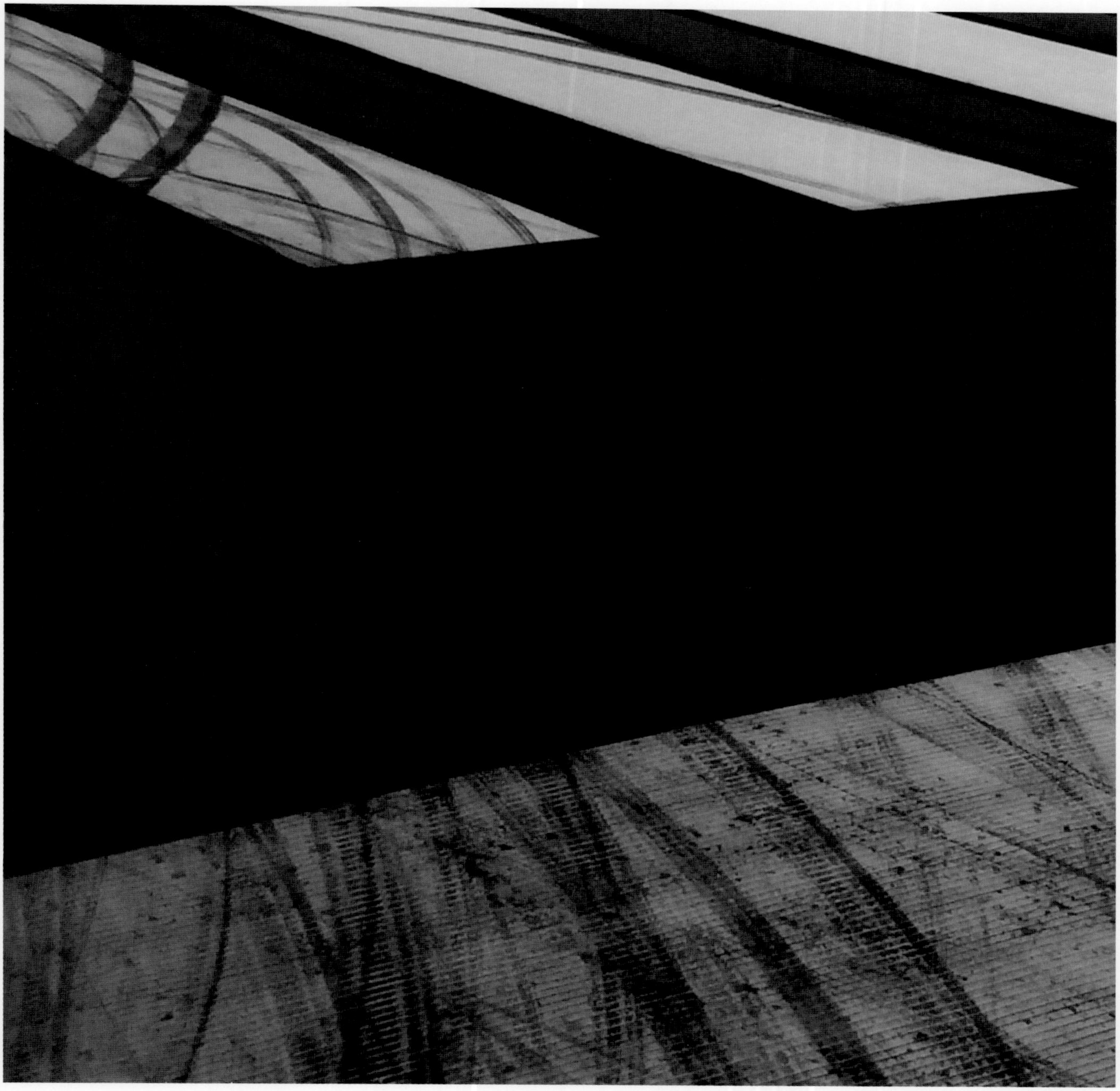

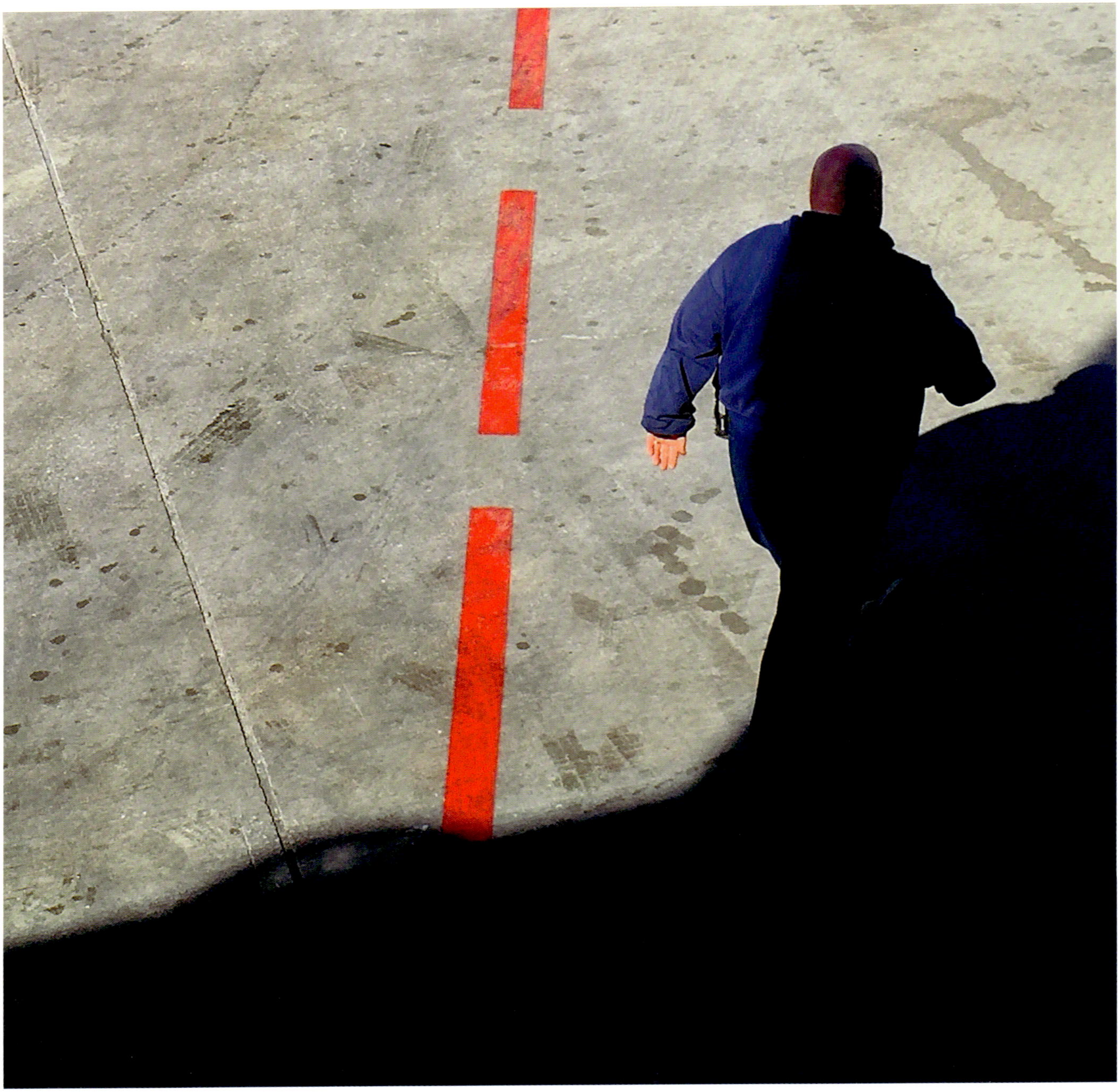

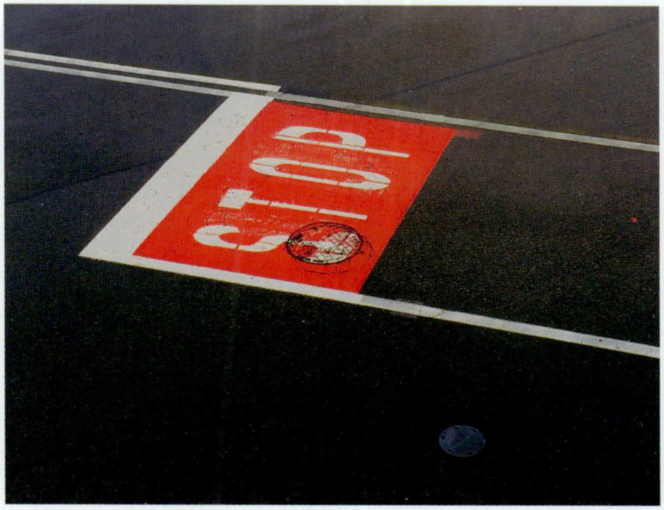
STOP

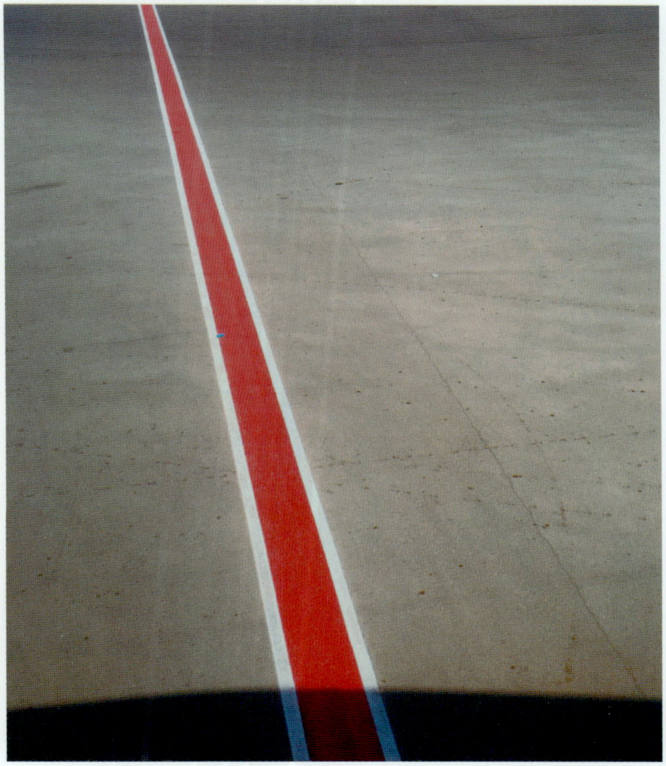

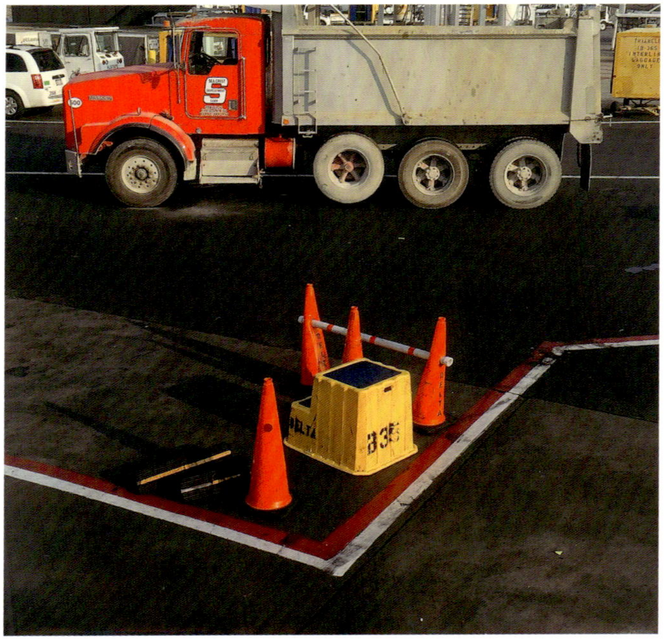

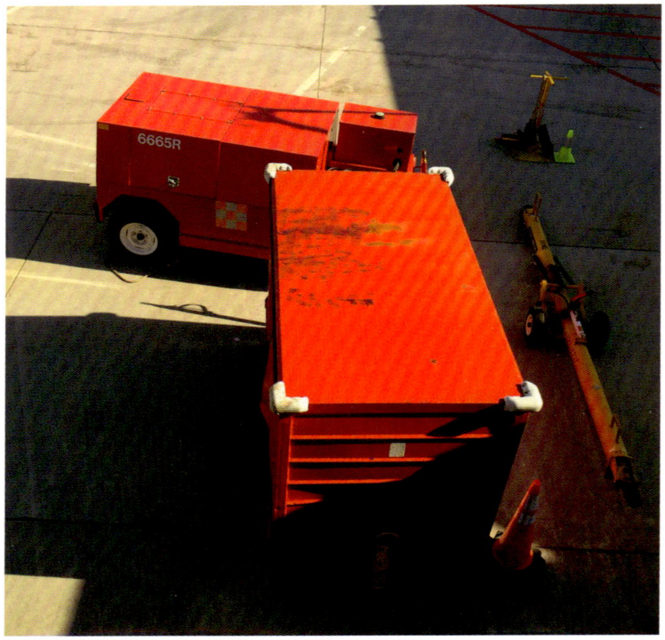
6665R

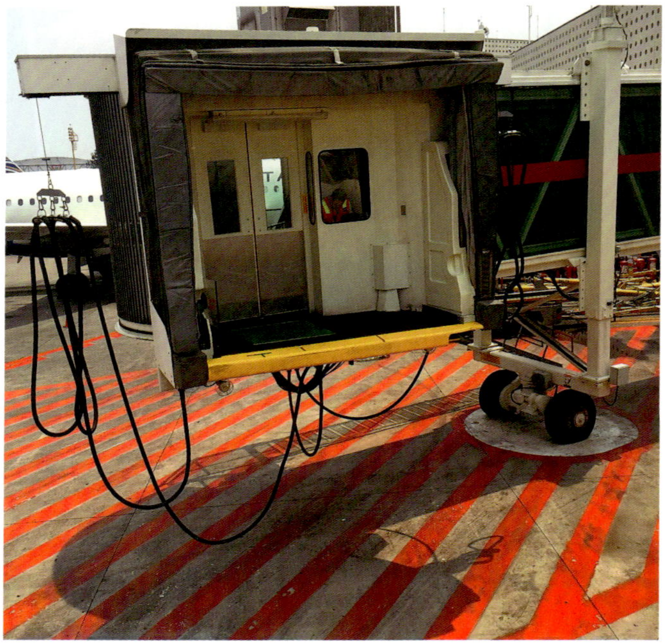

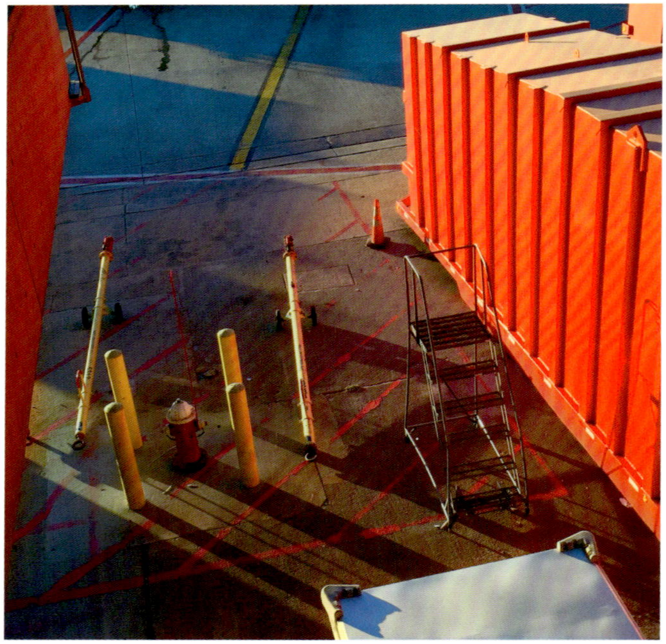

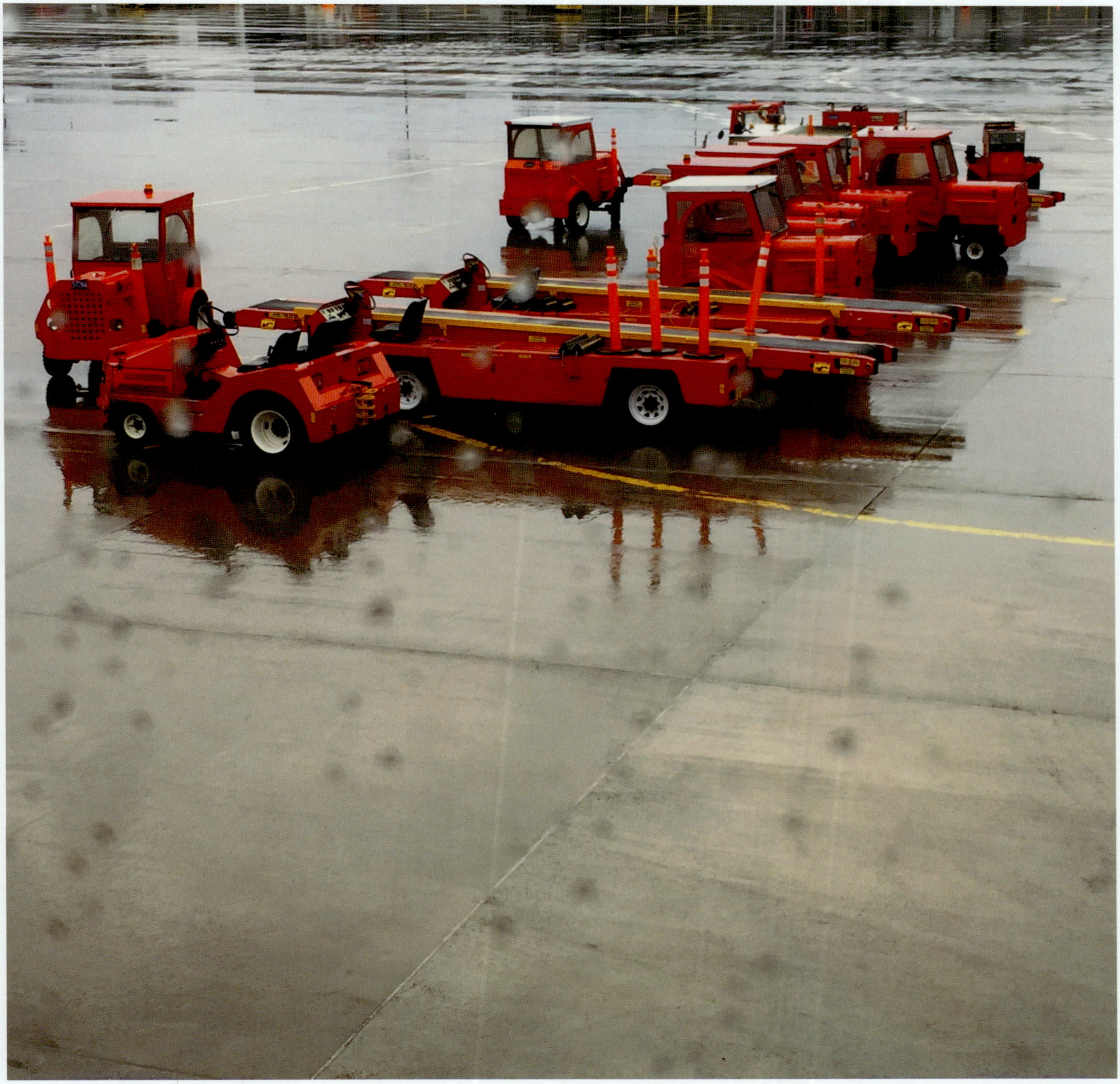

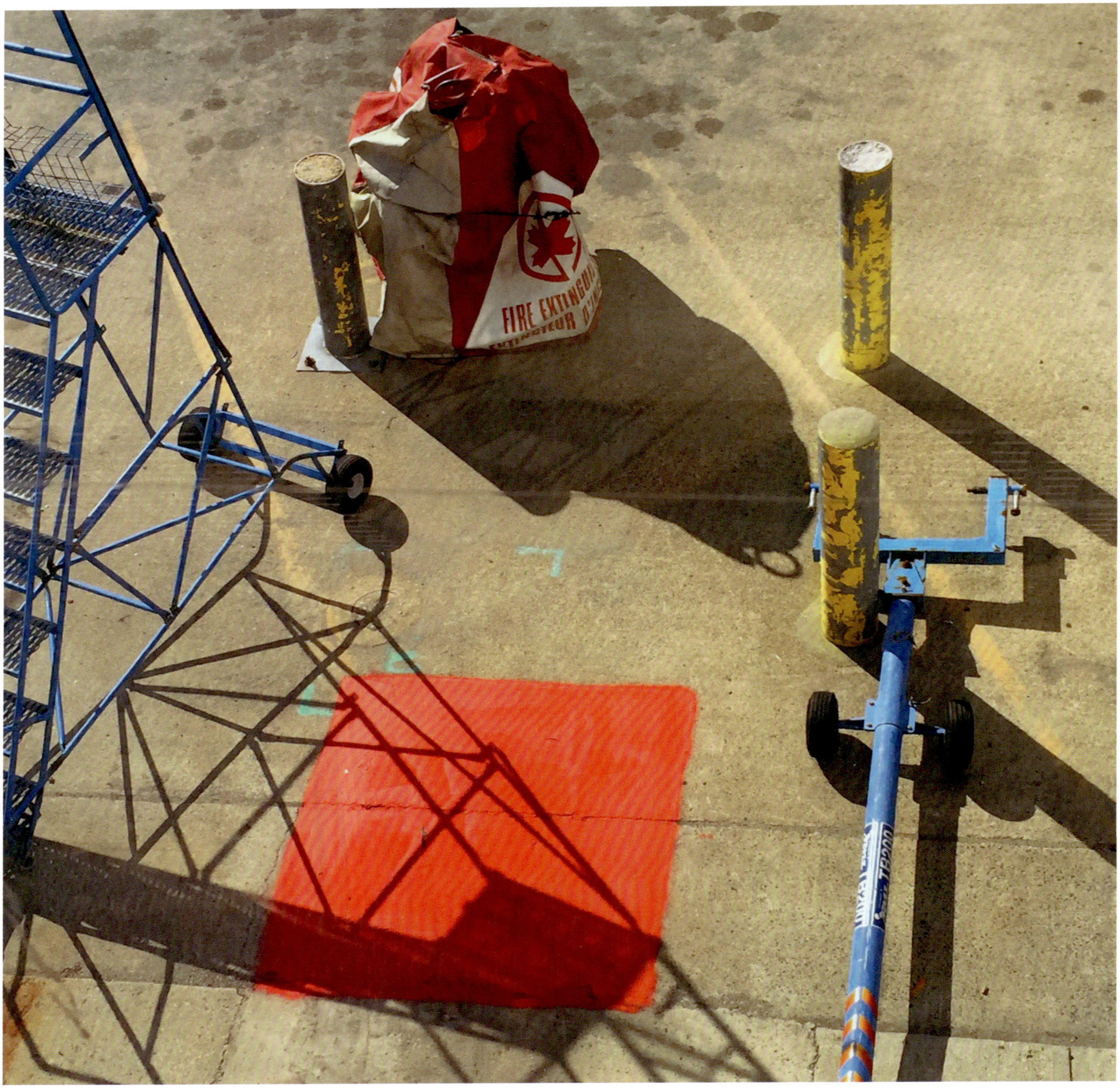

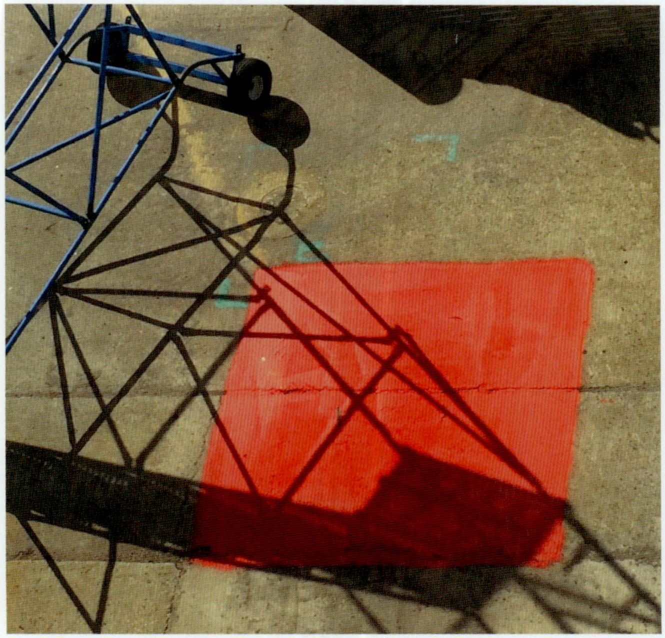

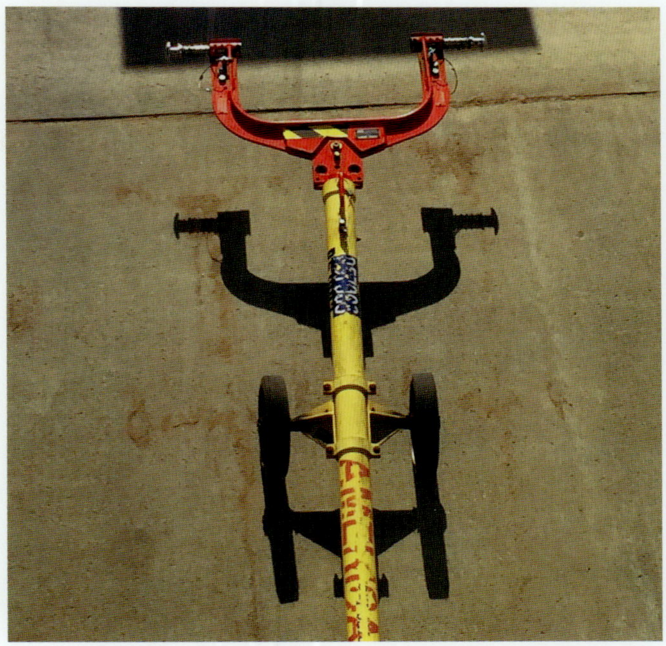

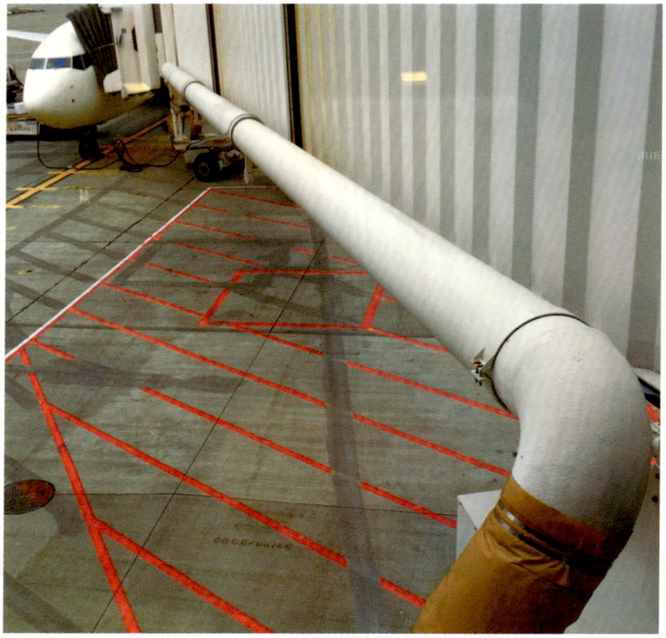

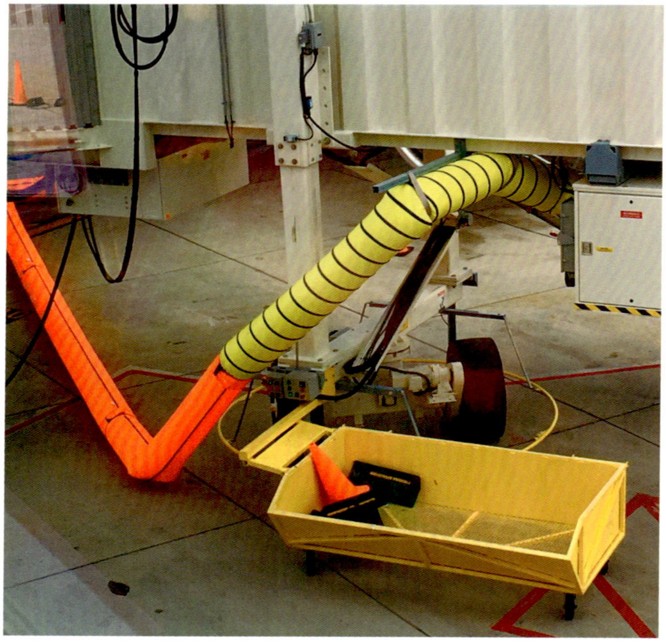

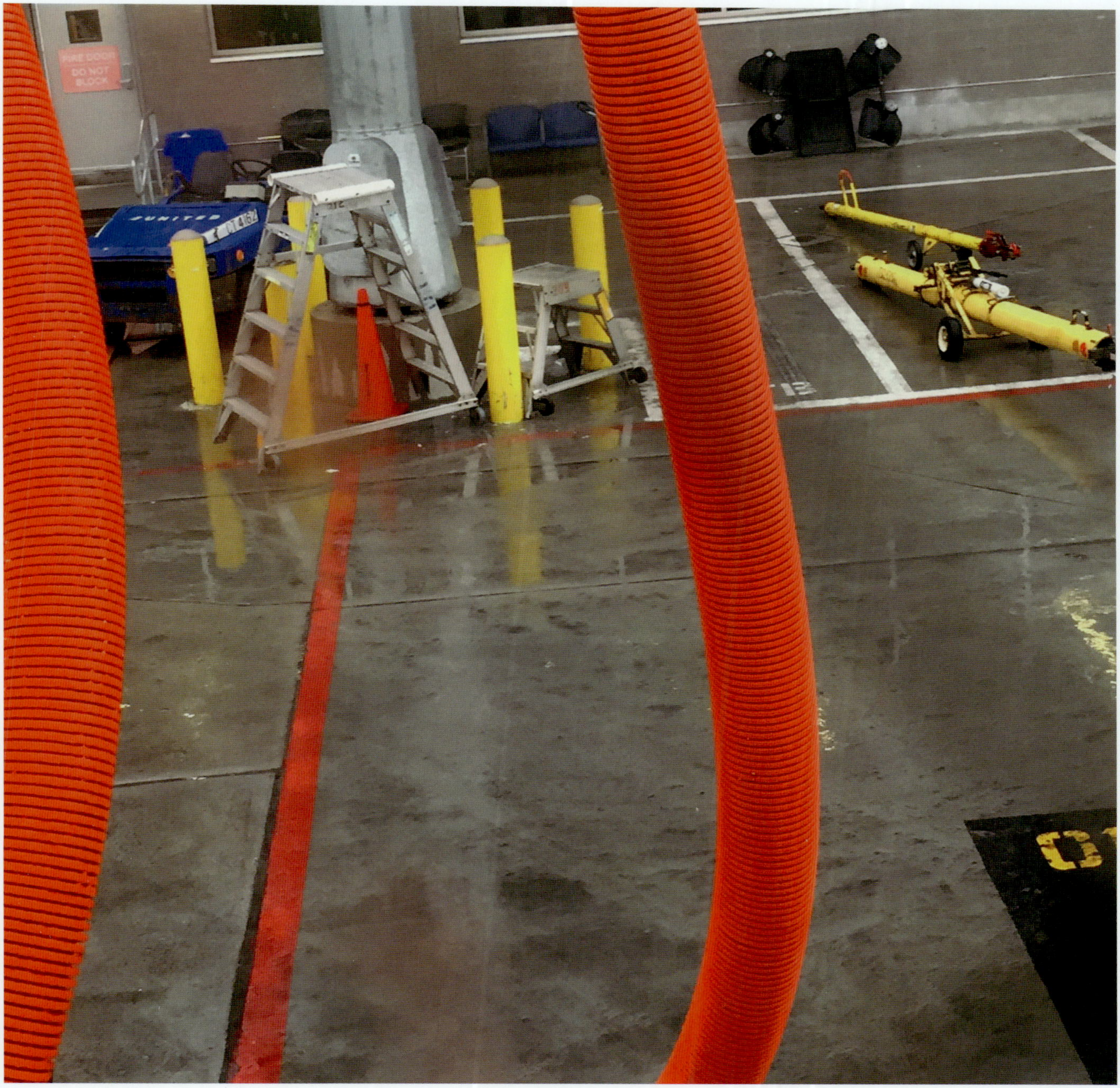

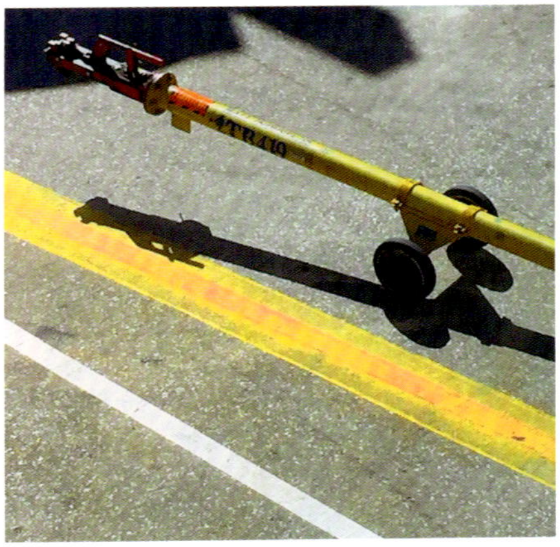
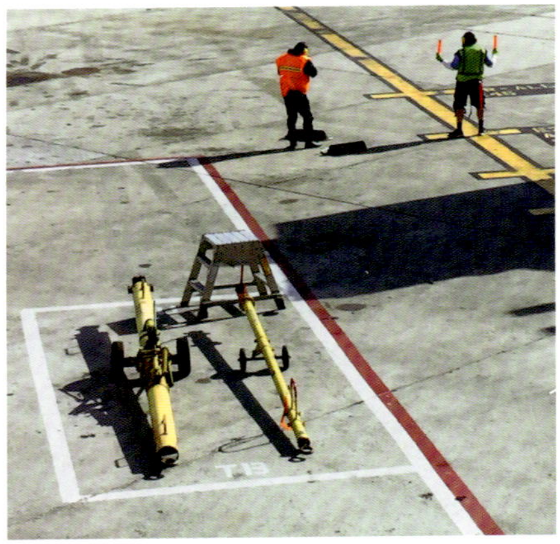
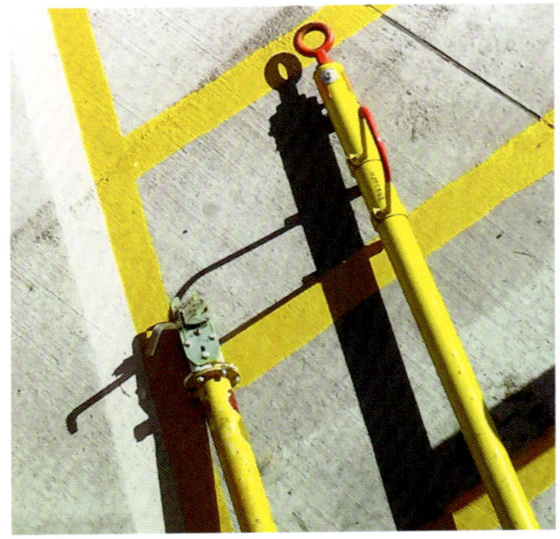
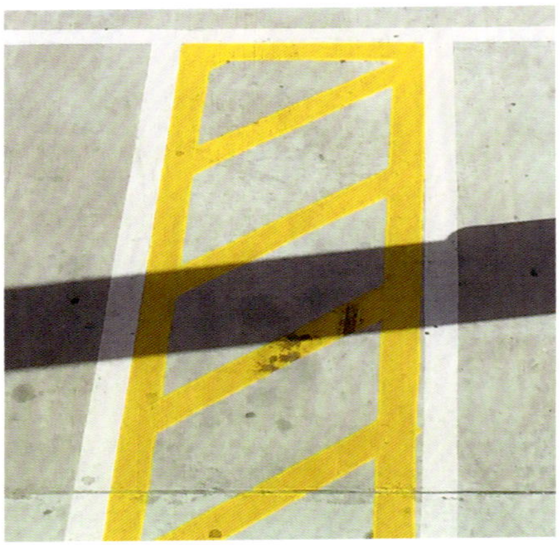
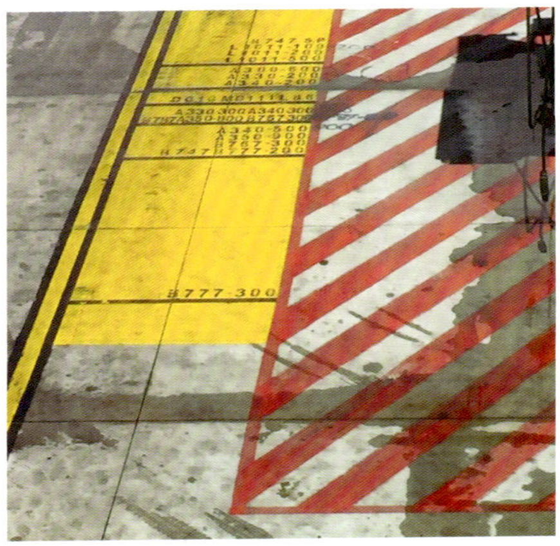
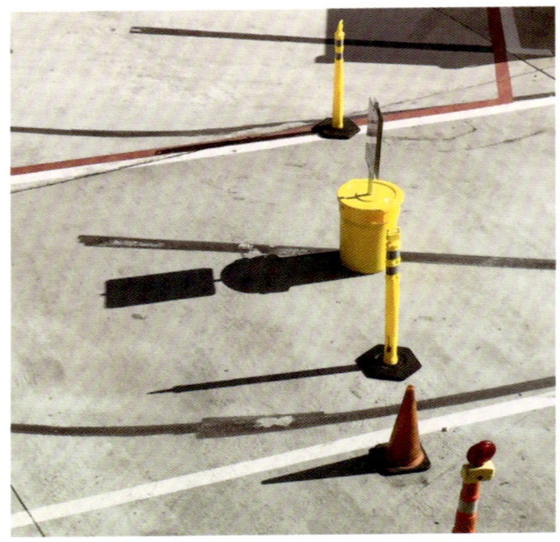
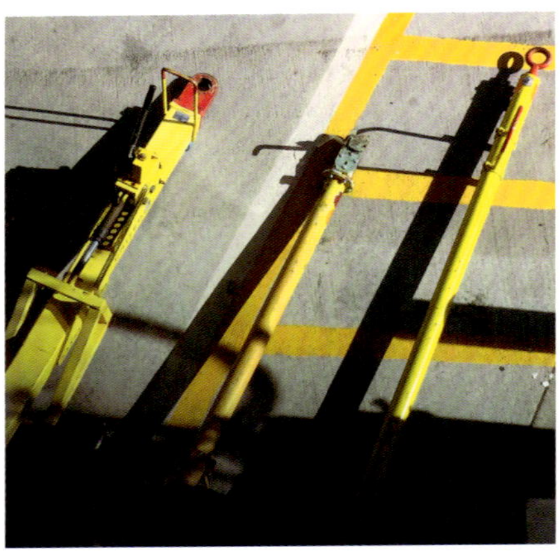
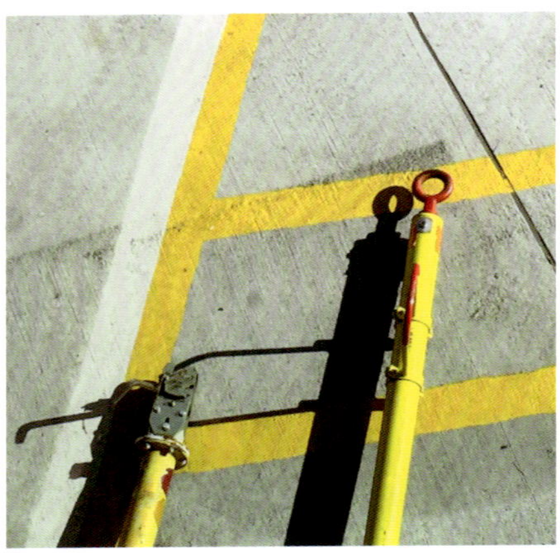
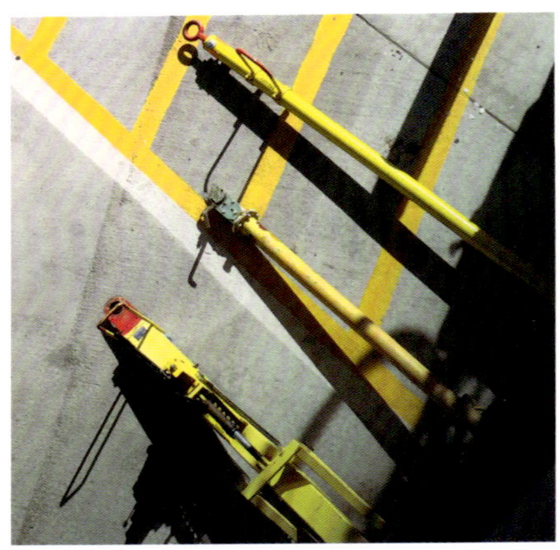

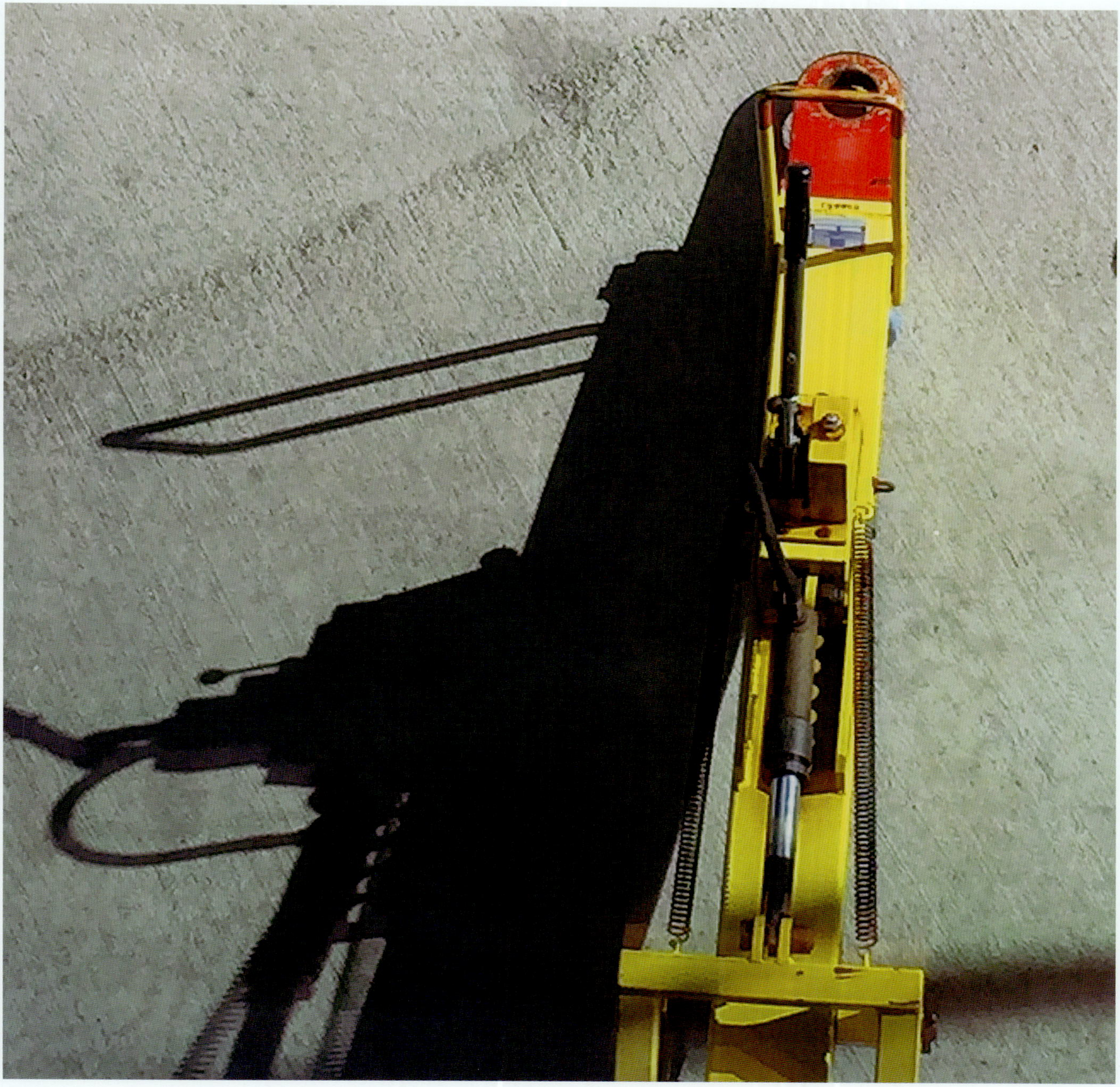

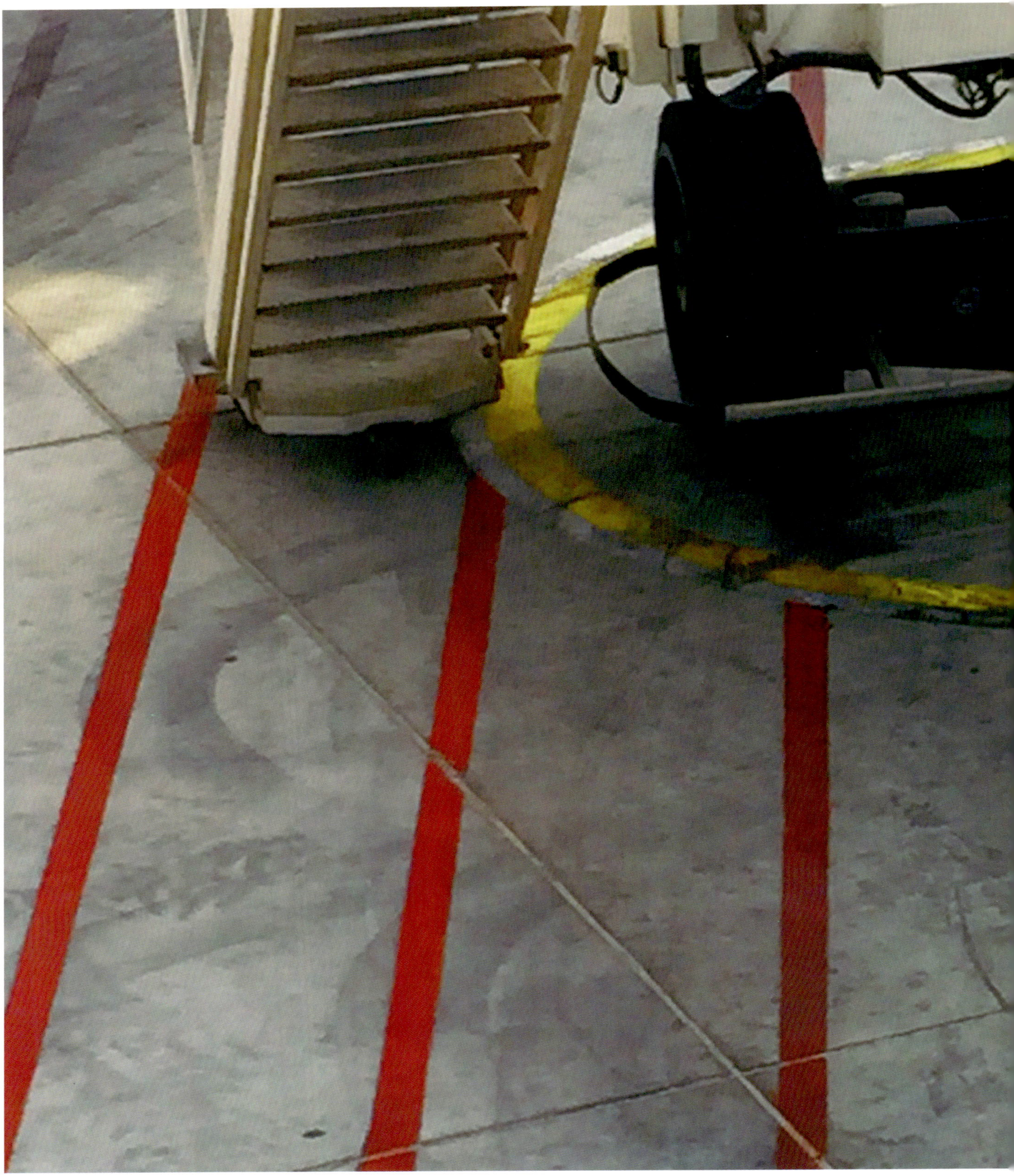

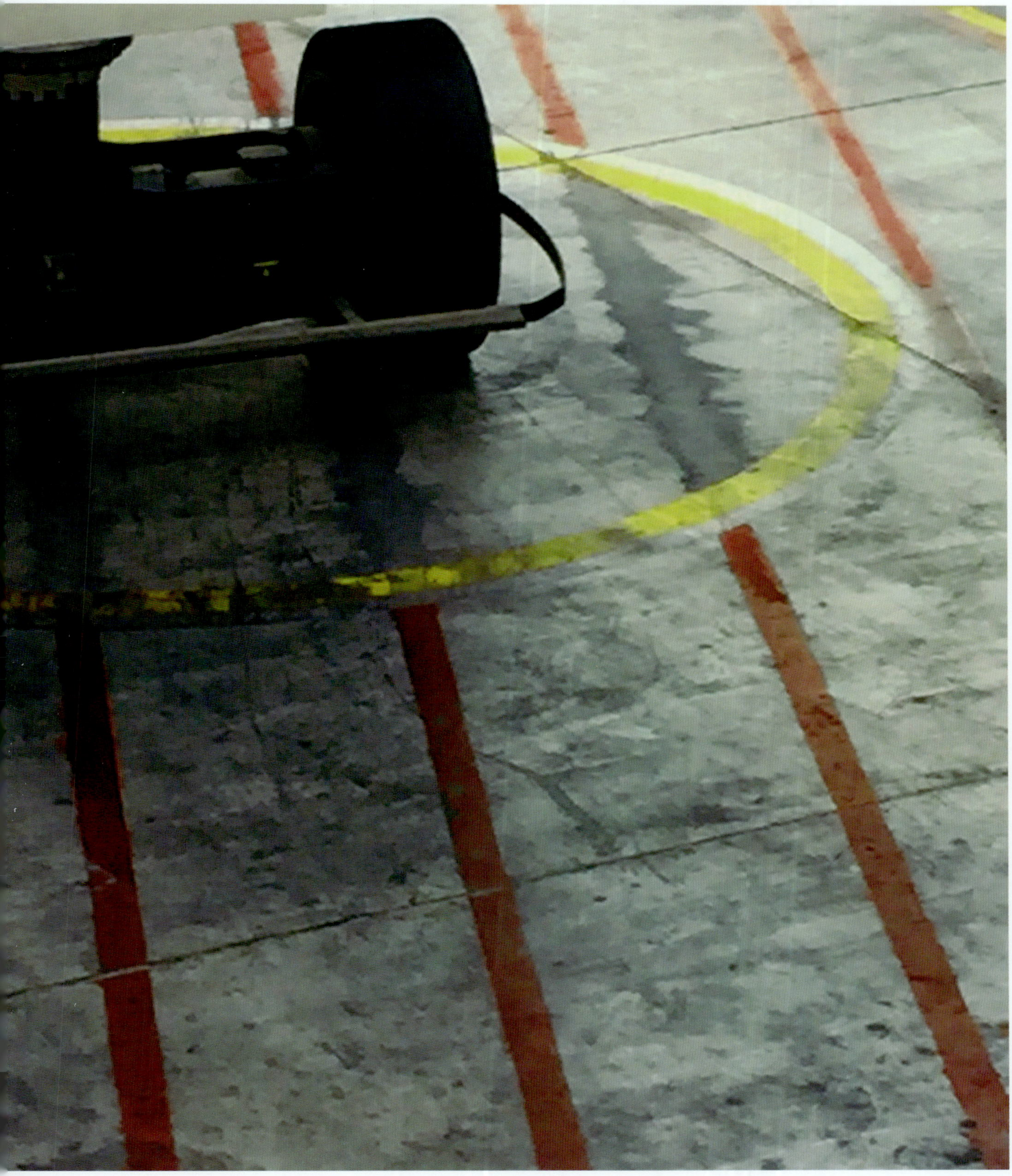

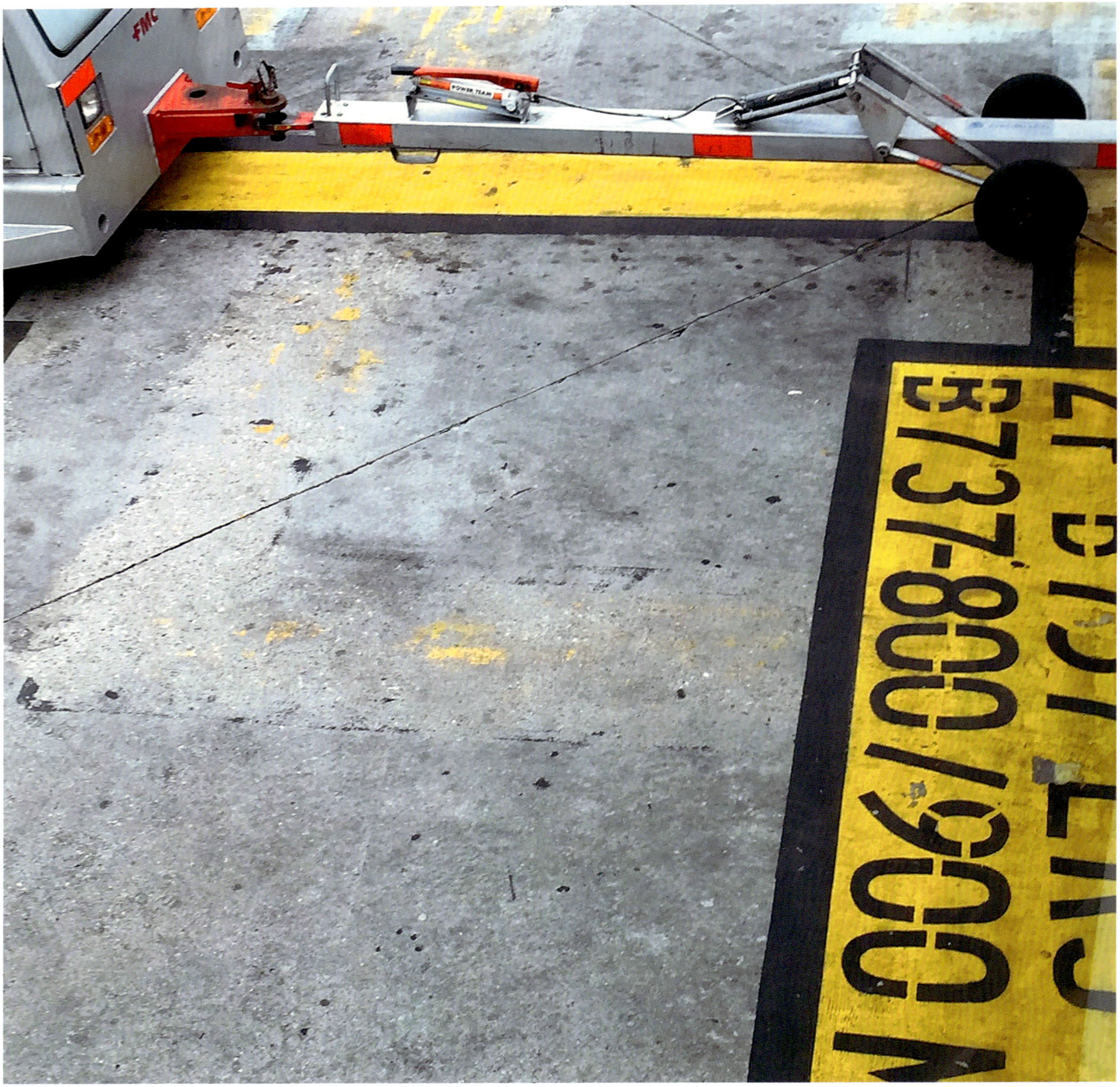
FMC
B737-800/900

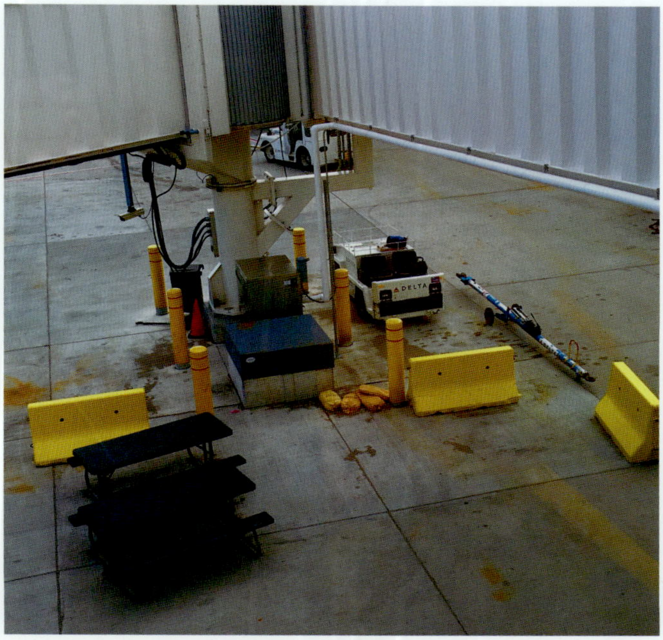

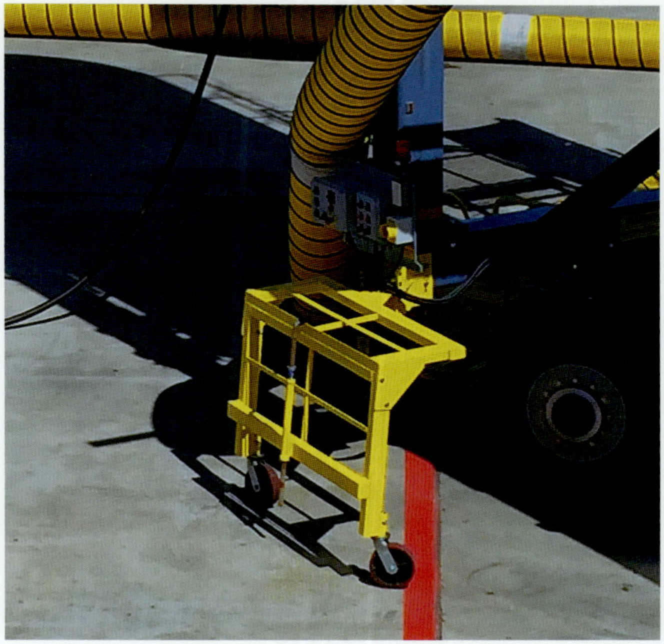

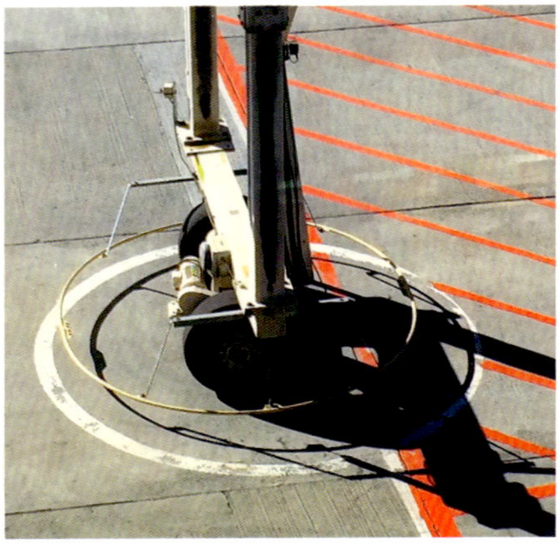

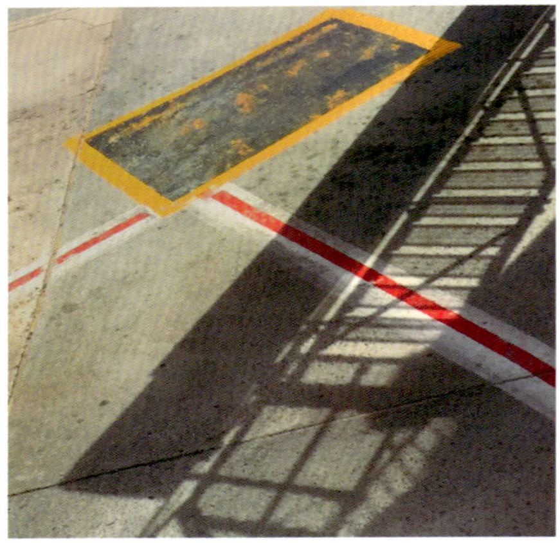

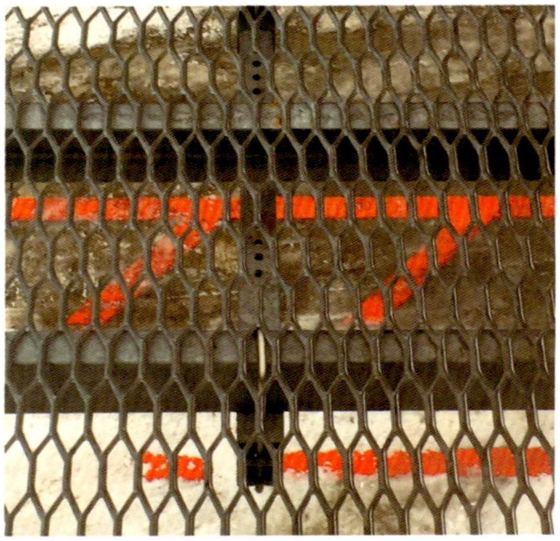

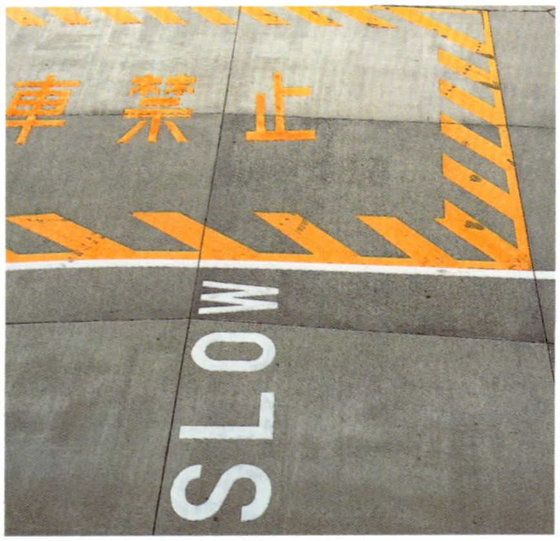
車禁止
SLOW

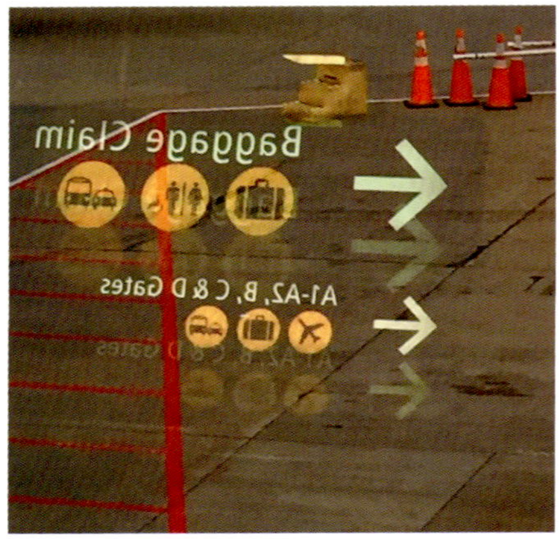
Baggage Claim
A1-A2, B, C & D Gates

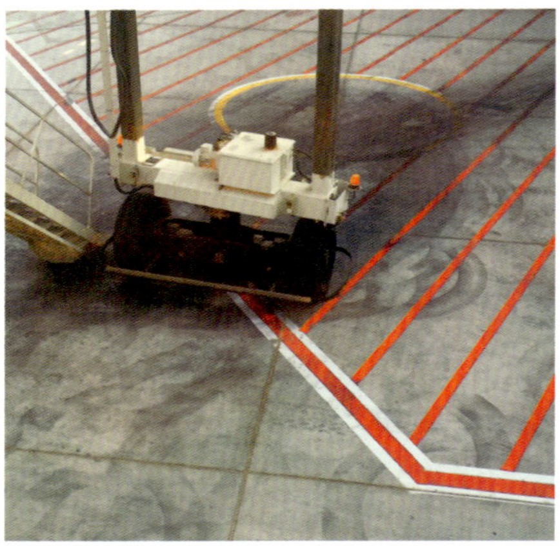

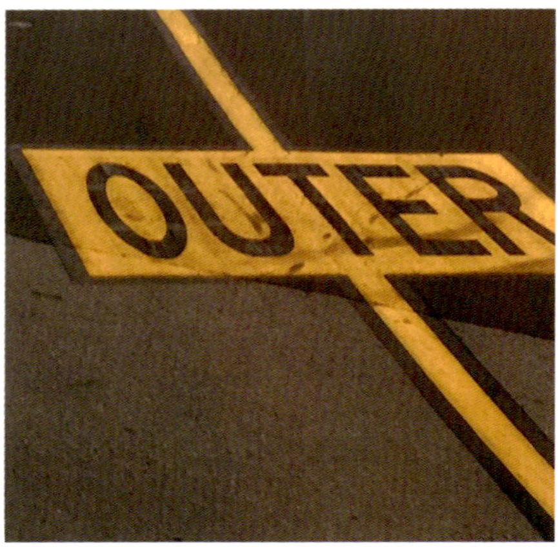
OUTER

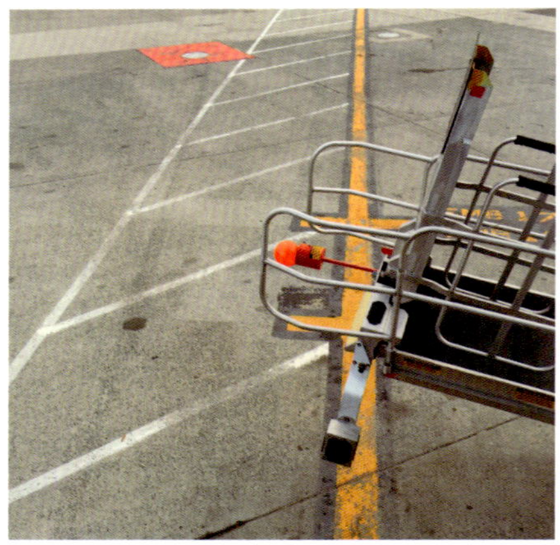

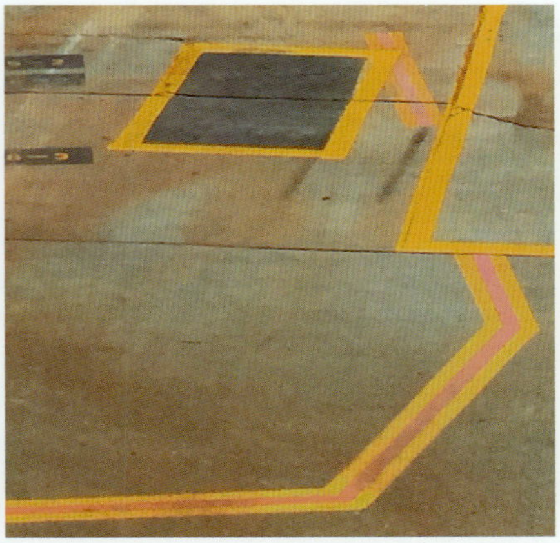
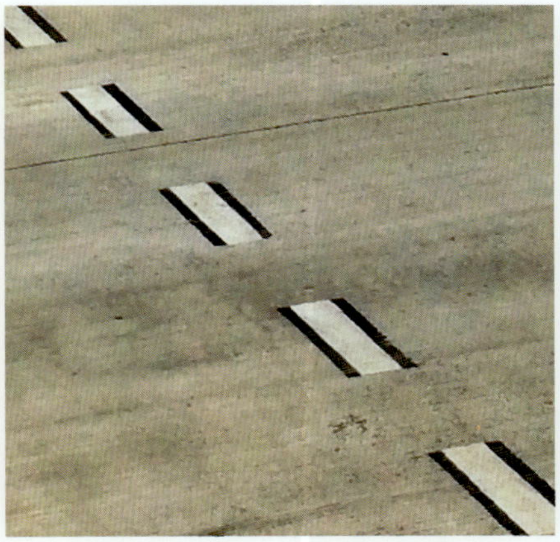
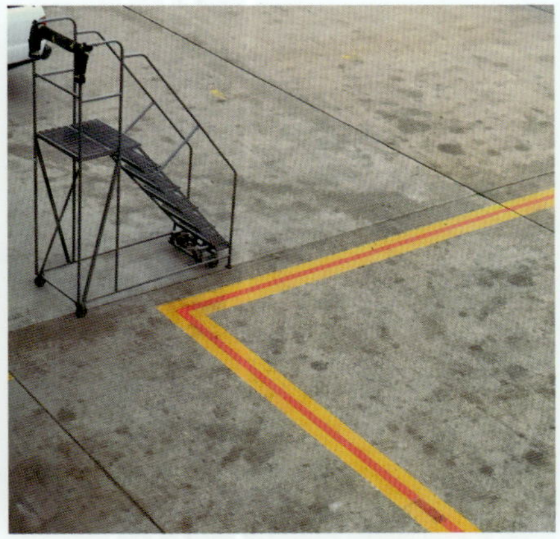
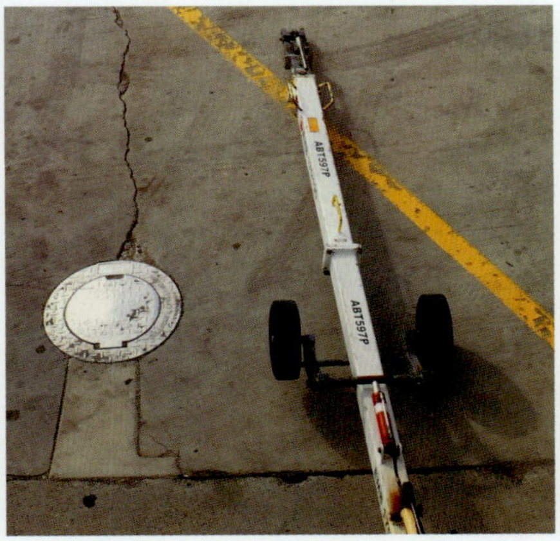
ABT597P
ABT597P
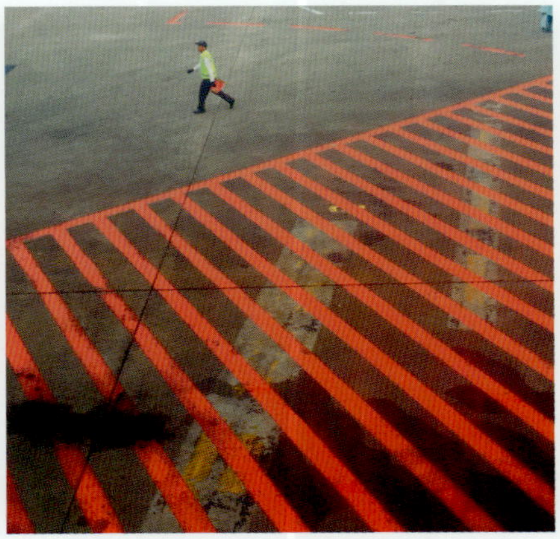
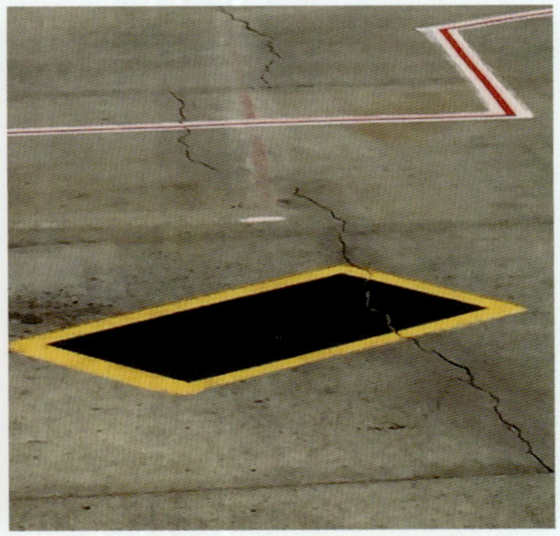

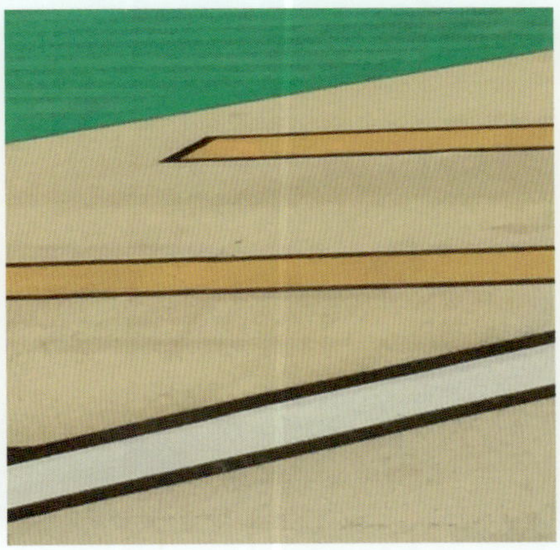
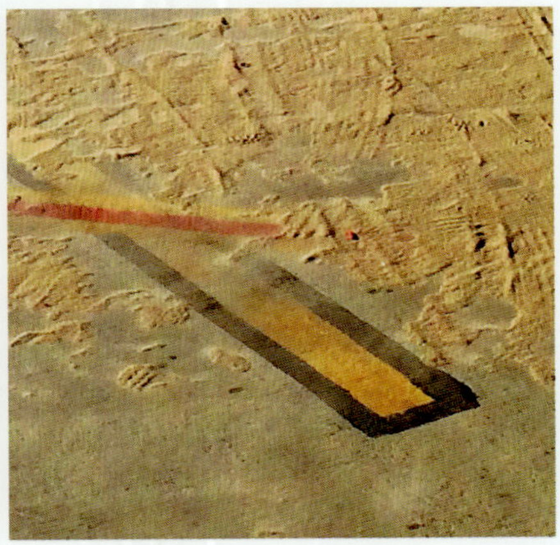

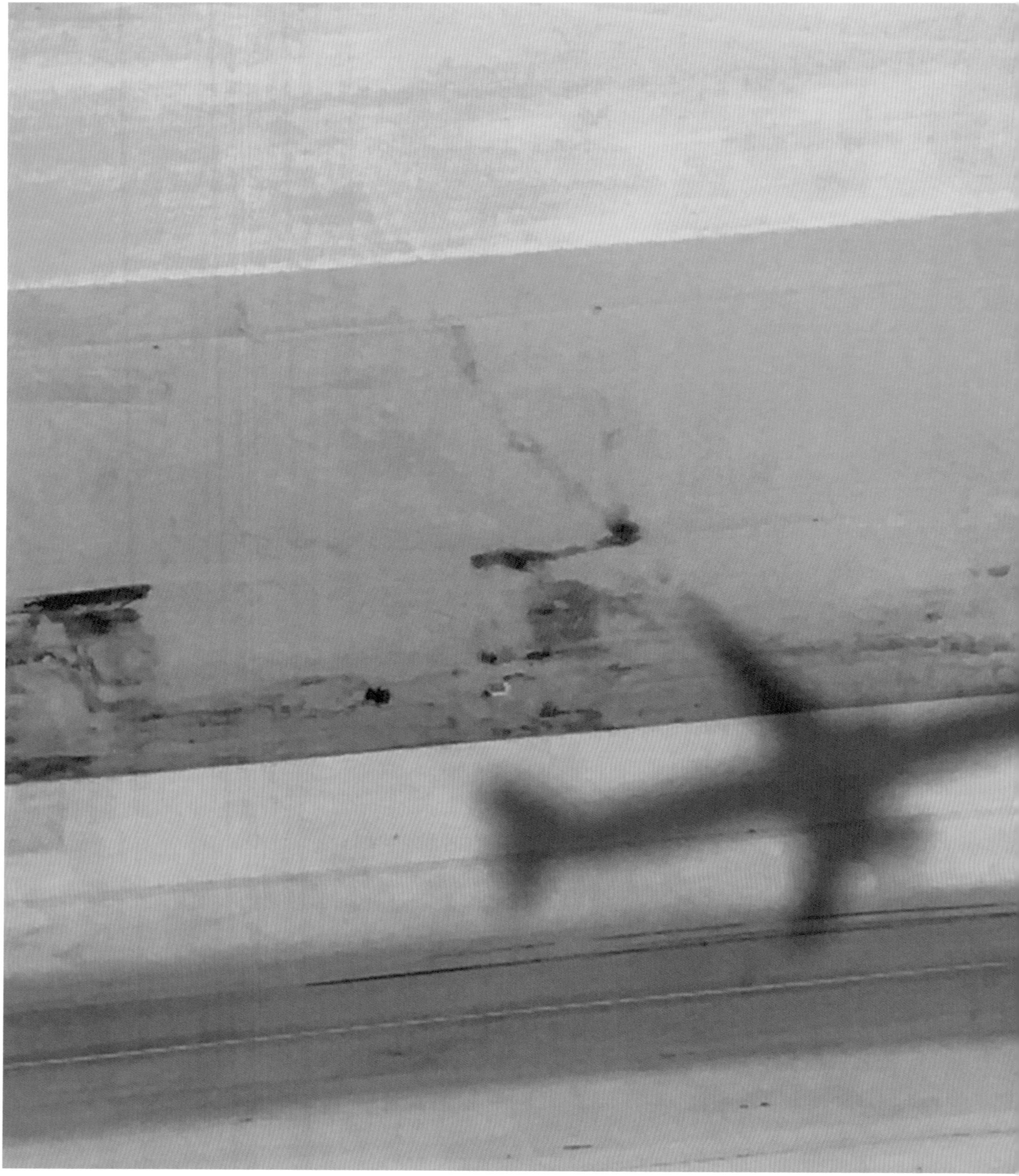

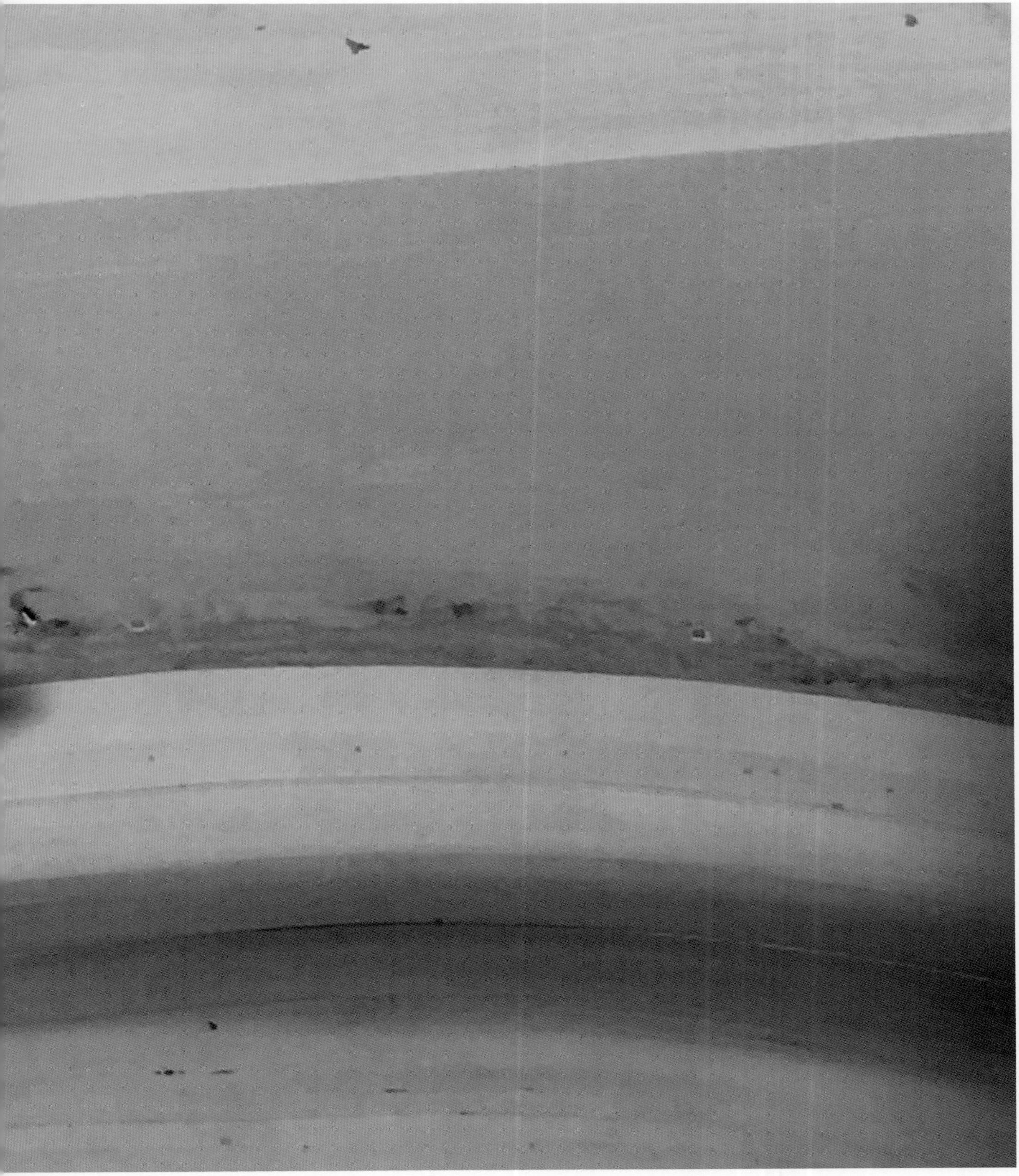

# APPENDIX

# EXHIBITION

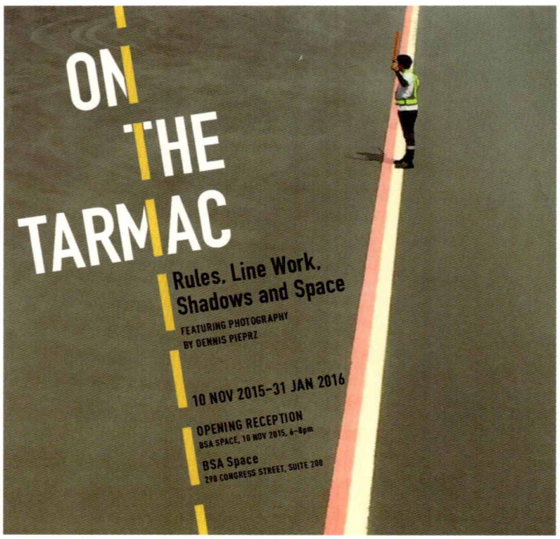
ON
THE
TARMAC
Rules, Line Work,
Shadows and Space
FEATURING PHOTOGRAPHY
BY DENNIS PIEPRZ
10 NOV 2015–31 JAN 2016
OPENING RECEPTION
BSA SPACE, 10 NOV 2015, 6–8pm
BSA Space
290 CONGRESS STREET, SUITE 200

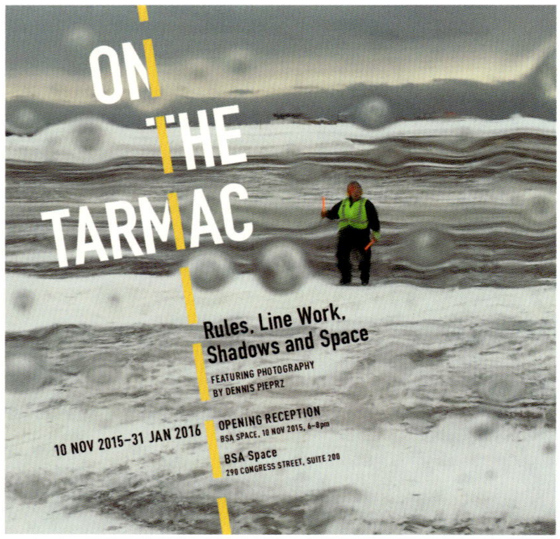
ON
THE
TARMAC
Rules, Line Work,
Shadows and Space
FEATURING PHOTOGRAPHY
BY DENNIS PIEPRZ
10 NOV 2015–31 JAN 2016
OPENING RECEPTION
BSA SPACE, 10 NOV 2015, 6–8pm
BSA Space
290 CONGRESS STREET, SUITE 200

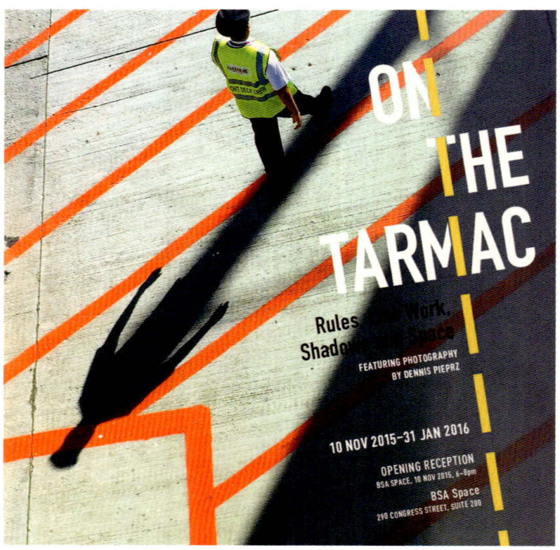
ON
THE
TARMAC
FEATURING PHOTOGRAPHY
BY DENNIS PIEPRZ
10 NOV 2015–31 JAN 2016
OPENING RECEPTION
BSA SPACE, 10 NOV 2015, 6–8pm
BSA Space
290 CONGRESS STREET, SUITE 200

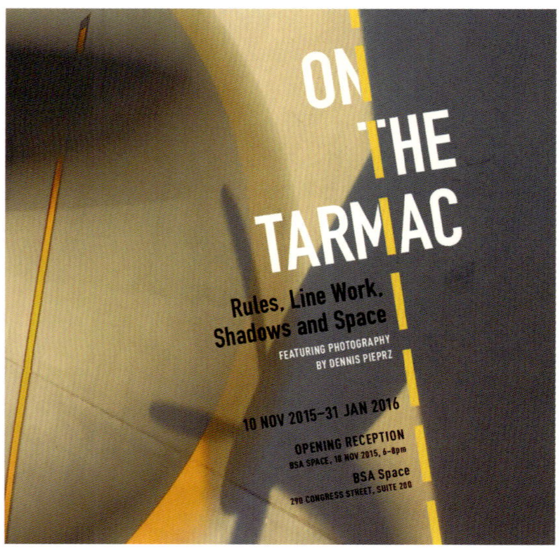
ON
THE
TARMAC
Rules, Line Work,
Shadows and Space
FEATURING PHOTOGRAPHY
BY DENNIS PIEPRZ
10 NOV 2015–31 JAN 2016
OPENING RECEPTION
BSA SPACE, 10 NOV 2015, 6–8pm
BSA Space
290 CONGRESS STREET, SUITE 200

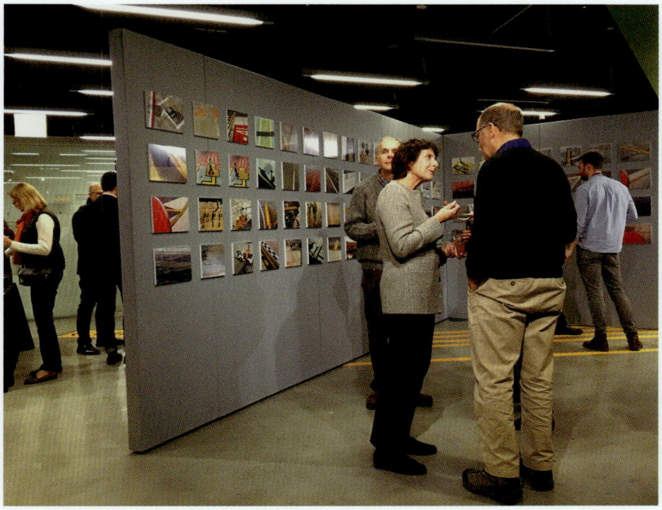

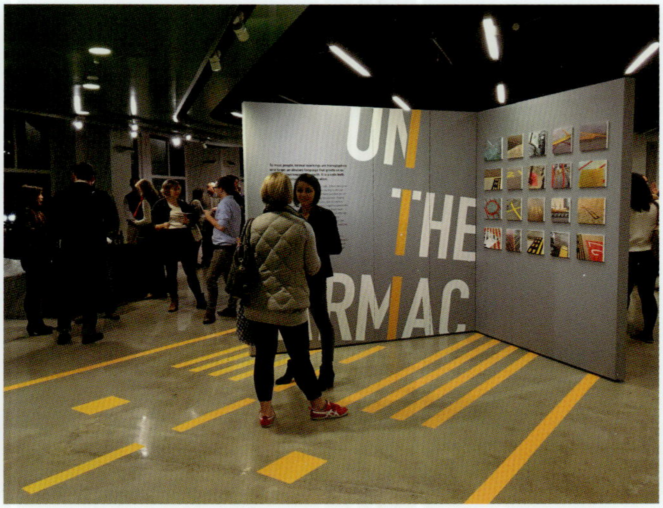
ON
THE
RMAC

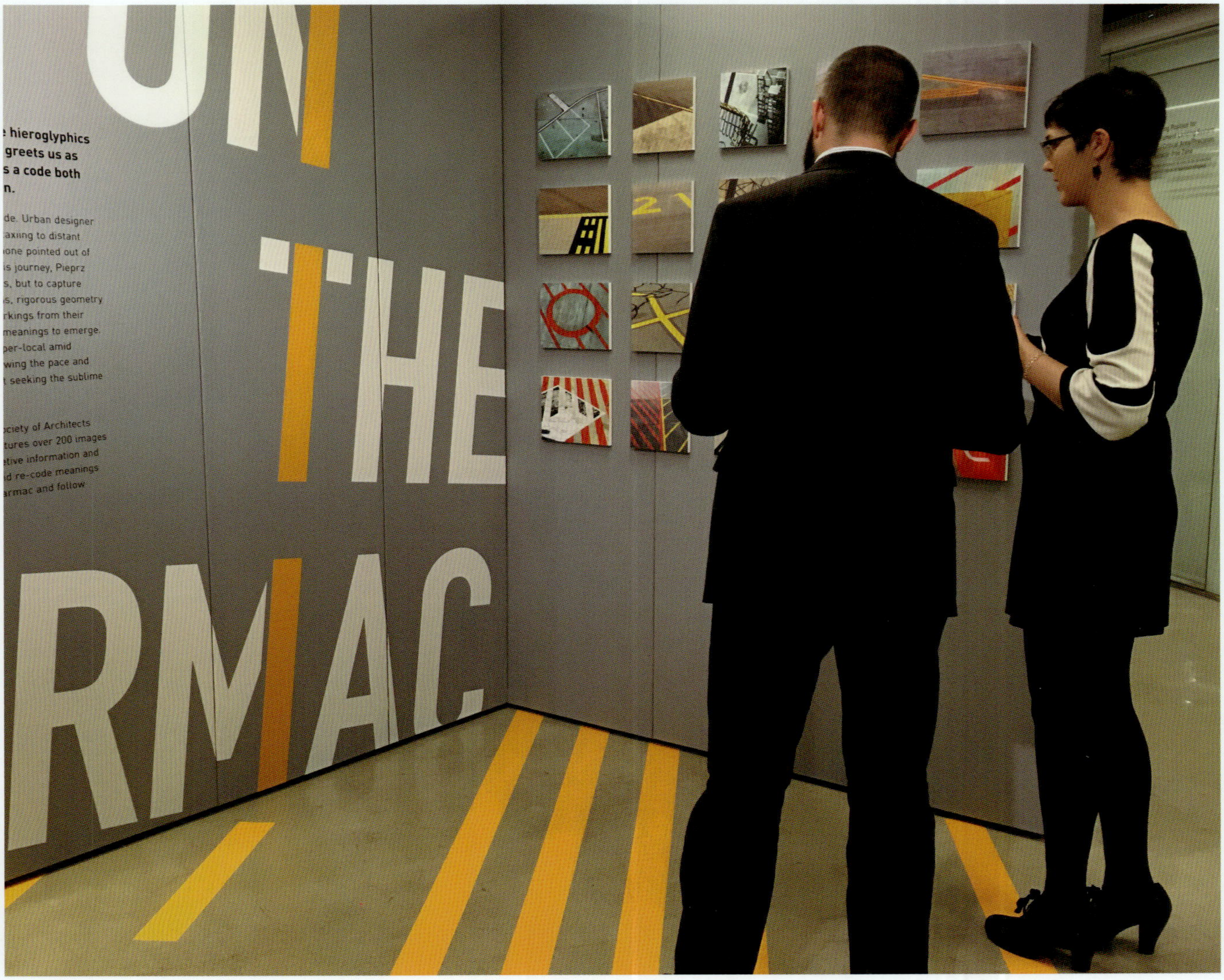
ON
THE
RMAC
hieroglyphics
greets us as
s a code both
n.
de. Urban designer
axiing to distant
one pointed out of
is journey, Pieprz
s, but to capture
s, rigorous geometry
rkings from their
meanings to emerge.
per-local amid
wing the pace and
seeking the sublime
ciety of Architects
tures over 200 images
tive information and
d re-code meanings
armac and follow

# PHOTOGRAPHER

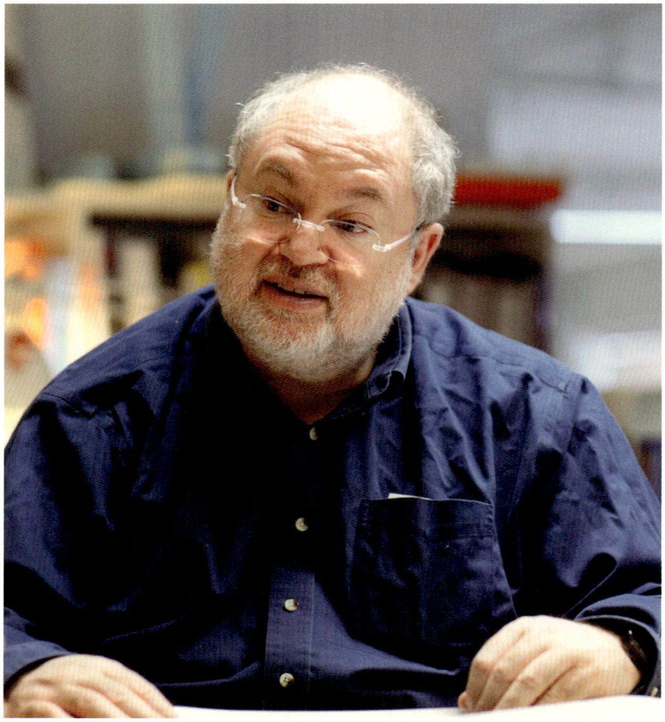

**"Life at 30,000 feet"**

Designer and urbanist Dennis Pieprz is passionate about cities. As a Principal and practitioner at Sasaki, his experience encompasses the design of urban districts, new communities, campus environments, waterfronts, and urban regeneration. Pieprz approaches his work with a critical understanding of the forces that shape contemporary cities.

While traveling to project locations around the world, Pieprz documents cities and people through the lens of his iPhone camera. A curious observer of daily life, Pieprz frames the world with the empathy of a designer and the precision of an ethnographer.

Educated at the Harvard Graduate School of Design and the University of Toronto School of Architecture, Dennis leads remarkable teams that have been honored with more than 50 design awards, including national recognition from the American Institute of Architects, the American Society of Landscape Architects, and the Society for College and University Planning. Dennis has been inducted as an honorary member of ASLA—a title bestowed upon only a handful of professionals nationwide.

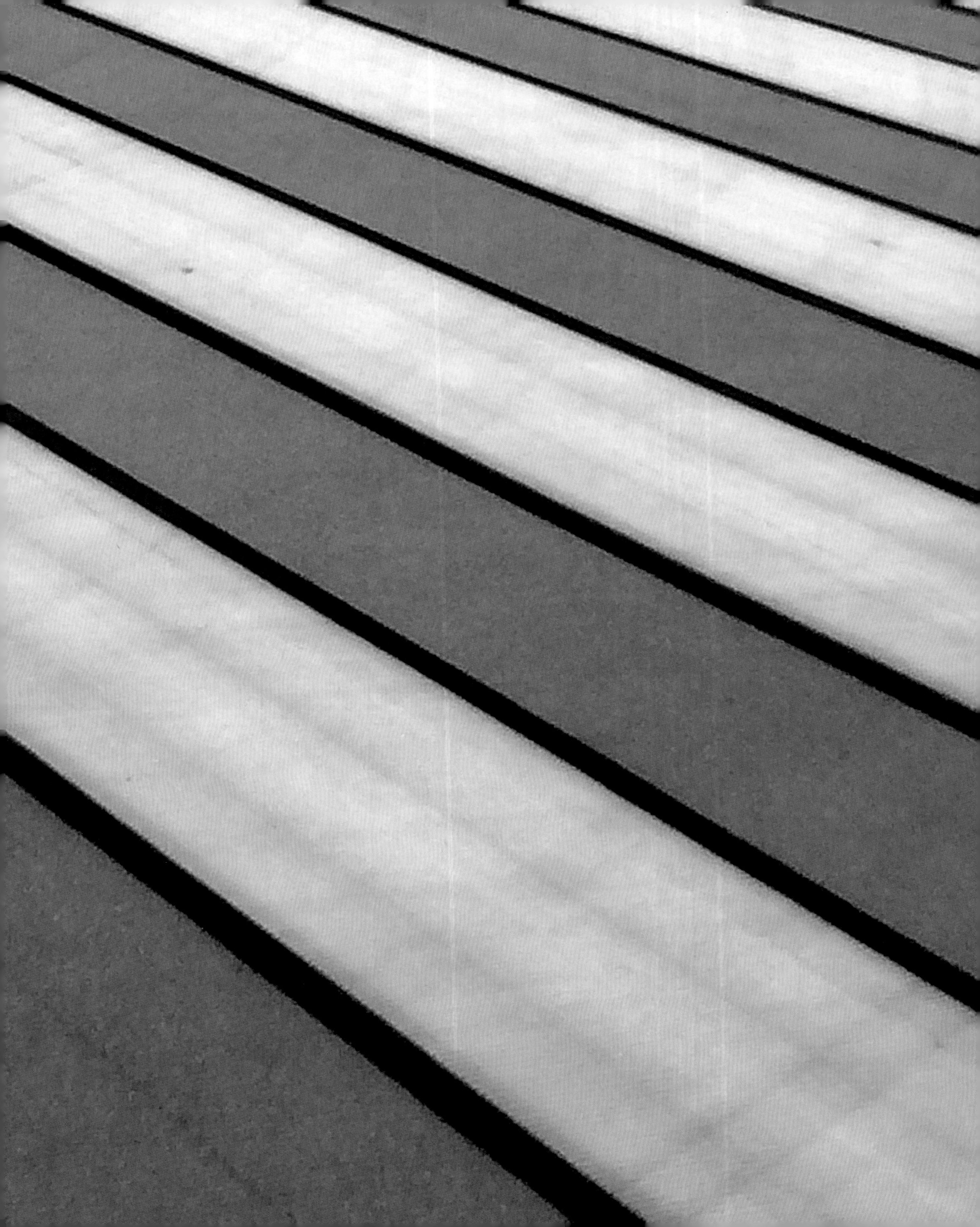

# CREDITS

The main source of inspiration and motivation for this book was an eponymous exhibition, presented at BSA Space in downtown Boston between November 2015 and January 2016. The exhibition included 214 photographs, along with supergraphics and interpretive materials that invited viewers to explore the language of tarmac markings. The author thanks the Boston Society of Architects -- and Mary Fichter in particular -- for organizing the exhibition and related events. And many thanks to the exhibition team at Sasaki, including Sam Pease, Jessica Grant, Erin Kim, Joanna Chow, Philip Barash, and Gina Ford, who was the muse of this project.

**Book Credits**

Creative Direction by Leo Malinow

Interior Page Layouts: Oscar Riera Ojeda

Copy editing by Brigette Brown

**OSCAR RIERA OJEDA**
PUBLISHERS



ISBN 978-988-13975-6-0

Published by Oscar Riera Ojeda Publishers Limited

Printed in China by Artron Art Center

Oscar Riera Ojeda Publishers Limited

Unit 6 22/F.,
Far East Consortium Building,
121 Des Voeux Road Central, Hong Kong
T: +852-5311-1625

Production Offices | China

Suit 19, Shenyun Road,
Nanshan District, Shenzhen 518055
T:+86-182-0098-3774

www.oropublishers.com | www.oscarrieraojeda.com

oscar@oscarrieraojeda.com